Gendered Memories

China Understandings Today

Series Editors: Mary Gallagher and Emily Wilcox

China Understandings Today is dedicated to the study of contemporary China and seeks to present the latest and most innovative scholarship in social sciences and the humanities to the academic community as well as the general public. The series is sponsored by the Lieberthal-Rogel Center for Chinese Studies at the University of Michigan.

Ethnic Minority Cinema in China's Nation-State Building
Kwai-Cheung Lo

Gendered Memories: An Imaginary Museum for Ding Ling and Chinese Female Revolutionary Martyrs
Xian Wang

Engineering Stability: Rebuilding the State in Twenty-First Century Chinese Universities
Yan Xiaojun

In Search of Admiration and Respect: Chinese Cultural Diplomacy in the United States, 1875–1974
Yanqiu Zheng

Seeking a Future for the Past: Space, Power, and Heritage in a Chinese City
Philipp Demgenski

China as Number One? The Emerging Values of a Rising Power
Yang Zhong and Ronald F. Inglehart

Paris and the Art of Transposition: Early Twentieth Century Sino-French Encounters
Angie Chau

The Currency of Truth: Newsmaking and the Late-Socialist Imaginaries of China's Digital Era
Emily H. C. Chua

A complete list of titles in the series can be found at www.press.umich.edu

Gendered Memories

An Imaginary Museum for Ding Ling and Chinese Female Revolutionary Martyrs

Xian Wang

University of Michigan Press
Ann Arbor

Published in the United States of America by the
University of Michigan Press
Manufactured in the United States of America
Printed on acid-free paper
First published February 2025

A CIP catalog record for this book is available from the British Library.

Library of Congress Cataloging-in-Publication data has been applied for.

ISBN 978-0-472-07719-9 (hardcover : alk. paper)
ISBN 978-0-472-05719-1 (paper : alk. paper)
ISBN 978-0-472-90481-5 (open access ebook)

DOI: https://doi.org/10.3998/mpub.12838586

The University of Michigan Press's open access publishing program is made possible thanks to additional funding from the University of Michigan Office of the Provost and the generous support of contributing libraries.

To Qing and Melody, with love and gratitude

CONTENTS

Digital materials related to this title can be found on the Fulcrum platform via the following citable URL: https://doi.org/10.3998/mpub.12838586

LIST OF ILLUSTRATIONS

PREFACE

When I was a child, my school's yearly spring excursion (*chunyou* 春游), held during the Qingming Festival (Tomb-Sweeping Day), always included a stop at a monument on Tortoise Mountain in Wuhan. We climbed the mountain to honor Xiang Jingyu, an early Chinese Communist Party (CCP) leader and female revolutionary martyr from Xupu, who died in Wuhan. Her statue is surrounded by tall, straight pine trees that lend a solemn air to the setting (see fig. 1). Our teacher, holding the red flag of the CCP, told us heroic stories about Xiang Jingyu and how she sacrificed her life for the salvation of the nation. Wearing our red scarves, we, as young pioneers, swore to learn from Xiang Jingyu and took turns placing flower wreaths in front of her statue. After paying tribute to Xiang Jingyu, we explored the mountain and found a spot to enjoy some snacks and a view of the Yangtze River, the Wuhan Yangtze River Bridge, and the Yellow Crane Tower. While there, our teacher taught us to recite Mao Zedong's lyrics, "Yellow Crane Tower—to the melody of *P'u Sa Man*," which Mao wrote during his visit to that very location in 1927. This was as the Great Revolution teetered on the brink of failure and just a year before Xiang Jingyu was executed by the Kuomintang (KMT) during the White Terror:

> Broad, broad
> through the country
> flow the nine tributaries.
> Deep, deep
> from north to south
> cuts a line.
> Blurred in the blue haze
> of the rain and mist
> The Snake and Tortoise Hills
> tower above the water

The yellow crane
has departed.
Who knows where it has gone?
Only this resting-place
for travellers remains.
In wine I drink
a pledge to the surging torrent
The tide of my heart
rises as high as the waves.[1]

My childhood memories of spring excursions during the Qingming Festival feature a mix of youthful excitement—the pleasure of sharing the beautiful views on Tortoise Mountain with friends and tasting the snacks I usually couldn't acquire at home—and solemnity, as we paid tribute to Xiang Jingyu and recited Mao Zedong's lyrics. In moments like these, the state shapes both personal and national memory, blurring the line between the individual and the revolutionary sublime. Large-scale statues, monuments, and museums serve as the most visible forms of national public storytelling; these sites become the spatial embodiment of both collective and personal memories.

The act of mourning patriotic role models plays an important role in the formation of these conjoined memories. As such, it is no surprise that after 1949, the CCP transformed the Qingming Festival, a traditional family holiday dedicated to commemorating ancestors, into a national memorial day honoring revolutionary martyrs.[2] According to Chang-tai Hung, "In declaring the Qingming Festival as Martyrs' Memorial Day, the communists essentially gave this traditional event an emotional moral appeal, equating the fallen with China's forebears."[3] Thus, through ritual, revolutionary martyrs take the place of family ancestors within the public consciousness. And yet, despite attempts by the state to regulate collective memory, memory can take alternate routes and develop in unexpected ways. "On the one hand, official agencies are in position to shape memory explicitly as they see fit, memory that best serves a national interest," James Young argues. "On the other hand, once created, memorials take on lives of their own, often stubbornly resistant to the state's original intentions."[4]

My journey from China to the United States for academic pursuits has allowed me to examine Chinese culture and society from a new perspective, leading to a unique phenomenon I describe as "memory shock." This term encapsulates the ongoing, profound questioning and reshaping of my past

Figure 1: The statue of Xiang Jingyu 向警予 (1895–1928) on Tortoise Mountain (Guishan 龟山) in Wuhan. The image is from Liu Shuiqing 刘水清, "Lingyuan li de yipian ye" 陵园里的一片叶 (A leaf in the cemetery), *Changjiang ribao* 长江日报 (Yangtze River daily), March 21, 2021.

memories. This influence, more powerful than the culture shock associated with adapting to a new physical environment, has reverberated throughout my scholarly research and continues to shape my life. For instance, while examining the Chinese revolution through the prism of diverse readings, my understanding of the revolutionary martyrs I learned about during my student years in China underwent a significant transformation. Previously overlooked figures, such as female martyr Lin Zhao 林昭 (1932–68), began to emerge in my reconstructed memories. Recollections of Xiang Jingyu, as recounted by early expelled leaders of the CCP like Zhang Guotao and Peng Shuzhi, have prompted me to contemplate more deeply the role of women in the revolution. Being in a different cultural environment has made me more attuned to these counternarratives and fostered a sensitivity toward the nuances of these revolutionary stories.

This book project grows out of my long-standing interests in ideological maneuvering, gender studies, and memory studies. In it, I intend to build an imaginary museum to house official memories, countermemories, personal memories, and, most importantly, the forgotten and repressed memories of Chinese female revolutionary martyrs. My ambition is to create a comprehensive understanding of these women's heroic deeds, struggles, and dilemmas. I have chosen celebrated female author Ding Ling, who endured the vicissitudes of Chinese revolutions and almost became a martyr herself, to guide us through this imaginary landscape. It is my hope that this imaginary museum of gendered memories provides readers with the proper space, time, and mood for contemplation, much like Xiang Jingyu's monument did for me as I sat on Tortoise Mountain.

ACKNOWLEDGMENTS

Unveiling the stories of female revolutionary martyrs in China has been akin to traversing an intricate maze of memories, emotions, and scholarly insights. My heart swells with gratitude when I think of those who walked alongside me, nurturing both my spirit and this book. Along this path, I was blessed to encounter three remarkable female scholars during my graduate years at the University of Oregon—the time when the seeds of this book first took root. My mentor, Maram Epstein, became my guide, leading me through the twists and turns of my journey with wisdom and patience. I still remember engaging in riveting discussions in her class that sparked my curiosity. Beyond her academic prowess, Professor Epstein has been a pillar of unwavering support, freely sharing her knowledge, time, and vivacity. My academic path was further illuminated by Wendy Larson, a beacon of wisdom and a source of inspiration. With a heart as vast as her knowledge, she not only taught me how to become a better scholar but also exemplified what it means to be a strong, resilient woman. In moments of doubt and darkness, she shared her own experiences, dispelling my apprehensions. Her counsel on navigating an academic career has been invaluable for my transformation from a graduate student to a professional scholar. I also had the good fortune of encountering Bryna Goodman, whose teachings were instrumental, pushing me to approach my research materials with precision and foster my unique academic voice. These three luminaries not only set the scholarly standard but also witnessed the nascent stages of my book's formation.

Upon joining the University of Notre Dame in 2018, I was welcomed by a bevy of supportive colleagues. Michel Hockx, a mentor beyond compare, has dedicated himself to nurturing young scholars like myself. He diligently read entire book manuscripts and draft proposals, offering invaluable insights and suggestions. Elisabeth Köll, with her steadfast support and timely guidance, played an essential role in keeping me on course. My gratitude extends to our past and present department chairs, Zhu Yongping and Yang Xiaoshan, whose support allowed me the time to pursue my research and complete this book. I also owe a debt of gratitude to Hye-Jin Juhn, our former East Asian Studies librarian, not only for her assistance with my research but also for her friendship. I offer my sincere thanks to Tarryn Chun, Emily Wang, Jennifer Huynh, Korey Garibaldi, and Sonja Stojanovic, my fellow members of our junior faculty writing group at Notre Dame, for their camaraderie and intellectual companionship.

There have been countless other scholars who, through fleeting conversations or enduring engagements, have shaped my thoughts. I am grateful to Louise Edwards, who generously shared her research and offered her guidance, and whose meticulous feedback significantly contributed to my book. To Tani Barlow, our unforgettable conversation as we meandered through the Notre Dame campus while discussing Ding Ling and her generation of revolutionaries remains etched in my memory. Conversations with Paola Iovene have always been a delightful dance of ideas. My resilience throughout this academic pursuit has been bolstered by fellow young scholars and friends like Ying Jia Tan, Hsin-Chin Hsieh, Dominic Meng-Hsuan Yang, Mara Yue Du, Calvin Hui, Cai Liang, and Wu Yidi. With them by my side, the oft-solitary quest of academia felt more like a journey shared with comrades. I'm thankful for their consistent support and cherished friendship.

To the team at the University of Michigan Press, I express my gratitude. To my editor, Sara Cohen, who has exhibited unwavering confidence and patience throughout this book's journey, and who expertly guided it through production. To the series editor, Emily Wilcox, who lent her support to this project. I am grateful to the copy editor, John Raymond, and the production editor, Marcia LaBrenz, for their assistance in the concluding phases of the book. I wish to thank the anonymous reviewers whose insightful comments and suggestions enriched the manuscript. This book is made possible in part by support from the Institute for Scholarship in the Liberal Arts, College of Arts and Letters, University of Notre Dame.

An earlier version of the chapter on Liu Hulan in this book appeared in "Contested Memories: An Imaginary Museum for a Chinese Female Revolutionary Martyr, Liu Hulan," *Modern China* 50, no. 2 (2024): 231–63, and I extend my appreciation to Kathryn Bernhardt for her guidance in its publication; it is reprinted here with permission. Special thanks to Katherine Thompson for her friendship and professional editing over the years. My research assistant, Wu Xiyun, played a pivotal role in obtaining photos from museum visits in Beijing for this book. I am grateful to Xin Zhaorui from the National Museum of Modern Chinese Literature for her generous assistance with archival materials and for connecting me with Ding Ling's former secretary, Wang Zengru. I appreciate the insightful conversations I had with Wang Zengru about Ding Ling. In a particularly poignant discussion, she remarked that Ding Ling is destined to be associated with the University of Michigan, harkening back to Yi-tsi Mei Feuerwerker's pioneering research on Ding Ling. I am delighted that this book has found a home at the University of Michigan Press, which is steeped in the legacy of Ding Ling's life.

Finally, I turn to my family with a heart overflowing with love and gratitude. This journey would have been impossible without their support. To my family, both in America and in China, I extend my deepest thanks. There are not enough words to convey my gratitude to my beloved parents, who have always encouraged me to pursue my dreams, even when they take me thousands of miles away from them. To my American family, John Moseley and Susan Moseley, whose unconditional love and care have been my emotional cornerstone since that autumn night in 2010 when they welcomed me at Eugene airport. To my husband, Qing, who has been my unwavering pillar of support and my most fervent cheerleader. To my precious daughter, Melody, who fills my life with boundless joy. Their presence has breathed life into my intellectual pursuits.

Introduction

Martyrdom, Memory, Museum

The Song of Death

Ding Ling 丁玲 (1904–86), the pen name for Jiang Bingzhi 蒋冰之, was a highly influential female writer and revolutionary of twentieth-century China. She was hospitalized in Beijing in July 1985. From July to September, while in the hospital and nearing the end of her life, she recorded one of her final essays, titled "The Song of Death" (*Si zhi ge* 死之歌).[1] In this essay, Ding Ling recalls numerous deaths that affected her and explains why she chose to live out her full life rather than die young as a martyr. She depicts two types of deaths she encountered in her life: those of her relatives and those of revolutionary martyrs, some of which overlapped.

"The Song of Death" begins with Ding Ling recalling her father's funeral when she was only three years old. She remembers wearing a white filial cap adorned with white pom-poms. The entire room was white, except for a black coffin in the center. "Death is so horrifying!" she laments.[2] Ding Ling was sensitive to death from an early age. The death of her cousin's wife was another lingering childhood memory. Ding Ling's cousin died before his wedding. His fiancée wed his spirit tablet, following the faithful maiden tradition. On the day of her wedding, she passed out crying. Within less than a year, she died as a Confucian chastity martyr. Ding Ling sympathized with her and was saddened by her death. In the spring of 1918, Ding Ling lost another close family member when her little brother died. She overheard her aunt say, "It would have been better if Bingzhi 冰之 had died. Why did the younger brother have to die?"[3] After experiencing the deaths of her cousin's wife and her younger brother, Ding Ling came to believe, out of despair, that girls have no future.

In her essay, Ding Ling explains how she was eventually inspired to escape her unfortunate fate as a woman, influenced by tales of both chastity and

Figure 2: Display of Ding Ling's study room at the National Museum of Modern Chinese Literature includes the sculpture of Ding Ling made by Zhang Dedi 张得蒂 in 1982 and Ai Xuan's 艾轩 painting of Ding Ling. Photo courtesy of Wu Xiyun.

revolutionary martyrs. Ding Ling and her mother's lives were significantly altered by her father's death. Ding Ling's mother gradually evolved from a virtuous wife with bound feet to a revolutionary. She often told Ding Ling tales of heroes and chastity martyrs (*gongchen lienü* 功臣烈女) and gave her related books to read.[4] Her favorite story to tell was about the female revolutionary martyr Qiu Jin 秋瑾. In this context, Ding Ling did not distinguish between female chastity martyrdom and revolutionary martyrdom. These stories established Ding Ling's general veneration of martyrs and martyrdom.

During the 1911 Revolution, Ding Ling's uncle was executed by Qing soldiers for being a revolutionary.[5] The assassination of the revolutionary leader Song Jiaoren 宋教仁 (1882–1913) in 1913 also profoundly influenced Ding Ling. She recounts delivering a speech, drafted by her mother, condemning the killing of revolutionaries.[6] Later in life, she was further impacted by the martyrdom of Liu Hezhen 刘和珍 (1904–26) and Li Dazhao 李大钊 (1889–1927). However, it was the martyrdom of Xiang Jingyu, whom she referred to as her ninth aunt, that ultimately drove her to join the revolution. Ding Ling

Figure 3: Ding Ling and her brother in Hunan, 1918. Source: Jiang Zulin 蒋祖林, *Ding Ling zhuan* 丁玲传 (Biography of Ding Ling), Beijing: Renmin wenxue chubanshe, 2015, 28.

shares that she later learned about the death of a fourteen-year-old girl in her hometown. The girl had participated in a few marches and was executed by the local government for having her hair styled in the short bob of a progressive woman. She was saddened by the news and wished she had followed Xiang Jingyu and led the girl in the revolution.[7] In May 1930, introduced by Pan Hannian 潘汉年 (1906–77), Ding Ling and her husband, Hu Yepin 胡也

频 (1903–31), joined the League of Left-wing Writers.[8] Ding Ling recounted, "When we joined the League of Left-wing Writers, we were aware that the revolutionaries would sacrifice their lives one day."[9] Tragically, Hu Yepin faced this fate and was ultimately executed by the Kuomintang (KMT) in 1931.

In "The Song of Death," Ding Ling's portrayal of martyrs reveals her obsession with martyrdom. This preoccupation was further shaped by her own personal experience of narrowly avoiding becoming a martyr when she was kidnapped by the KMT in 1933. After escaping captivity and fleeing to Shaanbei in 1936, Ding Ling became the subject of numerous investigations and spent the rest of her life defending her political loyalty to the CCP, even in her final essay. In "The Song of Death," she asserts that she was fully aware of the dangers involved in participating in the revolution and was prepared to become a martyr.[10] However, she also explains her desire to survive in order to reassure her comrades of her loyalty.[11]

Throughout the essay, Ding Ling emphasizes the challenge of staying alive. She contends, "To live is indeed difficult; however, death should not be an option. To live is to survive, to find ways to remain alive despite adversity."[12] In her 1983 memoir "The World of Demons and Monsters" (*Wangliang shijie* 魍魉世界), Ding Ling offers a detailed account of her days after being abducted by the KMT.[13] She describes that period as if she were dead but maintains that she preserved her integrity as a CCP member.[14] Although Ding Ling did not die as a martyr, her interest in martyrdom, particularly in female martyrdom, persisted throughout her life.

Female Martyrdom and Gendered Memory

Ding Ling's fascination with martyrdom, particularly female martyrdom, stems from both her personal experiences and historical origins. In China, female martyrdom has long been upheld as a testament of loyalty, both to the patriarchal family and the state. The analogies drawn between a wife's fidelity to her husband and an official's loyalty to the emperor, coupled with the strong bond between family and state, render female chastity martyrdom a fertile ground for politicized content and a potent narrative device for nation-building and the crafting of national memory. In her examination of the faithful maiden cult in late imperial China, Lu Weijing points out that "from the outset, female chastity was politicized in the moral philosophy of Confucianism."[15] Janet Theiss, in her research on female chastity cults in Qing

China, including female chastity martyrdom, illustrates how the Qing government leveraged female chastity to validate and reinforce its authority: "As the imperial state reached into the inner quarters of family life, seeking to mold behavior and moral intent, it placed women at the center of political culture, making female virtue integral to imperial state building and the civilizing project that legitimated it."[16]

The enduring legacy of the chastity cult continues to shape modern perceptions of female revolutionary martyrdom, reinforced by the state's narrative strategies. Revolutionary martyrs, whether male or female, are posthumously constructed for political purposes through narratives of their lives. Benedict Anderson points out that the narratives and memories of "exemplary suicides" and "poignant martyrdoms" are crucial to the establishment and legitimacy of a nation.[17] The shared grief over revolutionary martyrs contributes to the formation of national identity. Consequently, revolutionary martyrdom is inherently politicized. The construction of revolutionary martyrs is deeply entangled with the politics of collective memory, raising questions about who gets remembered, what is commemorated, what is forgotten, and who has the authority to make these determinations. Moreover, these commemorations of revolutionary martyrdom are shaped by gender considerations.

In this book, I explore the gendered dimensions of national memory by demonstrating that female revolutionary martyrs cannot be included in national memory without being constrained by traditional gender norms. As Louise Edwards argues in her research on women in wartime, there is a "rubric of 'crisis femininity'—where women are welcomed temporarily out of the confines of regular feminine expectations to meet the needs of a particular national or community crisis."[18] However, once the crisis is resolved, women who challenged the existing patriarchal structure either fade from national memory or have their stories restructured to conform to traditional gender expectations. Official narratives about female revolutionary martyrs thus exist in a paradox: they simultaneously grant women agency and confine them to the role of exemplary chastity martyrs. While chastity is seldom an issue in narratives about male martyrs, this traditional virtue becomes a pervasive concern in the accounts and literary representations of female revolutionary martyrs.

My book examines the commemorations and narratives surrounding Chinese female revolutionary sacrifices, with a specific focus on the concept of chastity in female revolutionary martyrdom. It investigates the transformation from traditional female chastity martyrs to female revolutionary martyrs and explores the politics of the gendered memory. By analyzing the changing narratives of female revolutionaries such as Qiu Jin 秋瑾 (1875–1907), Xiang Jingyu 向警予 (1895–1928), Zhenzhen 贞贞, and Liu Hulan 刘胡兰 (1932–47), all of whom are linked to Ding Ling's perception of martyrdom, I propose that female revolutionary martyrdom essentially reinforces rather than rejects the concept of female chastity martyrdom. It compels women to sacrifice both their bodies and lives for the nationalist cause. However, narratives that challenge established gender norms, particularly those surrounding female chastity, often remain silenced or overlooked in the collective memory of these female revolutionary martyrs.

To recover the silenced and overlooked voices in collective memories, this book aims to establish an imaginary museum of Chinese female revolutionary martyrs. This conceptual space would juxtapose regulated history and countermemories, helping us to understand the process of negotiating memories of female revolutionary martyrs and the construction of female revolutionary martyrdom both within and outside a nationalist framework. In examining gendered national memory, my book centers on the discursive construction and commemoration of female revolutionary martyrs rather than the female revolutionary martyrs themselves. While the state regulates national memory by defining who qualifies as a martyr and determining how such figures should be memorialized, personal memories and alternative narratives persist. From a broader sociopolitical perspective, the state strives to enshrine the importance of women's sacrifice through historical records, stone monuments, and museums, aiming to strengthen its own authority. At the same time, personal memories and the literary representations of female martyrs challenge the state-sanctioned discourse, shedding light on the experiences of individual women and their double sacrifice (*xianshen* 献身) for the Chinese revolution, offering both their bodies and their lives.

The Imaginary Museum

This book conceptualizes an imaginary museum for Chinese female revolutionary martyrs, exhibiting both memory and countermemory, in juxtaposition. Benedict Anderson underlines the pivotal role of museums in forming nationalist sentiment: "For museums, and the museumizing imagination, are both profoundly political."[19] Revolution museums, crafted to cultivate collective national memory, generally adhere to a rigid ideological agenda and exclude any dissenting narratives. Their exhibitions are meticulously curated for political objectives. Drawing upon Maurice Halbwachs's pioneering work on collective memory, which distinguishes between history and memory, Aleida Assmann advocates for the juxtaposition of the two as "complementary modes of cultural memory."[20] She considers the museum as a space that connects memory and history, explaining that "the juxtaposition or sequence of items in a spatial setting enables the observer to travel through history, offering a panorama of all the different eras at a single viewing. Time is thus transformed into space or, to be more precise, into the space of memory, in which it is constructed, represented, and perpetuated."[21] However, as Michel de Certeau points out, "Memory is a sort of anti-museum: it is not localizable. Fragments of it come out in legends. Objects and words also have hollow places in which a past sleeps, as in the everyday acts of walking, eating, going to bed, in which ancient revolutions slumber."[22]

In this book, I aim to merge Aleida Assmann's concept of juxtaposition with Michel de Certeau's notion of the "anti-museum" to construct an unlocalizable imaginary museum that preserves a gendered and pluralistic form of memory. This museum provides a space for negotiating between state-sanctioned historical narratives and countermemories, thereby enhancing our understanding of women's sacrifice during the Chinese revolution. At the heart of this imaginary museum stands Ding Ling, a central figure who came close to becoming a revolutionary martyr during her house arrest in Nanjing. Her survival, however, subjected her chastity and political loyalty to constant scrutiny by the CCP throughout the Chinese Communist revolution, spanning from the Rectification Movement in Yan'an to the Cultural Revolution. Ding Ling's life serves as a poignant symbol of the tumultuous journey of the Chinese revolution, and her preoccupation with martyrdom underscores the formidable challenges women faced during this period. It's worth noting that the word "martyr" carries the meaning of "witness" in Greek.[23] In this context, martyrs serve as witnesses to faith and truth. Ding Ling, as a witness of the Chinese revolution, embodies the essence of a martyr. Her life as an almost-martyr sheds light on the potential destinies of other female revolutionary martyrs had they survived.

Centered on Ding Ling's experiences and her fascination with martyrdom, this imaginary museum features five exhibitions, each dedicated to a different Chinese female revolutionary, including Ding Ling herself. The spatial construction of this imaginary museum mirrors the physical layout of actual museum exhibitions. Each chapter represents an exhibition that begins by showcasing an iconic image associated with the heroine, followed by a brief biography of the individual and an exploration of her connection with Ding Ling (except in the case of the exhibition on Ding Ling herself). Subsequently, the museum brings together contested fictional and historical records, objects, visual images, and stone monuments dedicated to the female revolutionary. This presentation exhibits both the official narrative and personal memories. This arrangement disrupts the conventional linear presentation found in real-life museums, offering plural memories that challenge a singular historical narrative.

In this imaginary museum, Exhibition I is dedicated to Ding Ling herself, unraveling the mysteries that surround her almost-martyrdom during her abduction in 1933 and the aftermath. The exhibition demonstrates the ups and downs in Ding Ling's revolutionary career and reveals the double burden that requires female revolutionaries to be both revolutionary and adherent to traditional gender norms. Female chastity remained a concern within the CCP, which was why Ding Ling's sexual relationship with the alleged traitor Feng Da was at the center of the controversy surrounding her. Through examining official records on the CCP's investigations of Ding Ling, personal memories, rumors, and gossip, I argue that a Chinese female revolutionary was expected to embody the roles of a *lienü* 列女 (exemplary woman), a *lienü* 烈女 (chastity martyr), and a *nülieshi* 女烈士 (female revolutionary martyr) at the same time.

Exhibition II explores the evolving reputation of Ding Ling's childhood inspiration, the martyr Qiu Jin, from a filial, chaste, and wrongfully convicted weak woman in the late Qing to a revolutionary icon by the time of the Yan'an era. I analyze the initial depiction of Qiu Jin in media and literature, where she was portrayed in a manner similar to the female character Dou E 窦娥 from a classic Chinese play who was also unjustly convicted.[24] This depiction served dual purposes of avoiding explicit political messages against the Qing government and confining the images of Qiu Jin within traditional gender norms. Following the fall of the Qing dynasty, Qiu Jin began to be hailed as a martyr for the nation. I examine how Qiu Jin was constructed as a female revolutionary martyr and integrated into the new collective national memory in the Republican era through various forms of commemorations such as memorial services, broadcasting, governmental orders, textbooks, and relic exhibitions. I argue that nationalism played a significant role in the invention of Qiu Jin as a revolutionary martyr. I also analyze the portrayals of Qiu

Jin as a revolutionary martyr in Xia Yan's 夏衍 (1900–1995) national defense drama, *The Spirit of Freedom* (*Ziyou hun* 自由魂, 1936), and Yan Yiyan's 颜一烟 (1913–97) play, *Qiu Jin* 秋瑾 (1940), which was written in Yan'an. These works evoke patriotism with different emphases and political agendas. In this exhibition, multiple memories and literary representations of Qiu Jin illustrate how female sacrifice becomes a fertile field for politicized and gendered narratives.

Exhibition III focuses on Xiang Jingyu, an early female Communist leader and a close family friend of Ding Ling, who was executed by the KMT in 1928. She demonstrated remarkable leadership in women's movements and made significant contributions to the May Thirtieth Movement. Nonetheless, women's movements were marginalized in the early CCP era. Female revolutionaries often took on roles related to women's issues, and their broader contributions to the revolution were not fully acknowledged within the party. These women were expected to be virtuous wives as well as committed revolutionaries, seen as devoted to both their husbands and the nation. In the CCP's official narratives, Xiang Jingyu is portrayed as a dedicated Communist revolutionary, and her marriage to another early CCP leader, Cai Hesen 蔡和森 (1895–1931), is held up as an ideal model for revolutionaries. However, personal memories from early CCP leaders who later distanced themselves from the party, such as Zhang Guotao 张国焘, Yang Zilie 杨子烈, Zheng Chaolin 郑超麟, Peng Shuzhi 彭述之, and Chen Bilan 陈碧兰, present a more complex image of Xiang Jingyu. Her extramarital affair with Peng Shuzhi complicates her image as a revolutionary martyr. Examining both the official accounts and private recollections of Xiang Jingyu underscores the gender hierarchy within the CCP and the subordination of the women's movement to broader national salvation. The tension between her revolutionary commitments and personal emotions reveals the challenges faced by female revolutionaries in a largely male-dominated political environment.

Exhibition IV explores the fine line between being a heroine and being labeled a prostitute in the narratives of female revolutionary sacrifice. This exhibit focuses on contested perspectives on Zhenzhen, a fictional character from Ding Ling's short story "When I Was in Xia Village" (*Wo zai Xiacun de shihou* 我在霞村的时候), which was inspired by a true story Ding Ling heard in Yan'an. I first examine Ding Ling's one-act play *Reunion* (*Chongfeng* 重逢, August 1937) and Lao She's 老舍 (1899–1966) two Chinese operas about women's wartime sacrifice, both of which were adapted by the Northwest Front Service Corps led by Ding Ling. These works reveal societal expectations for women to sacrifice both their sexual integrity and their lives for nationalism. I then analyze the representations of rape and sexual violence in Chinese wartime literature, demonstrating that women are unable to erase their pain and shame unless their stories are integrated into the grand historical narrative of Communist revolution and national salvation. Ding Ling's short story "When I Was in Xia Village" complicates and transcends the national salvation narrative by focusing on the wronged woman herself. To further explore the concept of *xianshen* 献身 (sacrifice body and life) for women during the revolution, I trace Zhenzhen's journey from the Catholic Church to a planned trip to a transformed Yan'an, from devoting herself to God to sacrificing herself for the CCP. I argue that patriarchal nationalism imposed on women the untenable burden of sacrificing sexually for the nation while miraculously reclaiming their chastity after the crisis had subsided. During the Anti-Rightist Movement in 1958, the character Zhenzhen's revolutionary credentials were revoked, and she was disparaged as nothing more than a military prostitute. This devaluation of female sacrifice demonstrates how women's individual sufferings during national crisis were often ignored.

In the criticism of Ding Ling and her fictional character Zhenzhen during the Anti-Rightist Movement, Liu Hulan, an iconic young female revolutionary, was often contrasted with Zhenzhen.[25] Liu Hulan was presented as the exemplary female revolutionary martyr who should be worshipped and included in national memory. Exhibition V examines both the state-sanctioned narratives and various reinterpretations of Liu Hulan. The exhibition aims to explore how the process of making Liu a martyr contributes to the formation of collective memory, how gender and sexuality either support or problematize state-sponsored ideology, and how contemporary rewritings of Liu's martyrdom interrogate state ideology and nationalism. I investigate some key display items such as the state inscriptions commemorating the martyr, the hay cutter used to execute Liu Hulan, paintings and statues, the soldiers' shoes that Liu made and collected to support the Eighth Route army, and a handkerchief, all relics that contribute to the evolving narratives of Liu Hulan that reflect the ideological changes in modern and contemporary China. I argue that the issue of chastity continues to present challenges in representations of female martyrdom. In contemporary artwork, Liu Hulan is portrayed either as an asexualized political model or as an oversexualized weapon against mainstream ideology.

The epilogue reflects on the poignant death of Guan Lu 关露 (1907–82) and explores the friendship between her and fellow writer and revolutionary

Ding Ling. These two women are mirror images of each other, having both faced lifelong scrutiny over their chastity and political loyalty. Additionally, the epilogue examines the controversy surrounding the commemoration of Ding Ling, highlighting the negotiation between official memory and personal memory. After Ding Ling's death on March 4, 1986, her husband, Chen Ming 陈明 (1917–2019), made several appeals to the Central Committee of the CCP, hoping that Ding Ling's body could be covered by the Chinese Communist Party flag to symbolize the official recognition of her contributions to both the party and the nation. However, the CCP denied his request. Ding Ling's body was eventually covered by a red flag, a gift from her friends from the Great Northern Wasteland (*beidahuang* 北大荒), where she and Chen Ming spent twelve years in exile performing hard labor. The words "Ding Ling is immortal" (*Ding Ling busi* 丁玲不死) were embroidered on it. Her suffering and sacrifice were remembered by those who truly knew her.

EXHIBITION I

Ding Ling

Almost a Martyr

Ding Ling 丁玲 (1904–86) emerged as a prominent female writer and revolutionary in modern China. Her ascent in the literary field was marked by her inaugural work, "Mengke" (*Mengke* 梦珂), and the subsequent acclaim for her notable short story, "Miss Sophia's Diary" (*Shafei nüshi de riji* 莎菲女士的日记) in 1928, both of which explored women's issues in China. In May 1930, she and her husband, Hu Yepin 胡也频 (1903–31), became affiliates of the League of Left-wing Writers. The execution of Hu Yepin by the Chinese Nationalist Party (KMT) in 1931 propelled Ding Ling to join the Chinese Communist Party (CCP) in 1932, intensifying her involvement in the Communist revolution. Tragically, the KMT abducted Ding Ling in 1933, and while in captivity in Nanjing, she gave birth to a daughter in 1934, whose father was Feng Da 冯达, an alleged traitor. She managed to escape to the CCP's headquarters in Yan'an in 1936, where she would continue to confront persistent doubts about her sexual chastity and political loyalty. In 1951, her novel *Sun Shines over the Sanggan River* (*Taiyang zhao zai Sanggan he shang* 太阳照在桑干河上) earned her the Stalin Prize, the pinnacle of recognition for socialist literature. Nevertheless, in a stark turn of events, she was exiled to the desolate *beidahuang* 北大荒 (Great Northern Wasteland) in 1958, where she endured a dozen years of strenuous labor. Vindicated by the CCP in 1984, her contributions and tribulations were finally acknowledged, and she passed away two years later. The story of Ding Ling's life poignantly echoes the turbulent shifts of Chinese revolution in the twentieth century.

Two Poems

The abduction of Ding Ling was a sensational story in China during the early 1930s. The renowned female writer was kidnapped by the KMT from her resi-

Figure 4: Ding Ling, 1931 in Shanghai, photo by Agnes Smedley (1892–1950). Source: *Ding Ling quanji*, vol. 1, 6.

dence within the Shanghai international settlement on May 14, 1933. Pan Zinian 潘梓年 (1893–1972), a leftist intellectual who happened to be visiting Ding Ling, also fell victim to the abduction. On that very same day, Ying Xiuren 应修人 (1900–1933), a leftist poet, was ambushed by KMT spies at Ding Ling's apartment. Choosing to leap from the window rather than succumb to his assailants, he sacrificed his life as a martyr. The shocking nature of the crime and the disappearance of a leftist female writer sparked a media frenzy.

Numerous newspapers published the news about Ding Ling's disappearance. Prominent figures from the public sphere, including Song Qingling 宋庆龄 (1893–1981), Cai Yuanpei 蔡元培 (1868–1940), and Yang Xingfo 杨杏佛 (1893–1933), took active roles in the endeavor to rescue Ding Ling and Pan Zinian. A coalition of progressive intellectuals organized the Association for Rescuing Ding Ling and Pan Zinian (*Ding Pan yingjiu hui* 丁潘营救会) and

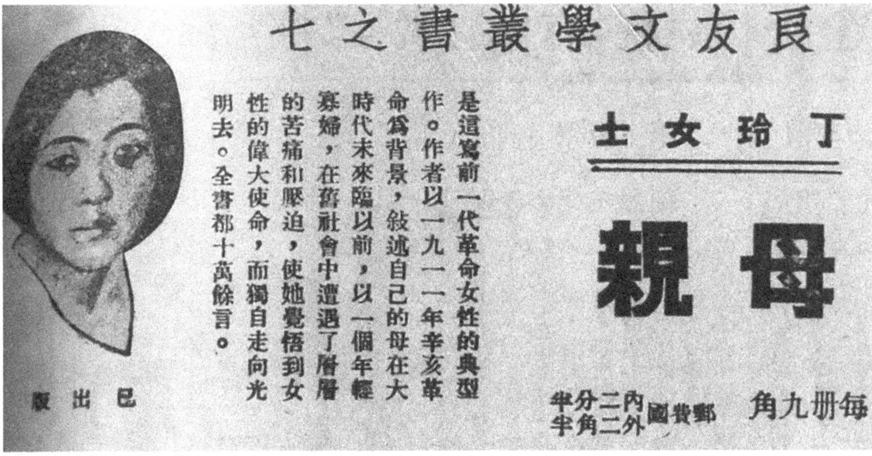

Figure 5: The advertisement for Ding Ling's novel *Mother* in *Liangyou* magazine. Source: *Liangyou* 良友 (The friendly companion) 78 (1933): 38. The portrait of Ding Ling on this advertisement was drawn by Cai Yuanpei's 蔡元培 daughter Cai Weilian 蔡威廉 (1904–39) in 1929.

issued the "Declaration from the Cultural Community for the Rescue of Ding Ling and Pan Zinian," urging the KMT government to release the captives.[1]

Furthermore, innovative strategies were employed to amplify awareness about Ding Ling's disappearance. For instance, the *Liangyou* literary series published Ding Ling's incomplete novel titled *Mother* (*Muqin* 母亲), and extensively promoted the publication to shed light on Ding Ling's abduction, thereby catalyzing efforts for her rescue (see fig. 5). The Domestic Product Retail Store, under the leadership of the patriotic entrepreneur Song Zejiu 宋则久 (1867–1956), released an advertisement asserting that Ding Ling, the proletarian writer, exclusively endorsed domestic products (see fig. 6). This approach aimed to concurrently boost domestic product sales and enhance awareness regarding the disappearance of Ding Ling.

After several months of unsuccessful endeavors, a prevailing notion emerged that Ding Ling had embraced the role of a revolutionary martyr, following the path of her deceased husband Hu Yepin.[2] A news report surfaced detailing a clandestine memorial service held for her in the Shanghai French Concession. According to the report, the service drew a significant gathering of leftist writers. The memorial hall was adorned with a magazine photograph of Ding Ling, accompanied by the inscription "neither arising nor

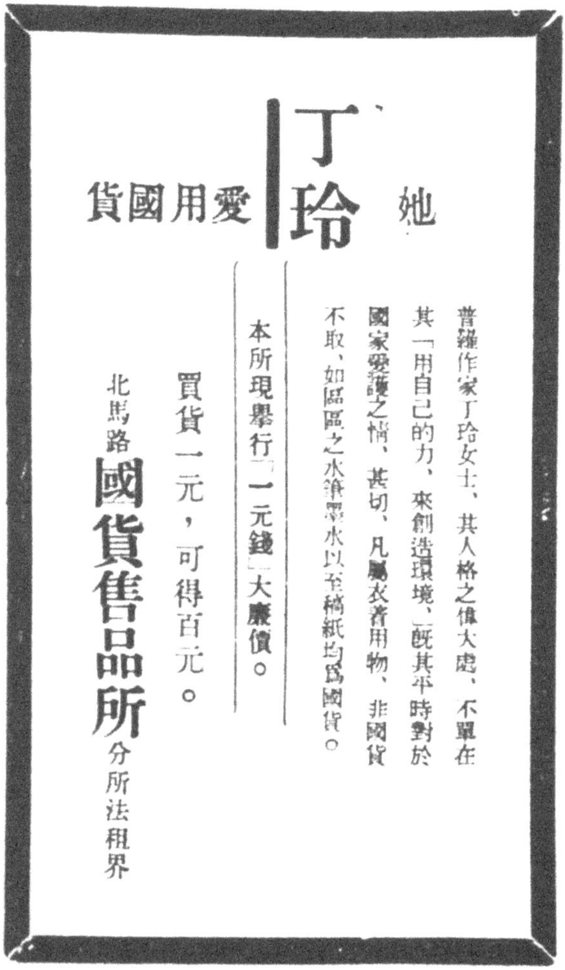

Figure 6: Domestic Product Retail Store's advertisement linking Ding Ling and domestic products. Source: *Yishi bao* (Tianjin), June 23, 1933.

ceasing" (*busheng bumie* 不生不灭) from Lu Xun 鲁迅 (1881–1936), along with Guo Moruo's 郭沫若 (1892–1978) mourning poem inscribed in oracle bone script.[3] While the origin of the report remained uncertain and could very well have been a piece of misinformation, numerous essays and poems were indeed written in memory of Ding Ling at the time.[4]

One notable tribute came from the prominent Chinese literary figure Lu Xun, who composed a classical Chinese poem titled "A Lament for Ms. Ding" (*Dao Ding jun* 悼丁君) to commemorate Ding Ling (see fig. 7):

On storied buildings endless night
weighs down like flagstones overhead;
Spring's breeze that once shaped willow trees
to autumn's ninety days has led.
The inlaid zither now dust-choked,
its clear and poignant music stops;
Alack that we're without the beauty
who shined on the mountaintop.[5]

The poem's closing line alludes to Qu Yuan's 屈原 (340–278 BC) lament in "Encountering Sorrow" (*Li sao* 离骚), where he mourns, "there is no beauty on the mountaintop" (*ai gaoqiu zhi wunü* 哀高丘之无女).[6] By referencing the early political martyr Qu Yuan and his "Encountering Sorrow," Lu Xun laments Ding Ling's fate while he praises her literary prowess. On September 21, 1933, Lu Xun wrote to Cao Juren 曹聚仁 (1900–1972), the editor-in-chief of *Taosheng Weekly*, requesting the publication of his poem in Cao's periodical.[7] Personal pleas for publication were an unusual occurrence in Lu Xun's writing career. The assumed demise of Ding Ling deeply saddened him, and he wished to share his grief with the public. The poem was indeed published in *Taosheng Weekly* on September 30, 1933.[8] Three years later, in 1936, while en route to Shaanbei, Ding Ling learned about Lu Xun's death. She adopted the pseudonym Yao Gaoqiu 耀高丘 (shining on the mountaintop) from "A Lament for Ms. Ding" to write a condolence letter to Lu Xun's wife, Xu Guangping 许广平 (1898–1968).[9] In her letter, Ding Ling invoked the poem to both commemorate Lu Xun and recall his poignant tribute.

Commemoration plays a crucial role in strengthening bonds within a community. Ding Ling and Lu Xun's friendship flourished through their shared acts of commemorating revolutionary martyrs. Their initial interaction occurred in 1925 when Ding Ling reached out to Lu Xun, seeking advice about the challenges she was facing.[10] Regrettably, due to misunderstandings, she never received a response from him. However, the shared sorrow over the loss of Ding Ling's first husband Hu Yepin in 1931 became the foundation of their friendship.

Following Hu Yepin's death, the CCP invited Ding Ling to become the chief editor of a new left-wing magazine, *Beidou* 北斗 (The plough). Seeking guidance on magazine editing, she turned to Lu Xun, who was the leader of the League of Left-wing Writers. Lu Xun introduced her to woodprint paintings and suggested including the German artist Käthe Kollwitz's (1867–1945)

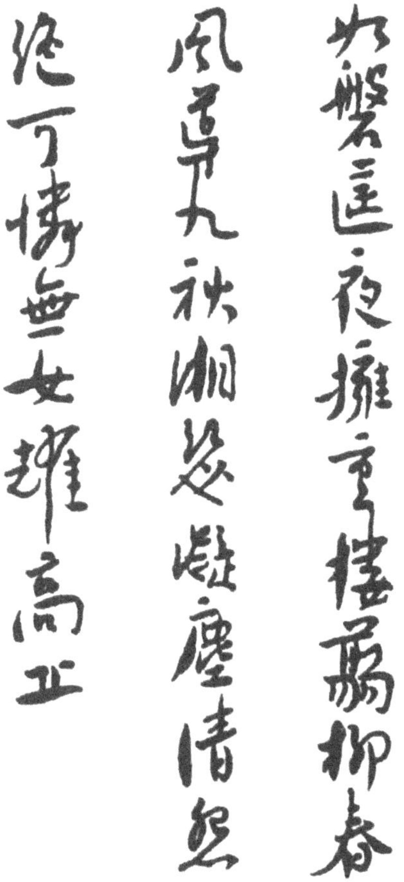

Figure 7: Lu Xun's handwritten piece of "A Lament for Ms. Ding." Source: Tu Shaojun 涂绍钧, *Tuben Ding Ling zhuan* 图本丁玲传 (Illustrated biography of Ding Ling), Changchun: Changchun chubanshe, 2015, 129.

work *Sacrifice* in *Beidou* to commemorate the five martyrs of the League of Left-wing Writers.[11] Influenced by the left-wing writer community, Ding Ling joined the CCP in 1932 while she was editing *Beidou*, solidifying her commitment to the cause.

After her kidnapping, Ding Ling lived under house arrest for three years with her then-husband Feng Da, who was suspected of betraying her to the KMT. It wasn't until 1936 that she reconnected with the CCP. On May 14, 1936, the three-year anniversary of Ding Ling's abduction, she excitedly informed her friends, "Today is my birthday; May 14 was once my day of death, but now is my birthday."[12] Ding Ling held the belief that the CCP could resurrect her. With the assistance of the CCP, Ding Ling managed to escape from Nanjing and arrived in Bao'an 保安, the CCP's headquarters at the time, in November 1936. Upon her arrival, prominent CCP leaders including Mao Zedong 毛泽东 (1893–1976), Zhou Enlai 周恩来 (1898–1976), Zhang Wentian 张闻天 (1900–1976), Deng Yingchao 邓颖超 (1904–92), and Li Kenong 李克农 (1899–1962) held a warm welcome party for Ding Ling in a *yaodong* 窑洞 cave house.[13]

Ding Ling embarked on her second life in Bao'an. Within days of her arrival, she played an instrumental role in establishing the Chinese Literature and Art Association (*Zhongguo wenyi xiehui* 中国文艺协会), marking the inception of the first literary organization within the Revolutionary Base Area. During the inaugural meeting of the Chinese Literature and Art Association, Mao Zedong delivered a speech that urged literary workers to venture to the front lines to inspire soldiers in battle.[14] Responding to Mao's call, Ding Ling enthusiastically volunteered to serve on the front line of the Red Army. Propelled by the resolution of the Xi'an Incident, which called for the KMT to cease the civil war, Mao Zedong conveyed his elation through a poem titled "The Immortals at the River: To Ding Ling" (*Linjiangxian: Gei Ding Ling tongzhi* 临江仙给丁玲同志, see fig. 8). He sent this poem to the front line via military telegram at the end of December 1936. General Nie Rongzhen 聂荣臻 (1899–1992) forwarded this special telegram to Ding Ling. The poem reads:

> The red banners on the wall flutter in the sinking afterglow,
> Over the solitary town whirls sweepingly the westerly blast.
> The characters in Bao'an are at once jubilant.
> In the cave dwelling is tendered a banquet,
> To regale the very soul who was once imprisoned as a convict.
> Who bears comparison with the slender pen?
> Three thousand crack troops with mausers as their equipment.
> The planned battle array is deployed toward the east on the Long Mount.
> A literate lady yesterday,
> And a martial general at the present.[15]

The poem is notable for its rarity in a time of war, as sending a telegram to the front line without explicit military content was uncommon. Additionally, it remains unique as Mao's sole poem dedicated to a writer. In this poem,

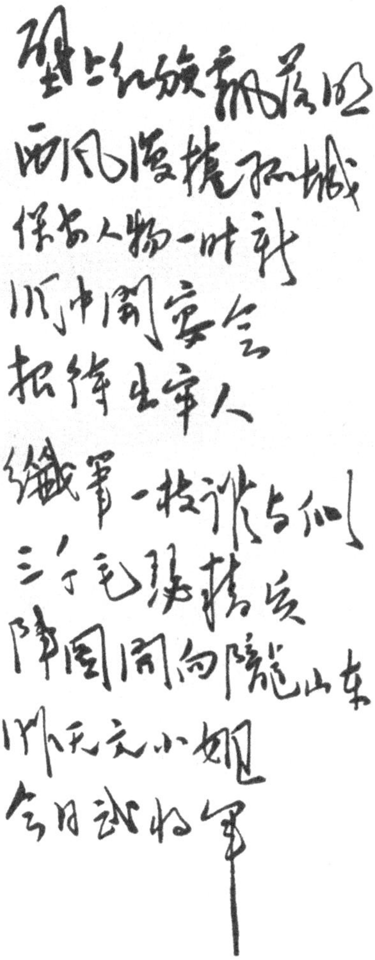

Figure 8: Mao Zedong's handwritten piece of "The Immortals at the River: To Ding Ling." Source: *Ding Ling* 丁玲, edited by Luo Guangda 罗光达 and Jiang Zulin, Shenyang: Liaoning meishu chubanshe, 1993, 9.

Mao draws a parallel between Ding Ling's literary prowess and the strength of military forces. The final two lines compare Ding Ling's past and present, symbolizing her rebirth as a female revolutionary. The poem holds significance for both Mao Zedong and Ding Ling. Mao handwrote it on several occasions throughout his life, including a version he gifted to Ding Ling upon her return to Yan'an in the spring of 1937. Around 1945, Mao handwrote the poem "To Ding Ling" once again, modifying the last line from "a martial general" (*wu jiangjun* 武将军) to "a female general" (*nü jiangjun* 女将军) in this rendition, acknowledging her as a heroine.[16] Mao's poem to Ding Ling can be regarded as a love letter from the CCP to a female intellectual. Unfortunately, this honeymoon phase did not endure for long.

The Problematic Note

Ding Ling found herself haunted by her days under house arrest in Nanjing during every purification movement led by the CCP. Her purity, both political and sexual, faced constant scrutiny. Upon her arrival in Yan'an, speculations circulated that Ding Ling had collaborated with the KMT while in captivity in Nanjing. Eager to vindicate herself, Ding Ling volunteered to be investigated by the party. Ren Bishi 任弼时 (1904–50) was the designated investigator for Ding Ling's case. Following the investigation, the CCP Organization Department outlined areas of suspicion regarding Ding Ling. These included the claim that she maintained a sexual relationship with the defector Feng Da while under house arrest. By 1940, the investigators concluded that there was no evidence of her surrender in Nanjing, her relationship with Feng Da was involuntary (*shenbu youji* 身不由己), and her commitment to the CCP remained steadfast.[17] This conclusion received the endorsement of the CCP leaders Chen Yun 陈云 (1905–95) and Li Fuchun 李富春 (1900–1975). Additionally, Mao Zedong appended his endorsement to the "1940 Conclusion," stating that "Comrade Ding Ling is still a loyal party member dedicated to the CCP and the revolution."[18]

To purify the CCP, Mao Zedong launched the Rectification Movement in Yan'an in 1941. During the heyday of this movement, Ding Ling underwent intense scrutiny and criticism. However, Mao's endorsement intervened in her favor, and was a gesture for which she remained deeply grateful. During a senior cadre meeting, Mao expressed that Ding Ling's essay "Thoughts on March 8" (*Sanba jie yougan* 三八节有感) not only critiqued but also offered valuable suggestions to the CCP. He drew a distinction between Ding Ling and Wang Shiwei 王实味, noting that while Wang Shiwei adhered to Trotskyism, Ding Ling was a comrade.[19]

Following the Rectification Movement, Ding Ling adjusted her writing style. Influenced by Mao's call for writers to spotlight workers, peasants, and soldiers, as articulated in his instrumental talks at the Yan'an Forum on Literature and Art, Ding Ling wrote a reportage in 1944 about the labor hero Tian

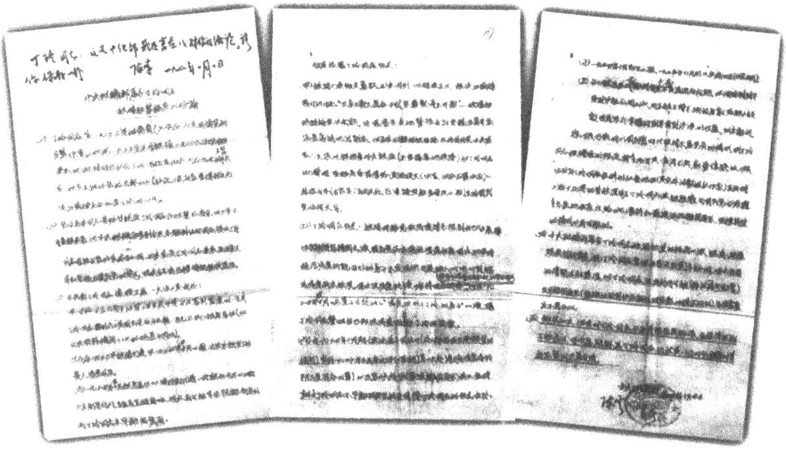

Figure 9: The original copy of the "1940 Conclusion." Source: *Ding Ling zishu* 丁玲自述 (Autobiography of Ding Ling), edited by Li Hui 李辉, Zhengzhou: Daxiang chubanshe, 2006, 170.

Baolin 田保霖. Upon reading Ding Ling's "Tian Baolin" and Ouyang Shan's 欧阳山 (1908–2000) reportage titled "Living in the New Society" (*Huo zai xin shehui li* 活在新社会里), Mao Zedong wrote a letter to the two writers. In it, he lauded their new writing style and extended an invitation for a conversation at his residence.[20]

On April 3, 1943, the party Central Committee released "Guanyu jixu kaizhan zhengfeng yundong de jueding" 关于继续开展整风运动的决定 (The Decision on Continuing the Rectification Movement).[21] Then, on July 15, Kang Sheng 康生 (1898–1975) delivered a speech on "Qiangjiu shizuzhe" 抢救失足者 (Rescuing the fallen), in which he exaggerated the number of spies within the CCP and advocated for a purge.[22] These developments, including the "Decision" and Kang Sheng's speech, intensified the radicalization of the Rectification Movement and resulted in the unjust convictions of numerous intellectuals.

In the spring of 1943, Ding Ling was assigned to the first sector of the Central Party School of the CCP (*dangxiao yi bu* 党校一部) for the purpose of ideological reform and cadre investigation (*shengan* 审干).[23] Under immense pressure during this investigation, Ding Ling wrote supplemental material detailing her activities in Nanjing, including a note she had written under the instruction of the KMT during her time under house arrest. The note roughly conveys, "The arrest is a misunderstanding; there is no interrogation; I have received preferential treatment; I will return home to take care of my mother and not engage in any political activities."[24] In her later years, Ding Ling explained the context of the note in her memoir:

> I've always regarded the note I wrote to the KMT as worthless. It neither signified betrayal nor submission. It did not suggest any wavering or compromising on my part. The note held no value for the enemy. However, to me, it served as a way to distance myself from the enemy. I believe that considering the political climate and my circumstances at that time, no one can rightfully accuse me of wrongdoing, let alone label me as politically problematic.[25]

This seemingly harmless note, however, caused Ding Ling significant problems within the realm of political movements. To begin with, during the 1940 investigation, Ding Ling did not disclose the fact that she had written a note to the KMT. The conclusion of the investigation with which Ding Ling cooperated in 1940 states that Ding Ling "did not provide any written communication to the KMT."[26] It is not surprising that Ding Ling initially regarded the note as insignificant and did not disclose this information when she reconnected with the CCP after years of house arrest in Nanjing. This can be attributed, in part, to the fact that Ding Ling was neither a professional revolutionary nor politically attuned.

While traveling from Nanjing to Bao'an, Ding Ling had an encounter with an old friend, Pan Hannian, a prominent secret agent for the CCP, in Xi'an. During their meeting, Pan strongly recommended that Ding Ling head to France instead of Bao'an to raise funds for the Red Army. Despite France being a place she had long desired to visit, Ding Ling's most fervent aspiration after three years was to be back within the "embrace of the Mother—the Party Central Committee."[27] Thus, she declined the tempting proposal from Pan Hannian and proceeded to Bao'an.

A few years later, Ding Ling crossed paths with Pan Hannian again in Yan'an. It is likely that Pan was aware of the numerous hardships and investigations Ding Ling had already undergone. The two did not engage in lengthy conversations, except on one occasion when Pan sincerely urged Ding Ling to "put forth effort in writing (*haohao xie wenzhang ba* 好好写文章吧)."[28] As an experienced professional revolutionary who played an important role in founding the League of Left-wing Writers, Pan Hannian was familiar with the suspicions and challenges intellectuals like Ding Ling might face in

Yan'an. During their encounters in both Xi'an and Yan'an, Pan Hannian subtly advised Ding Ling to avoid politics and focus on her role as a writer. Ding Ling, however, opted for the demanding path of being both a writer and a professional revolutionary.

Both Pan Hannian and Ding Ling saw their socialist revolutionary journeys unfold in strikingly similar ways. In 1943, Pan Hannian found himself deceived into a meeting with the Japanese collaborator Wang Jingwei 汪精卫 (1883–1944), yet he refrained from reporting this incident to the CCP out of concern that he might struggle to clarify it effectively.[29] Mao Zedong chose to place his trust in Pan, even quelling any rumors that circulated about him. Due to his invaluable intelligence efforts that contributed to the triumph of the Communist revolution, Pan Hannian was subsequently appointed as the deputy mayor of Shanghai after the establishment of the PRC. However, in 1955, prompted by the spirit of reporting individual historical issues to the party Central Committee, Pan Hannian admitted to his clandestine encounter with Wang Jingwei.[30] This confession led Mao Zedong to doubt Pan's reliability, eventually ordering his arrest. Pan spent the rest of his life in prison and died in 1977. It was not until 1982 that the CCP declared Pan's rehabilitation and restored his reputation.[31] Similarly, Ding Ling's decision to withhold the fact that she had written a note to the KMT cast a shadow of suspicion over her for the rest of her life.

Political purity stands as a fundamental principle within the CCP. During each political campaign, party members undergo rigorous scrutiny to ensure their loyalty to the CCP. This concept serves as means for the CCP to maintain tight control over its members and prevent ideological deviation. Furthermore, the CCP also uses the notion of political purity to legitimize and solidify its authority by positioning itself as morally superior. Although the note Ding Ling wrote to the KMT in 1933 showed no overt signs of betraying the CCP, its existence was a black mark on her revolutionary track record, given the party's emphasis on the notion of "purity." In 1943, under the immense pressure of the radical "Rescue the Fallen" movement, Ding Ling mentally collapsed and unwillingly confessed to having acted as a KMT spy.[32] The investigation into Ding Ling's activities throughout 1943 extended over several years without yielding conclusive results. In the spring of 1944, Ding Ling left the party school to assume a role at the Shanganning Border Region Culture Association (*Shanganning bianqu wenhua xiehui* 陕甘宁边区文化协会) focused on writing.[33]

In August 1945, three party school committee members drafted a "preliminary conclusion" (*chubu jielun* 初步结论), labeling the note Ding Ling composed for the KMT as a type of remorse letter (*huiguo shu* 悔过书) expressing regret for her involvement with the CCP.[34] This contentious "preliminary conclusion" was included in Ding Ling's political profile. In 2006, Li Xin 黎辛 (1920–2021), who had collaborated with Ding Ling on editing the *Jiefang ribao* 解放日报 (Liberation Daily) in Yan'an, highlighted that the frequently employed investigative method in Yan'an, known as *bi gong xin* 逼供信 (coercing confessions through torture and subsequently accepting them as credible), had led people to provide fabricated admissions of guilt during the cadre investigations.[35] He further argues that the "preliminary conclusion" lacks validity, as it was formulated after the cadre investigation movement and was never discussed by the party branch or sent to Ding Ling.[36]

Before departing Yan'an for northeast China in 1945, Ding Ling visited Ren Bishi, expressing her concerns about the pending cadre investigation case, despite her lack of awareness regarding the "preliminary conclusion." Ren Bishi assured Ding Ling of the CCP's trust in her and encouraged her to proceed to the front lines without worry.[37] It remains unclear whether Ren Bishi and Mao Zedong were aware of Ding Ling's note to the KMT and the existence of the "preliminary conclusion" during that period. However, considering Mao's commendation of Ding Ling's reportage titled "Tian Baolin" in 1944 and Ren's assurance, it is plausible that they were either uninformed about the "preliminary conclusion" or harbored skepticism regarding the documents associated with the "Rescue the Fallen" movement. The CCP maintained unwavering confidence in Ding Ling until the 1950s when she was questioned again about her political purity.

Ding Ling reached the pinnacle of her career during the early years of the PRC. She held the position of vice president at the Chinese Literature Association (*quanguo wenxie* 全国文协) and served as the inaugural editor-in-chief of *Wenyi bao* 文艺报 (Journal of Literature and Art), the official platform for the CCP's literary policies. In 1951, amid his busy schedule, Mao Zedong made a visit to Ding Ling while she was writing at Yihe Garden.[38] Despite her successes, which included winning the prestigious 1951 Stalin Prize for her novel *Sun Shines over the Sanggan River* (*Taiyang zhao zai Sanggan he shang* 太阳照在桑干河上), the highest honor for socialist literature, her days of acclaim turned out to be fleeting.

During the *Sufan* 肃反 (Party-cleansing) Movement, Ding Ling faced criticism for allegedly forming an antiparty clique alongside Chen Qixia 陈企霞 (1913–88). In 1955, at the China Writers Association Party group's expansion meeting, Zhou Yang 周扬 (1907–89) questioned Ding Ling's loyalty to the CCP. He labeled Ding Ling as a defector after she discussed her house arrest in Nanjing during the meeting.[39] In the same year, Lu Dingyi 陆定一 (1906–96), the minister of the Central Propaganda Department, submitted a report detailing Ding Ling's perceived faults to the Central Committee of the CCP, which Mao Zedong reviewed. With Mao's consent, the Central Propaganda Department organized a group to investigate the historical issues surrounding Ding Ling, including her note to the KMT in 1933.

In August 1956, Ding filed an appeal in response to the assertion that she was a member of the antiparty group. Alongside her appeal, she submitted an extensive essay titled "My Opinions on the Work Done by Comrade Zhou Yang from 1949 to 1952" (*1949 zhi 1952 nian wo dui Zhou Yang tongzhi gongzuo shang ceng youguo de yijian* 一九四九至一九五二年我对周扬同志工作上曾有过的意见) to the Central Propaganda Department.[40] In this essay, Ding Ling criticized Zhou Yang for his extramarital affair during the early PRC era. Her critique was widely circulated among many CCP officials, greatly infuriating Zhou Yang. Of all the criticisms from Ding Ling, he was particularly enraged by her condemnation of his extramarital relationship.[41] This likely became the primary reason why, for the rest of his life, Zhou Yang insisted that Ding Ling was unchaste and disloyal to the CCP. On October 24, 1956, the Central Propaganda Department released the document titled "The Conclusion of the Investigation on Comrade Ding Ling's Historical Issues" (*Guanyu Ding Ling tongzhi lishi wenti de shencha jielun* 关于丁玲同志历史问题的审查结论), stating that her time in Nanjing constituted an act of betrayal (*bianjie* 变节).[42] Unable to accept this conclusion, Ding Ling submitted another appeal to the Central Propaganda Department.

In the spring of 1957, Mao Zedong launched a campaign known as "speaking out loudly and freely" (*daming dafang* 大鸣大放) to encourage people to openly voice their criticisms of the CCP. In response to the democratic spirit in this campaign, Zhou Yang admitted that the criticism of Ding Ling in 1955 had gone too far and apologized to her during the China Writers Association Party group's expansion meeting on June 6, 1957.[43] However, the *daming dafang* campaign soon took a drastic turn as criticisms of the CCP exceeded Mao's expectations. Perceiving some of these criticisms as malicious attacks on the CCP, Mao shifted his strategy to *yinshe chudong* 引蛇出洞 (luring the snakes out of their holes) to identify the critics and label them as rightists. Consequently, the *daming dafang* campaign, initially intended to assist the

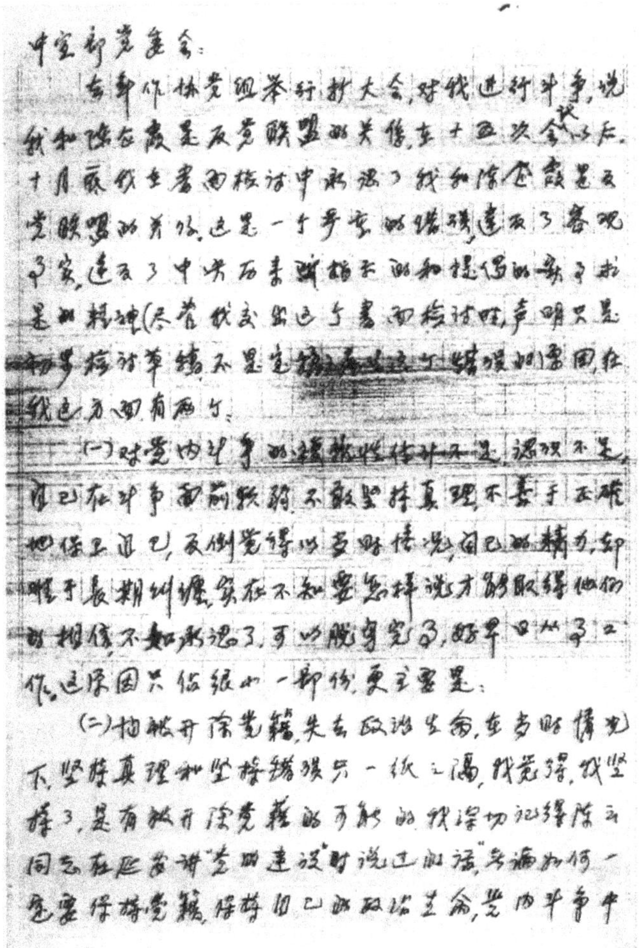

中宣部党委会：

　　去年作协党组举行扩大会，对我进行斗争，说我和陈企霞是反党联盟的关系。在十五次会议以后，十月底我在书面检讨中承认了我和陈企霞是反党联盟的关系，这是一个严重的错误，违反了客观事实，违反了中共历来所标示的和提倡的实事求是的精神（尽管我交出这个书面检讨时，声明只是初步检讨草稿，不是定稿）这个错误的原因，在我这方面有两个。

　　（一）对党内斗争[illegible]认识不足，自己在斗争面前软弱，不敢坚持真理，不善于正确地保卫自己，反倒觉得以当时情况，自己的精力，却陷于长期纠缠，实在不知要怎样说才能取得他们的相信，不如承认了，可以脱身完了，好早日从事工作。这原因只占很小一部份，更主要是：

　　（二）怕被开除党籍，失去政治生命，在当时情况下，坚持真理和坚持错误只一纸之隔，我觉得，我坚持了，是有被开除党籍的可能的。我深切记得陈云同志在延安讲"党的建设"时说过的话"无论如何一定要保持党籍，保持自己的政治生命，党内斗争中

Figure 10: A page excerpted from Ding Ling's appeal letter to the Central Propaganda Department in 1956. Source: Tu Shaojun, *Tuben Ding Ling zhuan*, 247.

CCP's rectification movement, turned into the Anti-Rightist Movement in the summer of 1957.

At the outset of the Anti-Rightist Movement, Zhou Yang reversed his stance and, during the China Writers Association Party group's expansion meeting on July 25, 1957, accused Ding Ling of "three disloyalties" (*san buzhong* 三不忠), referencing her alleged lack of loyalty in the Nanjing, Yan'an, and PRC eras.[44] This led to Ding Ling being labeled as a rightist. In September 1957, Mao Zedong publicly denounced Ding Ling during a meeting with a delegation from Czechoslovakia. He referred to Ding as a bourgeois intellectual who should be expelled from the party.[45]

In January 1958, *Wenyi bao*, for which Ding Ling had once served as the editor-in-chief, published a special issue titled "Criticism Again" (*Zai pipan* 再批判). This issue criticized Ding's works including "Thoughts on March 8," "In the Hospital" (*Zai yiyuan zhong* 在医院中), "When I Was in Xia Village," as well as certain essays published in the literary supplement of *Jiefang ribao*, which Ding Ling and Chen Qixia were in charge of during their time in Yan'an. Mao revised and approved the "Editorial Remarks in *Wenyi bao*" for the special issue. The "Editorial Remarks" state unequivocally that "Ding Ling wrote a letter of surrender (*zishou shu* 自首书) in Nanjing. She betrayed the proletarians and the CCP to Chiang Kai-shek. She gained the trust of the party through hiding and cheating."[46] The "letter of surrender" mentioned here refers to the note Ding Ling wrote to the KMT, which became critical evidence of Ding Ling's disloyalty to the CCP.

Drawing upon the writing style and tone of the "Editorial Remarks," Ding Ling deduced that Mao was the one who authorized "Criticism Again." Recognizing the limited options available to her at that point, she opted to withdraw her appeal. "Criticism Again" marked the conclusive downfall for Ding Ling. Following its publication, she found herself politically ostracized and was expelled from the CCP in May 1958.[47] Subsequently, she and her husband Chen Ming endured twelve years of exile in the desolate *beidahuang* 北大荒 (Great Northern Wasteland), engaging in arduous labor. Their lives took another turn when they were separated upon being transferred to the notorious Beijing Qincheng Prison, reserved for political detainees, in 1970. After five years, the Central Committee of the CCP's special investigation team announced "The Concluding Investigation Report on the Traitor Ding Ling" (*Dui pantu Ding Ling de shencha jielun* 对叛徒丁玲的审查结论).[48] Without presenting any new evidence, this conclusion escalated Ding Ling's criminal classification from a "surrenderer" to a "traitor." Ding Ling was moved from

Qincheng to a remote village near Changzhi in Shanxi, where she reunited with Chen Ming and resided for four years until her rehabilitation in 1979.

Many assumed that Ding Ling had died during the Cultural Revolution. Similar to her disappearance in 1933 when she was abducted, she vanished from public view after Mao condemned her as a rightist in 1958, imposing political death upon her. As Yi-tsi Mei Feuerwerker, a scholar who devoted years to studying Ding Ling, noted, "There had been no indication for over two decades as to whether she was still alive."[49] Thus, the news of the removal of Ding Ling's rightist label and her subsequent reappearance in Beijing captured headlines in 1979. Excited by the resurrection of Ding Ling, her old friend Shi Zhecun 施蛰存 (1905–2003) composed a collection of poems for her. The opening line of the first poem reads: "It is a miracle that Ding Ling did not die" (*Ding Ling busi zhen qiji* 丁玲不死真奇迹).[50]

The dilemma of whether or not to choose martyrdom haunted Ding Ling throughout her lifetime. In 1957, Zhou Yang accused her of "three disloyalties" to the CCP, which included publishing essays such as "Thoughts on March 8" and Wang Shiwei's "Wild Lilies" (*Ye baihe hua* 野百合花), that criticized the CCP in 1942, and forming an "independent kingdom" (*duli wangguo* 独立王国) with Chen Qixia in the early years of the PRC era.[51] Ding Ling's most significant betrayal, according to Zhou Yang, was writing that note to the KMT instead of embracing martyrdom like Ying Xiuren did in 1933.[52] In this context, to die or not to die was a matter of allegiance rather than mere survival. As a survivor of political oppression, Ding Ling not only received no sympathy, but was persistently questioned about her loyalty to the party. It seemed that martyrdom was the sole route for Ding Ling to cleanse herself of the shadow cast by her time in Nanjing.

Ding Ling was, in fact, unafraid of death. She was prepared to embrace martyrdom. In her memoir "The World of Demons and Monsters" (*Wangliang shijie* 魍魉世界), Ding Ling detailed her failed suicide attempt during her time of house arrest in Nanjing. She tore a dress into shreds, crafting a rope with which she intended to hang herself. Leaving behind a brief suicide note to Feng Da, she implored him to find a reliable source to forward her message to the CCP. In her memoir, Ding Ling explicitly declared, "I have chosen to die for the party. Death becomes my way to convey to both the people and my relatives that 'Ding Ling is innocent and loyal to her faith.' Death is the only way I can prove my devotion to the party."[53] Despite her resolute intentions, Ding Ling's suicide attempt failed, as Feng Da intervened and rescued her. She lamented, "Death is not easy!" (*Si ye bu rongyi a* 死也不容易啊).[54]

After 1933, being alive carried the weight of an original sin for Ding Ling. She spent the rest of her life defending her loyalty to the CCP. In April 1942, right before Mao's Yan'an Talks, Ding Ling was criticized for exposing the dark side of the CCP in her essay "Thoughts on March 8." Bearing the weight of her comrades' distrust and mourning the death of her fellow female writer, Xiao Hong 萧红 (1911–42), Ding Ling wrote a heartfelt essay titled "Commemorating Xiao Hong in Wind and Rain" (*Fengyu zhong yi Xiao Hong* 风雨中忆萧红) in 1942. In this reflective piece, she grieved not only for the premature death of Xiao Hong but also mourned the execution of early CCP leader and martyr Qu Qiubai 瞿秋白 (1899–1935) by the KMT, along with the political suspicions cast upon her friends Feng Xuefeng 冯雪峰 (1903–76) and Hu Feng 胡风 (1902–85).

Before his execution, Qu Qiubai wrote a short confessional essay titled "Superfluous Words" (*Duoyu de hua* 多余的话) in 1935, in which he candidly addressed his vulnerabilities and uncertainties in his revolutionary journey. Despite his heroic death, Qu Qiubai was labeled a traitor during the Cultural Revolution due to the controversies surrounding his essay "Superfluous Words." During her time in Yan'an, Ding Ling came across "Superfluous Words" and empathized with Qu Qiubai's views on revolution.[55] Ding Ling had been a student of Qu Qiubai at Shanghai University, and her first novel on revolution, *Wei Hu* 韦护 (1930), was based on Qu's romantic relationship with her close friend Wang Jianhong 王剑虹 (1901–24). In 1932, Qu Qiubai attended Ding Ling's CCP admission ceremony as the party representative.[56] Having navigated the intricate political landscape of Yan'an herself, Ding Ling gained profound insight into Qu's internal struggles. This sentiment of deep compassion for Qu Qiubai is evident in Ding Ling's essay "Commemorating Xiao Hong in Wind and Rain":

> Yesterday, in my moments of misery, I contemplated Qiubai. He had been immersed in politics for an extended period, yet he couldn't fully transform himself. Even before his death, the duality of his life compelled him to make appeals. I often blame him for making a superfluous appeal. However, I cannot help but be moved when I delve into the history of his inner struggles.[57]

In January 1980, after her rehabilitation, Ding Ling revisited Qu's final words again in her essay titled "Comrade Qu Qiubai as I Knew Him" (*Wo suo renshi de Qu Qiubai tongzhi* 我所认识的瞿秋白同志). In this essay, she lauded his unwavering commitment to communism and his courage in revealing his vulnerabilities and inner struggles. She states that "revolutionaries are not deities. Imperfections and mistakes are inevitable. However, if they confront themselves, engaging in introspection, aren't they more honorable than the hypocrites who mislead the masses?"[58] Thus, Ding Ling's tribute to Qu Qiubai also serves as her self-defense.

On October 19, 1980, the party Central Committee released "The Investigation Report on Comrade Qu Qiubai's Arrest and Martyrdom" (*Guanyu Qu Qiubai tongzhi beibu jiuyi qingkuang de diaocha baogao* 关于瞿秋白同志被捕就义情况的调查报告), which declared that "Superfluous Words" was not evidence of betrayal of the CCP or a surrender to the KMT.[59] The CCP reinstated the reputation of the revolutionary martyr Qu Qiubai and acknowledged his significant contributions to the Chinese Communist revolution.

On July 14, 1984, the Organization Department of the CCP issued "The Notification regarding the Restoration of Comrade Ding Ling's Reputation" (*Guanyu wei Ding Ling tongzhi huifu mingyu de tongzhi* 关于为丁玲同志恢复名誉的通知), confirming her status as a loyal CCP member (see fig. 11). Upon receiving this news in her hospital bed, Ding Ling remarked, "Now I can die" (*zhexia wo keyi si le* 这下我可以死了).[60] Qu Qiubai once likened Ding Ling to "a moth to a flame, ceaseless until its death" (*fei'e puhuo, feisi buzhi* 飞蛾扑火，非死不止).[61] Although Ding Ling might not fit the conventional mold of a martyr, she embodied a living martyr who, like a moth drawn to the fire, willingly embraced her destiny in pursuit of the "fire of truth" (*zhenli zhi huo* 真理之火).[62]

Gossip and Rumors

The official restoration of Ding Ling's reputation in 1984 addressed concerns regarding her political loyalty. However, doubts persisted regarding her chastity. Zhou Yang remained adamantly opposed to Ding Ling's rehabilitation up until his death, primarily due to her involvement with Feng Da, a traitor, which resulted in the birth of her daughter. This association with the traitor, according to Zhou Yang, permanently tarnished Ding Ling's political purity. When Ding Ling's daughter, Jiang Zuhui 蒋祖慧, confronted Zhou Yang about her mother's potential rehabilitation following the end of the Cultural Revolution in 1978, Zhou insisted that while the questionable point (*yidian* 疑点) about Ding as a faithful Communist might have been dispelled, the blemish (*wudian* 污点) on her record remained unchanged.[63]

中央组织部文件

中组发〔1984〕9号

各省、自治区、直辖市党委，中央各部委，国家机关各部委党组，各人民团体党组，解放军总政治部：

我部《关于为丁玲同志恢复名誉的通知》业经中央书记处批复同意，现发给你们，以消除影响。

中共中央组织部

一九八四年八月一日

（此件请转发至县、团级）

—1—

Figure 11: The first page of "The Notification Regarding the Restoration of Comrade Ding Ling's Reputation" in 1984. Source: Tu Shaojun, *Tuben Ding Ling zhuan*, 289.

In his later years, Xia Yan, the former deputy minister of culture, also "couldn't reconcile the fact that Ding Ling continued to have a sexual relationship with Feng Da."[64] In 1979, both Zhou Yang and Xia Yan opposed Ding Ling's request to have her CCP membership reinstated.[65] This highlights how female revolutionaries bear a dual burden encompassing both political loyalty and chastity. In Ding Ling's case, Wang Xiaojue points out, "Strikingly, the accusation of treachery is based not only on her 'contamination' of Communist purity but, more importantly, on the fact that she slept with the enemy—Feng Da the traitor. Here, the communist ideal of purity signifies the chastity norm for women."[66]

The double burden requires female revolutionaries simultaneously to uphold revolutionary ideals and conform to traditional gender norms. Female chastity remained a concern within the CCP. In this context, individuals such as Zhou Yang and Xia Yan bear resemblances to the moralists that Lu Xun satirized in his essay "My Views on Chastity" (*Wo zhi jielie guan* 我之节烈观, 1918):

> When a rough man swoops down on one of the weaker sex (women are still weak as things stand today), if her father, brothers, and husband cannot save her and the neighbors fail her too, her best course is to die. She may, of course, die after being defiled; or she may not die at all. Later on, her father, brothers, husband, and neighbors will get together with the writers, scholars, and moralists; and, no whit abashed by their own cowardice and incompetence, nor concerned about how to punish the criminal, will start wagging their tongues. Is she dead or not? Was she raped or not? How gratifying if she has died, how shocking if she has not! So they create all these glorious women martyrs on the one hand and these wantons universally condemned on the other. If we think this over soberly, we can see that, far from being praiseworthy, it is absolutely inhuman.[67]

In this context, Lu Xun condemns the deplorable reality where Confucian gender norms take precedence over basic humanity. Ding Ling was regarded as weak due to her prioritization of humanity over party principles. In her memoir, she explains her intimate relationship with Feng Da during their period of house arrest:

> Feng Da was my lover. However, in recent months, I treated him as if he were an enemy. Now that I'm stranded on this bleak mountain, the cold has frozen

> not only my towel, handkerchief, and tea, but also my soul. I really need some heat, even if it's just a little. Only a little heat can warm my frozen feet and reanimate my frozen heart. . . . I am a Communist Party member, but I am also a human being.[68]

The contrast between warmth and coldness symbolizes the disparity between intricate human emotions and unwavering party principles. Ding Ling distinctly demarcated herself from the traitor Feng Da in her confessions and thought reports throughout various political movements. However, her privacy was repeatedly violated due to disclosing her intimate relationships during these investigations. During the 1940 investigation, Ding Ling stated that she was deceived into believing that Feng Da had not betrayed her until Yao Pengzi 姚蓬子 (1905–69) informed her in April 1934 that Feng had disclosed her address to the KMT. It was at this point she ended her sexual relationship with Feng.[69] However, Ding Ling gave birth to a daughter, whose father was Feng Da, in October 1934.[70] Her determinization to raise her daughter also provided a compelling reason for her to remain alive.

Feng Da entered Ding Ling's life through Feng Xuefeng after Hu Yepin's martyrdom. At that time, Ding Ling was living alone in Shanghai and struggling with depression. She wrote letters to Feng Xuefeng, pouring out her passionate love for him.[71] However, Feng was already married, and his affection for Ding Ling was of a more restrained nature. He chose to temper the intensity of their emotions, maintaining a strong friendship instead. Ding Ling held deep admiration for Feng Xuefeng and continued to regard him as a revolutionary mentor throughout her life. In his capacity as a personal friend and mentor, Feng Xuefeng introduced Feng Da, who served as the secretary of Agnes Smedley, to Ding Ling. Around the end of 1931, Ding Ling and Feng Da moved in together.[72]

In her later years, Ding Ling depicted Feng Da in her account of the Nanjing days in a neutral light, refraining from portraying him as a traitor. She described him by saying that "he assisted me by adopting a tranquil living attitude. He lacked both heat and light. He didn't captivate me, but he didn't frighten or disturb me either. He was single and had never been in love. He was simply working quietly."[73] While Ding Ling's affection for Feng Da might not have equaled that for Feng Xuefeng, his calm and caring demeanor played a crucial role in helping her endure the challenging days following the death of Hu Yepin.

Feng Da attended to household chores, kept Ding Ling updated on global

Figure 12: Ding Ling and Feng Da in Shanghai, 1932. Source: Wang Zengru, "Jiaru meiyou nachang bangjia—Ding Ling yu Feng Da zai Bansong yuan de yizhang heying" 假如没有那场绑架—丁玲与冯达在半淞园的一张合影 (If there hadn't been that kidnapping—a photo of Ding Ling and Feng Da at Bansong garden), *Shiji* 2 (2016): 41.

communist movements through news, accompanied her on visits and interviews with flood refugees, and provided support for her writing.[74] These seemingly mundane yet consistently reliable actions endeared Feng Da to Ding Ling. Shen Congwen's 沈从文 (1902–88) perception of Feng Da echoed this sentiment: "When Ding Ling assigned a task to Feng Da, he executed it with remarkable efficiency. If she sought amusement, he accompanied her with great enthusiasm. If she desired solitude, he respected her wish and withdrew. While he lacked passion, his demeanor remained unfailingly gentle."[75] Feng Da might not have possessed the liveliness that normally appealed to Ding Ling, but he provided the necessary support during challenging periods, especially throughout their days of house arrest.

In September 1936, Ding Ling left Nanjing for Shanghai, where she awaited travel arrangements to Shaanbei. On September 30, 1936, Feng Xuefeng designated Nie Gannu 聂绀弩 (1903–86) to accompany Ding Ling.[76] In his self-examination materials written during the Anti-Rightist Movement in 1957, Nie Gannu recounted the vivid scene of Ding Ling's farewell to Nanjing. She described this scene to him in detail on their train journey from Shanghai to Xi'an:

> Ding Ling had a child with a spy. The man who had a sexual relationship with her came to bid farewell as she was departing. On that night, the sky was graced with a full moon. Unable to bear being apart, they walked back and forth along a road. The man, suffering from tuberculosis, spoke to her in a profoundly romantic manner. He acknowledged that he understood she had to leave. In his ailing state, he couldn't hold her back. With a promising future ahead, she should not long for him. He believed the revolution would eventually triumph. If she survived, they might reunite, but he remained uncertain about what that reunion might entail (or something to that effect). Both were tearful as they exchanged their goodbyes, reminiscent of lovers in a novel. I initially believed this man was Feng Da, yet Ding Ling refuted this notion. She refrained from disclosing his identity. In her narrative, the spy resembled a young revolutionary in many ways.[77]

In 1939, Ding Ling wrote an account of her train voyage with Nie Gannu.[78] Leaving Nanjing behind filled her with a sense of relief, and engaging in conversation with Nie brought her joy, despite it being their first encounter. While Ding Ling hesitated to disclose her romantic partner's identity, Nie's recollections seemed to align with characteristics of Feng Da. Feng had been diagnosed with tuberculosis prior to his detainment, and his health deteriorated during his days under house arrest. Following his doctor's advice of bed rest, he refrained from work. Aware of his limited time, Feng Da confided in Ding Ling, saying "we are destined to be separated. My health is in critical condition. My lungs have ached often in the last six months. I may not live long, but I hope to see you free."[79]

Ding Ling spoke openly about her past with Nie Gannu, but what caused her reluctance to reveal that the man she was parting ways with was Feng Da? Her main concern, I believe, stemmed from the complications of being associated romantically with an identified traitor, let alone portraying him as a revolutionary. Ding Ling recognized the necessity of establishing a clear boundary between herself and Feng Da, and she knew she would need to provide explanations upon her return to the party from Nanjing. The question remains: Why did she appear to be romantically connected to a traitor, thereby jeopardizing her political career?

Feng Da was silenced, and he was simply labeled as a traitor after the mysterious abduction of Ding Ling in Shanghai. Feng's perspective remains concealed; we never come to understand his side of the story. According to Ding Ling, on the morning of May 14, 1933, Feng Da, who was responsible for the *Truth* (*Zhenhua bao* 真话报), the official newspaper of the Jiangsu provincial party committee, set out to visit two correspondents. Meanwhile, Ding Ling was scheduled to attend a meeting at Zhengfeng College of Literature (*Zhengfeng wenxueyuan* 正风文学院).[80] To ensure their safety, the two agreed to return home before noon. Should one fail to return in time, the other would depart immediately.

Ding Ling returned at half past 11 without encountering Feng Da. She waited for a while, intending to leave by noon. Unexpectedly, Pan Zinian, the chief editor of the *Truth*, walked in. Though Ding Ling informed him of the agreement with Feng Da, Pan chose to stay, engrossed in reading a newspaper. He appeared to be waiting for someone's arrival. After a while, KMT spies, accompanied by Feng Da, forcibly entered the house, leading to the arrest of both Ding Ling and Pan Zinian. Later in the afternoon, Ying Xiuren, a left-wing poet and the minister of the Propaganda Department of the CCP Jiangsu Committee, was ambushed by the KMT spies at Ding's house and martyred himself. Ding Ling and Feng Da's residence served as a secret meeting place for the CCP. It is likely that Pan was awaiting a meeting with Ying Xiuren there and underestimated the danger of the situation.

Feng Da and Ding Ling were under house arrest following the abduction. Feng Da explained to Ding Ling that he had been apprehended by KMT spies while on his way to visit the two correspondents for the *Truth*. The spies insisted on visiting his home to verify his nonmembership in the CCP. Feng calculated that it should be safe after noon, assuming that the house search would not yield results since no one would be present. He employed every effort to negotiate with them, attempting to buy some time. Unfortunately, both Ding Ling and Pan Zinian were still there after the designated time.[81]

Ding Ling placed her trust in Feng Da as he refrained from providing any additional addresses or names to the KMT. Feng was also supportive of Ding's escape from house arrest. Although Feng Da had not intentionally betrayed Ding Ling, his action of disclosing the address, knowing it was a clandestine CCP meeting point, demonstrated his lack of vigilance and commitment as a revolutionary. This lapse in judgment resulted in significant damage to the party. Feng Da understood that the incident marked the end of his revolutionary career, closing the door on his potential return to the CCP.

He told Ding Ling that "his purpose for being alive is to express himself to her and assist her in escaping the vicious imprisonment and rejoining the CCP."[82] In April 1934, Feng Da accepted a translating position offered by the KMT, fully aware that this act would render him forever unacceptable to the CCP. He explained to Ding Ling that this move was a strategic one, intended to make the KMT perceive him as willing to collaborate with them, thus reducing their suspicion toward her.[83] Ding Ling was disappointed by his decision to collaborate with the enemy.

During the 1940 investigation in Yan'an, Ding Ling revealed that she ended her sexual relationship with Feng Da in April 1934 after learning from Yao Pengzi that Feng had disclosed her address to the KMT. This might have been one of the reasons she sought to sever ties with Feng Da. A more significant catalyst, however, was Ding Ling's realization that they were parting ways in April 1934 when Feng Da agreed to work for the KMT. Nonetheless, it remains plausible that a romantic connection between them persisted.

Around July 1936, Ding Ling traveled from Nanjing to Shanghai in search of a way to reach Shaanbei. Feng Xuefeng assigned Hu Feng to pick her up. According to Hu Feng's wife, Mei Zhi 梅志 (1914–2004), while Ding Ling was in Shanghai, she expressed concern about a possible pregnancy and requested to consult a Japanese doctor. Hu Feng accompanied her to the doctor and acted as her interpreter. Her relief was palpable upon discovering that she was not pregnant.[84] She stayed in Shanghai for a few days. Feng Xuefeng assessed the situation and concluded that it was not a secure moment for her departure, thus suggesting she return to Nanjing. After two months, Ding Ling made her second departure from Nanjing, successfully reaching Shaanbei this time. Before leaving Nanjing, she gave Feng Da her only available money and borrowed travel funds from Tan Tiwu 谭惕吾 (1902–97).[85] During the train journey from Shanghai to Xi'an, Ding Ling shared the romantic farewell story with Nie Gannu.

Under the weight of the double burden of chastity and political loyalty, Ding Ling found herself compelled to explain her relationship with Feng Da by disclosing details about her private life. A female revolutionary was expected to embody the roles of a *lienü* 列女 (exemplary woman), a *lienü* 烈女 (chastity martyr), and a *nülieshi* 女烈士 (female revolutionary martyr) simultaneously. Assuming Ding Ling died following her disappearance in May 1933, numerous writers dedicated essays to commemorate her. At the same time, numerous news outlets propagated rumors about her, particularly concerning her private life. The female "martyr," Ding Ling, was eroticized to satisfy the voyeuristic desires for a female revolutionary and to tarnish the reputation of the CCP.

In her memoir, Ding Ling recounted an incident of mental abuse she endured due to the manipulation of the KMT. During her days of house arrest, after a period of isolation, she requested novels and magazines to read. Among the materials she received was the *Social News* (*Shehui xinwen* 社会新闻) magazine, edited by two prominent KMT secret agents, Ding Mocun 丁默村 (1901–47) and Li Shiqun 李士群 (1905–43), with the intention of slandering Communists. Ding Ling was infuriated as she read an essay rife with rumors about her within the pages of this magazine.[86] This was one of the KMT's strategies to undermine Ding Ling's morale and coerce her into a confession (*zishou* 自首).

The essay, titled "Ding Ling before Her Fame" (*Wei chengming yiqian de Ding Ling* 未成名以前的丁玲), in *Social News* was written under the pseudonym Ping Jia 平斝. In this essay, a young Ding Ling was portrayed as a Lin Daiyu 林黛玉 character who was slender, beautiful, emotional, and prone to tears. It was mentioned that she gained weight after attending progressive schools in Changsha. According to the author, despite being engaged to her cousin, Ding Ling was involved in multiple romantic relationships, which eventually led to the breakup of the engagement. The author sneers that when encountering Ding Ling in the Shanghai French Concession in 1923, she "was even fatter, her plump buttocks were two times bigger than before."[87] Instances of body shaming and slut-shaming directed at Ding Ling became prevalent in the media once she was identified as a leftist writer. For instance, one author wrote, "Ding Ling appears round, with a pale complexion, a short, fat body, and high, protruding buttocks."[88] Another author wrote that she "has a fat and sensual body" (*shenti feipang, poyou rougan* 身体肥胖，颇有肉感).[89]

The circulation of rumors and gossip about her love affairs spurred sensational media coverage. In "Ding Ling and Pan Zinian" (*Ding Ling yu Pan Zinian* 丁玲与潘梓年), the author claims that Ding Ling was arrested while in the company of her lover, Feng Xuefeng. The essay depicts Ding as a shrew who frequently fought with Hu Yepin in the streets, to the extent that police intervention was required.[90] Other tabloids and pro-KMT newspapers fabricated sensational stories surrounding Ding Ling's romantic relationships with Tian Han, Shen Congwen, Yao Pengzi, Zhou Yang, her extramarital relationship with Yang Hansheng 阳翰笙 (1902–93), and even her alleged lesbian affair with Wang Jianhong, embellishing them with erotic details.[91] The shaming of

Figure 13: Ding Ling (left) and Wang Jianhong (right) in Hunan, 1923. Source: Jiang Zulin, *Ding Ling zhuan*, 42. Both from Hunan, Ding Ling and Wang Jianhong were classmates at Hunan No. 2 Women's Normal School. In 1922, inspired by Wang's encouragement, Ding Ling joined her to study in Shanghai, which deepened their strong bond of friendship. Wang married Qu Qiubai in January 1923 but tragically passed away due to tuberculosis shortly after their wedding in July 1923.

female revolutionaries in relation to their chastity, body, and private lives is a tactic frequently employed to discredit and undermine women, especially those who assume public and influential roles that challenge existing power structures. By focusing on Ding Ling's physical appearance or alleged sexual behavior, critics sought to devalue her intellectual contributions and political engagement. This was a strategy designed to marginalize her leftist stance. It reinforced traditional gender dynamics and discouraged other women from pursuing similar roles.

If the intention behind the rumors concerning her private life was to tarnish her reputation and depict a revolutionary woman as lascivious, then the slanderous claim that Ding Ling had engaged in a sexual relationship with the KMT secret agent Ma Shaowu 马绍武 would constitute a malicious endeavor to indicate her betrayal of the CCP. Shortly after her disappearance, *Dagong bao* released a news article stating that Ding Ling had been executed. According to the report, Ding Ling supposedly confessed to the KMT and began living with Ma Shaowu on May 17, only three days after her arrest. The two supposed lovers were described as inseparable, being "like paint and glue" (*ruqi rujiao* 如漆如胶).[92] Reportedly, Ma Shaowu was assassinated by CCP secret agents on June 14, following which Ding Ling was executed on June 15 under suspicion of complicity in the assassination.[93]

Enraged by the unfounded rumors surrounding Ding Ling, Lu Xun wrote a letter to a leftist journal called *Scientific News* (*Kexue xinwen* 科学新闻), stating, "There has been no news about Ding Ling. I think she has already been killed. Nonetheless, some journals continue to spread rumors about her. They are more ferocious than beasts."[94] These rumors and slander continued to haunt Ding Ling even during her time in Shaanbei. Zhu Zhengming 朱正明, under the pseudonym L. Insun, recounted in "Ding Ling in Shaanbei" (*Ding Ling zai Shaanbei* 丁玲在陕北) that the rumor about Ding Ling's relationship with Ma Shaowu reached Xi'an. After the Xi'an Incident (*Xi'an shibian* 西安事变), a local magazine alleged, "After Ding Ling's arrest in Shanghai, Ma Shaowu forced her into a sexual relationship. She agreed without hesitation."[95] In her memoir, Ding Ling lamented that "rumors kill" (*yaoyan sharen* 谣言杀人), stating: "I thought those rumors would ruin my entire life. Once my purity was tarnished by the KMT, I knew I could never completely cleanse the dirt they dumped on me, even if they eventually set me free."[96]

Beyond all the rumors, the fact remained that Ding Ling had a daughter with a known traitor, and this tainted both her political and sexual purity. After her abduction in 1933, Ding Ling was subjected to countless CCP investigations. The controversy surrounding her romantic involvement with Feng Da persisted even after the CCP officially restored Ding Ling's reputation in 1984. The notion of chastity remained important to the modern conception of female revolutionary martyrdom. Ding Ling, nearly a female martyr herself, was profoundly influenced by the concept of martyrdom, which defined her perspective on the role of women's sacrifice in revolution throughout her life. Qiu Jin, the topic of the next exhibit in this imaginary museum of martyrdom, was the initial figure that sparked Ding Ling's fascination with martyrdom, marking the beginning of her obsession with female sacrifice in revolution.

EXHIBITION II

Qiu Jin

Changing Images of a Female Revolutionary Martyr

Qiu Jin 秋瑾 (1875–1907), a native of Shaoxing, was a female revolutionary during the late Qing era. She married Wang Tingjun 王廷钧 (1879–1909), a man from a wealthy Xiangtan family, in 1896.[1] However, Qiu Jin was deeply dissatisfied with her marriage. Seeking personal and intellectual fulfillment, she left her family in 1904 to pursue education in Japan. During the summer of 1905, while back in Shanghai for vacation, Qiu Jin was induced by revolutionaries Tao Chengzhang 陶成章 (1878–1912) and Xu Xilin 徐锡麟 (1873–1907) to join the Restoration Society (*Guangfu hui* 光复会), a group opposing the Qing government.[2] In September of the same year, Qiu Jin met Sun Yat-sen 孙中山 (1866–1925) in Tokyo and joined the Revolutionary Alliance (*Tongmenghui* 同盟会).[3] By the end of 1905, Qiu Jin had returned to China, protesting against the Japanese government's "Regulations to Abolish Qing and Korean International Students" (*qudi Qing Han liuxuesheng guize* 取缔清韩留学生规则).[4] In the same month, she wrote a letter to her brother, Qiu Yuzhang 秋誉章 (1873–1909), revealing her resolve to divorce Wang Tingjun—an audacious step for a woman of her era.[5] In early 1907, Qiu Jin took on a leadership role at the Datong School (*Datong xuetang* 大通学堂), an institution established by Xu Xilin with the goal of nurturing revolutionaries. Furthermore, she initiated the publication of the *Chinese Women's News* (*Zhongguo nübao* 中国女报), a platform for advocating for women's liberation.[6] Tragically, on July 13, 1907, Qiu Jin was arrested at the Datong School for her involvement in a failed attempt to topple the Qing government and was executed two days later.[7]

Qiu Jin has remained an enduring source of inspiration for generations of Chinese female revolutionaries, including Ding Ling. In "The Song of Death," Ding Ling recalls: "My mother's favorite topic of conversation was Qiu Jin. I often leaned against her knees and listened to her recount stories about

Figure 14: Qiu Jin in menswear. Source: *Qiu Jin shiji* 秋瑾史迹 (Historical materials on Qiu Jin), Shanghai: Zhonghua shuju, 1958, 1.

Qiu Jin. Qiu Jin was the person my mother admired the most. She told me about Qiu Jin's participation in the revolution and her subsequent martyrdom. I have known these stories since I was a child."[8] By 1919, Ding Ling had transferred to Zhounan Girls' Middle School in Changsha, an institution that had nurtured a cadre of notable female revolutionaries, among them Xiang Jingyu 向警予 (1895–1928), Tao Siyong 陶斯咏 (1896–1931), and Cai Chang 蔡畅 (1900–1990). While at Zhounan Girls' Middle School, she attended a literature class taught by Chen Qiming 陈启明. Chen was a former classmate of Mao Zedong and a member of the New Citizen Study Society (*Xinmin Xuehui* 新民学会) led by Mao. He often recited Qiu Jin's final words written before her execution, "the sorrow of autumn wind and autumn rain kills" (*Qiufeng qiuyu chou sha ren* 秋风秋雨愁煞人), to his students.[9] The story of Qiu Jin sowed the seeds of revolution in Ding Ling's heart.

Qiu Jin has long been inscribed as an iconic female revolutionary martyr in modern Chinese history. However, the symbolic meanings of her death shifted along with the constant political turmoil. Qiu Jin's image transformed from that of a Dou E-like character in late Qing to a new Nora-like character in Yan'an. This chapter analyzes varying narratives surrounding Qiu Jin's death, spanning from the late Qing period to the Yan'an era, in order to trace the process of constructing a new form of chastity martyrdom that entails dying for the nation rather than for one's husband. The examination will delve into how the tenets of nationalism emerged as a new dimension of female martyrdom, and how the state repurposed Qiu Jin's death into a national symbol, thereby forming a collective memory and a new national ideology.

Qiu Jin as Dou E in Late Qing

In contrast to the typical portrayal of fearless revolutionary martyrs, late Qing narratives presented Qiu Jin as a wronged woman, a vulnerable victim of the corrupt Qing government. Initially, the story of Qiu Jin was interpreted by media and literature as a faithful reimagining of the Yuan dynasty playwright Guan Hanqing's 关汉卿 play *Dou E yuan* 窦娥冤 (The Injustice to Dou E), which depicts a helpless woman wrongfully convicted by a corrupt official. Guifu 贵福, the magistrate of Shaoxing who sentenced Qiu Jin to death, similarly faced condemnation as a corrupt official. The outcry against Guifu was so intense in Shaoxing that he was reassigned as the magistrate of Ningguofu 宁国府 in Anhui. The locals in Anhui also vehemently protested his new appointment because he "wrongly executed Qiu Jin" (*yuansha Qiu Jin* 冤杀秋瑾).[10] In October 1912, at Qiu Jin's memorial service at the Shaoxing Guild in Shanghai, people created a paste turtle with Guifu's name inscribed on it.[11] This gesture was meant as a public act of humiliation, as labeling someone a "turtle" is a customary insult in Chinese culture.

The death of Qiu Jin ignited fervent discussions in major newspapers in the late Qing era. Despite their varied political perspectives, the newspapers unanimously decried the treatment of Qiu Jin as unjust and likened her to a contemporary Dou E. *Shibao*, a newspaper that advocated for constitutionalism, criticized Zhejiang Province officials for their unlawful handling of the case. A week after the execution of Qiu Jin, *Shibao* reported a Shaoxing-based source's claim that the "local governor had instructed someone to collect letters written by Qiu Jin and then forge documents purporting her collaboration with revolutionaries by imitating her handwriting."[12] On July 29, 1907, *Shibao* published an essay urging the Qing government to publicly disclose the evidence pertinent to Qiu Jin's case.[13] About four months later, Qiu Jin's close friend Wu Zhiying 吴芝瑛 (1867–1933) stated in *Shibao* that she was collecting evidence with the aim of overturning the wrongful conviction of Qiu Jin.[14] In another instance, Xu Xilin, another friend of Qiu Jin's, was executed by the Qing government for orchestrating the uprising. As reported by the newspaper *Shenbao*, Xu's close associates falsely implicated Qiu Jin in the rebellion due to their fear of association with the case, despite the lack of supporting evidence.[15]

In addition to criticizing the local government for sentencing Qiu Jin to death without substantial evidence, the late Qing media regarded her case as unjust on the grounds that they perceived her as a frail woman without any intent to participate in the revolution. For instance, the author of "Lament for Qiu Jin's Case" (*Ai Qiu Jin an* 哀秋瑾案) portrays her as a "fragile beauty" (*juanjuan ruonü* 娟娟弱女).[16] In "Qiu Jin sihou zhi yuan" 秋瑾死后之冤 (The injustice after Qiu Jin's death), the author argues that Qiu Jin advocated solely for gender revolution and female independence, and therefore her execution was unjust. The author claims that "it is unprecedented to publicly accuse a frail woman and a dozen young students of rebellion in the county."[17] In an essay mourning Qiu Jin, an author for *Shenzhou Daily* (*Shenzhou ribao* 神州日报) directly likens Qiu Jin to the wrongly executed filial daughter Dou E in Guan Hanqing's play.[18] As a response to the unjust death of Qiu Jin, *Shenzhou Daily* published a serialized fiction titled "Resurrection at Xuanting" (*Xuanting fuhuo ji* 轩亭复活记), in which Qiu Jin is revived under the new name

Xia Yu 夏瑜 and embarks on English literature studies with a Japanese tutor, preparing for her journey to America.[19] It's worth noting that in Lu Xun's 1919 short story "Medicine" (*Yao* 药), the offstage male protagonist, a revolutionary martyr, shares the name Xia Yu, serving as a reference to Qiu Jin.

During the late Qing era, the media perceived the injustice in Qiu Jin's case as a reflection of a corrupt government, portraying her as a victim of a defective legal system. They acknowledged her advocacy for gender equality but denied her involvement in revolution. The poems, lyrics, and essays commemorating Qiu Jin during the late Qing era concentrated on the theme of injustice (*yuan* 冤). In her poem titled "Mourning Qiu Jin from Shanyin" (*Ai Shanyin* 哀山阴), Wu Zhiying wrote, "the verdict, every word dripping with the blood of a wronged citizen."[20] Xu Zihua 徐自华 (1873–1935), another close friend of Qiu Jin, wrote, "grieve over the injustice of the verdict, lament the cruelty of her fate."[21] Drawing a parallel to Dou E in Guan Hanqing's play, who swears before her execution that there will be snow in midsummer to prove her innocence, Qiu Jin's brother Qiu Yuzhang lamented that "an undeserved grievance turns into frost in June."[22] As Qiu Jin was also executed during the middle of summer, "frost in June" became a prevalent allusion in late Qing literary works symbolizing the injustice she faced.

Coinciding with the media frenzy, numerous literary works on Qiu Jin emerged in the initial years after her death. These included Xiaoshan Xianglingzi's 萧山湘灵子 *zaju* drama *Tragedy at Xuanting* (*Xuanting yuan* 轩亭冤, 1907) and Jingguanzi's 静观子 novel *Frost in June* (*Liuyue shuang* 六月霜, 1911). Both literary works portray Qiu Jin as a victim of a corrupted legal system, asserting her advocacy for a family revolution (*jiating geming* 家庭革命), rather than a radical racial revolution (*zhongzu geming* 种族革命) aimed at opposing Manchu rule and reviving the Han heritage. In these works, Qiu Jin is predominantly portrayed as adhering to traditional gender roles.

In fact, Qiu Jin undeniably embraced a revolutionary spirit. During her time studying abroad in Japan in 1905, she joined the Revolutionary Alliance, a political organization dedicated to opposing Manchu rule and the Qing government. She also voiced her anti-Manchu revolutionary ideas in her writings. In a poem addressed to Jiang Lushan 蒋鹿珊, Qiu Jin explicitly conveyed that all revolutionaries should "collaborate in harmonious unity to expel the Manchu oppressors" (*xieli tongxin qu mannu* 协力同心驱满奴).[23] Despite her resolute advocacy for overthrowing the Qing government, the portrayals of Qiu Jin in fictional narratives such as *Tragedy at Xuanting* and *Frost in June* adamantly differentiate her from revolutionaries (*geming dang* 革命党). In

Tragedy at Xuanting, Qiu Jin firmly refuses to identify herself as a revolutionary and even directs vehement reproach toward an official, exclaiming, "Fool official! How dare you falsely identify me as a revolutionary."[24]

In *Frost in June*, Qiu Jin repeatedly denies her association with revolutionaries. She draws a sharp distinction between family reform and anti-Qing revolution, claiming that her focus is solely on promoting gender equality and she has no connection with Xu Xilin. The novel begins with Yue Lanshi 越兰石, a character based on Wu Zhiying, reading about the execution of Qiu Jin in a newspaper. Qiu Jin then appears in Yue Lanshi's dream, explaining her revolutionary ideals. She tells Yue Lanshi, "I hate the new youths who study abroad in Japan. They lack patriotic sentiment but frequently discuss revolution. . . . My fundamental purpose and theirs are as incompatible as ice and fire."[25] When confronted by the county officials, Qiu Jin defends herself by contending that "my version of revolution is family revolution, not racial revolution."[26]

The author of *Frost in June* confines Qiu Jin's revolution to the women's field (*nüjie* 女界) and views any anti-Qing revolution as transgressive. In the novel, Yue Lanshi is portrayed as a conservative reformist who perceives Qiu Jin's "personality as excessively radical and her thoughts as overly innovative."[27] She befriends Qiu Jin in order to "guide her onto the correct path."[28] Qiu Yuzhang 秋裕章, another fictional character inspired by Qiu Jin's brother Qiu Yuzhang 秋誉章, is depicted as a timid individual who fears the term "revolution." In the novel, "Upon learning about his sister's revolutionary martyrdom, he was so frightened that he almost wanted to abandon his surname passed down from his ancestors. Although he was aware that his sister's death was unjust, he still refused to step forward and seek justice to redress the grievance on her behalf."[29] However, in reality, Qiu Yuzhang was an adamant revolutionary who wholeheartedly supported Qiu Jin.

In addition to refuting Qiu Jin's involvement in political revolution, the portrayals of Qiu Jin in both *Tragedy at Xuanting* and *Frost in June* predominantly adhere to traditional gender roles in Chinese society, despite acknowledging her support for women's rights. The divorce initiated by Qiu Jin to pursue her personal aspirations, a significant event that highlights her agency and independence, is ambiguously presented in *Tragedy at Xuanting*. In the *zaju* drama, the entire fourth act depicts Qiu Jin as a frail woman confined to her sickbed while studying in Japan, omitting the iconic images of her cross-dressing as a man or holding an unsheathed knife. In *Frost in June*, Qiu Jin is first introduced in Yue Lanshi's dream, described as "wearing a snow green silk gauze robe, layered with a short pink muslin gown underneath. She wears a black close-woven pleated skirt, complemented by black socks and damask rush shoes. A hint of her raspberry-pink muslin pants is visible in the breeze. Her hair is styled in the usual fashionable bun."[30] These detailed descriptions of Qiu Jin's elegant feminine clothing encourage readers to perceive her as a traditional beauty, diverting attention from her remarkable agency.

Instead of the more common motif of shedding blood in narratives of revolutionary martyrdom, both *Tragedy at Xuanting* and *Frost in June* prominently feature the motif of shedding tears. These narratives depict Qiu Jin as a vulnerable woman. In Jingguanzi's novel *Frost in June*, Qiu Jin appears too feeble to resist during her arrest: "Some soldiers searched the vacant room at the back and discovered a woman (Qiu Jin) crouching in a corner. They hurriedly approached; some pulling, some pushing, until they dragged her out. The unfortunate woman remained silent, tears welling in her eyes as she trailed behind the soldiers toward the front."[31]

In the *zaju* drama *Tragedy at Xuanting*, Qiu Jin's tears are ceaseless following her arrest.[32] The drama poignantly depicts Qiu Jin's sentiment: "My heart is like tangled hemp, the grievance is difficult to voice; it truly compels me to cry to the heavens and pound the earth, tears falling like beads."[33] According to Hu Ying's analysis, the depictions of Qiu Jin in the drama, particularly through the stage directions, "are consistent with the generic portrayal of a woman of good family confronting the legal system."[34] The initial portrayal of Qiu Jin followed both gender and literary conventions.

Qiu Jin's torrential tears also appeared in an elaborately depicted scene—her mourning for her mother—in both works. In *Xuting yuan*, saddened by her mother's passing, Qiu Jin cries so intensely that her "blood and tears flow together (*xue lei jiao liu* 血泪交流)."[35] The author paints Qiu Jin as a Confucian filial daughter, mourning her mother with deep reverence. The novel *Frost in June* dedicates an extended, tear-filled scene to depict Qiu Jin's heart-wrenching grief for her mother:

> Qiu Jin didn't care that relatives and friends were all present. She began crying right from the entrance, crying all the way in. She knelt before her mother's memorial tablet, sobbing uncontrollably. When the relatives and friends saw this, they too shed tears for her. Her elder brother, Qiu Yuzhang, hearing Qiu Jin's cries from inside the mourning hall, came out to help her up. The siblings met and were overcome with even greater sobs. . . . Before her brother could finish speaking, Qiu Jin was already crying so much that she was almost

> unrecognizable. Seeing their mother in such a state, her children started to sob. For a moment, the sound of crying was earth-shaking, as if they might awaken the dead.[36]

The depiction of Qiu Jin's mourning for her mother follows a conventional pattern, reminiscent of mourning stories in the biographies of filial daughters from ancient China. In late Qing literary imagination, the motif of Qiu Jin's tears aims to evoke empathy from readers while framing her as a virtuous woman and a filial daughter who adheres to Confucian norms.

The literary works concerning Qiu Jin during the late Qing merged traditional values and literary conventions, portraying her as a filial daughter and chaste woman, reminiscent of the wrongly convicted frail female character Dou E. In *Frost in June*, after the execution of Qiu Jin, the local populace of Shaoxing assembles to gossip about her potential romantic relationship with Xu Xilin. An esteemed elderly man initiates the discussion by critiquing Qiu Jin's radical notions of family revolution, contending that a woman should not abandon her spouse and parents to pursue independence. However, he subsequently dismisses the rumors about Qiu Jin's relationship with Xu Xilin and comes to her defense regarding her chastity, asserting that "while Qiu Jin's actions may have been unorthodox, she seemed to grasp the essence of upholding her chastity (*shoushen* 守身)."[37] The old man's commentary on Qiu Jin mirrors the stance of the reformist faction (*gailiang pai* 改良派) during the late Qing period, which accepted certain new ideas about women's independence, provided that they refrained from destabilizing the established foundations of the traditional family structure and the state.

Qiu Jin's transgressiveness, however, goes beyond even the perspective of a revolutionary like Zhang Binglin 章炳麟 (1869–1936). A few months after Qiu Jin's passing, Zhang Binglin published two essays in *Minbao* 民报, commemorating her under his style name Taiyan 太炎. One of the essays is dedicated to the martyrs of the Anqing 安庆 uprising, a group that includes Qiu Jin, Xu Xilin, Chen Boping 陈伯平, and Ma Zonghan 马宗汉. Despite their collective sacrifice for the same cause, Zhang Binglin labels the male martyrs as *zhishi* 志士 (aspiring men), while characterizing Qiu Jin as a *lienü* 列女 (exemplary woman).[38]

Zhang's second essay serves as a preface to a collection of Qiu Jin's works. In it, Zhang Binglin endeavors to position Qiu Jin in the category of traditional exemplary women by drawing a comparison between her and Cao E

曹娥, an iconic filial daughter from Chinese history who was also a Shaoxing native. While praising Qiu Jin's courage and literary talent, Zhang Binglin criticizes her for not adhering to the standards of "proper speech," a traditional virtue for Chinese women. He asserts that Qiu Jin did "not carefully choose her words" (*yuyan wu jianzi* 语言无简择), and met her execution by uttering indiscreet remarks (*yi louyan ziyun* 以漏言自殒).[39] As Hu Ying argues, Zhang's criticism stems from his "discomfort at Qiu Jin's transgression of gender norms."[40] According to Zhang Binglin, a female martyr must embody both heroism and virtue to warrant eulogization.

During the late Qing period, both media and literature portrayed Qiu Jin as a contemporary Dou E, partly as an attempt to avoid explicit political statements against the Qing government. Yet, even more significantly, their intention was to confine the images of Qiu Jin within the boundaries of traditional gender norms. The deliberate separation of family revolution from anti-Qing revolution in literary works pertaining to Qiu Jin during this era aimed to prevent the female martyr from penetrating the political sphere and unsettling the established gender hierarchy. It was not until the fall of the Qing dynasty and the emergence of nationalism that Qiu Jin gained recognition as a revolutionary martyr. At this juncture, women's liberation became intertwined with national salvation.

Qiu Jin as a Revolutionary Martyr after 1911

Wu Zhiying's writings on Qiu Jin epitomize the evolving perception of the image of Qiu Jin and the construction of the meanings of Qiu's death during the late Qing and early Republican era. As previously explored, prior to the 1911 Revolution that toppled the Qing dynasty, Wu Zhiying's essays and poems commemorating Qiu Jin primarily emphasized the theme of injustice. She refrained from depicting Qiu Jin as a revolutionary and approached discussions about revolution with caution.[41] However, after the 1911 Revolution, Wu Zhiying swiftly transformed Qiu Jin's identity from that of a wronged woman to that of a revolutionary martyr. Shortly after the establishment of the Republic of China, Wu published "Preface to the Posthumous Works of Qiu Jin" (*Qiu Jin yizhu xu* 秋瑾遗著序), explicitly identifying Qiu Jin as a pioneer of the 1911 Revolution. In it, Wu remarked that "during these times, the Wuhan Uprising rallied numerous heroic individuals and their supporters. . . . Unfortunately, Qiu Jin died before her aspirations could be fulfilled and she could witness the revolution. However, Qiu Jin would find solace in knowing that her dying wish has been realized."[42]

In 1912, Wu Zhiying and Xu Zihua advocated for relocating Qiu Jin's tomb to West Lake and organizing a grand assembly to honor her sacrifice. They exchanged letters to discuss these matters. In a letter dated March 10, 1912, Wu Zhiying addressed Xu, proposing that "the inscription on Sister Qiu's memorial stele should prominently feature the term 'revolution.' . . . It should read, 'the tomb of Qiu Jin, the first female revolutionary.' . . . As for the date on the tomb, it should be recorded as February 13, 1912, to coincide with the celebration of the abdication of the last Qing emperor" (see fig. 15).[43] Later the same year, Wu Zhiying entrusted Bu Songlin 卜松林 with several of Qiu Jin's relics for exhibition at the forthcoming commemorative event. Accompanying these relics was a letter from Wu to Xuzihua on July 17. She consistently referred to Qiu Jin as a *lieshi* 烈士 (martyr) throughout the letter (see fig. 16).[44]

After the 1911 Revolution, the newly established Republican China faced the imperative of constructing a fresh narrative for the state to legitimize its rule. Commemorating martyrs became essential in forming the collective memory. In less than a year, local governments organized a series of significant memorial ceremonies to honor revolutionary martyrs. On December 17, 1911, Chen Yingshi 陈英士 (1878–1916), the Shanghai military leader, organized an elaborate memorial event at Minglun tang 明伦堂 with over 10,000 people attending to pay tribute to the revolutionary martyrs.[45] During the ceremony, Qiu Jin's photograph graced the altar, and she was esteemed as a *nülieshi* 女烈士 (female martyr).[46] In his speech at the ceremony, Huang Fu 黄郛 (1880–1936) lauded "both the martyrs and the female revolutionary Qiu Jin [who] transcended the boundaries of familial loyalty and embraced freedom."[47] Qiu Jin was no longer confined to the realm of family revolution; instead, she was celebrated as a martyr for the entire nation.

In January 1912, Xu Zihua sent a telegram to Sun Yat-sen, the provisional president of the Republic of China, pleading for the restoration of Qiu Jin's grave at West Lake. She signed the letter as "Xu Zihua, a party member from Shimen" (*Shimen dangyuan Xu Zihua* 石门党员徐自华).[48] For the first time, Xu Zihua was not campaigning for the commemoration of Qiu Jin merely as a friend, but rather, she capitalized on her political identification as a member of the Revolutionary Alliance. This transformation elevated the act of commemoration from a personal endeavor to a communal and political pursuit. In the name of the Qiu Society (*Qiushe* 秋社), Xu Zihua hosted a grand memorial ceremony for Qiu Jin at the Dashan Temple (*Dashan Si* 大善寺) in

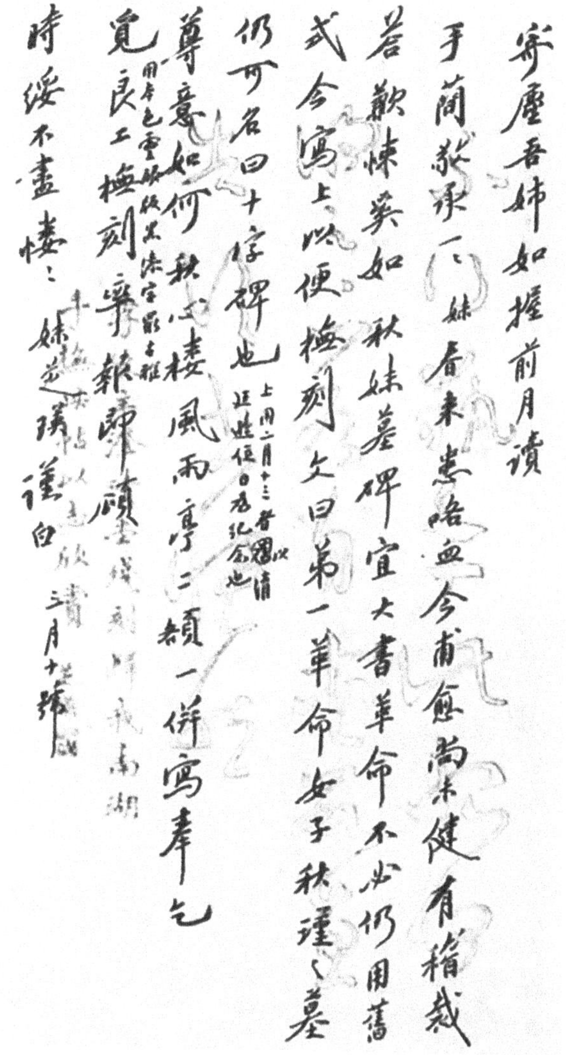
寄塵吾姊如握前月讀
手簡敬承一一 妹舊來患咯血今甫愈尚未健有稽裁
答歉悚奚如 秋妹墓碑宜大書革命不必仍用舊
式今寫上以便梅刻文曰第一革命女子秋瑾之墓
仍可名曰十字碑也
尊意如何 秋心樓風雨亭二額一併寫奉乞
覓良工梅刻寧報歸續
時綏不盡悽悽 妹芝瑛謹白

Figure 15: Wu Zhiying's letter to Xu Zihua, dated March 10, 1912, collection at the National Museum of China. Source: Xiong Guanqin 熊广琴, "Qiu Jin maigu, Xiling chuanqi—du Wu Zhiying zhi Xu Zihua xinzha" 秋瑾埋骨，西泠传奇—读吴芝瑛致徐自华信札 (Qiu Jin's resting place, a legendary tale in Xiling—reading Wu Zhiying's letters to Xu Zihua), *Rongbaozhai* 6 (2017): 251.

Shaoxing on January 26, 1912.[49] Just two days later, the memorial service in Hangzhou drew a gathering of over a thousand attendees to honor Xu Xinlin, Chen Boping, Ma Zonghan, Qiu Jin, and Tao Chengzhang.[50]

In March 1912, the Provisional Government proposed the conversion of the Shrines to Loyal Soldiers (*Zhaozhong ci* 昭忠祠) from the Qing dynasty into the Shrines of Great Han Loyal Martyrs (*Dahan zhonglie ci* 大汉忠烈

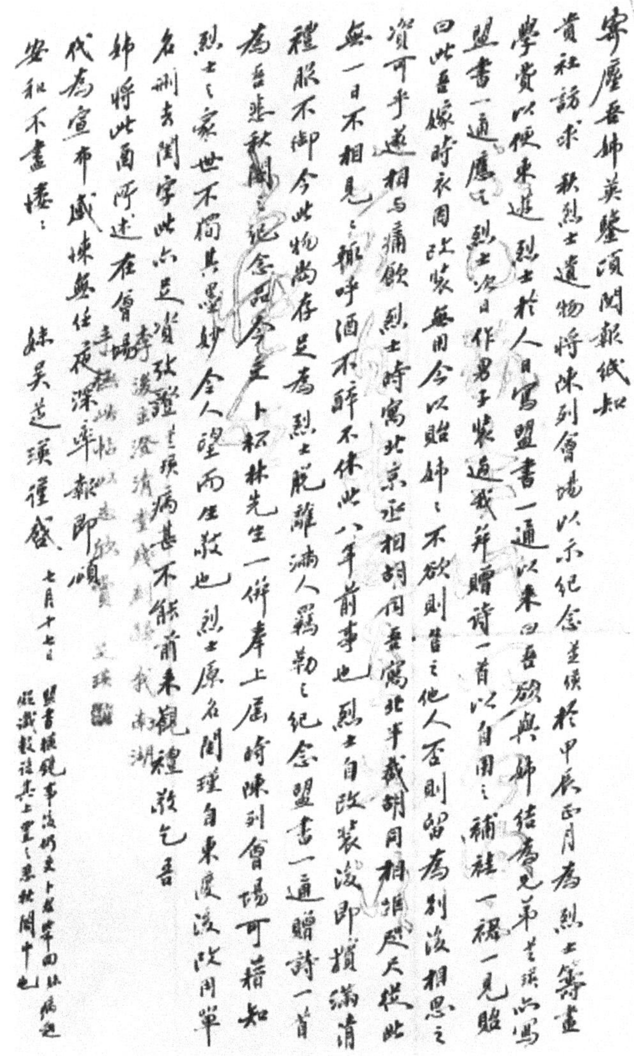

寄塵吾姊英鑒頃閱報紙知
貴社訪求 秋烈士遺物將陳列會場以示紀念並憶於甲辰正月為烈士籌畫
學費以便東渡 烈士於人日寫盟書一通以來四吾欲與姊結為兄弟芝瑛亦寫
盟書一通應之 烈士後日作君子歌遺我并贈詩一首以自用之補褂一襲一見贈
曰此吾嫁時衣用改裝無用今以贈姊之不欲則替之他人否則留為別後相思之
資可乎遂相與痛飲 烈士時寓北京西相胡同吾寓北半截胡同相距咫尺從此
無一日不相見之輒呼酒不醉不休此八年前事也 烈士自改裝後即損滿清
禮服不御今此物尚存足為 烈士脫離滿人羈勒之紀念盟書一通贈詩一首
為吾悲秋閣之紀念品今並上卜私林先生一併奉上屆時陳列會場可藉知
烈士之家世不獨其墨妙令人望而生敬也 烈士原名閨瑾自東渡後改用單
名刪去閨字此亦足資考證 芝瑛病甚不能前來觀禮敬乞吾
姊將此函所述在會場
代為宣布 感悚無任夜深草草報此即頌
安和不盡縷縷 妹吳芝瑛謹啟 七月十七日

Figure 16: Wu Zhiying's letter to Xu Zihua, dated July 17, 1912, collection at the National Museum of China. Source: Xiong Guanqin, "Qiu Jin maigu, Xiling chuanqi—du Wu Zhiying zhi Xu Zihua xinzha," 254.

祠), dedicated to "worshipping the martyrs who sacrificed themselves for the Republic of China (*jinzhong minguo sishi zhulie rusi qizhong* 尽忠民国死事诸烈入祀其中)."[51] The memorial services held for revolutionary martyrs and the transformation of the sacred sacrificial spaces in early Republican China aimed to erase old memories and establish new ones.

The commemoration of Qiu Jin in early Republican China reached its peak on June 6 of the lunar calendar in 1912, which marked the anniversary of her death. On this day, both Hangzhou and Changsha held elaborate memorial services for Qiu Jin. Xu Zihua delivered a speech at the ceremony in Hangzhou, where relics of Qiu Jin and archives of her case were exhibited.[52] In Changsha, Qiu Jin's son and daughter attended the memorial service. Zhounan Girls' Middle School, whose progressive views would later influence Ding Ling, paid tribute to the female martyr as part of the ceremony.[53]

During that period, Zhejiang, where Qiu Jin had grown up and become a martyr, and Hunan, where she had married and resided for a long time, were competing to claim authority over the commemoration of the iconic female revolutionary martyr. As Henrietta Harrison points out, in early Republican China, "By presenting well known local figures as martyrs they demonstrated the connection between national ideals and the realities of local politics."[54] Following the Qiu Society's campaign and negotiations between the Hunan and Zhejiang governments, the Hunan military leader Tan Yankai 谭延闿 (1880–1930) agreed to transfer Qiu Jin's remains to be buried at West Lake alongside other Republican martyrs.[55] Qiu Jin's son Wang Yuande 王沅德 (1897–1955) was disappointed by the decision as it would pose challenges for relatives in Hunan wishing to pay homage to his mother. However, he understood that his mother had "sacrificed her life for the country. [She] is a revolutionary giant and a public figure in the world. The family cannot claim her as private property."[56]

Qiu Jin's remains traveled from Hunan to Hangzhou and were reburied at West Lake on October 27, 1912.[57] Therefore, the private commemoration of Qiu Jin by her family and friends was transformed into a collective national memory. A month later, during his visit to Hangzhou, Sun Yat-sen paid tribute to Qiu Jin, praising her as the "best comrade" (*zuihao de tongzhi* 最好的同志).[58] This visit further solidified Qiu Jin's position as a revolutionary martyr. However, during Yuan Shikai's 袁世凯 (1859–1916) reign from 1913 to 1916, the significance of martyrs for the 1911 Revolution, including Qiu Jin, was deliberately downplayed. In August 1916, after Yuan's death, Sun Yat-sen revisited Qiu Jin's grave, reinstating her status as a revered revolutionary martyr.[59]

Figure 17: This group photo was taken after a visit to Qiu Jin's grave in Hangzhou on December 9, 1912. It includes Chiang Kai-shek 蒋介石 (1887–1975) (seated third from the left), Sun Yat-sen (seated fifth from the left), Xu Xiaoshu 徐小淑 (first on the right), Wu Zhiying (second from the right), and Xu Zihua (third from the right). Source: *Qiu Jin nüxia yiji* 秋瑾女侠遺集 (Remaining works of the woman warrior Qiu Jin), edited by Wang Canzhi 王灿芝, Beijing: Zhaohua chubanshe, 2018, 45.

Note: For photo descriptions, see Qian Xiaofo 钱小佛, "Xinhai geming wenxian zhanlanhui zhi yijiao: xianlie Qiu Jin nüshi shiji" 辛亥革命文献展览会之一角：先烈秋瑾女士事迹 (A corner of the Xinhai Revolution Archive Exhibition: The deeds of the female martyr Qiu Jin), *Chunqiu huabao* 春秋画报 (Spring and autumn pictorial) 10 (1947): 21; and "Sun Zhongshan liu lun Qiu Jin" 孙中山六论秋瑾 (Sun Yat-sen's six discussions on Qiu Jin), in *Qiu Jin nianbiao xibian*, 2.

The government of the Republic of China exerted significant efforts in creating a new national memory by commemorating revolutionary martyrs through rituals, education, and exhibitions. Among these revolutionary martyrs, Qiu Jin played an essential role in shaping this new collective memory. From June 6 to October 20, 1929, Hangzhou hosted the West Lake Exposition (*Xihu bolanhui* 西湖博览会), a global event that attracted people from around the world, including Hu Yepin, Ding Ling, Ding Ling's mother, Jiang Shengmei 蒋胜眉 (whose original name was Yu Manzhen 余曼贞), and Jiang Yiren 蒋毅仁, Jiang Shengmei's lifelong friend.

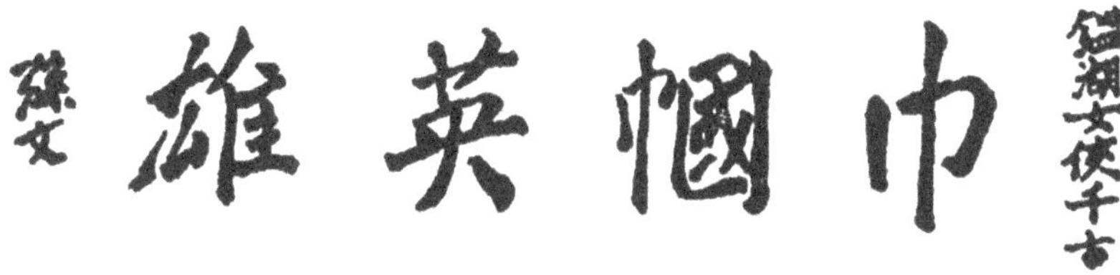

Figure 18: Sun Yat-sen's inscription for Qiu Jin, praising her as the "woman warrior," was written during his visit to Qiu Jin's grave on December 9, 1912. Source: *Qiu Jin nianbiao xibian* 秋瑾年表细编 (Detailed chronological biography of Qiu Jin), edited by Wang Qubing 王去病 and Chen Dehe 陈德和, Beijing: Huawen chubanshe, 1990, photo, 2.

In her memoir, Jiang Shengmei elaborately documented their journey to Hangzhou and their experience at the West Lake Exposition. She specifically mentioned that Ding Ling rented a house next to the Fenglin temple and a martyr's grave. Jiang Shengmei specified that the house belonged to a friend of the martyr.[60] Although Jiang Shengmei did not disclose the identity of the martyr, it becomes apparent that the martyr was likely Qiu Jin, given her grave's location at the Fenglin temple. For Ding Ling, it was a journey back to her childhood memories of Qiu Jin. However, Qiu Jin had transcended being a mere personal memory for Ding Ling; she had become a part of the nation's collective memory.

The West Lake Exposition was dedicated to showcasing Chinese merchandise and culture to the world. Notably, this commercially oriented international fair featured a Revolutionary Memorial Hall (*Geming jinianguan* 革命纪念馆), a Revolutionary Memorial Hall Library (*Geming jinianguan tushu bu* 革命纪念馆图书部), and a newly established Revolutionary Memorial Tower (*Geming jinian ta* 革命纪念塔) designed for patriotic education and the dissemination of political messages.[61] Li Chaoying 李超英, the director of the Revolutionary Memorial Hall at the Exposition, claims that "the Revolutionary Memorial Hall bears the responsibility of spiritual construction, while the other exhibition halls are tasked with the responsibility of material construction."[62] In the essay titled "Politicized West Lake Exposition" (*Danghua de Xihu bolanhui* 党化的西湖博览会), Hu Yong 湖傭 explains that the purpose of the West Lake Exposition is to "promote domestic products" (*tichang guohuo* 提倡国货).[63] However, Hu argues that the approach to pro-

Figure 19: From left to right: Hu Yepin, Ding Ling, Jiang Yiren, and Ding Ling's mother, taken during their visit in Hangzhou in the summer of 1929. Source: Jiang Zulin, *Ding Ling zhuan*, 113.

moting Chinese goods at this Exposition was distinct: "It contains enthusiastic revolutionary spirit and a strong party-oriented emphasis."[64] As Kirk Denton points out, "The consumerism in the exposition as a whole is also framed as a form of patriotism (e.g., buy national products [*guohuo*]) that is quite consistent with the nationalist rhetoric of the Revolutionary Memorial Hall."[65] Nationalism was seamlessly woven into the fabric of the 1929 West Lake Exposition.

The Revolutionary Memorial Hall at the Exposition was meticulously designed to evoke nationalist sentiments. At the entrance, the flag of the Nationalist Party fluttered, and the illuminated characters "Geming jinianguan" 革命纪念馆 (Revolutionary Memorial Hall) beckoned. Upon stepping inside, visitors commenced their journey by paying tribute to Sun Yat-sen. The visitor guidelines required all visitors to bow three times before Sun's portrait.[66] The Hall comprised six exhibition rooms displaying the relics of

Figure 20: The front entrance of the Revolutionary Memorial Hall at the West Lake Exposition. Source: *Xihu bolanhui canguan bixie*, photo, 3.

the revolutionary martyrs, collections from the 1911 Revolution, and photographs depicting moments of national humiliation. Additionally, it included a room where visitors could take a break while listening to revolutionary songs and speeches broadcast through radios and phonographs.[67]

Notably, the Revolutionary Memorial Hall prominently featured a dedicated section honoring Qiu Jin. This section displayed photographs of Qiu Jin leading the women's movement in Shaoxing, images of her wearing men's attire and a traditional kimono. It also showcased personal items such as her frequently used knife, the kimono she wore, and her handwritten poems and letters.[68] Qiu Jin played a significant role in the Republic of China's endeavor to create a new national memory and generate nationalist sentiments.

Qiu Jin was commemorated through various means during the Republican era. Around six months after the West Lake Exposition, the Shaoxing government erected a Monument to the Martyr Qiu Jin (*Qiu Jin lieshi jinian bei* 秋瑾烈士纪念碑) at the location of her execution (see fig. 21). The story of Qiu Jin was also promoted by the Nationalist government through broadcast-

Figure 21: Monument to the Martyr Qiu Jin in Shaoxing. Source: *Qiu Jin shiji* 秋瑾史迹 (Historical materials on Qiu Jin), Shanghai: Shanghai guji chubanshe, 1991, 17.

ing. The Nationalist Government Radio Station (*Guomin zhengfu zhongyang guangbo diantai* 国民政府中央广播电台), established in 1928, emerged as a primary conduit for disseminating KMT propaganda messages. To expand its coverage, the Nationalist government constructed a new broadcasting station in November 1932.[69] One of the initial programs aired on this new station was the *bajiao gu* 八角鼓 (eight-cornered drum) rendition of *Qiu Jin's Martyrdom* (*Qiu Jin jiuyi* 秋瑾就义), performed by He Zhichen 何质臣.[70] This program was later recorded and distributed by Pathé Orient (*Shanghai Baidai* 上海百代). The Propaganda Committee for the Nationalist government issued official directives (*xunling* 训令), instructing local governments and educational departments to acquire recordings of *Qiu Jin's Martyrdom.* The directive stated that "the recording serves as an effective tool for propagating revolutionary deeds."[71] On October 14, 1935, the Nationalist government issued an official decree to eulogize Qiu Jin.[72]

On October 10, 1936, which marked the National Day of the Republic of China, the Exhibition Hall for Historical Materials of the KMT (*Guomindang zhongyang dangshi shiliao chenlieguan* 国民党中央党史史料陈列馆) was inaugurated for public access in Nanjing (see fig. 22).[73] Its primary aim was to present the official narrative of the history of the KMT and to offer a space for fostering patriotic education. The Exhibition Hall encompassed a collection of Qiu Jin's relics titled "The Martyr Qiu Jin" (*Qiu Jin lieshi* 秋瑾烈士), which included photographs of her dressed in men's attire and traditional kimono, information on the military organizational structures she established for the Restoration Army (*Guangfu jun* 光复军, see fig. 23), her handwriting, a compilation of her works, and a ceramic vase that belonged to her.[74] In 1937, Qiu Jin's daughter, Wang Canzhi 王灿芝 (1901–67), donated a pair of her mother's jade bracelets to the Exhibition Hall.

The bracelets were gifts given by Qiu Jin to Xu Zihua in 1907. According to Xu Zihua's account in "A Record of Returning the Bracelets" (*Fanchuan ji* 返钏记), Qiu Jin sought her assistance with military expenses for an upcoming uprising in Zhejiang. Xu generously offered all her jewelry to help Qiu. As a token of respect, Qiu Jin took off her bracelets and gifted them to Xu. The two then made an agreement to be buried at West Lake after their passing. Xu Zihua faithfully upheld this pact, investing significant effort into constructing Qiu Jin's grave at West Lake. She also founded the Jingxiong Girl's School (*Jingxiong nüxiao* 竞雄女校) in Shanghai as a tribute to Qiu Jin.

As Wang Canzhi grew older, Xu entrusted her with the responsibility of overseeing the school and returned Qiu Jin's bracelets to her in 1927.[75] Xu Zihua later wrote an essay titled "A Record of Returning the Bracelets" to address Qiu Jin's passion for the revolution, their friendship, and her aspiration for Wang Canzhi to inherit both the bracelets and Qiu Jin's revolutionary spirit. The essay found its place in numerous textbooks during the Republican era, aimed at educating the next generation to emulate exemplary citizens like Qiu Jin.[76] In a teaching methodology manual that complements a textbook, there is a suggestion for educators to incorporate visual aids such as maps of Zhejiang and West Lake, photographs of Qiu Jin, images of her gravesite, and the adjacent architectural landmarks.[77] These resources help students grasp the revolutionary ethos and friendship encapsulated in the

Figure 22: Front door of the Exhibition Hall for Historical Materials of the KMT in Nanjing. Source: "Zuijin luocheng zhi dangshi shiliao chenlieguan" 最近落成之党史史料陈列馆 (The recently completed Exhibition Hall for Historical Materials of the KMT), *Zhongyang dangwu yuekan* 中央党务月刊 (Central Party affairs monthly) 100 (1936): 9.

essay "A Record of Returning the Bracelets." Catering to young students, both textbooks and teaching guides have played a pivotal role in shaping the collective memory of Qiu Jin as a revolutionary martyr.

Upon donating the bracelets to the Exhibition Hall for Historical Materials of the KMT in 1937, Wang Canzhi wrote an essay to elucidate the historical significance of these items. In the essay, she expressed that the bracelets would possess even greater value when "gazed upon by future generations, admired, and immortalized. How could I keep them to myself? How could I not display them to honor my ancestor's aspirations?"[78] Through the contribution of her mother's relics, Wang Canzhi's personal memorial was transformed into a shared collective memory.

To celebrate National Day in 1947, Shanghai hosted a Xinhai Revolution Archive Exhibition at the French Children's School (*Fatong xuexiao* 法童学

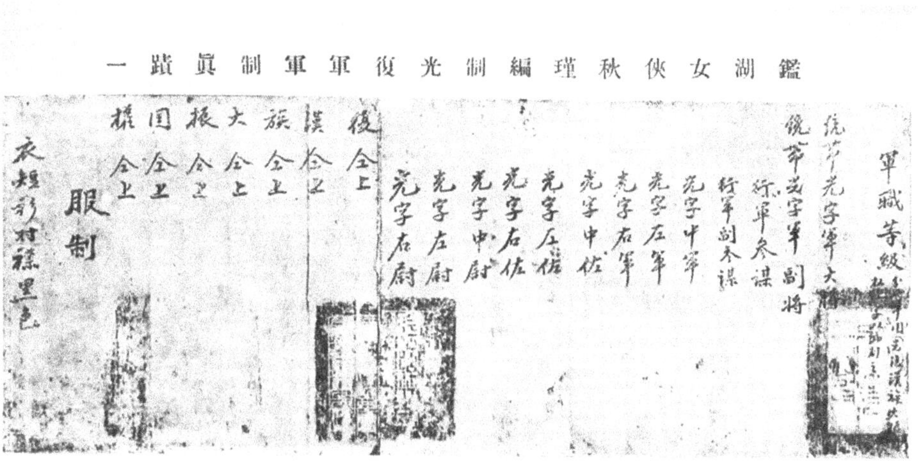

Figure 23: The military organizational structures of the Restoration Army, established by Qiu Jin, the female knight-errant of Mirror Lake (authentic handwriting, no. 1). Source: *Jiansu geming bowuguan yuekan* 江苏革命博物馆月刊 (Jiangsu Revolutionary Museum monthly) 2 (1929): 1.

Note: Established in 1929, Jiangsu Revolutionary Museum was one of the earliest public museums in the Republic of China. Chen Qubing 陈去病 (1874–1933), a core member of the Qiu Society, served as the director of the museum. The museum collected a large number of items related to the 1911 Revolution, including photos of Qiu Jin. However, it began to decline after Chen Qubing resigned from his position in 1931.

校) from October 10 to 17. At the opening ceremony, Wang Canzhi inaugurated the event, and the bracelets were displayed at the exhibition (see fig. 24).[79] For this occasion, Wang Canzhi changed her surname to Qiu, strengthening her connection to her revolutionary heritage.[80] In May 1948, under her new name Qiu Canzhi, she organized another exhibition at the Baxianqiao YMCA (*Baxianqiao qingnianhui* 八仙桥青年会) in Shanghai. This exhibition showcased Qiu Jin's relics, including photographs, bloodstained clothing, a firearm, and legal documents from Qiu Jin's case.[81]

The journey of Qiu Jin's bracelet from a personal gift to Xu Zihua, then a cherished family heirloom for Wang Canzhi, and ultimately to a public memorial, exemplifies the shifting images of the female martyr. As Hu Ying argued, in Xu's accounts, the bracelets underwent a transformation from a symbol of sisterhood to "Qiu Jin's token of gratitude for Xu's financial support of an explicitly revolutionary uprising, thus transforming their signifi-

Figure 24: Photo of Qiu Jin's emerald green jade bracelets displayed at the Xinhai Revolution Archive Exhibition in 1947. Source: *Xinhai geming wenxian zhanlanhui jiniance* 辛亥革命文献展览会纪念册 (Memorial brochure for the Xinhai Revolution Archive Exhibition), Xinhai geming tongzhihui 辛亥革命同志会 (The Alliance of the Comrades of the Xinhai Revolution), 1947, photo, 3.

cance from private gift to support for a public, political cause."[82] The return of the bracelets to Qiu Jin's daughter elevated these ostensibly feminine adornments into symbols of revolutionary spirit to be inherited. Lastly, donating the bracelets to the Exhibition Hall for Historical Materials of the KMT symbolizes Qiu Jin's integration into the official narrative of the 1911 Revolution. She is no longer a wrongly convicted vulnerable woman, mourned only by her close friends such as Wu Zhiying and Xu Zihua. Instead, she emerges as a nationally acclaimed revolutionary martyr, occupying a significant place in the collective memory.

Through the relocation of Qiu Jin's remains from Hunan to Hangzhou, numerous public memorial services, broadcasts, and governmental directives, textbook education, and exhibitions of her relics, the image of Qiu Jin as a revolutionary martyr became firmly established in early Republican China. As she became integrated into the collective memory of the 1911 Revolution, the founding of the Republic of China, and the KMT, Qiu Jin's role as an advocate for women's revolution receded to the background. Through examining two wartime plays centered around Qiu Jin—Xia Yan's *The Spirit of Freedom* (*Ziyou hun* 自由魂, 1936) and Yan Yiyan's *Qiu Jin* 秋瑾 (1940)—the following sections present an alternative viewpoint to the national defense literature movement and the CCP's perspective regarding the relationship between women's revolution and national salvation.

Qiu Jin in National Defense Drama

The year 1936 was designated as the "Year of Qiu Jin" (*Qiu Jin nian* 秋瑾年) to commemorate the thirtieth anniversary of her martyrdom.[83] On March 8, 1936, to celebrate International Women's Day, both Nanjing and Shanghai held commemorative gatherings and passed a proposal to establish the day of Qiu Jin's martyrdom as "Chinese Women's Day" (*Zhonghua funü jie* 中华妇女节).[84] In Shanghai, over 2,000 people attended the gathering at the Sichuan Road YMCA. Leaders of the women's movement, including He Xiangning 何香凝 (1878–1972), Shi Liang 史良 (1900–1985) and Wang Canzhi, delivered speeches at the meeting. Following the conclusion of the assembly at 4 p.m., attendees initiated a patriotic march from Sichuan Road to Nanshi district (*Nanshi* 南市), advocating for women's rights and national salvation along the way. The parade garnered the participation of over 10,000 people, effectively merging the causes of the women's movement and national sentiment within this event.[85]

Nationalism played an important role in the commemoration of Qiu Jin in 1936, driven by China's deep entanglement in a severe national crisis. On September 18, 1931, Japan initiated its invasion of Manchuria and subsequently gained control over northeast China by 1932. On January 28, 1932, the Japanese Army attacked Shanghai. On December 9, 1935, thousands of students marched through Beijing to protest the KMT's policy of "stabilizing the country before repelling foreign invaders" (*annei rangwai* 安内攘外) and vehemently demanded proactive behavior from the Nationalist government against the Japanese invasion. Within this complex landscape, national salvation was the paramount concern in China in 1936.

In 1936, Shen Zijiu 沈兹九 (1898–1989), the founder and the chief editor of the magazine *Women's Life* (*Funü shenghuo* 妇女生活), published an essay titled "Why We Should Commemorate Qiu Jin" (*Women weishenme yao jinian Qiu Jin* 我们为什么要纪念秋瑾). In this essay, she articulates that "in this critical moment when we face the peril of national subjugation and the potential extinction of our race, we need passionate soldiers, adept organizers capable of rallying comrades, and sowers propagating revolutionary messages. . . . [Qiu Jin] is indeed a revolutionary sowing machine."[86] She proceeds to contend that commemorating Qiu Jin could ignite the spirit of resistance against foreign invaders and contribute to the salvation of the nation. At the end of the essay, Shen calls upon novelists, playwrights, and filmmakers to rectify the misrepresentations of Qiu Jin in late Qing literature, such as the novel *Frost in June*, and to create new versions of this female revolutionary martyr.

Shortly after Shen Zijiu's invocation, in late 1936, Xia Yan published his three-act, five-scene play script titled *The Spirit of Freedom*, which revolved around the life of Qiu Jin.[87] This play emerged within the backdrop of the national defense theater (*guofang xiju* 国防戏剧) movement, with the aim of generating nationalist sentiments and rallying public support for national salvation. It achieved this by focusing on antiforeign (*fandi* 反帝) and anti-traitor (*fan hanjian* 反汉奸) themes.[88] Prior to *The Spirit of Freedom*, Xia Yan had already published a seven-act historical play script titled *Sai Jinhua* 赛金花 in April 1936. This play was acclaimed as the representative work of national defense theater. It tells the story of a famous late Qing courtesan, Sai Jinhua, who strategically leveraged her romantic relationship with the German general Alfred von Waldersee to contribute to national salvation during the Boxer Rebellion.

Sai Jinhua quickly became a popular sensation upon its premiere by the 40s Drama Club (*Sishi niandai jushe* 四十年代剧社) in November 1936. However, it generated controversy over its allusion to the Nationalist government's policy of kowtowing to Japan and the portrayal of a prostitute as a national heroine. During a performance of *Sai Jinhua* in Nanjing on February 22, 1937, some audience members threw bananas, oranges, and even spittoons onto the stage in protest of the scene featuring a Manchu diplomat's kowtow to Waldersee. In response, the 40s Drama Club had to swiftly switch to performing the play *Qiu Jin* instead on the following day.[89]

The 40s Drama Club introduced Xia Yan's two plays centered around patriotic heroines to Nanjing in February 1937. They changed the title *Ziyou hun* to *Qiu Jin* to enhance comprehension and align it with the other play's title, *Sai Jinhua*.[90] In contrast to the controversial heroine Sai Jinhua, Qiu Jin is portrayed as an adamant revolutionary in the Republic of China. The advertisement for the 40s Drama Club's debut of *Qiu Jin* in Nanjing highlights Qiu Jin's role as a revolutionary. It states that "she actively points out the path Nora should tread after leaving the house" (see fig. 25). Additionally, the advertisement underlines that the production features the same playwright and cast as the popular play *Sai Jinhua*, aiming to secure commercial success for *Qiu Jin*.

Xia Yan drew inspiration for *The Spirit of Freedom* from his reading of Qiu Jin's collected works, his translation of German Marxist August Bebel's *Woman and Socialism* (1879), and the heroic martyrdom of the female

Figure 25: Advertisement for the 40s Drama Club's premiere of *Qiu Jin* in Nanjing in February 1937. Source: *Zhongyang ribao*, February 24, 1937.

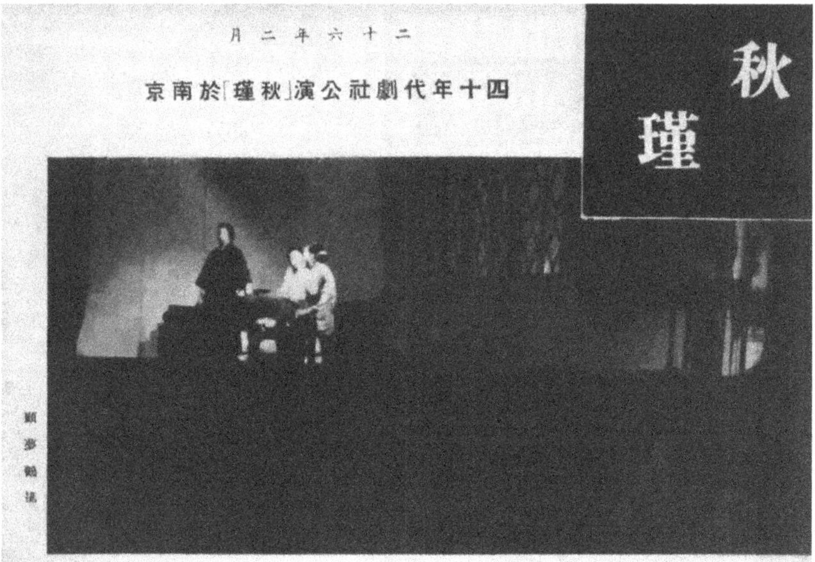

Figure 26: A scene from *Qiu Jin*, photo by Gu Menghe 顾梦鹤. Source: Gu Menghe, "Sishi niandai jushe gongyan 'Qiu Jin' yu Nanjing 四十年代剧社公演《秋瑾》于南京" (Public performance of *Qiu Jin* by the 40s Drama Club at Nanjing), *Xinhua huabao* 新华画报 (New China pictorial) 4 (1937): 15.

revolutionary Feng Keng 冯铿 (1907–31).[91] In *The Spirit of Freedom*, Xia Yan portrays Qiu Jin as a nationalist hero, depicting her as a revolutionary who perceives her commitment to revolution as her life's calling, surpassing even her familial ties. Contrasting with the frail and feeble portrayals common in late Qing literature, Xia Yan's rendition of Qiu Jin is as a transgressive woman who "usually wears men's clothing and rides horses."[92] The conventional depiction of Qiu Jin mourning her mother, emblematic of filial piety in late Qing narratives, is entirely absent from Xia Yan's play. Xia Yan fundamentally rejects filial piety, a core value of Confucian ideology that came under vehement criticism during the New Culture Movement, as suitable for a revolutionary heroine.[93]

Confronting her imminent death, Qiu Jin, as penned by Xia Yan, transforms into an unwavering martyr, diverging from the sorrowful Dou E archetype prevalent in late Qing narratives. The play describes a scene in which "prison guards march Qiu Jin onto the stage. Her hair is disheveled, wrists bound behind her back, and she wears heavy ankle shackles. Yet, she stands defiantly, refusing to kneel."[94] In her final speech before her execution, Qiu Jin states: "You can chop off my head, but you cannot change my determination. . . . As revolutionaries, it is our duty to die for benevolence and righteousness."[95] This depiction is drastically different from the similar scenes in *Frost in June* and *Tragedy at Xuanting*, where Qiu Jin constantly cries and denies her revolutionary identity.

While depicting Qiu Jin as a heroic revolutionary martyr in his play, Xia Yan simultaneously casts doubts on her sacrifice. In Xia Yan's play, Qiu Jin's loyal comrade, Cheng Yi 程毅, endeavors to persuade her to evade her imminent arrest. He contends that "being fully aware of the danger but refusing to escape is detrimental to the revolution . . . Revolutionaries don't sacrifice themselves for naught."[96] However, Qiu Jin remains resolute in her determination to sacrifice herself and rejects the idea of fleeing. Another revolutionary, Wang Jinfa 王金发, criticizes Qiu's unnecessary martyrdom. He sneers at her, remarking, "You have been ruined by reading those archaic books promoting the five cardinal virtues of Confucianism."[97] Xia Yan portrays Cheng Yi and Wang Jinfa as more mature male revolutionaries who attempt to guide Qiu Jin toward a path that avoids unnecessary death, thereby preserving revolutionary forces.

The apparent deflation of Qiu Jin's heroic martyrdom in *The Spirit of Freedom* faced criticism from Guo Moruo and Tian Han.[98] Guo Moruo claims that "knowing that death is avoidable but still facing it with great composure—this is the true spirit of the female knight of Jianhu."[99] However, it is important to consider that Xia Yan's decision to portray Qiu Jin as a flawed revolutionary martyr was deeply influenced by the political and cultural climate of the time, as well as his personal involvement in clandestine activities for the CCP.

Following the collapse of the first KMT-CCP collaboration in 1927, the KMT initiated both military and cultural suppression campaigns against the CCP. In December 1930, for its cultural suppression (*wenhua weijiao* 文化围剿) campaign, the Nationalist government promulgated the Publication Law to tighten control over newspapers, magazines, and books, while also censoring messages critical of the KMT.[100] In May 1932, another measure was introduced titled "Standards for Inspecting Propaganda Materials" (*Xuanchuanpin shencha biaozhun* 宣传品审查标准), which categorizes "propaganda for communism and encouragement for class struggle" as reactionary propaganda.[101] On June 10, 1935, the "Directive Urging Citizens to Foster Friendly Relations with Other Nations" (*Shenjing guomin duiyu youbang wudunmuyi ling* 申儆国民对于友邦务敦睦谊令), was issued. Additionally, on February

20, 1936, the "Emergency Measures for Maintaining Public Order" (*Weichi zhi'an jinji banfa ling* 维持治安紧急办法令) were implemented, prohibiting anti-Japanese movements and granting military police the authority to apprehend individuals identified as leftists and anti-Japanese activists.[102] During the White Terror period, a significant number of Communists, including Xia Yan, went underground. Simultaneously, the national defense drama gravitated toward historical topics to mirror the contemporary national crisis while avoiding censorship by the Nationalist government.

Foreign invasion and traitors, the two central themes in national defense dramas, are significant in Xia Yan's *The Spirit of Freedom*. Despite Qiu Jin's historical focus on challenging the Manchu government without directly confronting imperialism, Xia Yan includes a fictional prelude in the play where Qiu Jin expresses anti-foreign-invasion sentiments. Notably, she extends help to a peasant whose land was seized by a Chinese Christian during the *gengzi* 庚子 year (1900) national crisis. Furthermore, Xia Yan introduces the character Jiang Ji 蒋纪, a despicable traitor who betrays Qiu Jin and fellow revolutionaries in the storyline. In a letter to the adaptors of the Peking opera version of *The Spirit of Freedom*, Xia Yan elaborates on this creative choice:

> The themes of the play, anti-imperialism and antifeudalism, are evidently clear. However, certain plot elements, such as the depiction of Jiang Ji, Qiu Jin's failure to remain vigilant against the hidden traitor, and the debate between Wang Jinfa and Qiu Jin regarding whether to engage in desperate fighting like trapped animals or to conserve strength for a future resurgence in act 3, have specific purposes within the context. After 1934, the KMT experienced repeated failures in both military and cultural repression. They changed their strategy, employing traitors to undermine the revolutionaries and cause damage. In KMT-controlled areas, our Communists held deep disdain and aversion for traitors. . . . On one hand, I wrote about Qiu Jin's perseverance and courage. On the other hand, I subtly critiqued her for her limited understanding of revolutionary strategies.[103]

Incorporating insights drawn from his personal experiences as an underground Communist, particularly his involvement in the "strange Westerner incident" (*guai xiren shijian* 怪西人事件) in Shanghai, Xia Yan wove his thoughts about revolutionary strategies into *The Spirit of Freedom*. In May 1935, secret agents from the KMT military intelligence bureau (*juntong* 军统) arrested a foreign spy who refused to answer any inquiries and even withheld

Figure 27: A stage photo from the Peking opera adaptation of Xia Yan's *The Spirit of Freedom*, depicting Jiang Ji's betrayal of the revolution. From left to right: Qiu Jin, Wang Jinfa, Jiang Ji, and Cheng Yi. Source: Wang Yan, *Qiu Jin zhuan (Jingju)*, photo, 2.

his name. The incident made headlines, with newspapers referring to him as a "strange Westerner." Joseph Walden (real name Yakov Bronin), the leader of the Soviet intelligence bureau in China, was this so-called strange Westerner. Alongside him, Yuan Shu 袁殊 (1911–87), a legendary CCP secret agent who also worked for the Soviet intelligence bureau in China, was exposed due to the treachery of Lu Haifang 陆海防, a traitor. To prevent further harm to the CCP and preserve their forces, Xia Yan, who maintained close ties with Yuan Shu, retreated to a secure apartment on Carter Road in Shanghai for a span of three months.[104] During his period of seclusion, Xia Yan managed to complete the writing of the national defense drama *Sai Jinhua*.

Set against the backdrop of national defense literature and enriched by Xia Yan's experiences as an underground Communist, *The Spirit of Freedom* eulogizes revolutionaries while vehemently condemning traitors. Xia Yan's critique of Qiu Jin in the play was not intended to undermine her martyrdom; rather, it functions as a cautionary reminder against unnecessary sacrifice during the White Terror and a contemplation of the attributes of a mature revolutionary. Focusing on delivering the message of national salvation, Xia Yan's portrayal of Qiu Jin serves more as a symbol of patriotism. Her role in advocating for women's rights is downplayed. In a separate setting far removed from KMT-controlled Shanghai, female writer Yan Yiyan wrote a play titled *Qiu Jin* in Yan'an, the headquarters of the CCP. This particular play provides a perspective on the relationship between women's emancipation and national liberation.

Qiu Jin as the New Nora in Yan'an

In 1940, Yan'an organized a series of three plays showcasing heroic women as a tribute to International Women's Day. These plays included *Mother Yue Tattooing Characters [on Her Son Yue Fei's Back]* (*Yuemu cizi* 岳母刺字), *Liang Hongyu* 梁红玉, and *Qiu Jin*. The three women honored through plays were deliberately chosen by the March 8 celebration committee because they are "famous female warriors in history."[105] The primary aim of these three plays was to galvanize the populace, particularly women, to resist Japanese invaders. Notably, the four-act spoken drama *Qiu Jin* was written by Yan Yiyan, a female playwright who led the screenwriters' group for the Counter-Japanese Military and Political University performance troupe.[106]

Yan Yiyan had attended a performance of Xia Yan's play, *The Spirit of Freedom*, in Shanghai and found herself greatly impressed. However, she decided to create a fresh production that would directly address the prevailing issues and concerns in Yan'an during 1940, focusing on different facets of the female martyr. As she explains, her play emphasizes "unwavering spirit even in the face of death . . . a revolutionary's integrity and perseverance in the revolution."[107] In Yan Yiyan's adaptation, the theme of questioning of Qiu Jin's decision to forgo escape upon arrest, as seen in Xia Yan's play, was eliminated. Instead, her revised version introduced two fictional female characters: Xu Shufang 徐淑芳 and Xia Zhenguo 夏振国. These characters represented, respectively, the repressed Chinese woman and the successor of Qiu Jin's legacy. Through this alteration, the play conveyed a distinct and pronounced message concerning women's liberation in China.

Yan Yiyan's play *Qiu Jin* was performed by students and faculty at the newly established Chinese Women's University (*Zhongguo nüzi daxue* 中国女子大学) in Yan'an. In 1939, Mao Zedong proposed the establishment of a women's university for the CCP to cultivate female cadres for the revolution. On July 20, 1939, CCP leaders, including Mao Zedong, Zhou Enlai, and Wang Ming 王明 (1904–74), attended the inauguration ceremony of the Chinese Women's University and delivered speeches. Mao Zedong's talk emphasized the significance of women's roles in the Anti-Japanese War of Resistance. He concluded his speech by proclaiming, "The day all women in China rise up is the moment of China's revolutionary victory."[108]

In their speeches, both Zhou Enlai and Wang Ming hailed Qiu Jin as an exemplary female revolutionary. In Zhou Enlai's talk, he affirmed that Qiu Jin was one of the female role models for women to follow. He also praised Ding Ling for leading the Northwest Front Service Corps, recognizing her as a New Woman.[109] Earlier that same year, Zhou Enlai revisited Shaoxing, his and Qiu Jin's hometown. During this visit, he wrote a couplet for his cousin Wang Qubing, stating, "Never forget the legacy of the female knight of Jianhu, aspire to honor our eastern Zhejiang daughters" (see fig. 28). Through his talk and writings, Zhou Enlai solidified Qiu Jin's position as an inspirational figure, encouraging women's active participation in the revolution.

Wang Ming, the president of the Chinese Women's University and the director of women's work for the CCP's Central Committee (*Zhonggong zhongyang funü gongzuo weiyuanhui zhuren* 中共中央妇女工作委员会主任), presented a comprehensive report outlining the rationale behind establishing a women's university in Yan'an, the university's current status, and the type of female cadres the CCP aimed to train.[110] In the report, Wang Ming summarized the attributes that the Chinese Women's University should cultivate in its female cadres:

> On the one hand, they don't rely on men. They are revolutionary women with independent personalities, lives, and work, capable of fighting independently. On the other hand, they are exemplars of the new virtuous wife, good mother, and filial daughter. . . . The new type of good mother that China needs today resembles figures like Mother Yue, who teach their sons to serve the country with devoted loyalty; new virtuous wives are talented women like Liang Hongyu, who can assist their husbands on the front lines; new filial daughters are heroines like Hua Mulan, who join the army in place of their fathers.[111]

Wang Ming proceeded to list a group of exemplary female revolutionaries, including Qiu Jin, Song Qingling, He Xiangning 何香凝 (1878–1972), Xiang Jingyu 向警予 (1895–1928), Deng Yingchao 邓颖超 (1904–92), Kang Keqing

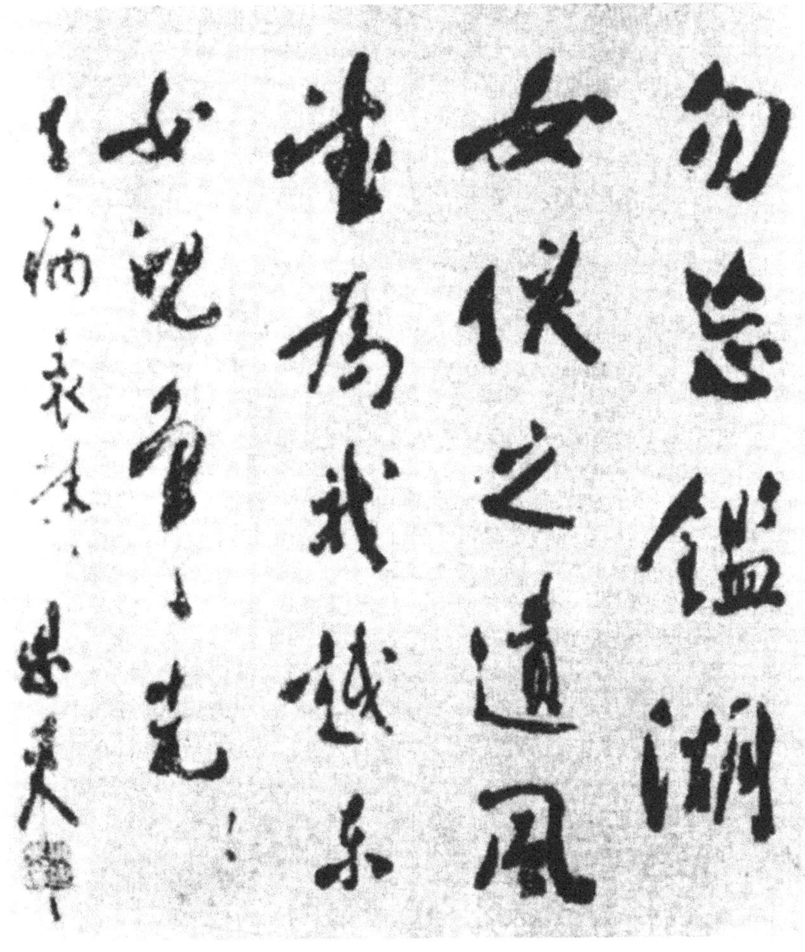

Figure 28: Zhou Enlai's handwritten couplet for his cousin Wang Qubing, March 29, 1939. Source *Qiu Jin nianbiao xibian*, photo, 3.

康克清 (1912–92), Cai Chang 蔡畅 (1900–1990), and Huang Youmei 黄友梅 (1870–1954). Notably, Huang Youmei, a supporter of the Communist revolution, was the mother-in-law of the revolutionary martyr Zhao Shiyan 赵世炎 (1901–27). Among the talented and independent female revolutionary figures mentioned in Wang's report, the majority were wives of male revolutionaries and they aligned with his criteria for virtuous wifehood.[112] An exception to this pattern was Qiu Jin, who did not fit the mold of a traditional virtuous wife or a good mother. She notably left her children behind to pursue studies in Japan and divorced her husband. This raises the question: Why was Qiu Jin's name included on the list?

Wang Ming's reference to the CCP's interpretation of the new virtuous wife and good mother (*xin xianqi liangmu* 新贤妻良母) directly counters the KMT's version. Back in 1934, Chiang Kai-shek, the leader of the Nationalist government, initiated the New Life Movement (*xin shenghuo yundong* 新生活运动) to rejuvenate the nation by resurrecting Confucian virtues such as propriety, justice, integrity, and conscience (*li, yi, lian, chi* 礼义廉耻).[113] This movement, influenced by the severe restrictions placed on women's employment in Nazi Germany and Fascist Italy, led to a surge in the revival of Confucianism and called for women to return to the home (*funü huijia* 妇女回家).[114] The doctrine of new virtuous wives and good mothers (*xin xianqiliangmu zhuyi* 新贤妻良母主义) generated heated debates in the media.

In 1935, *Women's Weekly* (*Funü zhoukan* 妇女周刊), a supplement of *Central News Daily* (*Zhongyang ribao* 中央日报), the official organ of the Nationalist Party, published a series of essays promoting the concept of the new virtuous wife and good mother.[115] *Women's Resonance* (*Funü gongming* 妇女共鸣) magazine released a special issue titled "The Question of Being Virtuous" (*xianliang wenti* 贤良问题), expressing a similar conservative view that placed family responsibilities as women's priority.[116] In contrast, the leftist women's magazine *Women's Life* (*Funü shenghuo* 妇女生活) strongly criticized this movement. Luo Qiong 罗琼 disputed the essays in the special issue in *Women's Resonance*, asserting that "the more important duty for women is to participate in social production to reform the unjust social system."[117] Shen Zijiu, the chief editor of *Women's Life*, pointed out that "the notion of 'women returning home' and the concept of a 'virtuous wife and good mother' were poisons used by the Fascists to numb and deceive women . . . to cultivate them into numerous tamed lambs."[118] She urges women to step outside their homes and join the fight for national salvation.

To counter the rising influence of the new virtuous wife and good mother movement, in 1935 and 1936, progressive media and intellectuals once again brought back the image of Nora, aiming to motivate women to break free from their domestic confines.[119] On New Year's Day in 1935, the leftist Mofeng Art Troupe (*Mofeng yishe* 磨风艺社) staged *A Doll's House* at Taotao Grand Theater in Nanjing. The performance was met with resounding success; however, the actresses involved faced repercussions such as dismissal from their jobs or expulsion from their schools.[120] Wang Guangzhen 王光

珍 (1916–90), an elementary school teacher who portrayed Nora in the play, was among those fired. The "Nora" was forced to return home. This ignited intense discussions in the media and became known as the "Nora incident" (*Nala shijian* 娜拉事件).

The bimonthly publication *New Society* (*Xin shehui* 新社会) released a special issue on "Nora" (*Nala teji* 娜拉特辑), consisting of four articles that offered commentary on the Nora incident. This special issue criticized the new virtuous wife and good mother movement, contending that the incident signified a regression, harking back to the old society that oppressed women. One of the authors in the special issue lamented, "The Nora question remains relevant and contemporary, as it has yet to be resolved."[121] Mao Dun, writing under his alternate pen name Weiming 微明, observed, "It seems unbelievable that 'Nora' could still cause trouble these days; however, from another perspective, 'Nora' is still considered dangerous in China because she dares to challenge the traditional responsibilities of a wife and mother."[122] *Women's Life* magazine organized a Nora symposium (*Nala zuotan* 娜拉座谈) to discuss the future of Chinese Noras. During this symposium, Chinese "Noras" Yifan 伊凡, Luo Qiong 罗琼, Junhui 君慧, Bai Wei 白薇, Shen Zijiu, and Biyao 碧遥 shared their personal experiences of leaving their families, breaking free from arranged marriages, pursuing education, and establishing their professional paths.[123]

The image of Nora resurfaced as a response to the pressures urging Chinese women to return to their homes during the 1930s. However, the future of Nora remained uncertain. In "Why We Should Commemorate Qiu Jin," Shen Zijiu criticizes the notion of confining women to domestic spheres. She draws a parallel between Qiu Jin and the character Nora from Ibsen's play, suggesting that while Ibsen's Nora primarily seeks individual freedom, Qiu Jin, the "Chinese Nora," left home to pursue the liberation of the nation. Thus, Qiu Jin should serve as the exemplar for Chinese women.[124]

Published in the CCP's official organ *New China Daily* (*Xinhua ribao* 新华日报) in 1942, Guo Moruo's essay "The Answer to Nora" (*Nala de da'an* 娜拉的答案) commemorates Qiu Jin. In his essay, Guo praises Qiu Jin as the quintessential model of the new woman. He lauds the martyrdom of Qiu Jin and posits that she is the answer to Lu Xun's question about "what happens after Nora leaves home,"[125] stating:

> Where should Nora go after she leaves the doll's house? She should study and acquire the skills to live independently; fight to achieve women's emancipa-

tion in the context of national liberation; take on women's responsibilities in national salvation; and not fear sacrificing her life to accomplish these tasks—these are the right answers.[126]

According to both Shen Zijiu and Guo Moruo, the future embodiment of Nora ought to be a female revolutionary. From their perspective, the realization of personal freedom hinges on the attainment of national liberation, with women's emancipation intricately woven into the broader mission of national salvation.

The intellectual community in Yan'an was acutely conscious of the ongoing debates surrounding the idea of reintroducing women to traditional domestic roles and the Nationalist government's active promotion of the concept of virtuous wife and good mother. Issued on March 3, 1939, the "Guidance Letter from the CCP Women's Committee regarding the Principles and Tasks of the Current Women's Movement" stated: "We don't merely oppose the 'virtuous wife and good mother' slogan with empty words. Instead, we should offer a new interpretation of it and nurture countless exemplary wives, mothers, daughters, daughters-in-law, and mothers-in-law for the Anti-Japanese War and the revolution."[127]

Discussion regarding the "women return home" slogan persisted throughout the 1940s. In early 1940, Zhang Qinqiu 张琴秋 (1904–68), a prominent female CCP leader, wrote to support women postal workers in Shanghai who were fighting against the new restrictions placed on female employment in post offices.[128] Later that same year, Deng Yingchao wrote a critical response to Duanmu Luxi's 端木露西 essay titled "A Touch of Gray in Azure" (*Weilan zhong yidian andan* 蔚蓝中一点黯淡), which promotes the idea of women's retreat to domestic spheres.[129] Commemorating International Women's Day in 1942, Bai Shuang 白霜 contributed an essay to *Jiefang Daily*, arguing that women's independence and contentment could only be realized by venturing beyond their homes, engaging in employment, participating in social activities, and contributing to the War of Resistance.[130] In his essay "On 'Virtuous Wife and Good Mother' and Motherhood" (*Lun 'xianqiliangmu' yu muzhi* 论"贤妻良母"与母职), Zhou Enlai argues that motherhood should be promoted based on principles of gender equality and should not serve as a pretext to prohibit women from pursuing professional paths.[131]

In response to the Nationalist government's regressive policies toward women, Wang Ming presented the CCP's interpretations of virtuous wife and good mother in his address during the opening ceremony of the Chinese

Women's University. He notably positioned Qiu Jin as a leading female role model. Qiu Jin defied the conventions of a traditional virtuous wife and good mother. However, as a pioneer of the Chinese revolution, she was portrayed as the symbolic maternal figure for female revolutionaries in Yan Yiyan's play.

Yan Yiyan play introduces Xia Zhenguo 夏振国, a young woman who escapes an arranged marriage to join Qiu Jin. In the play, Qiu Jin regards Xia Zhenguo as her own daughter and nurtures her as the torchbearer for the upcoming generation of female revolutionaries. She affectionately addresses Xia as "my child" (*wo de haizi* 我的孩子).[132] Wang Jinfa refers to Xia Zhenguo as "your [Qiu Jin's] good daughter" (*nide hao nü'er* 你的好女儿), emphasizing the concept of "like mother, like daughter" (*you qimu biyou qinü* 有其母必有其女).[133] Determined to martyr herself, Qiu Jin implores Xia Zhenguo to pledge her unyielding allegiance to the revolution, even if it entails sacrificing her own life. Qiu Jin entrusts Xia with her ring, a symbol of her leadership in the revolutionary army. Qiu Jin as portrayed in Yan Yiyan's play therefore epitomizes the CCP's version of a good mother—an independent woman who raises her "daughter" to be a revolutionary. The play exemplified the primary goal of the newly established Chinese Women's University in Yan'an, which was to cultivate the next generation of female CCP cadres.

Yan Yiyan's writing of the play *Qiu Jin* was supported and assisted by Wang Ming, the director of women's work in the CCP, and Wu Yuzhang 吴玉章 (1878–1966), the president of the Lu Xun Academy of Art and Literature.[134] In the beginning of 1940, Yan Yiyan participated in a performance of Cao Yu's 曹禺 (1910–96) play *Sunrise* (*Richu* 日出) in Yan'an. It was during the interlude between performances that Wu Yuzhang proposed the idea of Yan Yiyan writing a script centered around Qiu Jin. Subsequently, Yan Yiyan engaged in daily discussions with Wu about Qiu Jin's life and experiences, benefiting from his insights and participating in script revisions.[135] Meanwhile, Wang Ming's leadership position enabled her to endorse the CCP's perspective on the concept of a virtuous wife and good mother, thereby embedding political messages in the play.

In 1939, to commemorate the second anniversary of the Anti-Japanese War of Resistance, Mao Zedong wrote "The Greatest Crisis under Current Circumstances" (*Dangqian shiju de zuida weiji* 当前时局的最大危机), in which he advocated for active resistance against the Japanese and the strengthening of the anti-Japanese united front.[136] Mao's views on the war were reflected in the plays staged for International Women's Day in 1940. For instance, one of the themes presented in the newly adapted traditional opera *Liang Hongyu*

梁红玉 in Yan'an was the debate between militarists (*zhuzhan pai* 主战派) and pacifists (*zhuhe pai* 主和派) during the Southern Song dynasty.[137] The opera effectively delivered the message of resistance during wartime.

Yan Yiyan's play *Qiu Jin* advocates for wartime resistance. In the play, the character Gui Fu, a magistrate, is portrayed as an oblivious official who confuses Wang Jinfa for Mr. Han (*Han xiansheng* 汉先生) and engages in a discussion with him about the strategy of suppressing bandits instead of prioritizing the fight against the foreign invaders.[138] Thus, the play satirizes the KMT's policy of "stabilizing the country before repelling foreign invaders," while advocating for a united front against invaders.

Another central political message in Yan Yiyan's play revolves around the significance of unity. In the play, Qiu Jin articulates, "Anyone who seeks to overthrow the Qing dynasty, expel foreign invaders, and save China is our friend. This is regardless of their association or party. We should sincerely unite with them and cooperate."[139] She emphasizes the importance of uniting with peasants, remarking, "You must not look down on the peasants! Just think about how many peasant uprisings have occurred throughout history. I even feel that the peasants we have been in contact with are too few."[140] In response to Xu Xilin's failed uprising, she highlights, "Revolution must unite forces from all aspects and rely on support from the masses; otherwise, it will inevitably lead to failure. I have learned another painful lesson from this incident."[141]

Traitors emerge as another significant theme in Yan Yiyan's play. Similar to Xia Yan's inclusion of the traitor Jiang Ji in his play *The Spirit of Freedom*, Yan Yiyan also introduces a traitor named Mrs. Ding in her play, with the unique aspect that the traitor she depicts is a woman. During the 1940s, one of the primary objectives of the women's movement in Yan'an was to denounce the female traitor Chen Bijun 陈璧君 (1891–1959), who was the wife of Wang Jingwei 汪精卫 (1883–1944) and who collaborated with the Japanese, earning the label of a national traitor. On February 1, 1940, the Central Committee of the CCP issued instructions to the party branches for International Women's Day, emphasizing the need for the CCP to unite women from different classes and motivate them to stand against the female traitor Chen Bijun.[142]

In the essay titled "New Tasks in the Women's Field for This Year's International Women's Day" (*Jinnian sanbajie funüjie de xin renwu* 今年三八节妇女界的新任务), Xiu Yan 修岩 states that women in China should be conscious of Chen Bijun's involvement in assisting Wang Jingwei's collaboration with the Japanese.[143] An open letter from women in Yan'an to women across the nation, the essay draws a parallel between Wang Jingwei and Qin Hui 秦桧, the infamous traitor from the Song dynasty, while likening Chen Bijun to Qin Hui's wife. The letter encourages Chinese women to "raise sons unlike Wang Jinwei and have daughters unlike Chen Bijun."[144] Yan Yiyan's portrayal of a female traitor in the play *Qiu Jin* was a direct response to the campaign against Chen Bijun in Yan'an.

The evolution of Qiu Jin from a modern-day Dou E to a revolutionary martyr was a gradual process. In late Qing literature, Qiu Jin was initially depicted as a wrongly accused traditional virtuous woman. It was not until the success of the 1911 Revolution that Qiu Jin underwent a transformation into a revolutionary martyr, with nationalism playing an important role. Qiu Jin's firm installment as a revolutionary martyr served to legitimize the newly established Republican government. Nonetheless, the meaning of Qiu Jin's martyrdom underwent shifts over time, as evident in works like Xia Yan's *The Spirit of Freedom* and Yan Yiyan's *Qiu Jin*. The multifaceted depictions of Qiu Jin illustrate how female martyrdom serves as a fertile ground for politicized and gendered narratives.

EXHIBITION III

Xiang Jingyu

Married to the Proletariat

Xiang Jingyu 向警予 (1895–1928), originally from Hunan and a close family friend of Ding Ling, was one of the few female leaders during the early years of the Chinese Communist Party. She was well versed in both traditional and modern education. In 1919, she joined the New Citizen Study Society established by Mao Zedong and Cai Hesen. By January 1920, Xiang Jingyu and Cai Hesen embarked on a work-study program in France, where they married in May, forming the renowned Xiang Cai Alliance. Upon returning to China in 1922, Xiang Jingyu took charge of various women's movements within the CCP, contributing actively through her writings for the *Guide Weekly* (*Xiangdao* 向导) and *Women's Weekly* (*Funü zhoubao* 妇女周报), which aimed to disseminate both Communist and feminist ideas. Her notable efforts significantly impacted women's movements in China during the 1920s. Xiang Jingyu's life was cut short on May 1, 1928, when she was executed by the KMT in Wuhan during the purge targeting Communists and their supporters.

In a 1936 interview with Edgar Snow (1905–72) in Yan'an, Mao Zedong lauded Xiang Jingyu as the only female founder of the CCP.[1] He commemorated her martyrdom for the liberation of women and the proletariat during his speech at a 1939 conference celebrating International Women's Day, urging everyone to draw inspiration from her.[2] At the inauguration of the Chinese Women's University in Yan'an in July 1939, Zhou Enlai praised Xiang Jingyu as an important role model for Chinese women.[3] The CCP's official narratives extol Xiang Jingyu as a devoted Communist revolutionary, lauding her marriage to Cai Hesen as an exemplary revolutionary union. Yet personal recollections from former CCP leaders paint a more complex image of Xiang Jingyu. These accounts bring to light her extramarital relationship with Peng Shuzhi, which unsettles her portrayal as a female paragon of revolutionary sacrifice. A balanced examination of both official and personal accounts of

Figure 29: Photo of Xiang Jingyu. Source: *Xiang Jingyu jinian wenji* 向警予纪念文集 (Collected works in memory of Xiang Jingyu), Changsha: Hunan renmin chubanshe, 2005, 1.

Xiang Jingyu's life reflects on the CCP's stance on female chastity and the prevailing gender hierarchy within the party.

Xiang Jingyu is remembered as a leading figure in the early CCP and women's movement in China. However, she never received official appointments as a Central Committee member or as the minister for women.[4] As Andrea McElderry pointed out, "Careful examination of Xiang's activities tends to support the conclusion that the women's movement was accorded a low priority and that Xiang's position in the Party reflected this in spite of her posthumous elevation to high status."[5] Nonetheless, this does not diminish her prominence in the early Chinese Communist movement. Xiang Jingyu played a pivotal role in laying the groundwork for the Communist women's movement in China during the 1920s. She was a direct influence on both Ding Ling and Ding Ling's mother, encouraging their involvement in the revolution.

Ding Ling, Her Mother, and Xiang Jingyu

> The horrifying death of Liu Hezhen and the martyrdom of Li Dazhao deeply shook me. For many years afterward, I was reluctant to visit Tian'anmen. After liberation, I went to Tian'anmen to pay my respects to Comrade Li Dazhao's place of sacrifice, and I felt that my heart was still trembling. However, what truly pierced my heart was the martyrdom of Comrade Xiang Jingyu.[6]
>
> —DING LING

After the split of the first KMT-CCP Alliance in 1927, the KMT launched a purge of Communists and their sympathizers. This period of White Terror inflicted profound spiritual anguish upon Ding Ling. In her quest for healing and to explore the path to revolution, she turned to writing.[7] In 1927, she published her first short story, "*Mengke*" (*Mengke* 梦珂), followed by the celebrated work "Miss Sophia's Diary" (*Shafei nüshi de riji* 莎菲女士的日记) in 1928.

On May 1, 1928, Xiang Jingyu, an early female Communist leader and a close family friend of Ding Ling, was executed by the KMT in Wuhan during the purge. Xiang Jingyu's martyrdom marked a pivotal moment in Ding Ling's political consciousness. It shook Ding Ling's earlier anarchist beliefs and drew her closer to leftist ideas. In an essay commemorating Xiang Jingyu, Ding Ling reflected on the influence of the martyrdom on her own life:

> For a long time, I had not found the desired way out. I kept hitting walls repeatedly, feeling the pain as I struggled and strived. Meanwhile, after the failure of the Nationalist Revolution in 1927, I received a lot of devastating news. The sorrowful news about Aunt Xiang Jingyu's glorious martyrdom shocked my soul like thunder, weighing heavily on my heart like a stone. I remembered her beautiful and sublime image that had been in my heart since my childhood. She was the light and fire that warmed both me and my mother, guiding us when we were alone, stumbling through our lives.[8]

Inspired by Xiang Jingyu's revolutionary martyrdom, Ding Ling ardently embraced the cause of revolution. In May 1930, she joined the League of Left-wing Writers alongside Hu Yepin. The following year saw the sacrifice of Hu Yepin, who gave his life for his revolutionary ideals. After his martyrdom in March 1931, Ding Ling returned to Hunan accompanied by Shen Congwen. She entrusted her four-month-old son, Jiang Zulin, to her mother's care. During this brief homecoming, she was exposed to tales of families, peasants, landlords, and officials from her village. These narratives ignited her imagination, leading her to conceptualize a novel that would capture the societal transformations in China from the late Qing to the failure of the revolution in 1927, all against the backdrop of a small town in Hunan.[9]

Ding Ling began to write the novel after receiving an invitation from Lou Shiyi 楼适夷 (1905–2001) to contribute to *Continental News* (*Dalu xinwen* 大陆新闻). The novel, titled *Mother* (*Muqin* 母亲), was serialized in *Continental News* from June 15, 1932 until the KMT's shutdown of the daily on July 3 of the same year. Following a request from Zhao Jiabi 赵家璧 (1908–97), the editor of the *Liangyou* literary series, Ding Ling resumed writing the novel in September 1932 and continued until her abduction in May 1933.[10]

Ding Ling's initial plan was to write a novel of 300,000 words, but her writing endeavor was abruptly curtailed due to her abduction. Lu Xun, upon the counsel of Zhao Jiabi, suggested releasing the unfinished novel through the *Liangyou* literary series and advertising the publication extensively. The intention behind this publication was to generate awareness of the abduction of Ding Ling and initiate efforts for her rescue. Influential newspapers and magazines, including the *China Times* (*Shishi xinbao* 时事新报), *Shenbao*, and *Liangyou*, carried advertisements about the novel. These advertisements highlighted 100 author-signed copies available for purchase on June 28, 1933, the first day of the book release.[11] On that very day, Lu Xun received a signed copy and wrote the poem "A Lament for Ms. Ding." The book release achieved success and drew significant attention to Ding Ling's mysterious disappearance.

Ding Ling's unfinished novel, *Mother*, traces the transformation of Yu Manzhen 于曼贞, a newly widowed gentry woman from Hunan, from a woman with bound feet to a revolutionary on the brink of the 1911 Revolution. The novel is semiautobiographical in essence. The female protagonist Yu Manzhen is based on Ding Ling's own mother, Yu Manzhen (1878–1953), while the character of Xiaohan 小菡, the daughter, is modeled after Ding Ling herself. This novel shares common themes such as sisterhood, education, and revolution, with Qiu Jin's unfinished semiautobiographical *tanci* fiction *The Stones of Jingwei* (*Jingwei shi* 精卫石). *The Stones of Jingwei* tells a story of five female friends who courageously break free from the chains of their oppressive families to pursue an education in Japan, with the greater ambition of liberating women in China and the nation as a whole.[12] Similarly, in *Mother*, Yu Manzhen forms a sisterhood with her classmates at a women's normal school, exploring revolutionary ideas. Yu's closest sworn sister in the novel, Xia Zhenren 夏真仁, is modeled after Xiang Jingyu.

Xiang Jingyu, originally named Xiang Junxian 向俊贤, was born into a business family in Xupu 溆浦 County in Hunan in 1895. She was among the first group of girls to attend school in Xupu in 1903. Influenced by her brother Xiang Xianyue 向先钺, who was one of the founders of the elementary school she attended, Xiang Jingyu began to read *People's News* (*Minbao* 民报) and *New Citizen Journal* (*Xinmin congbao* 新民丛报), which engaged in debates about whether China should opt for a path of reform or revolution.[13]

During the autumn of 1910, Xiang Jingyu commenced her studies at Changde Women's Normal School, where she was joined by Ding Ling's mother, Jiang Shengmei, who was then thirty-two years old.[14] By spring 1911, Xiang Jingyu and Jiang Shengmei, along with five classmates who frequently gathered to deliberate on women's issues and national affairs, solidified their bond as sworn sisters at Ding Ling's uncle's house (see fig. 30).[15] They jointly wrote "Oath of the Seven Sisters" (*Qi zimei shici* 七姊妹誓词), which reads:

> Seven sisters here, we pledge our commitment to raising women's aspirations, devoting ourselves to study, striving for gender equality, being strong and victorious, achieving the goal of national salvation through education.[16]

The sight of the seven sisters taking their oath left a profound impression on Ding Ling. She recalled that despite being the youngest among them,

Xiang Jingyu displayed a remarkable maturity and wisdom, earning admiration from Jiang Shengmei.[17] In Ding Ling's mother's memoir, Xiang Jingyu is referred to as her closest cross-generational friend, and she is lauded for excelling both academically and morally during their time at school.[18]

Ding Ling's novel *Mother* portrays the friendship between Yu Manzhen and Xia Zhenren, the characters inspired by Ding's mother and Xiang Jingyu. In the novel, Xia Zhenren encourages Yu to break free from foot binding and participate in gymnastics classes at school. The two companions often discuss news about the nation. Yu Manzhen proposes mobilizing people for the revolutionary cause to save the nation. In response, Xia Zhenren concurs, expressing, "if there is a need for me, I have no fear of martyrdom."[19] The two later organize a group of progressive female students, pledging to support one another. Ding Ling includes a pivotal scene in which they take an oath to become sworn sisters in the novel.[20]

In *Mother*, Yu Manzhen and Xia Zhenren embody the emergence of new women during a period of transition in China, around the time of the 1911 Revolution. They step out of their boudoirs to pursue education and to form a women's alliance in order to contribute to the national salvation. The sisterhood in both Qiu Jin's *The Stones of Jingwei* and Ding Ling's *Mother* mirrors the burgeoning women's movement in early twentieth-century China.

In the autumn of 1912, Xiang Jingyu and Jiang Shengmei moved to Changsha to study at Hunan No. 1 Women's Normal School, as Changde Women's Normal School had closed.[21] After a year, due to financial difficulties, Jiang Shengmei left school and took a position as an elementary school teacher in Taoyuan 桃源. During this period, she entrusted the care of Ding Ling to Xiang Jingyu, leaving her at the kindergarten attached to Hunan No. 1 Women's Normal School. Xiang would visit Ding Ling every day after school, bringing her food and playing with her. By the autumn of 1914, Xiang Jingyu followed the progressive educator Zhu Jianfan 朱剑凡 (1883–1932), the former principal of Hunan No. 1 Women's Normal School, to Zhounan Girls' Middle School, which he had founded.[22] At this transition, she changed her name from Junxian, signifying beauty and virtue, to Jingyu, meaning self-alert.

Following her graduation from Zhounan Girls' Middle School in the summer of 1916, Xiang Jingyu returned to her hometown to establish Xupu Girls' School.[23] Adhering to the seven sisters' oath, which emphasized gender equality and identified education as a pathway to national salvation, she penned the school anthem. The anthem proclaims: "Our sisters are united, loving one another. Now that men and women are equal, natural selection

Figure 30: A photo of the seven sisters at Changde Women's Normal School in 1911, including Ding Ling's mother Jiang Shengmei (standing on the right), Xiang Jingyu (seated third from the left), Jian Wanrong 翦万容 (Historian Jian Bozan's 翦伯赞 aunt), Tang Wanfen 唐畹芬, Hu Shanlun 胡善伦, Xu Youlian 许友莲, and Yu Zimin 余紫敏. Source: *Ding Ling quanji*, vol. 1, 2. For the names of the seven sisters, see "Xiang Jingyu shengping dashi nianbiao," 316.

shocks our eyes and awakens our minds! Our students shall be prepared to illuminate the women's field."[24]

Xiang Jingyu exerted significant effort in advancing women's education in Xupu. Faced with Xupu's isolation and conservatism, the school initially experienced low enrollment. Xiang Jingyu corresponded with the county magistrate, urging each district in the county to identify a group of girls for enrollment.[25] In order to encourage more girls to attend school, she visited numerous families in the area to promote gender equality and the importance of women's education. Through her dedicated work, the school's enrollment surged from a handful to three hundred. Following the stabilization of the student population, Xiang Jingyu further championed the concept of coeducation.[26]

Xiang Jingyu campaigned for physical education and the discontinuation of foot-binding for girls. She regularly delivered speeches with patriotic messages and organized student performances of patriotic plays. Moreover, she rallied students to clean up the streets in Xupu, aiming to make contributions to society. During her two years as the principal of Xupu Girls' School, Xiang Jingyu introduced student-centered educational approaches as well as new ideas, including democracy and gender equality, to Xupu.[27] As noted by Christina Gilmartin, "Here she combined her nationalist and feminist objectives."[28]

With the expansion of Xupu Girls' School, Xiang Jingyu recruited her friends and former classmates from Hunan No. 1 Normal School and Hunan No. 1 Women's Normal School to teach in Xupu. The school evolved into a fertile ground for nurturing new Chinese citizens. Meanwhile, in April 1918, Mao Zedong and Cai Hesen, two classmates from Hunan No. 1 Normal School, founded the revolutionary group New Citizen Study Society in Changsha, which later made significant contributions to the establishment of the CCP and the development of Marxism in China.

Shortly after its establishment, the New Citizen Study Society advocated for the aforementioned work-study program in France. Xiang Jingyu, acquainted with Mao Zedong and Cai Hesen through Cai Chang 蔡畅 (1900–1990), her schoolmate at Zhounan Girls' Middle School and Cai Hesen's sister, found herself inspired by the New Citizen Study Society's ideals. Motivated by this, Xiang Jingyu made the bold decision to resign as the principal of the Xupu Girls' School and embark on the work-study program. In June 1918, the New Citizen Study Society sent Cai Hesen as its representative to Beijing to seek support from the Sino-French Education Association (*Fahua jiaoyu hui* 法华教育会) founded by Cai Yuanpei, Li Shizeng 李石曾 (1881–1973), Wu Zhihui 吴稚晖 (1865–1953), and Wu Yuzhang.[29] Meanwhile, during this period, Xiang Jingyu traveled from Xupu to Changsha to commence her preparations for studying abroad in France.

In summer 1918, Xiang Jingyu visited Jiang Shengmei in Changde on her way to Changsha. Jiang was immersed in grief over the death of her son that spring. Xiang Jingyu accompanied her every day during the visit to comfort her. She encouraged Jiang Shengmei to shift her attention to the women's movement and education. Following Xiang Jingyu's advice, Jiang Shengmei took the initiative to establish a work-study mutual aid group (*gongdu huzhu tuan* 工读互助团) to offer educational opportunities to women who lacked financial resources.[30] She also founded Women's Frugal and Moral Society (*Funü jiande hui* 妇女俭德会) with the aim of leading the women's liberation movement in Changde. Additionally, she established an affiliated elementary school as part of

Figure 31: A sculpture of the Xiang Cai Alliance at the Museum of the Chinese Work-study Program in Montargis. Source: Gong Shuguang 龚曙光, *Mengda'er jinianguan zhounian ji* 蒙达尔纪念馆周年纪 (One-year anniversary of the Museum of the Chinese Work-study Program in Montargis), Changsha: Hunan renmin chubanshe, 2017, 52.

the Women's Frugal and Moral Society's efforts. Just as Xiang Jingyu had experienced in Xupu, the elementary school encountered challenges in enrolling female students. Inspired by Xiang's approach, Jiang Shengmei visited families in rural areas in Changde, promoting the importance of women's education.[31] Xiang Jingyu therefore entrusted the responsibility of women's education to her beloved sister, Jiang Shengmei, and set forth on her next expedition to explore the paths leading to the nation's salvation.

The Xiang Cai Alliance

During the autumn of 1918, Xiang Jingyu traveled to Beijing and visited Cai Yuanpei, one of the founders of the work-study program in France. She reunited with Cai Hesen in Beijing, where they discussed their plans for studying abroad.[32] The conversation strengthened their friendship. As the May Fourth Movement erupted in Beijing, Cai Hesen actively participated in it, while Xiang Jingyu, back in Xupu, organized a protest march to boycott Japanese goods to support the patriotic movement. Her trip to Beijing and her involvement in the May Fourth Movement further solidified Xiang Jingyu's revolutionary beliefs. In August 1919, Cai Chang invited Xiang Jingyu to join her in organizing the Zhounan Girls Work-study in France Association. Subsequently, Xiang relocated to Changsha and resided with Cai Hesen's family. In the autumn of 1919, Xiang Jingyu became one of the first female members of the New Citizen Study Society.[33]

The early New Citizen Study Society took an active role in the debate over the abolition of arranged marriages. In November 1919, Zhao Wuzhen 赵五贞, a twenty-three-year-old educated woman from Hunan, committed suicide. She had been betrothed to a wealthy antique merchant, Wu Fenglin 吴凤林, who was considerably older than she was. Dissatisfied with her arranged marriage, Zhao concealed a razor in her leg wraps and slit her own throat in the bridal sedan chair on the way to the wedding. The suicide of Zhao Wuzhen sparked heated debates over marriage and women's liberation in China. The Changsha *Dagong bao* closely followed this sensational event.[34] As a regular contributor to the Changsha *Dagong bao*, Mao Zedong was vocal about the suicide case, publishing nine essays on it in the newspaper. Mao argued that the social environment, Zhao's natal family, and the family of her future in-laws together formed an inescapable web that strangled Zhao to death.[35] He ferociously criticized traditional arranged marriage and used Zhao's case to advocate for the concept of free love.

Mao Zedong discussed the case of Zhao Wuzhen with Xiang Jingyu and suggested that a meeting should be held to hear women's perspectives. In response, Xiang and her classmates at Zhounan organized a commemorative event for Zhao Wuzhen. During this gathering, Xiang delivered a passionate speech denouncing arranged marriage and advocating for women's liberation.[36] Xiang Jingyu actively participated in the women's movement in Changsha. She played a significant role in contributing to the publication of *Women's Bell* weekly (*Nüjie zhong* 女界钟), which was edited by students at Zhounan. She also helped in establishing a people's school for women (*pingmin nüxiao* 平民女校) to provide an opportunity for maids working for wealthy families to receive an education.[37]

In the same period as Zhao Wuzhen's tragic suicide, another mournful

Figure 32: Photo of Li Chao. Source: Hu Shi, "Li Chao zhuan," 266.

event took place in Beijing on November 30, 1919. This was a grand memorial service held in honor of Li Chao 李超, a former student at Beijing Women's Normal University. Li Chao, a native of Cangwu in Guangxi Province, graduated from Wuzhou Normal School for Women in 1915 and continued her studies in Guangzhou. In July 1918, against her family's wishes, she decided to attend Beijing Women's Normal University on the advice of a friend. Consequently, her family cut off her financial resources and pressured her to marry. Overwhelmed, distressed, and depressed, Li Chao died of pneumonia on August 16, 1919.[38] After her untimely passing, her friends discovered her poignant writings and family letters, which revealed the profound sufferings she endured. They forwarded these materials to Hu Shi 胡适 (1891–1962). Drawing from these documents, Hu Shi wrote "The Biography of Li Chao" (*Li Chao zhuan* 李超传), in which he addressed four critical issues faced by women in China, including the patriarchal family system, women's education, women's rights to inherit family wealth, and gender equality within the family.[39]

In November 1919, the death of Li Chao captured public attention and garnered extensive media coverage. A commentary in Changsha *Dagong bao* drew parallels between this incident and the suicide of Zhao Wuzhen, highlighting that both tragedies demonstrated the shift among Chinese women from sacrificing themselves for parents or husbands to fighting for their own independence.[40] Inspired by Li Chao's story, students at Beijing Women's Normal University wrote and performed a play titled *Evil Family* (*E Jiating* 恶家庭).[41] On November 30, 1919, a memorial service for Li Chao drew a crowd of over a thousand attendees, including prominent educators and New Culture Movement pioneers such as Cai Yuanpei, Hu Shi, Chen Duxiu, Li Dazhao, Liang Shumin 梁漱溟, Jiang Menglin 蒋梦麟, Huang Rikui 黄日葵, Luo Jialun 罗家伦, and Zhang Guotao 张国焘. These figures delivered speeches condemning the feudal family system while advocating for women's educational rights and the concept of free marriage.[42] Copies of Hu Shi's "The Biography of Li Chao" were distributed at the memorial service.[43] The commemoration of Li Chao evolved into a public forum for Chinese intellectuals to discuss women's emancipation.

The deaths of Zhao Wuzhen and Li Chao had a profound impact on Xiang Jingyu's views on marriage, women's education, and China's future. She realized that while education can serve as a tool for societal transformation, a fundamental revolution was imperative for China. Even educated women like Zhao Wuzhen and Li Chao could not break free from oppression. Xiang Jingyu's conviction that women's emancipation was contingent upon a national revolution became even more pronounced during her work-study trip in France.

On December 25, 1919, Cai Hesen, Cai Chang, their mother Ge Jianhao 葛健豪 (1865–1943), and Xiang Jingyu departed Shanghai for France. During the journey, Xiang Jingyu and Cai Hesen engaged in numerous in-depth conversations and gradually developed romantic feelings for each other.[44] After arriving in France in February 1920, Xiang Jingyu studied at Montargis Women's School as a part-time student while working at a rubber plant and a textile mill.[45] Cai Hesen attended Montargis Men's School, which was conveniently close to Xiang's school. Under the influence of Cai Hesen, a staunch socialist advocate, Xiang Jingyu explored Karl Marx's works. This exploration led to a shift in her beliefs, and she transitioned from seeking to save China through education to embracing the idea of saving China through a socialist revolution.

In May 1920, while in France, Xiang Jingyu wrote an essay titled "A Discussion about Women's Liberation and Transformation" (*Nüzi jiefang yu gaizao de shangque* 女子解放与改造的商榷), which marked her initial endeavor to apply Marxism to analyze women's issues in China. In the essay, Xiang draws on the examples of Zhao Wuzhen and Li Chao to demonstrate that individual efforts are insufficient to combat an oppressive society. To address this, she proposes the formation of self-determined marriage alliances (*hunyin zijue tongmeng* 婚姻自决同盟) among women, fostering mutual support.[46] Meanwhile, Xiang critiques the new family and bourgeois representative system, acknowledging that while it may provide certain Chinese women with personal happiness and financial independence, it comes at the cost of sacrificing the majority of the proletariat who will continue to endure suffering. Consequently, she contends that women's issues cannot be adequately resolved under such circumstances.

In "A Discussion about Women's Liberation and Transformation," Xiang Jingyu argues against private ownership of property, asserting it is the ultimate social ill due to its infringement on the rights of the proletariat. Reform is only worthwhile if it tries to bring happiness to all individuals.[47] She therefore contends that true women's emancipation can only be accomplished alongside the liberation of the proletariat. Xiang Jingyu envisions a twentieth-century shift from individual free competition to a system of socialist mutual support.[48] To achieve the goal of liberating Chinese women, she proposes the establishment of research institutes to foster women's movements. She advocates organizing self-determined marriage alliances to dismantle the traditional family system. Additionally, she suggests establishing specialized banks to provide financial aid to women for educational purposes, organizing public child care facilities, work-study mutual aid groups, cooperative entities, and new villages.[49] Xiang asserts that women's liberation is an integral aspect of the broader social revolution, and she envisions socialism as the path toward the future of the Chinese revolution.

In May 1920, Xiang Jiangyu married Cai Hesen in France, the same month she wrote the essay advocating for a socialist women's movement in China. Their marriage, known as the "Xiang Cai Alliance" (*Xiang Cai tongmeng* 向蔡同盟) or the "looking upward alliance" (*xiangshang tongmeng* 向上同盟), was revolutionary. At their wedding ceremony, they read heartfelt poems they had written for each other. In a powerful symbol of their shared beliefs in Marxism, their wedding photo captured them engrossed in reading Marx's *Capital* together.[50]

The "Xiang Cai Alliance" represented a novel and revolutionary form of

Figure 33: Photo of Xiang Jingyu and Cai Hesen. Source: Chen Bilan, *Zaoqi Zhonggong yu tuopai: Wo de geming shengya huiyi*, 6.

marriage, grounded in the principles of individual freedom and shared revolutionary beliefs. Before entering into this alliance, Xiang Jingyu and Cai Hesen had each taken vows of celibacy, dedicating themselves wholeheartedly to the revolutionary cause. During an interview conducted by Helen Snow in Yan'an, Cai Chang reminisced about the bond between Cai Hesen and Xiang Jingyu:

> At first their love was only platonic and did not change until later. They wrote poems to each other, which were collected into a volume in France and published under the title 'Look Upward Together' . . . these poems were part pure romance and described marriage as spiritual love and perfect harmony of ideas. The other part told of their dreams to return to China and fight together in the revolution.[51]

Rather than opting for traditional arranged marriages, Xiang Jingyu and Cai Hesen forged an alliance rooted in their shared revolutionary ideals. The unique bond blended revolution with romance, with a strong emphasis on "looking upward" together toward a common future.

It is not a coincidence that Xiang Jingyu and Cai Hesen, two members of the New Citizen Study Society, titled their joint poem collection *Looking Upward Together*. The concept of "looking upward" (*xiangshang* 向上) held great significance within the New Citizen Study Society. As stated in the "Report on the Affairs of the New Citizen Study Society" (*Xinmin xuehui huiwu baogao* 新民学会会务报告), the group was dedicated to exploring ways to bring "the lives of individuals and human beings upward."[52] The New Citizen Study Society aimed to "revolutionize academics, cultivate morality and conduct, and reform customs and minds."[53] According to the "Report," to become members, individuals had to embody purity, sincerity, and a commitment to upward progress.[54]

Upon marrying Cai Hesen in France, Xiang Jingyu sent a letter to her parents, accompanied by a postcard featuring two babies together. She wrote in the letter that "Hesen is Jiu'er's true love. Our aspirations and goals are the same. The two babies on this postcard perfectly represent us. We were born in 1920, as children of the twentieth century."[55] She reassured her parents that she was committed to "striving to be a good person and making upward progress."[56] As members of the New Citizen Study Society, Xiang Jingyu and Cai Hesen's marriage was akin to a miniature revolutionary alliance. Love was redefined, as their shared commitment to revolution took precedence.

The Xiang Cai Alliance was praised by the members of the New Citizen Study Society as the ideal way to break the traditional marriage system. Cai Hesen announced his alliance with Xiang Jingyu in a letter to Mao Zedong on May 28, 1920, stating that "Jingyu and I bonded over love. We will send you a printed brochure later."[57] A few days later, Xiang Jingyu wrote to Tao Yi 陶毅 and Ren Peidao 任培道, two female members of the New Citizen Study Society, encouraging them to rally more women to join the work-study program in France. She also proposed the establishment of an institute to research women's issues and the expansion of the *Women's Bell* weekly. In the same letter, she revealed her alliance with Cai Hesen.[58] In his letter to Mao Zedong and Peng Huang 彭璜, Xiao Zizhang 萧子暲 (1896–1983) explained that "Xiang and Cai were not engaged in a conventional sense. The so-called 'Xiang Cai Alliance' was founded upon the principle of free love."[59]

Mao Zedong lauded the "Xiang Cai Alliance" as an exemplary couple who rejected marital norms. He further advocated for the creation of a "Marriage Refusal Alliance," as he stated in a letter to Luo Xuezan 罗学瓒:

> A marriage system based on capitalism is completely unacceptable. In theory, it represents the legal protection of the most unreasonable form of rape while prohibiting the most reasonable free love. In practice, this marriage system is the source of numerous complaints from men and women worldwide. I believe many people have spoken out against it, but none have taken concrete action, likely due to fear. Hearing about the "Xiang Cai Alliance" delighted me, as they dispelled fear and rejected marriage. I believe we should follow their lead and form a "Marriage Refusal Alliance."[60]

Mao Zedong's proposal to establish a "Marriage Refusal Alliance" found its inspiration in both the "Xiang Cai Alliance" and the discussions on family and marriage reform conducted by the New Citizen Study Society members in Montargis and Changsha. From July 6 to July 10, 1920, members of the New Citizen Study Society in France held a weeklong meeting at Montargis, during which they deliberated on strategies for reforming China and the world.[61] At this meeting, Cai Hesen and Xiang Jingyu passionately argued for China to follow the path of the October Revolution in Russia, pursuing socialism and establishing a Communist Party.[62] This meeting played a significant role in the founding of the CCP.[63]

During the Montargis meeting, where the future of China was a topic of discussion, members of the New Citizen Study Society also talked about family reforms. They unanimously agreed that family issues were the most pressing problems in China. In the report to Mao Zedong about the meeting, Luo Xuezan states, "To reform society, we must first reform the family, and to reform the family, we must first reform the marital system. . . . During our recent discussion of family issues at the Montargis meeting, there was an outpouring of sadness. Family! Family! It is the prison that suffocates every Chinese!"[64] Mao Zedong's praise for the Xiang Cai Alliance in his letter to Luo Xuezan on November 26, 1920 was a response to Luo's comments on family and marriage reform.

Following the discussion on family and marriage during the Montargis meeting, the members of the New Citizen Study Society in Changsha continued the discussion on the same subjects at their New Year meeting in 1921. On January 3, at the Changsha meeting, Chen Zhangfu 陈章甫 presented reports from the members in France, highlighting the prevalence of family

Figure 34: A photo of the meeting in Montargis in July 1920, which includes thirteen members from the New Citizen Study Society. Xiang Jingyu (first from right), Cai Chang (first on the right side of the last row), and Cai Hesen (second on the right side of the last row). Source: *Xinmin xuehui ziliao*, photo, 3.

issues among Chinese youths.[65] The attendees then addressed their own family problems and provided various suggestions. The New Citizen Study Society considered arrangements like the Xiang Cai Alliance as a way to tackle family and marriage issues in China. Taking it a step further, Mao Zedong proposed the idea of forming a "Marriage Refusal Alliance."

The concept of abolishing family and marriage originated in anarchism and early twentieth-century family reform discussions in China. In his work *The Book of Great Unity* (*Datong shu* 大同书, 1901), Kang Youwei 康有为 (1858–1927) advocated for the abolishment of the traditional family structure to cultivate world citizens and realize an egalitarian utopia. According to his radical proposition, men and women should have the freedom to sign a marriage contract for a maximum term of one year, allowing for flexible and voluntary relationships.[66]

Similarly, Cai Yuanpei's short story "New Year's Dream" (*Xinnian meng* 新

年梦, 1904) envisions an anarchist world without institutionalized marriages, where people in love can publicly announce their engagement in a park and then cohabit without the constraints of traditional husband-wife roles.[67] Hanyi's 汉一 "On Destroying Families" (*Huijia lun* 毁家论), published in the late Qing anarchist feminist journal *Heavenly Justice* (*Tianyi bao* 天义报), condemns the institution of the family as the root of evil, arguing that after forming families, people become selfish, and women are subjected to male dominance.[68] *New Century* (*Xin shiji* 新世纪), another influential anarchist journal of that time, published Li Shizeng's essay "Revolution in the Three Bonds" (*Sangang geming* 三纲革命), which advocates for the abolition of marriage and family.[69] It is worth noting that both Cai Yuanpei and Li Shizeng were organizers of the Sino-French Education Association, which promoted the work-study program in France. Their writings had a significant impact on the Chinese youths of that era.

The discussion surrounding marriage and family reform persisted into the May Fourth Movement, alongside the growing trend of *dushen zhuyi* 独身主义 (celibatarianism). In May 1920, *Awakening* (*Juewu* 觉悟), a supplement to *Republican Daily*, published over twenty essays and corresponding letters that explored the idea of abolishing marriage. Intellectuals and early Chinese Communist leaders such as Shi Cuntong 施存统, Shao Lizi 邵力子, Ke Qingshi 柯庆施, and Fei Zhemin 费哲民 actively engaged in these discussions.[70] Many early Chinese Communist leaders, including Mao Zedong, Zhou Enlai, Deng Yingchao, Cai Hesen, and Xiang Jingyu, took an oath of celibacy as a form of resistance against traditional marriage. By doing so, they could devote themselves fully to revolutionary pursuits.

In the diary he maintained during his studies abroad in Japan, Zhou Enlai explored his thoughts on marriage and his resolute decision to remain single. He made a clear distinction between love and marriage, stating that "love is born from passion . . . whereas the institution of marriage solely serves the purpose of procreation."[71] He, therefore, argues, "free love does not discriminate between men and women. Why insist on having a wife and child in life."[72] In another entry, he documented reading the *New Youth* magazine both in the morning and upon returning home in the evening. He expressed strong agreement with the magazine's ideas, particularly those relating to anti-Confucianism and celibatarianism.[73]

In September 1919, Zhou Enlai established the Awakening Society (*juewu she* 觉悟社) to lead the patriotic movement in Tianjin. Among the founding members was Deng Yingchao, his future lifelong spouse. In her later years,

Deng recalled that during the May Fourth Movement, she held a pessimistic view about marriage, believing that a woman's life would come to an end once she got married.[74] The members of the Awakening Society pledged to abstain from romantic relationships and marriage. Deng learned about Zhou Enlai's advocacy for celibatarianism and supported him in his pursuit of this goal.[75] During the May Fourth era, celibatarianism served as a means for revolutionaries to resist traditional marriage and fully devote themselves to revolutionary endeavors.

The Xiang Cai Alliance provided an example for revolutionaries to transcend celibatarianism and achieve a harmonious balance between revolution and love. Mao Zedong and other members of the New Citizen Study Society acclaimed them as the perfect revolutionary couple. The wedding photo of Xiang and Cai, reading Marx's book together, beautifully illustrates that their marriage was built upon a shared belief in communism. Their heartfelt "Look Upward Together" poems exchanged during their wedding ceremony served as both their wedding vows and a solemn pledge to their revolutionary alliance. By choosing an alliance over traditional marriage, they resolved the dilemma between their desire for romantic relationships and their advocacy for abolishing the marriage system, which was common among revolutionary youths. However, did this new form of alliance actually break away from traditional family gender roles? What was Xiang Jingyu's position in a male-dominated party environment in the early years of the CCP? Was the Xiang Cai Alliance unbreakable? For years, Cai Hesen and Xiang Jingyu worked closely together as leaders of the CCP's Propaganda Department and women's movement, displaying a strong relationship. However, in 1925, Xiang Jingyu's extramarital relationship with another CCP leader, Peng Shuzhi 彭述之 (1895–1983), led to the separation of what was once considered an ideal revolutionary couple.

Xiang Jingyu and the Early CCP's Women's Movements

In June 1920, shortly after marrying Cai Hesen, Xiang Jingyu wrote a letter to Peng Huang and Mao Zedong, expressing her profound change in perspective. In the letter, she says, "Since I left Xupu, I have come to realize that my past actions were all mistakes and wrongdoings. I am afraid that even if I were to travel by airship from now on, I wouldn't be able to catch up. My energy is limited and insufficient to fulfill my ambition. What can I do? The only thing

I can do is work diligently to achieve my goals so that I can repay our comrades in the years to come."[76] The letter was a declaration that Xiang Jingyu had abandoned the idea of saving the country through education, as she had attempted in Xupu. Instead, she committed to a socialist revolution. While she continued to advocate for education, particularly women's education, as a means to reform the country, she now firmly believed that only through the path of socialist revolution could China be truly saved.

In September 1920, Mao Zedong wrote a letter to the members of the New Citizen Study Society in France, advocating for the idea of a violent socialist revolution rather than gradual reform through education. He argues that "education requires money, personnel, and institutions. In today's world, money is largely in the hands of capitalists. Those who oversee education are often capitalists themselves or their slaves. The two most important educational institutions in the world, schools and newspapers, are also under the control of capitalists."[77] Both Xiang Jingyu and Cai Hesen agreed with Mao Zedong's argument, and fervently promoted socialism during their time in France. The New Citizen Study Society, originally a group founded by progressive young people in Changsha to discuss state affairs, transformed into an association for early Chinese socialist activists with the goal of disseminating Marxism in both China and Europe. However, some members, such as Xiao Zisheng, who did not embrace the idea of a socialist revolution in China, gradually drifted away from the association. The New Citizen Study Society fulfilled its historical task after the founding of the CCP in July 1921.

The Xiang Cai Alliance actively propagated Marxism and led the February 28 Movement, which advocated for the rights of work-study program students to live and study in France. In January 1921, the Sino-French Education Association released a statement announcing the discontinuation of financial support for work-study students in France, effective from the end of February.[78] On February 28, Xiang Jingyu and Cai Hesen led approximately 400 work-study students in a protest in front of the Chinese embassy in Paris.[79] About ten student representatives, including Xiang and Cai, were arrested by the French police during the demonstration. They were later released. Due to mounting pressure from the protest, the Chinese embassy eventually agreed to provide three months of financial support to the students.[80] Meanwhile, the Sino-French Education Association collaborated with the French government to establish a Chinese university in Lyon, funded by the Boxer Indemnity (*gengzi peikuan* 庚子赔款). The work-study students requested to be enrolled at the new Lyon Sino-French University.

On May 30, 1921, Xiang Jingyu, Cai Chang, and ten other female work-study students wrote and signed a petition. They requested the Lyon Sino-French University not to limit the number of female students and to establish an equal enrollment quota for both male and female students. Additionally, they sought exemption for female students from the entrance exam and provision of tutoring and tuition subsidies.[81] However, the university issued a statement stating that students needed both financial and graduate certificates and must pass the entrance exam to be eligible for enrollment.[82] Infuriated by this statement, on September 21, 1921, Cai Hesen, Chen Yi 陈毅 (1901–72), and Li Lisan 李立三 (1899–1967) led a group of over 100 students in occupying a building at the university.[83] There were 104 students, including Cai Hesen, arrested by the French military police during this occupy Lyon Sino-French University movement. Consequently, Cai Hesen was deported from France on October 13.[84] Meanwhile, Xiang Jingyu, who was pregnant at the time, decided to return to China in early November.[85]

In early 1922, Xiang Jingyu and Cai Hesen officially joined the CCP after returning to China. Shortly after, on April 1, 1922, Xiang gave birth to their daughter, Cai Ni 蔡妮 in Shanghai.[86] The name of their daughter was chosen to commemorate the establishment of the Xiang Cai Alliance in Montargis (*Mengdani* 蒙达尼). In July 1922, the couple attended the Second National Congress of the CCP in Shanghai. During the congress meeting, Cai Hesen was elected as one of the Central Committee members in charge of the CCP's Propaganda Department.[87] Meanwhile, Xiang Jingyu assumed leadership of the CCP's women's movement. In September of the same year, Cai Hesen founded and became the chief editor of the *Guide Weekly*, the CCP's publication dedicated to promoting anti-imperialism and antiwarlord messages.[88] Xiang Jingyu provided assistance in editing the weekly and also wrote over thirty short political commentaries for it, using the pen name Zhenyu 振宇.[89] However, her focus later shifted, and in September 1923, Xiang Jingyu began editing and writing for *Women's Weekly*, a supplement to *Republican Daily*.

After the Second Congress, Xiang Jingyu became actively involved in leading the women's movement. Unlike those who focused only on the women's suffrage movement, she believed that real change for women in China would not come solely from gaining voting rights. Instead, she saw the potential of women laborers (*laodong funü* 劳动妇女) as the primary force behind the Chinese women's revolution. In August 1922, Xiang Jingyu participated in supporting strikes alongside female workers in Shanghai silk factories.[90] During these strikes, Xiang Jingyu sought to elevate these economic struggles to political ones by empowering and educating women workers. Recognizing that most of these female workers were uneducated, she advocated for CCP members to forge personal connections by becoming sisters and friends with them. Through these bonds, they could then educate the women about their exploitation under capitalism and imperialism, and assist them in forming unions to demand their rights.[91] To support women workers on strike, Xiang Jingyu organized female intellectuals, including Wang Yizhi 王一知 (1901–91) and Ding Ling, two Hunanese students studying at the People's School for Women (*pingmin nüxiao* 平民女校), to take to the street to promote the strikes and raise funds for the cause.[92]

The People's School for Women in Shanghai played an important role in the early Chinese women workers' movements, which were spearheaded by Xiang Jingyu. This educational institution was established by Chen Duxiu and Li Da 李达 (1890–1966), prominent early CCP leaders, in February 1922. Its primary aim was to cultivate future leaders of the women's movement. Wang Jianhong, who had been Ding Ling's former schoolmate at Hunan No. 2 Women's Normal School, collaborated with Wang Huiwu 王会悟 (1898–1993), one of the organizers of the People's School for Women and Li Da's wife, on the *Voice of Women* (*Funü sheng* 妇女声) biweekly, which was founded by the CCP. Encouraged by Wang Jianhong, Ding Ling decided to pursue her studies at the People's School for Women in Shanghai. In February 1922, Ding Ling, along with Wang Yizhi, Wang Jianhong, and three other female students from Hunan, traveled to Shanghai to attend the school.[93] Shortly after they arrived in Shanghai, Ding Ling and Wang Yizhi visited Xiang Jingyu. Xiang Jingyu had maintained contact with Ding Ling's mother while she was in France, regularly exchanging letters to introduce new thoughts and ideas. In one of these letters, she included the wedding photo of herself reading Marx's *Capital* with Cai Hesen.[94]

Ding Ling was eager to reunite with her aunt Xiang after her return from France. Wang Yizhi's association with Xiang Jingyu predated their meeting in Shanghai. After graduating from the Hunan No. 2 Women's Normal School in 1921, Wang Yizhi accepted a teaching position at the Xupu Girls' School, which was founded by Xiang.[95] The prospect of finally meeting Xiang in person in Shanghai filled Wang Yizhi with excitement. Her first impression of Xiang Jingyu was that she was approachable and dressed modestly in the style of rural Hunan. Xiang's dedication to promoting Marxism impressed Wang Yizhi, as she prioritized substantive matters over trivialities in daily life.[96] Under the influence of Xiang Jingyu, many progressive female students, such as Ding Ling and Wang Yizhi, explored the concept of socialism. Inspired by Xiang Jingyu, Wang Yizhi later joined the CCP while studying at the People's School for Women.

Under Xiang Jingyu's leadership, students from the People's School for Women, including Ding Ling, participated in the silk factory women workers' strikes in Shanghai in 1922. Xiang Jingyu strongly advocated for intellectuals to support and join female workers in the Chinese women's movement. In her interview with Helen Snow in Yan'an, Ding Ling shared her fundraising experience with fellow students from the People's School for Women to support the female strikers:

> We collected money on the streets and went out to do propaganda for the strike, to encourage the workers and explain the reasons for their action. We went from one group of the girl-workers to another, but it was hard to talk with them because of different dialects and some of us had to have an interpreter. The girl-workers were surprised to get support from the students and much interested in us.[97]

This valuable firsthand account provides insight into the early women's movement organized by the CCP. Xiang Jingyu played a pivotal role in urging female intellectuals to participate in the workers' strikes, which became a guiding principle in the CCP's women's movements. Ding Ling's account addressed challenges that arose in the collaborations between intellectuals and workers, such as language barriers and the unfamiliarity between the two groups.[98] Recognizing these issues, Xiang Jingyu took proactive measures to bridge the gap between herself and the women workers. She made earnest efforts to befriend them and improve her communication with them and other audiences during her street speeches. One of her endeavors was practicing Mandarin tirelessly to reduce her Hunan accent.[99] As a pioneering figure in the early CCP's women's movements, Xiang Jingyu played a crucial role in unifying intellectuals and workers, as well as nurturing female intellectuals to become future leaders in the party.

The CCP acknowledged Xiang Jingyu for her groundbreaking contributions to the women's movements. In June 1923, both Xiang Jingyu and Cai Hesen attended the Third National Congress of the CCP in Guangzhou. The Congress passed a "Resolution about the Women's Movement" (*Funü yundong jueyi'an* 妇女运动决议案) drafted by Xiang Jingyu. The "Resolution" emphasized the importance of women workers' movements. Moreover, it advocated for the integration of shared antiwarlord and anti-imperialism slogans to unite various other women's movements, such as the feminist movement, women's suffrage movement, and abolition of prostitution movement, which were organized by female activists at that time.[100] This strategic approach aimed to strengthen the overall women's movement under the umbrella of the CCP's vision.

Following the Third Congress, Xiang Jingyu published a detailed report on the state of women's movements in China. In her analysis, she classified Chinese women's movements into three distinct groups: the women workers' movement, feminist and women's suffrage movement, and Christian women's movement.[101] While recognizing the contributions of the feminist and women's suffrage movement in advocating for women's rights in politics, marriage, and education, Xiang Jingyu pointed out that it failed to become a mass movement with widespread participation, often involving only a few elite female representatives in government. To create substantial and lasting change in women's status in China, she argued that the feminist and women's suffrage movement must unite with the broader population of women across the country.[102]

In the report, Xiang Jingyu praised the Christian women's movement in China for its particular focus on women workers. This movement took significant steps to establish schools and childcare facilities in factories, as well as educate women about birth hygiene and discourage harmful habits such as smoking, drinking, and gambling.[103] However, she also noted that the Christian women's movement relied on foreign capital, making it different from the independent Chinese women's movement, which she deemed essential for national salvation.[104] In the conclusion of her report, Xiang Jingyu emphasized the revolutionary potential of women workers and advocated for their central role in driving the Chinese women's movements. This argument was instrumental in shaping the early CCP women's movements. Over the next two years, Xiang Jingyu worked as the editor of *Women's Weekly*. Through this platform, she actively promoted women workers' movements and other Communist ideas pertaining to women's movements, publishing approximately forty essays on related topics.

Xiang Jingyu assumed the role of editor for *Women's Weekly* following the confirmation of the CCP-KMT collaboration during the CCP's Third Congress. After the Third Congress, the central office of the CCP relocated to Sanzengli 三曾里 in Shanghai, where Mao Zedong, Xiang Jingyu, Cai Hesen, and Luo Zhanglong 罗章龙, resided together for a year, starting from the

Figure 35: Group photo of the KMT Shanghai Executive Committee in May 1924. Xiang Jingyu (first on the right side of the first row), Mao Zedong (second on the left side of the last row), and Luo Zhanglong (second on the right side of the last row). Source: *Xiang Jingyu wenji*, 2011, photo, 7.

summer of 1923.[105] They were all from Hunan, which is a part of what was the Chu 楚 region in ancient China, and were former members of the New Citizen Study Society. They referred to their residence as the Three Households Mansion (*sanhu lou* 三户楼), alluding to the saying that "even if there are only three families left in the state of Chu, Chu would be the state to destroy Qin" (*Chu sui sanhu, wang Qin bi Chu* 楚虽三户，亡秦必楚).[106] The Three Household Mansion served as the headquarters of the CCP and the CCP-KMT collaboration.

In January 1924, the First National Congress of the KMT marked the official CCP-KMT collaboration. As part of this collaboration, CCP members were allowed to join the KMT as individuals. Following the First National Congress, the KMT established the Shanghai Executive Committee (*Shanghai zhixingbu* 上海执行部), where both Mao Zedong and Xiang Jingyu became actively involved. Xiang Jingyu served as the assistant to Ye Chucang 叶楚伧 (1887–1946), who held the position of minister of the Women's Department in the committee.[107] During the same period, from September 1923 until the CCP-KMT collaboration began to unravel in May 1925, Xiang Jingyu worked as the editor of *Women's Weekly*.

Women's Weekly was a supplement to *Republican Daily*, the official publi-

Figure 36: Group photo of the Women's Department of the KMT Shanghai Executive Committee. Xiang Jingyu (first on the left side of the last row). Source: *Xiang Jingyu wenji*, 2011, photo, 8.

cation of the KMT, which was founded by Ye Chucang. Xiang Jingyu's editorial role allowed her to actively contribute to the dissemination of ideas related to women's movements and communist principles. In her essays published in *Women's Weekly*, Xiang Jingyu focused on three main themes: reforming women's education, supporting the Shanghai Women's Association for Facilitating the People's Assembly (*Shanghai nüjie guomin huiyi cucheng hui* 上海女界国民会议促成会), and advocating for women workers' movements.

Regarding women's education, Xiang Jingyu passionately advocated for mass education for women, urging a modern educational approach that cultivated women to become new citizens rather than conforming to traditional roles as virtuous wives and mothers. She actively supported various student movements aimed at reforming women's education. For example, she wrote in support of the movement at Zhili No. 2 Women's Normal School, which sought to remove Principal Yan Shiqi 燕士奇 for stifling student organizations, firing progressive teachers, and imposing restrictive dress codes on female students. Xiang also supported movements to remove Principal Yang Yinyu 杨荫榆 of Beijing Women's Normal University, who restricted students' revolutionary activities, and Principal Zhou Min 周敏 of Hubei Women's Normal School, who prohibited students from attending the meeting to commemorate Sun Yat-sen.[108]

Xiang Jingyu emphasized the connection between politics and education, stating that "education is the byproduct of politics and is greatly influenced and controlled by it."[109] She attributed the backwardness of Chinese education, particularly women's education, to political corruption.[110] As a result, Xiang believed that the key to reforming education in China lay in political reform. Thus, she actively promoted the People's Assembly (*guomin huiyi* 国民会议) proposed by Sun Yat-sen and advocated for women's participation in it as a means to bring about significant political and educational changes in the country.

In November 1924, Feng Yuxiang 冯玉祥 (1882–1948) overthrew the Zhili warlord Cao Kun's 曹锟 (1862–1938) government and invited Sun Yat-sen to Beijing for discussion on the situation in China. Supported by Feng, Duan Qirui 段祺瑞 (1865–1936) became the head of the Provisional Government of the Republic of China. On November 10, 1924, Sun Yat-sen issued a manifesto, which emphasized the need for anti-imperialism and antiwarlord movements and proposed the People's Assembly as an inclusive forum.[111]

While on his way to Beijing, Sun Yat-sen visited Shanghai, and Xiang Jingyu attended the meeting to welcome him. As a representative of the Women's Department at the KMT Shanghai Executive Committee, Xiang drafted an official letter expressing her support for the People's Assembly and women's right to participate in it.[112] However, Duan Qirui organized the Aftermath Conference (*shanhou huiyi* 善后会议), which controversially excluded civilian representatives and passed the Regulations on People's Representatives Meetings (*Guomin daibiao huiyi tiaoli* 国民代表会议条例) in April 1925. These regulations excluded women from the election process,[113] sparking nationwide protests, including strong opposition from women's groups.

Xiang Jingyu played a vital role as one of the leaders within the women's group, supporting Sun Yat-sen's proposal for a People's Assembly, while protesting against the Aftermath Conference and the Regulations on People's Representatives Meetings. Her passionate advocacy for women's active participation in national conferences concerning state affairs was showcased through her speeches and essays, which were published in *Women's Weekly*. As one of the organizers, Xiang Jingyu delivered a compelling speech during the inaugural meeting of Shanghai women's groups, where she promoted the concept of the People's Assembly. In her speech, Xiang Jingyu proposed to establish new laws to promote feminism and gender equality.[114] She argued that only people's groups could represent all citizens, emphasizing that women's identities as citizens were equal to men's.[115] Xiang Jingyu further contributed to the cause through several essays, delving into the importance of women's presence in the People's Assembly and encouraging female students to propagate the People's Assembly during the winter break.[116] Additionally, she elaborated on the intrinsic relationship between women's movements and the People's Assembly, underscoring the important role women could play in shaping the nation's future through their active participation in political affairs.

In response to the Duan Qirui government's Regulations on People's Representatives Meetings, Xiang Jingyu organized the Shanghai Women Citizens' Meeting (*Shanghai nü guomin dahui* 上海女国民大会) in March 1925 and delivered a powerful speech on women's rights to political participation (see fig. 37). Xiang claimed in her speech that the Women Citizens' Meeting was not merely a narrowly defined feminist movement aimed at electing a few elite women as government representatives, but rather an inclusive platform for demanding rights and equal opportunities for all women across China.[117]

While actively supporting the People's Assembly, Xiang Jingyu engaged in women workers' movements, advocating for female intellectuals to lend their support as well. In a remarkable display of solidarity, she intervened to save Wang Xichun 王熙春, a female worker at a Shanghai silk factory who had been arrested by the police. To address this injustice, Xiang Jingyu wrote the powerful piece titled "What Crime Did the Ninth Girl Commit?" (*Jiu guniang fanle hezui?* 九姑娘犯了何罪?).[118] Furthermore, she encouraged women's organizations in Shanghai and women workers employed in silk factories to come together in a united front. Her rallying cry urged them to fight against the capitalists, demanding reduced working hours and increased salaries for women workers in the silk industry.[119] Xiang Jingyu's dedication was evident through her tireless efforts to advance the rights and improve the welfare of women workers in China.

Alongside her publications in *Women's Weekly*, Xiang Jingyu actively participated in women's movements. Notably, she mobilized female intellectuals to engage in the women workers' movements. In an essay, Xiang Jingyu categorized female Chinese intellectuals into three distinct groups: those inclined towards family, those interested in professional pursuits, and those supporting romantic ideals. She criticizes the first and third groups for prioritizing individual happiness over collective welfare. Although professional women

Figure 37: Xiang Jinyu speaking at the Shanghai Women Citizens' Meeting, photo by Pow Kee Photography Studio. Source: Baoji 宝记, "Shanghai zhi nü guomin dahui" 上海之女国民大会 (Shanghai Women Citizens' Meeting), *Tuhua shibao* 图画时报 (Pictorial times) 243 (1925): 7.

contributed to society, they, according to Xiang Jingyu, lacked a sense of the greater good.[120] She orchestrated the collaboration of female students from Shanghai University with women workers and founded the association for Shanghai women workers in silk factories.[121] In June 1924, Xiang Jingyu successfully led the Shanghai silk factory strikes, drawing the participation of over 15,000 women workers.[122] Following these strikes, she led the Nanyang Tobacco Company strike in September, involving 7,000 workers advocating for improving working and living conditions.[123]

While serving as a member of the KMT Shanghai Executive Committee and as the editor of *Women's Weekly*, Xiang Yingyu demonstrated an impressive capacity for orchestrating women's groups and political campaigns. She adeptly united female intellectuals and women workers. The CCP's Fourth Congress lauded the party for initiating influential women's groups during the People's Assembly movement, which successfully bridged the gap between intellectuals and workers.[124] Xiang Jingyu stood out as one of the architects and leaders of the movement. Seizing the opportunity, she expanded the CCP's networks and played a pivotal role in organizing nationwide women's groups.

In February 1925, Xiang Jingyu dispatched Liu Qingyang 刘清扬 (1894–1977) and Zhong Fuguang 钟复光 (1903–92) as representatives of the Shanghai Women's Association for Facilitating the People's Assembly to attend the National Conference on Facilitating the People's Assembly in Beijing. During their visit, they paid their respects to Sun Yat-sen, who was critically ill. Unfortunately, Sun passed away on March 12, 1925, before realizing his aspiration of convening a People's Assembly. As a spokesperson for the women's groups, Xiang Jingyu delivered a speech to propagate revolutionary ideas during the commemoration of Sun Yat-sen at the Shanghai Public Stadium (*Shanghai gonggong tiyuchang* 上海公共体育场).[125] At the same time, she urged Liu Qingyang and Zhong Fuguang to collaborate with other female representatives at the Beijing Conference, aiming to establish a nationwide women's organization. On April 29, the Chinese United Women's Association (*Zhongguo nüjie lianhehui* 中国女界联合会) was founded in Beijing, with Liu Qingyang assuming the role of its chairperson.[126] Meanwhile, Xiang Jingyu established the Women's Liberation Association (*Funü jiefang xiehui* 妇女解放协会), which was primarily focused on women workers. This organization rapidly expanded its influence across the nation and emerged as a significant driving force in the socialist movements.[127]

Beyond acknowledging women workers as the driving force of the Chinese revolution, Xiang Jingyu also directed her attention toward uniting women intellectuals, extolling them as the guiding figures of the women's movements.[128] In May 1925, she participated in the inaugural meeting of the Chinese Women's Association (*Zhongguo funü xiehui* 中国妇女协会), presided over by Kang Youwei's daughter, Kang Tongbi 康同璧 (1887–1969). During the assembly, Xiang Jingyu delivered a speech in which she commended elite women like Kang Tongbi for their engagement in women's movements, expressing hopes that the Chinese Women's Association could advocate for women workers and fight for the rights of all women in China.[129]

Xiang Jingyu frequently visited another elite woman, Song Qingling, after the latter returned to Shanghai following her husband Sun Yat-sen's funeral. These interactions exerted a notable influence on Song's adoption of leftist political perspectives.[130] Subsequently, Song Qingling attended the inaugural meeting of the Shanghai United Association for Women of All Sections (*Shanghai gejie funü lianhehui* 上海各界妇女联合会) on June 5, an event organized by Xiang Jingyu. Within this context, the association orchestrated initiatives including fundraising, speeches, and patriotic theatrical performances during the May Thirtieth Movement.[131] Xiang Jingyu's persistent efforts in organizing women's movements, both in Shanghai and across China, coupled with her connections with both women workers and intellectuals, laid the groundwork for the CCP's leadership in the May Thirtieth Movement in 1925.

During the Fourth Congress in January 1925, the CCP clarified its relationship with the KMT and confirmed the proletariat's role in spearheading the national revolution. As outlined in the Fourth Congress's "Resolution on National Revolutionary Movements" (*Duiyu minzu geming yundong zhi yijue'an* 对于民族运动之议决案), the KMT was categorized into three factions: leftists, rightists, and moderates. The CCP aimed to amplify the influence of the leftist faction within the KMT and fight against the KMT's policies that oppressed workers and peasants.[132]

After the Fourth Congress, the CCP's attention gravitated toward workers' movements. In February 1925, the Eighth Cotton Mill in Shanghai, owned by the Naga Wata Kaisha company, replaced a group of adult workers with child laborers. This move incited around 40,000 workers from Japanese cotton mills in Shanghai to stage a strike, protesting against this exploitative practice.[133] To support the strikers, Xiang Jingyu organized the Support Group for Shanghai Japanese Cotton Mills Strikers (*Shanghai dongyang shachang bagong gongren houyuanhui* 上海东洋纱厂罢工工人后援会).[134] The strikes in February bolstered the workers' confidence to assert their rights to fair treatment and paved the path for the May Thirtieth Movement.

The Breakup of the Xiang Cai Alliance

Led by the CCP, the May Thirtieth Movement emerged as a crucial labor and anti-imperialist endeavor. This movement held profound significance as it empowered the Chinese working class to assume a leading role in the pursuit of national salvation. It also marked a turning point for the Xiang Cai Alliance. In early May 1925, workers at Shanghai Naga Wata Kaisha company resorted to striking once again, this time with the objective of initiating negotiations with the company management.[135] However, tensions escalated on May 15 when Japanese guards employed by the company fatally shot a worker named Gu Zhenghong 顾正红.

This tragic event ignited outrage, prompting the Shanghai Students Union to swiftly organize fundraising campaigns and deliver speeches condemning the incident.[136] In response to the killing of Gu Zhenghong, the CCP held emergency meetings to strategize the planning of protests.[137] During these discussions, Cai Hesen suggested a broader expansion of the workers' strikes into a comprehensive anti-imperialist national movement on a national scale.[138] The CCP, under the leadership of Chen Duxiu, the general secretary of the Central Committee, issued two official announcements.[139] These proclamations pledged assistance to the striking workers and heralded the initiation of an anti-Japanese-imperialism movement.

On May 30, 1925, the CCP organized an anti-imperialist protest, rallying thousands of workers, students, and other citizens who marched toward the British concession on Nanjing Road. British police resorted to gunfire, resulting in multiple fatalities and injuries among the protesters. Later that evening, on May 30, the CCP made the decision to advocate for a tripartite strike involving workers, students, and markets (known as *bagong, bake, bashi* 罢工，罢课，罢市) across Shanghai.[140] The Nanjing Road massacre sparked a wave of nationwide anti-imperialist sentiment.

On June 5, the CCP released a nationwide appeal in the form of a letter, urging widespread participation in the anti-imperialist movement.[141] Among the leaders of the May Thirtieth Movement was Xiang Jingyu, who coordinated students' attendance at the memorial service for Gu Zhenghong on May 24.[142] As the leader of the Shanghai Women's Association for Facilitating the People's Assembly, Xiang drafted pamphlets bearing anti-imperialist and patriotic messages for protests.[143] During the movement, she raised funds, disseminated flyers, and delivered street speeches during the day, while engaging with workers at night.[144] To support the movement in Shanghai, the CCP organized the Guangzhou–Hong Kong Strike in June and dispatched Xiang Jingyu to Guangzhou to participate.[145] Tragedy struck on November 4, 1925, when Cai Hesen's brother, Cai Linzheng 蔡林蒸 (1889–1925), who led the workers' picket team during the Guangzhou–Hong Kong Strike, was fatally shot.[146]

In the wake of the sacrificial deaths during the revolutionary uprisings and ensuing protests, the May Thirtieth Movement witnessed a notable surge in the nationwide influence of the CCP. This period saw a significant influx of individuals aligning themselves with either the CCP or the Communist Youth League of China. At the same time, local Communist organizations underwent rapid expansion. For example, Jiang Shengmei took charge of the Communist Youth League in Changde, playing a pivotal role in advocating for the May Thirtieth Movement, while Ding Ling provided support to her mother through propagandist endeavors.[147] Remarkably, the number of CCP members grew from a mere 994 at the beginning of 1925, coinciding with the Fourth Congress, to around 10,000 by the end of the year.[148]

Upon becoming aware of the increasing influence of the CCP, Dai Jitao 戴季陶 (1891–1949), a prominent KMT propagandist, wrote a short book in July 1925 titled *The National Revolution and the KMT* (*Guomin geming yu Zhongguo Guomindang* 国民革命与中国国民党), disseminating anti-Communist and anti-proletarian-revolution messages. In the book, Dai advocated for a purified and unified KMT to take the reins of the national revolution.[149] His book wielded a significant impact on the KMT's view on party policies, especially following the death of Sun Yat-sen, and generated debates within the CCP. In September of that year, shortly after the publication of Dai Jitao's book, The *Guide* book series (*Xiangdao congshu* 向导丛书), a publishing venue affiliated with the CCP, published *Countering Dai Jitao's Views on the National Revolution* (*Fan Dai Jitao de guomin gemingguan* 反戴季陶的国民革命观). This compilation featured Qu Qiubai's essay and Chen Duxiu's letter addressed to Dai, both of which criticized him for his role in dividing the united front.[150]

The May Thirtieth Movement marked a phase of expansion for the CCP, which in turn exacerbated the rift between the CCP and the KMT after the death of Sun Yat-sen. Additionally, the rapid growth of the CCP posed a serious challenge to the party's organizational structure and leadership. Peng Shuzhi, one of the CCP's Central Committee members and the minister of propaganda, advocated for the notion of centralizing authority, an approach supported by Chen Duxiu. However, other Central Committee members such as Cai Hesen, Qu Qiubai, and Zhang Guotao believed that the Central Committee should grant local CCP members some flexibility to adapt to prevailing circumstances. They criticized Peng Shuzhi, attributing his dogmatism to his lack of practical experience.[151] The CCP found itself contending not only with the KMT but also with internal discord within its Central Committee. Adding to this complexity, Xiang Jingyu's extramarital relationship with Peng Shuzhi during this time further complicated the conflicts among the CCP leaders.

In June 1925, the May Thirtieth Movement took its toll on Cai Hesen's health, exacerbating his asthma due to the strenuous efforts he exerted. The CCP decided to send him to Beijing for rehabilitation. Peng Shuzhi assumed the responsibilities of overseeing the *Guide Weekly* in place of Cai Hesen.[152] Sharing a common Hunan heritage with Cai Hesen and Xiang Jingyu, Peng Shuzhi had received his education in Changsha and Shaoyang 邵阳. He was introduced to the Shanghai Communist Group (*Shanghai gongchan zhuyi xiaozu* 上海共产主义小组) by He Minfan 贺民范 (1866–1950), a pioneering Marxist in Hunan. In September 1920, Peng Shuzhi traveled to Shanghai, where he became part of the group founded by Chen Duxiu.[153] He dedicated five months to Shanghai, actively participating in the Marxism Study Society (*Makesi zhuyi yanjiuhui* 马克思主义研究会) and immersing himself in learning Russian. In February 1921, he left Shanghai to attend the Communist University of the Toilers of the East in Moscow.[154] During his three years of study there, Peng Shuzhi took on the role of the secretary of the CCP in Moscow.[155]

In July 1924, Peng Shuzhi left Moscow to join the CCP in Shanghai.[156] His initial residence was a house on Moulmein Road, which was rented by the couple Shi Cuntong and Wang Yizhi, along with Qu Qiubai. Qu Qiubai's wife and Ding Ling's closest friend, Wang Jianhong, died of tuberculosis in July 1924. Following Wang's funeral, Qu Qiubai traveled to Guangzhou. Ding Ling rushed to Shanghai after receiving a telegram from Wang's cousin, only to find out about Wang Jianhong's death and Qu's departure.[157] She briefly stayed in the Moulmein Road house with Qu Qiubai's brother Qu Yunbai 瞿云白 (1902–58), before eventually making her way to Beijing. Shortly after, Cai Hesen and Xiang Jingyu moved in.[158] With several CCP leaders making it their residence, the house also served as the CCP's headquarters.

During the Fourth Congress of the CCP, Peng Shuzhi, Chen Duxiu, Cai Hesen, Qu Qiubai, and Zhang Guotao were elected to the Politburo Standing Committee.[159] Peng taught a historical materialism class at Shanghai University, while working closely with Xiang Jingyu and Cai Hesen to lead the Shanghai Japanese cotton mills strikes in February 1925. In March, shortly after commencing his duties as a CCP leader, Peng Shuzhi fell seriously ill, leading to his hospitalization due to tracheitis.[160] Upon his discharge from the hospital in September, the tumultuous May Thirtieth Movement was winding down, and Cai Hesen went to Beijing for rehabilitation.

Around the time of Mid-Autumn Festival, Zheng Chaolin, the secretary of the Propaganda Department, Peng Shuzhi, and Xiang Jingyu relocated to a house on Fusheng Road.[161] The first floor was used as the office of the CCP's Propaganda Department. Xiang Jingyu resided on the third floor, while Peng Shuzhi and Zheng Chaolin occupied the second floor and a pavilion room (*tingzi jian* 亭子间). To celebrate the recovery of Peng Shuzhi, the Mid-Autumn Festival, and their recent relocation, Peng Shuzhi, Zheng Chaolin, and Xiang Jingyu invited Zhang Bojian 张伯简 (1898–1926), Shen Zemin 沈泽民 (1900–1933) and his wife, Zhang Qinqiu, over for a gathering. Following a delightful dinner, Peng Shuzhi graced the event with a dance performance,

Zhang Qinqiu performed a song, and Xiang Jingyu recited a lyric poem. After the departure of their guests, Xiang Jingyu took the opportunity to express her affection for Peng Shuzhi.[162] After grappling with his feelings for a few days, Peng eventually reciprocated Xiang's sentiments.

After Cai Hesen returned from rehabilitation in Beijing in early October, Xiang Jingyu confessed to him about her involvement with Peng Shuzhi. Following the revelation, Cai Hesen called a meeting that included all members of the Politburo Standing Committee: Chen Duxiu, Qu Qiubai, Zhang Guotao, and Peng Shuzhi. Xiang Jingyu attended the meeting as a special guest. During the meeting, Xiang Jingyu openly admitted her feelings for Peng Shuzhi, while also expressing her enduring affection for Cai Hesen. She emphasized that she had no intention of harming Cai Hesen. In light of these circumstances, she requested to be sent to Moscow for studies. Chen Duxiu consented to dispatching both Cai Hesen and Xiang Jingyu to Moscow.[163]

The extramarital relationship between Xiang Jingyu and Peng Shuzhi not only shattered the highly esteemed Xiang Cai Alliance within the party but also accentuated conflicts among the CCP leaders. The top leaders were already divided on how to guide the growing CCP membership. While Peng Shuzhi and Chen Duxiu promoted the authority of the Central Committee, Qu Qiubai, Cai Hesen, and Zhang Guotao advocated for greater flexibility among local branches.

Despite his limited practical experience and relatively modest standing within the party, Peng Shuzhi, dispatched by the Communist International from Moscow, ascended to a top leadership role within the CCP. Peng Shuzhi's affair with Xiang Jingyu deepened feelings of discontent among other CCP leaders. Qu Qiubai criticized Peng for his lack of theoretical training and political experience, asserting that he was not qualified for a leadership position within the CCP.[164] Qu further condemned Peng's indiscretion in his private life, which caused pain and destroyed the relationship between two prominent CCP leaders. Qu Qiubai advocated for Peng Shuzhi's removal from the Central Committee and his reassignment to local branches to gain experience.[165] Qu also directed his criticism at Chen Duxiu, questioning his decision to protect Peng and challenging his leadership. These concerns were shared with Zhang Guotao, who resided with Qu at the time. Zhang was tasked with conveying these opinions to Chen Duxiu. During a meeting with Chen, Zhang Guotao communicated Qu's viewpoints and additionally recommended Peng's removal from the Central Committee. However, Chen Duxiu rejected the proposal and criticized Qu Qiubai for overstepping boundaries.[166] After the exchange between Zhang and Chen, rumors circulated within the party suggesting that Qu Qiubai, Zhang Guotao, and Cai Hesen had formed an opposing alliance. This rumor persisted despite Cai being unaware of the discussed matters.[167]

During the Fifth Congress of the CCP held in late April and early May of 1927 in Wuhan, Qu Qiubai and Cai Hesen fiercely criticized Chen Duxiu and Peng Shuzhi's rightist opportunism, which they believed was impeding the progress of workers' and peasants' movements, and undermining the leadership of the proletariat. Qu Qiubai disseminated a 70,000 word comprehensive pamphlet titled *Controversial Issues in the Chinese Revolution* (*Zhongguo geming zhong zhi zhenglun wenti* 中国革命中之争论问题) to the attending representatives. In the pamphlet, Qu asserted that "our party is sick, and the name of the illness is Peng Shuzhi-ism."[168]

Peng Shuzhi had ceased to be a member of the CCP's Political Bureau following the Fifth Congress. On July 15, Chen Duxiu drafted a letter to the Central Committee, expressing his desire to step down from the general secretary position.[169] Subsequently, on August 7, the CCP convened an urgent meeting in Wuhan, rectified Chen Duxiu's rightist opportunism, and entrusted Qu Qiubai with leadership responsibilities within the party.[170] The meeting also led to the establishment of the Northern Bureau of the CCP, which was headed by Cai Hesen, Peng Shuzhi, and Wang Hebo 王荷波 (1882–1927). Wang Hebo was arrested and subsequently executed by warlords in late 1927. Following this, Cai Hesen reported to the Central Committee that either Peng Shuzhi or his subordinates had betrayed Wang Hebo.[171] However, these accusations could not be substantiated, and it was unclear if they were motivated by a desire to retaliate. Nevertheless, Xiang Jingyu's affair with Peng Shuzhi played a significant role in shaping the dynamics and interactions among the early CCP leaders. As Andrea McElderry noted, "Ironically, Xiang's most lasting influence on the Central Committee occurred because of a sexual involvement not because of her political work."[172] Despite her significant contributions to the revolution, Xiang's political capacity was overshadowed by her personal life.

Xiang Jingyu's extramarital relationship with Peng Shuzhi tarnished her reputation and resulted in her removal from her position as a core member of the CCP.[173] In a male-dominated party, Xiang Jingyu exhibited a dual nature in response to the juxtaposition of revolutionary ideals and her personal emotions as a female CCP leader. Despite her relatively young age of around thirty, Xiang Jingyu earned the nickname "Old Grandma" (*lao zumu* 老祖

母) within the party because of her stern demeanor and simple attire. Yang Zilie, Zhang Guotao's wife and a collaborator with Xiang on women's movements, recalled that Xiang typically "wore an ill-fitting light blue *qipao*; sometimes, she would don a blue blouse and a black cloth skirt . . . She worked diligently and vigorously, with a solemn and austere demeanor, resembling a 'grandmother'—that's what comrades playfully called her behind her back. However, at the same time, comrades held great admiration and respect for her."[174] Upon their initial encounter, Wang Yizhi observed that Xiang Jingyu, fresh from her work-study program in France, had not succumbed to the influence of Western fashion; rather, her appearance and manner remained authentic to her Hunan countryside roots.[175] A similar impression was shared by Zheng Chaolin who perceived Xiang Jingyu as wholly devoted to the revolutionary cause, untouched by the superficiality prevalent in Shanghai.[176]

Xiang Jingyu wrote an essay in which she asserted that women's inclination toward adornments and cosmetics stemmed from the necessity to please men upon whom they relied for economic and social support.[177] She advocated for women's independence, urging them to consider more than just a man's outward appearance and social status when choosing a partner. Instead, she urged a focus on the individual's commitment to revolution.[178] Xiang Jingyu's audacity shone through when she confronted Chen Duxiu over inappropriate jokes related to romantic relationships.[179] Within the party, Xiang Jingyu evoked a sense of trepidation because of her seriousness. Thus, the revelation of her extramarital affair came as a shock to her comrades. This paradox led to questions of her authenticity. How do we reconcile the seeming contradictions within Xiang Jingyu's character?

Xiang Jingyu's characteristics and ideological foundations were shaped by a blend of traditional and modern education. After Xiang Jingyu's martyrdom, even though they had already parted ways, Cai Hesen enthusiastically wrote "The Biography of Comrade Xiang Jingyu" (*Xiang Jingyu tongzhi zhuan* 向警予同志传). In it, Cai Hesen explained that women's education in 1910s Hunan still focused on cultivating virtuous wives and good mothers.[180] The traditional education that Xiang Jingyu received led to her being hailed as a saint (*shengren* 圣人) because of her elevated moral principles. Her peers also elected her as the head of morality (*daode buzhang* 道德部长), a testament to her ethical standing.[181]

Xiang Jingyu's diaries from her time at Zhounan Girls' Middle School offer insights into the influence of Confucian ethics and Neo-Confucianism on her thoughts and behaviors. One of her diary entries detailed a teacher-led ceremony on Confucius's birthday, demonstrating the imprint of Confucianism on her experiences.[182] In another entry, she reflected on her conduct while laughing with peers and resolved to cultivate herself in accordance with the concept of "respect" (*jing* 敬) promoted by Cheng Yi 程颐 (1033–1107), a Neo-Confucian philosopher of the Song dynasty.[183] Interestingly, Qu Qiubai labeled Xiang Jingyu a "Marxist Neo-Confucian scholar" (*Makesi zhuyi Songxue jia* 马克思主义宋学家),[184] melding two seemingly divergent ideologies and thereby exposing contradictions within Xiang Jingyu's persona.

While influenced by traditional education, Xiang Jingyu was also exposed to progressive teachings advocating for women's emancipation. As Peng Shuzhi noted, "Her personality encapsulates the paradoxes faced by modern Chinese women of her time. Her actions reflect the enduring influence of the stringent 'virtuous wife and good mother' tradition. Yet, at the same time, her immersion in the May Fourth Movement and her studies in Western Europe enabled her to break free from the restrictions of traditional Chinese ideology."[185] Zhang Guotao observed that while Xiang Jingyu exhibited passion, she was simultaneously constrained by conventional rituals.[186]

There appeared to be a contrasting facet of Xiang Jingyu, calling into question her "Old Grandma" reputation. She was passionate about gymnastics and displayed remarkable proficiency in the discipline.[187] This commitment did not waver, even during her confinement in Wuhan, where she persisted in practicing gymnastics.[188] Yang Zilie's memoir details a lively visit to Xiang Jingyu's Fusheng Road residence with Zhang Guotao. Xiang Jingyu proposed a postdinner game in which everyone could sing, dance, share a story, or tell a joke for entertainment. When it was Xiang Jingyu's turn, she captivated everyone by performing a handstand, showcasing her gymnastic skills. In that moment, her countenance transformed. The customary cool demeanor of the "Old Grandma" was replaced by a joyful, youthful disposition.[189]

Xiang Jingyu's fervor extended to her passion for public speaking as well. Cai Hesen recalled that during the May Fourth Movement, Xiang Jingyu would address the public daily, promoting patriotism. Her emotions ran deep, often leading to uncontrollable tears when discussing state affairs.[190] Cai Chang recollected occasions when her passion during public speeches grew so overpowering that she came close to collapsing or fainting.[191] From these accounts, it becomes evident that beneath her usual stern appearance, Xiang Jingyu possessed the heart of a passionate and emotionally expressive young woman.

Xiang Jingyu's seriousness emanated from her steadfast dedication to revolutionary endeavors. The Xiang Cai Alliance was, at its core, a union grounded in revolution. On the surface, Xiang Jingyu and Cai Hesen earned the admiration of numerous revolutionaries as an exemplary couple dedicated to the cause, living an ascetic lifestyle. Peng Shuzhi recalled that "they abstained from gossip during meals, rarely wore smiles in casual interactions, and their conversations centered solely around politics. All else held little interest, as it did not pertain to their pure revolutionary consciousness."[192] Both Cai Hesen and Yang Zilie likened Xiang Jingyu to a missionary.[193] Cai Chang recounted how she effectively propagated revolutionary ideals among the masses, leading people to refer to her as a "new missionary."[194] Cai Hesen was likewise regarded as a saint solely dedicated to Marxism and revolutionary duties.[195]

Xiang Jingyu and Cai Hesen appeared as impeccable partners in the realm of revolutionary movements. However, in the course of their daily lives, not everything unfolded seamlessly. As recounted by Zhang Guotao, who shared a living space with Cai Hesen for a period in 1923, Cai's routine predominantly revolved around reading and writing, and he scarcely engaged in conversation. His severe asthma frequently led to labored breathing and gasping. He would neglect meals, and when exhaustion would set in, he would collapse into bed, sometimes even leaving his shoes on. His room bore a disorganized and untidy appearance.[196] According to Zhang Guotao, Cai Hesen's lifestyle may have strained the couple's marital bond.[197] Conversely, Peng Shuzhi was known as an "amorous scholar" (*fengliu caizi* 风流才子), successfully striking a balance between his professional commitments and personal life.[198]

After the revelation of Xiang Jingyu's affair with Peng Shuzhi, the CCP arranged for Xiang Jingyu and Cai Hesen to travel to Moscow with the intention of helping them reconcile their relationship. In late October 1925, the couple embarked on a journey from Shanghai to Vladivostok, accompanied by Shen Zemin, Li Lisan and his wife Li Yichun 李一纯, to await the train to Moscow.[199] In Vladivostok, they reunited with Yang Zilie, who had been dispatched by the CCP to study in Moscow. On the eve of their departure from Vladivostok, Xiang Jingyu complained about Cai Hesen's personal hygiene and stayed up late writing a letter. Entrusting the letter to Yang Zilie, she requested that it be mailed to Shanghai. Yang Zilie accidentally discovered that Xiang had handed her a six-page love letter addressed to Peng Shuzhi.[200]

As this letter portended, the bond between Cai Hesen and Xiang Jingyu waned in Moscow, ultimately leading to the dissolution of the once-admired Xiang Cai Alliance. During Cai Hesen's period of personal turmoil, Li Yichun, who was the spouse of Li Lisan, extended care and support. The party exhibited considerable tolerance toward Cai's romantic involvement with Li Yichun and toward the end of 1926, the pair were wed in Moscow.[201] Meanwhile, Xiang Jingyu attended the Communist University of the Toilers of the East and had a romantic relationship with a student from Mongolia.[202]

In addition to the emotional turmoil in her personal life, Xiang Jingyu faced challenges within her revolutionary pursuits. She demonstrated remarkable leadership skills in steering women's movements and made significant contributions to the May Thirtieth Movement. Nonetheless, women's movements were marginalized during the early CCP era, leading to a lack of equitable recognition for Xiang's contributions within the party. Yang Zilie noted that women during the initial stages of the CCP were not officially designated roles within the party. Xiang Jingyu led women's group that held meetings to discuss matters concerning women workers and child laborers.[203] The participants of this women's group included Xiang Jingyu, Yang Zilie, Li Yichun, Wang Yizhi, Kong Xianzhi 孔宪之 (1897–1970), Yang Zhihua 杨之华 (1901–73), Zhang Qinqiu, and He Baozhen 何葆珍 (1902–34)—all of whom were wives of the CCP leaders.[204] The recognition of women within the party frequently hinged on their associations with male party members, reflecting the male dominance that prevailed during the early years of the CCP. Peng Shuzhi recalled that it was not until the Fourth Congress of the CCP that a Women's Department was established in the Central Committee. Xiang Jingyu was entrusted by the CCP to manage women's issues without holding an official title.[205]

Xiang Jingyu's aspirations extended beyond women's initiatives. Cai Hesen described Xiang as an ambitious individual driven by a desire to make substantial changes.[206] She longed for accomplishments that could reshape the world. She became depressed after marrying Cai Hesen, as she found the notion that women were inferior to men to be deeply offensive. She was dissatisfied with merely participating in women's movements and being lauded solely as an exemplary female revolutionary.[207] Cai Hesen acknowledged that Xiang Jingyu possessed the ability to lead the CCP, not just women's movements. He also recognized that the early CCP had committed job assignment mistakes, notably by confining female revolutionaries to roles solely within women's movements.[208]

During the early years of the CCP, the women's movement was often regarded as subsidiary to the broader cause of national salvation, with the premise that women's liberation was intertwined with the liberation of the nation. Women revolutionaries usually assumed roles within women's movements, and their contributions to the revolution often went unrecognized in the male-dominated party environment. A prevalent pattern among early female CCP members was their marriage to male CCP members. As Lee Haiyan points out, "Women's access to the nation, however, is invariably mediated through the family or the romantic nexus."[209] Female revolutionaries were expected to embody the dual roles of virtuous wives and dedicated revolutionaries. They were perceived as wives to both their spouses and the nation itself.

In 1918, Zhou Zefan 周则范, a warlord in Xupu, proposed marriage to Xiang Jingyu. Pressured by Zhou's power, Xiang's father consented to the match. However, Xiang Jingyu staunchly declined the proposal, affirming her commitment "to marry the nation and remain celibate for life" (*yishen xuguo, zhongshen buhun* 以身许国，终身不婚).[210] The idea of marrying the nation was not new by 1918. In 1902, an influential biweekly journal, the *New Citizen Journal* (*Xinmin conbao* 新民丛报), founded by Liang Qichao 梁启超 (1873–1929) in Japan, featured an essay that introduced famous figures from around the world, including Queen Elizabeth I of England. The essay extolled Elizabeth I for her patriotism, citing her response to a query about her decision to lead a celibate life in which she said, "I have already married, and the name of my husband is England (*Wu yi jiade yifu, mingyue Yingjili* 吾已嫁得一夫，名日英吉利)."[211] Similarly, in late Qing fiction *Prophecy about the Tragic Fate of the Dissection of China* (*Guafen canhuo yuyan ji* 瓜分惨祸预言记, 1904), the heroine Xia Zhen'ou 夏震欧 states that "China is my husband. China is dead means my husband is dead."[212] Slightly altering Xiang Jingyu's expression "*yishen xuguo*," the last words of the first female Communist, Miao Boying 缪伯英 (1899–1929), were "[I] pledged to marry the party" (*yishen xudang* 以身许党).[213] Through making a commitment to "marry" the party or the nation, women reshape their gender identity into a political identity. However, the patriarchal logic persisted, whether women were dedicated to a husband or to the service of their nation.

"*Yishen xuguo*" and "*yishen xudang*" both carry the implication of sacrificing one's life for the nation and the party. Xiang Jingyu fulfilled this commitment by sacrificing her life. After returning from Moscow in March 1927, Xiang embarked on leading workers' movements in Wuhan from April onwards. She worked at the CCP Hubei Propaganda Department and assumed responsibility for *Great River* (*Dajiang* 大江), the underground party newspaper. Unfortunately, she was betrayed by traitors, leading to her

Figure 38: The first page of Cai Hesen's "Biography of Comrade Xiang Jingyu." Source: *Xiang Jingyu wenji*, 1980, 2.

execution by the KMT on May 1, 1928.[214] Upon receiving the disheartening news, Cai Hesen wrote the biography of Xiang Jingyu in Moscow. In it, Cai Hesen attributes their separation to their mystical perspective on love, which in turn brought about mystical suffering.[215] In concluding the biography, Cai Hesen wrote, "Great Jingyu, courageous Jingyu, you have not died, you will never die! You are not my personal beloved; you are the eternal lover of the Chinese proletariat!"[216]

Xiang Jingyu achieved a form of immortality by "marrying," or dedicating herself, to the entire proletarian class. The official narratives surrounding Xiang Jingyu, including the biography authored by Cai Hesen, deliberately avoided any discussion about her extramarital relationship with Peng Shuzhi.[217] In these accounts, Cai Hesen and Xiang Jingyu persist as an ideal revolutionary couple, meticulously crafted to project an impeccable image of the revolutionary martyr. This is not only to maintain the pristine nature of their legacy but also to address the notion of chastity within the realm of female revolutionary martyrdom. For female revolutionaries, the concepts of "*yishen xuguo*" and "*yishen xudang*" encompass not only the sacrifice of their lives (*xiansheng* 献生) but also their physical bodies (*xianshen* 献身). Ding Ling's short story "When I Was in Xia Village" (*Wo zai Xiacun de shihou* 我在霞村的时候) presents an extreme instance of female sacrifice in the context of revolution. This narrative reveals gendered memories of female revolutionaries.

EXHIBITION IV

Zhenzhen

Chastity and Female Revolutionary Sacrifice

Zhenzhen 贞贞, whose name means chastity, is a fictional character in Ding Ling's short story "When I Was in Xia Village." The piece was first published in Yan'an in June 1941.[1] It was reprinted in the "July literary series" (*Qiyue wencong* 七月文丛), edited by Hu Feng in 1944. Additionally, it appeared in the anthology *Collection of Short Stories in the Liberated Areas* (*Jiefangqu duanpian chuangzuo xuan* 解放区短篇创作选), edited by Zhou Yang in 1946.[2] In 1950, Ding Ling revisited the short story, implementing notable revisions that softened the politically sensitive points present in the original version.[3] "When I Was in Xia Village" draws its inspiration from an account Ding Ling gleaned from a fellow comrade. It tells the story of a girl named Zhenzhen from Xia village, who is abducted by the Japanese and coerced into serving as a military sexual slave. She endures both physical and mental torment while working as a spy for the CCP, gathering intelligence on Japanese troops. The short story later became a pretense for criticizing Ding Ling's chastity and loyalty to the CCP during the Anti-Rightist Movement in the 1950s.

This chapter begins with an examination of Ding Ling's early wartime writings, which discuss the themes of female chastity and sexual violence. It explores her selection of Lao She's wartime operas that depict women's chastity sacrifices for national salvation, as performed by the Northwest Front Service Corps. These works illustrate the expectation that women must sacrifice both their bodies and lives to the cause of national salvation. The discussion then moves to how rape and sexual violence are portrayed in Chinese wartime literature, highlighting that women's pain and humiliation can only be mitigated when their experiences are woven into the larger historical narratives of the Communist revolution and national redemption. I further trace Zhenzhen's journey from the Catholic Church to a planned trip to Yan'an, as she transitions from dedication to God to self-sacrifice for

Figure 39: Cover of the Ding Ling's short story collection *When I Was in Xia Village* (*Wo zai Xiacun de shihou* 我在霞村的时候), Guilin: Yuanfang shudian, 1944. It is on display at the National Museum of Modern Chinese Literature. Photo courtesy of Wu Xiyun.

the CCP. This section analyzes the dual *xianshen*—the anticipated sacrifice of both life and body imposed on women. Yet, when the national emergency waned and the Anti-Rightist Movement gained momentum, Zhenzhen came to be perceived as a lowly military prostitute rather than a heroine, unveiling the paradoxical expectation of patriarchal nationalism: women were to sacrificially offer themselves to the nation and yet, implausibly, were expected to reclaim their chastity after the crisis.

Female Revolutionary Martyrdom: New Wine in Old Bottles

Ding Ling initially received a warm welcome in Yan'an upon her arrival in 1936. However, her situation took a turn shortly thereafter, as she became the subject of incessant inquiries and speculation concerning both her political and sexual purity during her period of house arrest in Nanjing. In spring 1937, Earl Leaf, an American photojournalist, interviewed Ding Ling in Yan'an. During the interview, Ding Ling asserted, "Records of the Party show that many men comrades have confessed under imprisonment and torture but no girl member has confessed regardless how painful or humiliating her suffering. Many have died in the torture chamber and many more were executed by sword and gun."[4] This statement was a clear defense of her unwavering political integrity. Ding Ling's writings during her early years in Yan'an reveal her constant anxiety about sexual violence and chastity.

In "An Unfired Bullet" (*Yike wei chutang de qiangdan* 一颗未出膛的枪弹, April 1937), the first short story Ding Ling wrote in Yan'an, she portrays a child soldier of the Red Army, around thirteen years old, who is almost raped by a Northeast Army soldier.[5] Facing his imminent death, the child begs his enemies to kill him with a knife in order to spare a bullet to kill Japanese invaders. Moved by the child's words, the company commander of the Northeast Army halts the execution. The short story extols the purity and bravery of the child while advocating for a united front in resisting Japanese invasion. Two months later, Ding Ling wrote another short story titled "Affair in East Village" (*Dongcun shijian* 东村事件, June 1937).[6] In the story, Qiqi 七七, a fifteen-year-old *tongyangxi* 童养媳 (child bride) is given to the landlord Zhao in exchange for the possible release of her imprisoned father-in-law, who owes money to the landlord. The landlord confines Qiqi to a cage and rapes her. Infuriated by the landlord Zhao's sexual exploitation of his wife,

Qiqi's husband Chen Delu 陈得禄 joins forces with other oppressed peasants to fight against the landlord.

The sexual violence in these two stories reflects underlying concerns about national crisis and class struggles. At the time, Ding Ling focused her writing more on grand historical narratives and political propaganda than on individuals. Her emphasis on the metaphorical relationship between chastity and national salvation grew more pronounced as the national crisis escalated, notably after the Marco Polo Bridge Incident (*Qiqi shibian* 七七事变) on July 7, 1937. This incident marked the commencement of Japan's comprehensive invasion of China, thereby intensifying the urgency and significance of Ding Ling's thematic undertones.

The Marco Polo Bridge Incident sparked a fervent sense of patriotism in Yan'an, leading everyone, including Ding Ling, to aspire to join the battlefront against the Japanese invaders. In collaboration with Wu Xiru 吴奚如 (1906–85), Ding Ling organized a group primarily composed of students from the Anti-Japanese Military and Political University (*Kangri junzheng daxue* 抗日军政大学). This group, which included Chen Ming, took on the task of disseminating patriotic and anti-Japanese messages through newsletters, political cartoons, plays, dance, and songs as they made their way to the front lines.[7]

Formed on August 12, 1937, this semimilitary and semipropagandist group adopted the official title of the Northwest Front Service Corps (*Xibei zhandi fuwutuan* 西北战地服务团), with Ding Ling serving as its director.[8] Prior to their march to the front lines, the Corps engaged in thorough political and cultural preparation. They invited the CCP leaders, including Mao Zedong, to address their gatherings. During one such meeting, Mao Zedong gave a talk on "The Popularization Question" (*Dazhonghua wenti* 大众化问题).[9] To increase their cultural readiness, the Corps rapidly composed songs and plays. Noteworthy among these creations is Ding Ling's one-act play titled *Reunion* (*Chongfeng* 重逢, August 1937).

In Ding Ling's play *Reunion*, set during the War of Resistance against Japan, the female revolutionary Bai Lan 白兰 is arrested and imprisoned by Japanese Special Agents (*Riben tegao ke* 日本特高科). Yamamoto, the director of the Japanese Special Agents, is captivated by Bai Lan's beauty and attempts to convince her to marry him and work for Japan. Faced with Bai Lan's rejection, Yamamoto sends Ma Daming 马达明 to persuade her.[10] At that time, Bai Lan makes the astonishing discovery that Ma, the envoy, is none other than her long-lost lover, now seemingly aligned with the Japanese. The reunion takes a tragic turn as Bai Lan, believing Ma Daming to be a traitor, fatally stabs him. Only then does Bai Lan discover that Ma Daming is a spy for the CCP. The play concludes on a poignant note, as Ma Daming entrusts crucial Japanese intelligence to Bai Lan and assists her in her escape from prison.

The character name Ma Daming 马达明 in Ding Ling's play might be a subtle reference to two of her lovers, Feng Da 冯达 and Chen Ming 陈明. Feng Da, though suspected of treachery, supported Ding Ling's plan to escape from Nanjing. Bai Lan, the female protagonist of the play, bears a striking resembles to Ding Ling as a female intellectual and revolutionary. Both women are suspected of being traitors by their fellow comrades, stemming from their survival while in enemy custody. Ding Ling, poised to embrace martyrdom during her house arrest in Nanjing, saw her life spared by the KMT. This real-life event was echoed in Bai Lan's situation, as her fellow comrades who were captured after her detention began to question her political purity.

Among her fellow comrades stands Qi Xin 齐新, whose name alludes to "united heart" (*Qixin* 齐心). Qi Xin questions Bai Lan, remarking "you are fortunate to still be alive. Most of our imprisoned comrades have been martyred! Why have you been spared such a fate?"[11] In response, Bai Lan asserts, "I was willing to embrace death without fear, but they didn't kill me. I was equally prepared for torment and suffering. I was confident I wouldn't make a sound. Yet, [the executioners] never arrived."[12] This exchange reinstates the faith of her fellow comrades in her dedication. With renewed trust, they implore her to protect her identity and cooperate with the Japanese as a spy for the CCP, even if it entails sacrificing her chastity. Qi Xin argues, "Death is easy in the monstrous hands of the enemy. However, staying alive and continuing to work for the revolution in their grasp is an immense challenge."[13] Qi Xin's perspective resonates with Ding Ling's defense of her choice to endure suffering under the custody of the KMT, remaining alive and committed to her revolutionary ideals.

Ding Ling's play *Reunion* premiered successfully in Yan'an. It was later published in the literary journal *July* (*Qiyue* 七月), edited by Hu Feng. The play swiftly garnered widespread acclaim, becoming a favorite among local troupes across the nation.[14] On August 15, 1937, a farewell event took place in Yan'an, honoring the departure of the Northwest Front Service Corps to the front lines. Mao Zedong attended the gathering and delivered an inspiring speech, urging the Corps to "use pens and mouths to fight against

Figure 40: Photo of Ding Ling (second from the right) with the actors Chen Ming (first from the right), Wang Yuqing 王玉清 (fourth from the right), and the actress Xia Gefei 夏革非 (third from the right) after the performance of her play *Reunion* in Yan'an in 1938. Source: Tu Shaojun, *Tuben Ding Ling zhuan*, 159.

the Japanese."[15] As part of their regular programming, the Corps prepared a repertoire of songs, dances, and plays, including Ding Ling's *Reunion*. On September 22, they departed Yan'an for the front lines in Shanxi.[16] In 1938, the play was translated into English with the title "An Unexpected Reunion," and it was eventually performed at Visva-Bharati University in India in February 1940.[17]

Despite its success, Ding Ling was not satisfied with the play. In a letter to Hu Feng in early 1938, Ding Ling expressed that while she had written *Reunion* to meet the needs of the Corps, she believed it should not be performed frequently due to its focus on intellectuals.[18] She acknowledged Bai Lan as a generally commendable revolutionary. However, she felt compelled to critique Bai's excessive emotional display toward the end of the play. Ding Ling observed that even after Bai Lan's act of stabbing Ma Daming, audiences continued to sympathize with her, a reaction that solidified her conviction against frequent performances.[19] Ding Ling's primary concern did not rest on the artistic quality of the play, but rather on the potential diversion it posed from the political propaganda that the Corps ought to emphasize during that period. In response, she revised the play, diminishing the romantic aspect between Bai Lan and Ma Daming while highlighting patriotic messages. Even so, during the second collaboration between the KMT and the CCP, the KMT political leadership viewed the romantic element in *Reunion* as overshadowing its intended political message about denouncing traitors. Consequently, on November 7, 1939, the Propaganda Department of the KMT issued an official letter prohibiting the performance of Ding Ling's *Reunion*, arguing that the play conveys confusing messages that could undermine people's determination to eliminate traitors.[20]

Focusing on propaganda campaigns, the Northwest Front Service Corps dedicated five months to their endeavors in Shanxi before departing for Xi'an in March 1938. During their time in Xi'an, Ding Ling directed her efforts toward popularizing literature and art, aiming to convey propagandist messages with greater efficiency. Prior to their departure from Yan'an to the front lines, Ding Ling sought counsel from Mao Zedong. Mao told Ding that "propaganda needs to be popularized. Whether it is 'new wine in new bottles' (*xinping xinjiu* 新瓶新酒) or 'new wine in old bottles' (*jiuping xinjiu* 旧瓶新酒), it should be straightforward and concise to suit the wartime environment and resonate with the masses."[21]

In accordance with Mao Zedong's suggestion, Ding Ling mentioned in an interview conducted in Xi'an that their performances represented "new wine in old bottles" (*jiuping zhuang xinjiu* 旧瓶装新酒), ensuring that people from diverse class backgrounds could all appreciate them.[22] Throughout the War of Resistance against Japan, this "new wine in old bottles" stood as a guiding writing principle. This approach often intertwined new patriotic and anti-Japanese messages with traditional art and literature such as Peking opera, *dagu shu* 大鼓书 (big drum songs) and *zhanghui xiaoshuo* 章回小说 (chapter-divided novels), aiming to reach a larger audience and inspire them to fight against the Japanese.[23] Lao She emerged as a prominent advocate and practitioner of the "new wine in old bottles" writing principle. He wrote numerous traditional operas and big drum songs, among which were the Peking operas *The Loyalists and Martyrs* (*Zhonglie tu* 忠烈图) and *A Chaste Woman Martyred for the Nation* (*Liefu xunguo* 烈妇殉国), promoting the war against Japanese invasion through traditional art.[24]

The Northwest Front Service Corps orchestrated three public performances during their time in Xi'an. For the first two shows, they performed

Figure 41: Ding Ling (seated first from the right), Xiao Hong (seated first from the left), and Xia Gefei in Xi'an, spring 1938. Source: "Zai qianxian de nüzi" 在前线的女子 (Girls at the front), *Dongfang huakan* 东方画刊 (The Eastern pictorial) 1, no. 2, 1938: 8. Xiao Hong participated in writing the play *The Sudden Attack* for the Northwest Front Service Corps.

dances, small tunes (*xiaodiao* 小调), cross talk (*xiangsheng* 相声), and the play *The Sudden Attack* (*Tuji* 突击). *The Sudden Attack* was composed collaboratively by Xiao Hong, Sai Ke 塞克, Duanmu Hongliang, and Nie Gannu. Ding Ling noted the popularity of traditional operas in Xi'an, whereas the audience for modern plays typically comprised intellectuals who attended for artistic appreciation rather than to receive political education.[25] Given this observation, Ding Ling opted to conclude their public performance in Xi'an stage with two of Lao She's Peking operas, both of which centered on female chastity and martyrdom. Ding Ling's decision to stage Lao She's two Chinese operas rather than her own play, *Reunion*, primarily stemmed from propagandistic motives. Though *Reunion* reflected her personal experiences as a woman navigating revolutionary times, Ding Ling realized that the play was

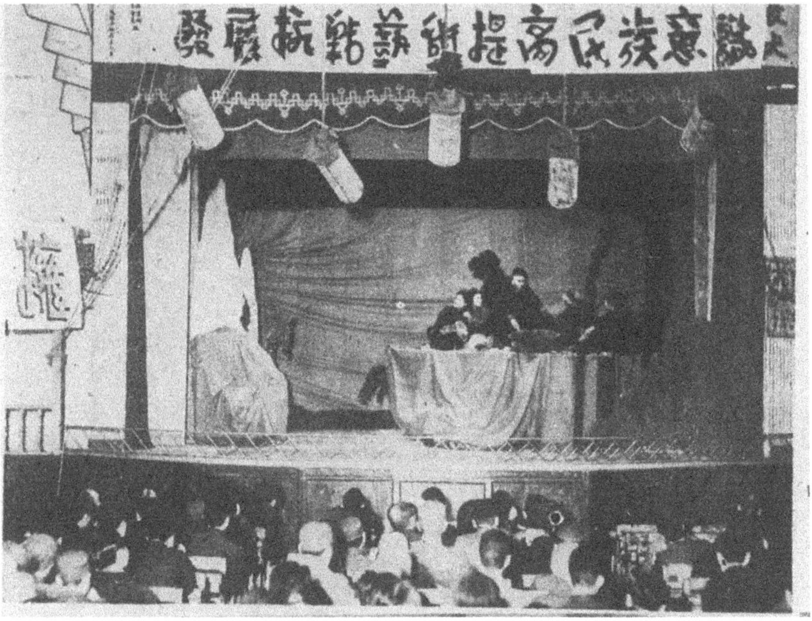

Figure 42: A scene from the Northwest Front Service Corps' performance of the play *The Sudden Attack* in Xi'an in 1938, photo by Zhao Dingming 赵定明. The banner on stage reads "developing antiwar art, elevating national consciousness," articulating the propagandist objective of the Corps. Source: Zhao Dingming, "Xibei zhandi fuwutuan" 西北战地服务团 (The Northwest Front Service Corps), *Zhonghua* 中华 (The China pictorial) 68 (1938): 23.

not ideal for effectively disseminating propaganda. In *Reunion*, the female revolutionary Bai Lan hesitates to embrace a suggested male revolutionary's proposition that she become a sex spy (*taose jiandie* 桃色间谍), adding complexities to the play's intended political messages.[26]

For their final performance in Xi'an, the Corps retained Lao She's *The Loyalists and Martyrs* in its Peking opera form and adapted *A Chaste Woman Martyred for the Nation* into *Qinqiang* 秦腔 (Shaanxi opera). This final performance proved to be the most successful among the three. In *The Loyalists and Martyrs*, the female protagonist Widow Chen's husband martyred himself on the front line fighting against the Japanese invaders. She agrees to remarry the bandit Zhao Hu 赵虎 under the condition that he joins the fight against the Japanese. In *A Chaste Woman Martyred for the Nation*, the traitor

Figure 43: Advertisement for the Northwest Front Service Corps' performance of antiwar traditional operas in Xi'an, including *The Loyalists and Martyrs* and *A Chaste Woman Martyred for the Nation*. Source: *Gongshang ribao* 工商日报 (Industrial and commercial daily), July 12, 1938.

Liu Liqiu 刘璃球 plots to surrender his sister-in-law to the Japanese forces, subjecting her to military sexual slavery, while selling out his own brother who is an anti-Japanese spy. Liu's wife, Xue Erniang, informs the couple of Liu's treacherous intentions and suggests that Liu's brother should kill her husband. After assisting the couple's escape, Xue Erniang is burned to death by the Japanese collaborator Gao Sihu 高四虎.

In these two Chinese operas, Lao She repurposed traditional notions of loyalty to the emperor and female chastity to fit the modern framework of nationalism. As highlighted by Liu Long-hsin, in Lao She's practice of "new wine in old bottles," "loyalty to the emperor in Chinese drama could be sub-

Figure 44: A scene from the Northwest Front Service Corps' performance of the opera *A Chaste Woman Martyred for the Nation* in Xi'an. Source: Yuan Peili 袁培力, "Kangzhan chuqi Xizhantuan zai Xi'an de sanci gongyan" 抗战初期西战团在西安的三次公演 (Three public performances of the Northwest Front Service Corps in Xi'an during the early stage of the Anti-Japanese War), *Gejie* 9 (2019): 75.

stituted by patriotism to the nation, and chivalry could be replaced by sacrifice for a righteous cause. In this way, the old structure and old thinking could be made useful for arousing popular sentiment in the Anti-Japanese War."[27]

Following the concept of "new wine in old bottles," Lao She introduced new moral standards for women through his writings, replacing the traditional Confucian gender norms. In 1938, Lao She rewrote *Classic for Girls* (*Nü'er jing* 女儿经), a three-character verse that outlined women's moral duties in premodern China. He infused this text with new messages aimed at inspiring women to contribute to the War of Resistance against Japan.[28] He reinterpreted the notions of female chastity and martyrdom, inventing new narratives of female martyrs in his war resistance Peking operas.

In *A Chaste Woman Martyred for the Nation*, Xue Erniang exposes her husband's identity as a traitor, defying the traditional idea that a wife must be submissive and loyal to her husband. She shifts her allegiance to the nation, ultimately sacrificing her life in its service. For Xue Erniang, the nation becomes her new husband. In a similar vein, Widow Chen in *The Loyalists and Martyrs* defies the traditional Confucian norm that expects women to maintain their chastity and remain widowed after the deaths of their husbands. She remarries a bandit, driven by the goal of persuading him to participate in national salvation. In the opera, Widow Chen justifies her remarriage by stating that "it is reasonable to sacrifice one's own body for the sake of the nation; considerations of chastity ought to be set aside when it comes to national matters."[29] Widow Chen emerges as a groundbreaking archetype of chastity, one who transitions her loyalty from her husband to the nation.

However, Lao She acknowledges in the preface to the opera that tackling the topic of Widow Chen's remarriage presented significant challenges. He lists three specific reasons for this difficulty: "First, it is necessary to break free from traditional notions of female chastity. Second, to show commitment, both men and women must be willing to sacrifice themselves for the nation, and the physical body should be of little concern. Third, considering the reality of Japanese aggression and the widespread rape and killing of women, why shouldn't Chinese women offer their bodies to our own soldiers?"[30] In this manner, Lao She normalizes women's sacrifice of both their lives and sexual reputations in service to the nation. Women's liberation is subordinate to national salvation. The nation effectively replaces the husband, assuming the role of a new patriarchal authority over women. This transformation from conventional womanhood rooted in chastity to a revolutionary form of female martyrdom can be viewed as a modern reinterpretation of traditional ideas, or new wine in old bottles.

In July 1938, the Northwest Front Service Corps performed the two Chinese operas adapted from Lao She's scripts a total of seven times over a span of three days. Remarkably, each performance drew a packed audience.[31] These performances marked the culmination of their ten months of propagandist works on the front lines. While stationed in Xi'an, Ding Ling received a letter from Feng Da. However, she handed this letter to Lin Boqu 林伯渠 (1886–1960), who was in charge of the Eight Route Army office in Xi'an, without offering a reply.[32] This decision by Ding Ling eliminated the possibility of their reunion, and she maintained no further contact with Feng Da.

The Northwest Front Service Corps returned to Yan'an in August 1938. On August 13, the Corps staged a public performance in Yan'an, featuring the Peking opera *The Loyalists and Martyrs* and the Shaanxi opera *A Chaste Woman Martyred for the Nation*. Among the audience members was Chen Xuezhao 陈学昭 (1906–91), a female intellectual who had recently arrived in Yan'an. She recalled that the performance took place in the grand meeting hall attached to the small Christian church in Yan'an. She recounted: "On that evening, both the Peking opera and Shaanxi opera were profoundly moving, prompting enthusiastic applause from the audience. . . . The plays' content revolves around the War of Resistance, yet they employ traditional forms."[33] The concept of "new wine in old bottles" found a welcoming audience in Yan'an. Following the performance in Yan'an, Ding Ling wrote an essay on the reformation of Peking opera.[34] With her responsibilities as leader of the Northwest Front Service Corps concluded, Ding Ling had more time to reflect and write. Some of her writings concerning women in wartime and revolution shifted the narrative's focus from pure political propaganda to individual enlightenment, sparking debates and controversies.

Giving Her Voice (*xiansheng* 献声): Recounting Wartime Sexual Violence

In November 1938, Ding Ling and Chen Ming commenced their studies at Yan'an Marxism-Leninism Institute (*Yan'an MaLie Xueyuan* 延安马列学院), a training center for CCP cadres. Kang Sheng, a faculty member of the Marxism-Leninism Institute, publicly cast doubts on Ding's political integrity, claiming that she lacked the qualifications for enrollment in the Marxism-Leninism Institute.[35] Furthermore, gossip circulated about a romantic relationship between Ding Ling and Chen Ming.[36] Even though Ding Ling later

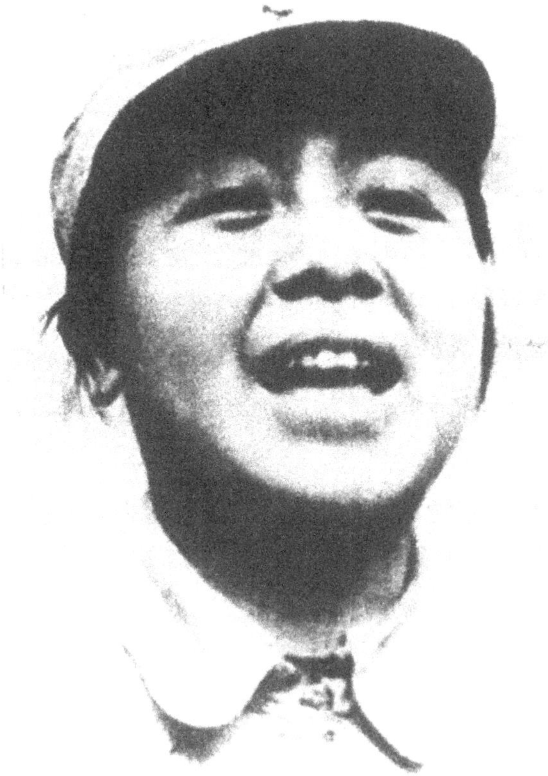

Figure 45: Ding Ling in Yan'an, 1938. Source: Jiang Zulin, *Ding Ling zhuan*, 298.

claimed that she remained unaware of Kang Sheng's remarks until 1940, she should have been conscious of the concerns surrounding her time in Nanjing during that period.[37] Infuriated by Kang Sheng's comments, Ding Ling formally requested that the CCP conduct a comprehensive background investigation on her. Despite her contributions, including leading the Northwest Front Service Corps for the CCP's propagandist efforts, Ding Ling's political loyalty came under scrutiny.

In distress, Ding Ling wrote two stories, "New Faith" (*Xin de xinnian* 新的信念, spring 1939) and "When I Was in Xia Village" (*Wo zai Xiacun de shihou* 我在霞村的時候, 1941), exploring the trauma of rape and sexual violence. While at the Marxism-Leninism Institute, she wrote a short story initially published in *Literary Front* (*Wenyi zhanxian* 文艺战线) under the title "Faith in the Eyes Dimmed by Tears" (*Leiyan mohu zhong zhi xinnian* 泪眼模糊中之信念), later retitled as "New Faith."[38] Ding Ling's "New Faith" recounts the story of Granny Chen, who is raped by Japanese soldiers and also witnesses the rape of her granddaughter Yingu 银姑 and the killing of her grandson Tongguan 同官. Deeply traumatized by her horrifying experience, Granny Chen finds the inner strength to speak out, embarking on village tours to share her stories and inspire people to fight against the Japanese. Upon hearing of Granny Chen's passionate rallies, two female CCP cadres invite her to join the Women's Organization (*Funü hui* 妇女会), thereby augmenting her influence in mobilizing the masses. Through her engagement in the revolutionary cause, Granny Chen discovers a renewed sense of hope and faith.

"Telling" is the predominant theme in Ding Ling's "New Faith." In contrast to Qiqi in Ding Ling's "Affair in East Village," who, though also a victim of rape, remains silent throughout the narrative, Granny Chen courageously opts to vocalize her experiences, even in the face of the potential shame her stories might bring. Telling her story becomes a means of healing for Granny Chen. In Ding Ling's portrayal, following the trauma inflicted by the Japanese, Granny Chen's initial emergence is as more of a "living thing" than a human being. Ding Ling writes, "There was only one living thing moving about on the plain. Then it too collapsed. Covered with snow, had it not begun instinctively to crawl forward again, it would have been impossible to spot. Gradually this living thing moved into the village. It was human."[39] As Yan Haiping notes, "While women who died as the results of colonial assaults could be and were rendered into political resources to stir up public anger and mobilize resistance, the survived and surviving bodies of raped, deformed, damaged females remained difficult sights to see, approach, confront, and relate to."[40]

In "New Faith," Granny Chen reclaims her sense of personhood through sharing her stories. She begins to tell women in her family about the rape of Yingu and the killing of Tongguan with graphic descriptions of their sufferings. However, initially, she avoids recounting these stories in the presence of her sons; "she was afraid of their searching glances, and besides, the personal shame and sorrow she felt kept her from going on when they were around."[41] She then proceeds to share her stories with her neighbors, recounting the ordeal of her abuse by the Japanese. She bares the scars on her body as evidence and guides them through the village, pointing out the locations where her sufferings occurred. Upon conclusion, she consistently addresses the villagers with an impassioned question, "You're not going to forget this now, are you?"[42] Granny Chen's storytelling endeavors serve as a conscious effort to resist forgetfulness and foster a collective memory within the community.

Granny Chen's storytelling takes on a new dimension when her youngest son returns home, sharing his experiences battling the Japanese on the front lines. This prompts her to travel to nearby villages. There, she first recounts the sufferings caused by the Japanese, then weaves in her son's firsthand narratives of the battles against the Japanese, ultimately rallying people to join the front lines. By connecting her personal ordeals to the overarching narrative of national salvation, Granny Chen rediscovers the meaning of her life. Assumedly like a missionary, she embarks on journeys to enlighten and preach to others. Her speeches hold such compelling power that numerous individuals heed her call and join the front lines. The sense of shame she once felt in front of her sons dissipates. Jingu 金姑, her granddaughter, follows in her footsteps, attending her speeches and adopting her words. The collective memory of the suffering past and the shared aspiration for the eventual defeat of the Japanese foster a closer bond within the family.

In "New Faith," the CCP recognizes Granny Chen's influential ability to mobilize, extending an invitation for her to become a part of the Women's Association. Embracing this opportunity, she not only joins the Women's Association herself but also enlists her granddaughter, Jingu, and her two daughters-in-law. As highlighted by Tani Barlow in her introduction to "New Faith," "As the story shows very accurately, the triumph of Yan'an policy on women was that it really did convince old women like the grandmother to expand their power and reach beyond the family through the new political bond of citizen and state."[43]

Granny Chen actively participates in the Women's Association, mobilizing the masses. While delivering a speech at a grand assembly organized by the association, her fervor leads her to momentarily lose her voice: "Finally the old woman gathered all her remaining strength: 'We must fight to the end!' An enormous roar answered her, the sound of a tidal wave crashing on the beach in a storm."[44] Her individual voice seamlessly merges into a formidable collective one. The story concludes with her moment of enlightenment: "She saw the collapse of the old, the radiance of the new, and though tears blurred her vision, it was a radiance that sprang from her own steadfast faith."[45] The new revolutionary ideology erases Granny Chen's pain and humiliation, giving her a new life.

The power of telling also emerges in other wartime writings depicting women who were subjected to Japanese military sexual slavery. Ma Feng's 马烽 fiction "Jinbao's Mother" (*Jinbao niang* 金宝娘), written in 1948, draws from his participation in land reform in the Jinsui border regions in 1947.[46] It tells a story of Cuicui 翠翠, Jinbao's mother, a peasant woman coerced by a landlord to be a Japanese military sexual slave. Her life takes a transformative turn following the CCP's land reform.

In the story, Cuicui staunchly refuses to have a sexual relationship with the landlord, Liu Guicai 刘贵财. In retaliation, Liu spreads rumors suggesting Cuicui's husband, Li Genyuan 李根元, is affiliated with the CCP, leading to his arrest and imprisonment. Displaying remarkable determination, Cuicui orchestrates her husband's escape from confinement, enabling him to evade his home village. Subsequently, Liu Guicai forces Cuicui to serve as a military sexual slave for Japanese soldiers. Upon her return from this traumatic experience, Cuicui finds herself without farmland and means of self-support. Faced with these dire circumstances, she is left with no choice but to resort to prostitution to support Jinbao and care for her mother-in-law. Labeled as a "woman idler" (*nü erliuzi* 女二流子), she endures the degrading ordeal of a public parade through the village streets.[47] The narrator "I" is a CCP cadre dispatched to the village in 1947 to supervise the land reform. Initially harboring disdain toward Cuicui, his sentiment undergoes a transformation as he becomes acquainted with the misery of her past. Motivated by empathy, he assists Cuicui in participating in a speaking bitterness (*suku* 诉苦) meeting and securing her land during the process of land redistribution.

Suku meetings during the CCP's land reform provided a platform for peasants to air their grievances and denounce the landlords. Through the act of storytelling, peasants empowered themselves. This dynamic is evident in "Jinbao's Mother," where Cuicui recounts her experience of being forced her to be a sexual slave in the Japanese military by Liu Guicai during one such speaking bitterness meeting. She "initially begins talking while crying. Then, she faints from anger. After people spray cold water on her, she suddenly goes crazy, jumping up with her hair disheveled. She grins foolishly, revealing her teeth, and pounces on the landlord Liu Guicai, biting him wildly."[48] Speaking out about her bitterness and participating in the struggle session against the landlord serves to alleviate Cuicui's pain and shame. With Liu Guicai's downfall, her husband is able to return home. As a token of appreciation, Cuicui gifts the CCP cadre a pair of her handcrafted black cloth shoes, a sharp contrast to the broken red shoes she wore at the beginning of the story. This gesture hints at the term "broken shoes" (*poxie* 破鞋), commonly used to label licentious women or prostitutes, and symbolizes transformation through the intervention of the CCP.

In both "New Faith" and "Jinbao's Mother," the CCP ultimately guides the act of storytelling to shape a unified political voice. Contrastingly, two other wartime short stories about women sexually abused by the Japanese—Cao Ming's 草明 "The Humiliated" (*Shouru zhe* 受辱者, 1940) and Liu Qing's 柳青 "A Woman Who Has Been Humiliated" (*Bei wuru le de nüren* 被污辱了的女人, 1941)—provide instances of women's voices emerging in the absence of political intervention.[49] In "The Humiliated," Liang Akai 梁阿开, a woman worker at a silk factory in Shunde 顺德, is abducted by Japanese soldiers and forced to serve as a sexual slave in the Fifth Team for Comfort Women (*Funü laojun diwu xiaodui* 妇女劳军第五小队).[50] After returning home, she repeatedly lies to her friends about her whereabouts during her disappearance, driven by the fear of being judged if she were to tell the truth. In "The Humiliated," for Liang Akai, the act of telling lies serves as a means to avoid potential further humiliations. However, a local hooligan who collaborates with the Japanese discovers Liang's secret and exploits it for blackmail. Her web of lies is at risk of exposure. Adding to her woes, her lone hope of regaining employment evaporates when the silk factory's machines are sold to the Japanese. In an act of desperation, Liang Akai corrodes one of the machines using nitric acid, eventually collapsing beside it. Devoid of political guidance, Liang is unable to reclaim her dignity or reinstate her job. In contrast to the optimistic ending of Ding Ling's "New Faith," Cao Ming's story concludes in a depressing tone, as "the boundless darkness of the night descends upon the earth, growing heavier as it falls."[51]

Liu Qing's "A Woman Who Has Been Humiliated" tells the story of Zhao Kuan's wife (*Zhao Kuan sao* 赵宽嫂) who endures the horrifying experience of being abducted by Japanese soldiers for a month. She later makes the unsettling discovery that she is pregnant, but the identity of the child's father remains uncertain—she is unsure whether the father is Zhao Kuan or one of the Japanese soldiers who raped her. After giving birth to a son, she once again falls victim to another abduction by the Japanese forces, which ultimately leads to her descent into mental illness. Upon her return home, she tragically kills her child and wanders the streets, repeatedly telling people how she was forced to "comfort the Japanese army" (*weilao huangjun* 慰劳皇军).[52] This narrative parallels that of Xianglin's wife (*Xianglin sao* 祥林嫂) from Lu Xun's short story "The New Year's Sacrifice" (*Zhufu* 祝福), who tirelessly tells her story of suffering and the heartbreaking loss of her son.[53] In contrast to Granny Chen's meticulously structured speeches with their messages of national salvation, Zhao Kuan's wife presents her story in a disorganized manner, without the CCP's guidance. In Liu Qing's fiction, the story of Zhao Kuan's wife is framed as a tale told by an elementary school teacher to a silent, unnamed Eight Route Army soldier, a representative of the CCP.

In the stories discussed above, the act of telling, even telling lies, is cathartic and therapeutic for women who have been sexually abused by Japanese soldiers during the war. Yet women's voices are insufficient to completely erase their pain and shame. For true healing to occur, their voices must be seamlessly woven into the grand historical narrative of the Communist revolution and national salvation. Embedded within the revolutionary ideology is the perspective that the loss of chastity is not merely a personal tragedy but a vulnerability that resonates on a national scale. According to this view, the alleviation of women's suffering hinges upon their active engagement in the revolutionary cause. It is through their participation in the larger struggle that they can transcend their individual trauma and become integral contributors to the narrative of national salvation.

From a contemporary literary perspective, Ding Ling's short story "When I Was in Xia Village" is distinctive in that it introduces intricate layers of complexity that transcend the boundaries of the revolutionary doctrine. In doing so, the story elevates itself beyond the confines of established ideology. Rather than solely incorporating the afflicted woman into the grand historical narrative, Ding Ling's narrative focuses on a woman as an individual with her own unique identity and experiences. This shift in perspective challenges the tendency to reduce women's stories to mere instruments of ideological unity and underscores the importance of acknowledging their individuality and agency. Through Ding Ling's storytelling, the suffering woman emerges not just as a participant in history but as a multifaceted individual whose pain, struggles, and strength deserve recognition on their own terms.

Sacrificing Her Body (*Xianshen* 献身): Zhenzhen and the Church Image in "When I Was in Xia Village"

In 1940, Ding Ling volunteered to be investigated by the CCP in response to rumors that labeled her a traitor and Kang Sheng's concerns about her political loyalty, as expressed during a meeting at the Marxism-Leninism Institute. Depressed by the ongoing investigation and the atmosphere of distrust within the party, Ding Ling confided in her close friend at the time, Xiao Jun 萧军 (1907–88).[54] Xiao Jun's diary offers detailed accounts of his interactions and conversations with Ding Ling throughout her tumultuous experiences in 1940. In an entry dated August 19, 1940, Xiao Jun recounted an evening walk he took with Ding Ling to the cooperative at Women's University (*Nüda hezuoshe* 女大合作社). In the same diary entry, he recorded a story titled "A Woman Escaped from Humiliation" (*Yige cong wuru zhong taochu de nüren* 一个从侮辱中逃出的女人), which he intended to develop into a novel.

The story is about a female CCP member who is abducted and raped by the Japanese forces in Hebei before being sent to Taiyuan. Eventually, she reconnects with the Eighth Route Army in Taiyuan and becomes actively involved in their operations. The CCP later arranges her relocation to Yan'an for the treatment of a venereal disease she contracted during her ordeals.[55] It is most likely that Xiao Jun acquired knowledge of this story through Ding Ling. In Ding Ling's recollections concerning the primary source of inspiration for "When I Was in Xia Village," she recounted being informed by a friend who had returned from the front lines. The friend shared details about a female comrade affiliated with the CCP who had been raped by the Japanese and subsequently sought treatment upon returning to Yan'an.[56] This account prompted Ding Ling to contemplate writing a story about the woman's self-sacrifice for the revolution.

According to Xiao Jun's diary, by September 1940, Ding Ling's stress and anxiety due to the ongoing investigation had escalated to the point where she felt compelled to relinquish her CCP membership.[57] She claimed, however, that even if she were to sever ties with the party, her affection for the CCP would persist.[58] When discussing the ongoing investigation with Xiao Jun, Ding Ling displayed intense emotions, shedding tears on multiple occasions.[59] The burden of her distress temporarily eased upon the CCP's conclusion of the investigation on October 4, confirming her political loyalty.

In January 1941, Ding Ling wrote the short story titled "When I Was in Xia Village," which can be interpreted as a mirror on her own sufferings. The story begins with the narrator "I," an educated female CCP cadre who is dispatched to Xia village for rehabilitation by comrade Mo Yu 莫俞, whose name holds dual connotations signifying "no speaking" (*moyu* 莫语) and "not cured" (*moyu* 莫愈). This reassignment transpires due to "noise" (*caoza* 嘈杂) within the Political Department, despite "I" having already regained physical health.[60] The noise is an indication that the narrator might have made political errors, resulting in her being exiled by the party.

In contrast to the narrator "I" in Ma Feng's "Jinbao's Mother," who journeys to the village to lead the land reform and enlighten the local peasants, the narrator in "When I Was in Xia Village" remains detached from political movements in Xia village. Shortly after the narrator's arrival, Comrade Ma, a leader in Xia village, invites the narrator to address the masses. Surprisingly, despite being a CCP cadre, the narrator seems disinterested, reflecting, "I had seen many young men like him at the Front. When I first met them, I was always amazed. I felt that these youth, who were somewhat remote from me, were really changing fast."[61] "I" evades his request and steers the conversation in a different direction. In the original version of the story, Ding Ling included the detail that "upon encountering too many of them, [I] lost enthusiasm to pursue understanding of them."[62] During the Anti-Rightist Movement in 1957, based on his reading of the original version of the story, Lu Yaodong 陆耀东 criticizes the narrator for maintaining an emotionally distant stance from the masses. He attributes the problematic portrayal of the CCP cadre to inherent issues with Ding Ling's political consciousness.[63]

Ding Ling establishes a sense of distance and coldness at the story's outset. A female cadre named Agui 阿桂 from the Propaganda Department accompanies the narrator to Xia village during the depths of winter. Guided by Agui's introduction, "I" anticipates that the village will be "hot and noisy" (*renao* 热闹).[64] However, the narrator states, "When we entered it, not even a single child or dog was to be seen. The only movement was dry leaves twirling about lightly in the wind. They would fly a short distance, then drop to earth again."[65] Agui then expresses sorrow over an abandoned elementary school in the village, explaining, "A year and a half ago, this area was full of life. Every evening after supper, the comrades gathered here to play soccer or basketball."[66] The underlying implication is that the fervor and spirit of revolution are diminishing in the village.

Despite the cold and quiet atmosphere, the village resounds with fervent chatter and gossip, all focused on Zhenzhen, an eighteen-year-old local girl who had recently returned from the Japanese Army. Rumors concerning Zhenzhen had already reached the narrator's ears even before they met face-to-face. These rumors revolved around Zhenzhen's perceived lack of chastity. For instance: "I hear her disease has even taken her nose. That's because she was abused by the Jap devils."[67] Or, "That girl was always frivolous. You saw the way she used to roam around the streets."[68] Even, "It's said that she has slept with at least a hundred men. Humph! I've heard that she even became the wife of a Japanese officer. Such a shameful woman should not be allowed to return."[69] Unlike the "telling" of sexual abuse in Ding Ling's "New Faith," which empowers Granny Chen, the words spoken by the villagers serve to further harm Zhenzhen, adding an additional layer of pain to her plight.

In Ding Ling's depiction of the bleak environment in Xia village, "a very beautiful Catholic church that had escaped destruction" emerges as a striking element.[70] The story reveals that Zhenzhen had taken refuge in this village's Catholic church, where she sought sanctuary from an arranged marriage, aspiring to dedicate her life (*xianshen* 献身) to God by becoming a nun. Tragically, the church proved incapable of shielding her, leading to her capture by Japanese forces and her coercion into becoming a military sexual slave.

At the time, the transformation of churches in Yan'an served as a representation of changing ideologies. Ding Ling was familiar with the churches in the Yan'an area. During their journey toward the front lines, the Northwest Front Service Corps held its first public performance within a Catholic church located in Ganguyi 甘谷驿 in September 1937. Chen Ming provides a detailed account of how the Corps converted the religious space into a revolutionary sphere:

> The church here is splendid, adorned with numerous beautiful patterns painted on its light-yellow wall. The foreigners fled long ago, while the locals, including some Catholics, have diligently maintained the church. They left it unused, as if unsure of its purpose. Upon our arrival in Ganguyi, the locals accommodated us in the church. As we entered, their excitement matched that of Catholics worshiping Mary. . . . We tidied up the meeting place, hanging red curtains with pale white square characters. . . . Despite the encroaching darkness, the concert could not be halted. Although we hadn't arranged for illumination, our concerns were eased as some people lit the candle chandeliers in the church. . . . Amidst the candlelight, the crowd shouted: "One more, one more!" . . . Our people love the Chinese Communist Party. They refuse to be nationless slaves. We sang for them. . . . In this splendid hall, originally used to preach about the Heavenly Father and Mary, we sang of the hearts of hundreds of millions. We sang of our determination to emerge victorious in the anti-Japanese war.[71]

Instead of singing Catholic hymns in the church, the Corps performed songs like "The Internationale," "La Marseillaise," and local anti-Japanese small tunes.[72] The locals warmly embraced and enjoyed their performances. The Corps repurposed the church to spread the message of communism and national salvation.

The Northwest Front Service Corps concluded their one-year propagan-

Figure 46: The front of the Ganguyi Catholic Church. Source: Wang Li 王莉 and Yu Changfei 于长飞, *Shaanbei jindai jianzhu yanjiu* 陕北近代建筑研究 (Research on modern architecture in Northern Shaanxi), Xi'an: Xibei gongye daxue chubanshe, 2015, 29.

dist march with a presentation at the small Christian church in Yan'an, where they staged Lao She's war of resistance traditional operas. After studying at the Yan'an Marxism-Leninism Institute, Ding Ling was appointed deputy director of the Border Region Cultural Association (*bianqu wenxie* 边区文协), headquartered at the same small Christian church in Yan'an.[73] The most prominent church in Yan'an was the Qiao'ergou 桥儿沟 Catholic Church, which underwent transformation into the iconic Lu Xun Academy of Art and Literature (*Lu Xun yishu wenxueyuan* 鲁迅艺术文学院, hereafter referred to as "Luyi"), which served as the training ground for CCP artists.

Established in April 1938, Luyi found its new home in the Qiao'ergou Catholic Church on August 2, 1939.[74] The former Catholic church underwent a transformation into the cultural center in Yan'an. He Jingzhi 贺敬之 (1924–), who was raised in a Catholic family and attended a Catholic elementary school, arrived in Yan'an in July 1940 at the age of sixteen, enrolling as a student at Luyi.[75] A few months later, he wrote a poem dedicated to Luyi, in which he extolled revolutionary ideology for superseding religious belief. His poem reads:

In the journey of time,
Church
Quenched the flames,
Jesus,
Descended the steps . . .
Today,
"Lu Xun"
Guiding us,
We assemble under the flag.
Today, here,
Red star shines,
Hammer embraces sickle
Dancing.[76]

In the poem, Lu Xun emerges as the newfound savior. The red star, hammer, and sickle have taken the place of the cross. The new ideology had remodeled the architectural space of the church. As Wei Mingxing 危明星 points out, in the poem, "class space has replaced religious space."[77] In 1941, He Jingzhi wrote two additional poems, "In the Church" (*Zai jiaotang li* 在教堂里) and "Christmas" (*Shengdan jie* 圣诞节), which highlight class disparities within religious belief and illuminate how impoverished individuals find no refuge even in their faith in God.[78]

Chen Huangmei 陈荒煤 (1913–96), a faculty member at Luyi, wrote a short story titled "The Person Who Sings at the Church" (*Zai jiaotang gechang de ren* 在教堂歌唱的人, 1941), which portrays a young man whose experience mirrors that of He Jingzhi.[79] In the story, the narrator, "I," overhears a conversation between two young men in Yan'an. One of them admits that upon arriving at Luyi, he felt a sense of unease when seeing the Catholic church. He recounts growing up in a destitute family, under the influence of a devout Catholic grandmother who took him to Mass every week starting when he was around ten years old. He later joined the choir and attended the Catholic Church's elementary school. Due to financial constraints, he could not afford new clothing and was embarrassed to attend church in shabby attire. He therefore decided to abstain from accompanying his grandmother to Mass. Tragedy struck when his grandmother stumbled on her way to the church, passing away two months later. At the age of sixteen, he left home just two days after her demise, harboring a growing aversion to the church and its symbols. However, his perception of the church underwent a transformation upon witnessing the illumination of the red star and hearing the rendition of "The Internationale" at Luyi. This experience led him to view the Yan'an Catholic church as a symbol of the new era.[80]

Gu Yuan 古元 (1919–96), then a student at Luyi, crafted a compelling woodblock print titled *The Bible Era Is Gone* (*Shengjing shidai guoqu le* 圣经时代过去了, 1940, see fig. 47).[81] This work encapsulated the transformation of the Catholic Church in Yan'an. In an essay, Gu Yuan explains his motivation for creating the woodblock print of Luyi: "The transformation from a church disseminating religion into a revolutionary academy reflects the changes of the era. I wish to demonstrate this new phenomenon in my work."[82] As explained by Gu Yuan, the woodblock print portrays "a young student, engrossed in reading a book beneath the shelter of a tree outside the church, wearing a military cap and straw shoes while reclining on a toppled wooden chair. His attire and posture indicate that he is not reading a Bible but rather a Marxist book."[83] In the woodblock print, the two trees stand parallel to and surpass the height of the church. The presence of the young man at the center, relaxing and enjoying his reading, disperses the dominance of religious symbols. This suggests that an individual equipped with a new revolutionary ideology, rather than religious belief, serves as the impetus for transformative change. In this landscape woodblock print, the focal point is the new man of Yan'an.

In May 1940, the celebrated writer Mao Dun 茅盾 (1896–1981), accompanied by his family, journeyed from Xinjiang to Yan'an, spending four months at Luyi. During his stay in Yan'an, he wrote several essays praising the CCP's transformation of the remote and barren Yellow Earth Plateau through both culture and labor endeavors. In one of his essays, titled "Cultivate the Wasteland" (*Kaihuang* 开荒, 1941), he hails the dual cultivation in Yan'an, both of the land and culture.[84] In this respect, Luyi served as the center of cultural cultivation in Yan'an. In another essay by Mao Dun, titled "An Account of the Lu Xun Academy of Art and Literature" (*Ji Lu Xun yishu wenxueyuan* 记鲁迅艺术文学院, 1941), he references Gu Yuan's woodblock print *The Bible Era Is Gone*, and commends the transformed church as "a symbol of new power in China" (*Zhonghua minzu xinsheng liliang* 中华民族新生力量).[85]

The transformation of the Qiao'ergou Catholic Church is also depicted in

Figure 47: Gu Yuan, *Shengjing shidai guoqu le* 圣经时代过去了 (The Bible era is gone), 1940. Source: Gu Yuan, "Wo zai Yan'an chuangzuo de liangfu muke," 484. The original title of the work was *Xiri de jiaotang* 昔日的教堂 (Church in the past). Gu Yuan later changed the title to *The Bible Era Is Gone* following advice from Tian Lan 天兰. See Gu Yuan, "Wo zai Yan'an chuangzuo de liangfu muke," 484–85.

other woodblock prints, such as Li Qun's 力群 (1912–2012) *The Landscape of Lu Xun Academy of Art and Literature* (*Yan'an Luyi xiaojing* 延安鲁艺校景, 1941, see fig. 48) and Liu Mengtian's 刘蒙天 (1918–2008) *My Alma Mater Lu Xun Academy of Art and Literature* (*Wo de muxiao Yan'an Luyi* 我的母校延安鲁艺, 1945, see fig. 49). Li Qun's work depicts locals riding in a carriage and others strolling casually near the Catholic church, all while a soldier stands guard with a gun. The revolutionaries have taken the place of priests and nuns in the church. On December 2, 1992, Li Qun added a note on the woodblock print that "this is a church. However, in this church, we don't preach God, but promote Marxism. This is a church. However, in this church, we don't recite

Figure 48: Li Qun, *Yan'an Luyi xiaojing* 延安鲁艺校景 (The landscape of Lu Xun Academy of Art and Literature). Source: https://auction.artron.net/paimai-art5149490716, accessed August 15, 2023.

Figure 49: Liu Mengtian, *Wo de muxiao Yan'an Luyi* 我的母校延安鲁艺 (My Alma Mater Lu Xun Academy of Art and Literature), 1945. Source: *Yan'an wenyi dang'an*, vol. 53, 603.

the Bible, but teach 'The Communist Manifesto.' We are atheists, determined to dismantle the old world. However, I am grateful for this church because it's where I mastered the weapons of revolutionary thought."[86]

Liu Mengtian's work presents the church in a less solemn manner, as it appears flat rather than three-dimensional and lacks the inclusion of a cross. The small square in front of the church bustles with people gathered to watch a performance. Judging from the costumes and props of the actors and the band depicted in the woodblock print, it is highly probable that the performance is the *yangge* opera (*yangge ju* 秧歌剧) *Brother and Sister Reclaim the Wasteland* (*Xiongmei kaihuang* 兄妹开荒, 1943). This opera was written and performed by the students and staff of Luyi to promote the Great Production Movement. The piece clearly shows how the church has undergone a transformation from a space of devotion to God into a realm of politics.

During the Rectification Movement in 1944, Ding Ling wrote "Tian Baolin" 田保霖, a reportage promoting a labor hero in alignment with Mao Zedong's "Talks at the Yan'an Conference on Literature and Art." Mao Zedong praised the reportage, which alleviated some of the pressure on Ding Ling during the cadre investigation. Ding Ling's reportage is an account of how Tian Baolin transformed from a church worker into a model revolutionary worker leading a cooperative in the Border Region. Tian Baolin "had kowtowed to the priest for eight years, yet still couldn't have a full stomach. It was only the revolutionary regime that saved him."[87] In Ding Ling's experience and writings, the transformation of the church symbolizes a broader ideological shift. Her short story, "When I Was in Xia Village," depicts Zhenzhen's journey as she transitions from the Catholic Church to a reformed Yan'an and from her devotion to God to self-sacrifice, offering her body (*xianshen* 献身) for the CCP. This journey illustrates the personal impact of the significant ideological change occurring in Yan'an, a transformation mirrored in the narrative of the church itself.

From a Revolutionary Heroine to a Military Prostitute: *Criticism Again* in 1958

Following her disappointment with the village's Catholic church, Zhenzhen from "When I Was in Xia Village" anticipates traveling to Yan'an, which houses a reformed Catholic church serving as a sanctuary for oppressed individuals like Zhenzhen. Nonetheless, Ding Ling's narrative suggests a lack of optimism regarding Zhenzhen's future in Yan'an. The story concludes with the line "I **seemed** to see the bright future that Zhenzhen had before her."[88] In contrast to the bright new future Granny Chen envisions at the end of the "New Faith," the ending of "When I Was in Xia Village" remains uncertain and dim. David Der-Wei Wang contends, "Even if she could recover from her physical ailment, chances are that Zhenzhen would end up like her creator, Ding Ling, spending the rest of her life in a cycle of political illness and rehabilitation."[89]

Zhenzhen is a reflection of Ding Ling, encapsulating various facets of her life. In Ding Ling's short story, both the narrator and Zhenzhen embody different dimensions of her own experiences. During the composition of the story of Zhenzhen in Yan'an, Ding Ling grappled with questions concerning her own purity. Before arriving in Yan'an, Ding Ling made three attempts to leave

Nanjing. In May 1936, Ding Ling made her initial trip from Nanjing to Beijing under the pretense of visiting friends. During this journey, she engaged with Li Da, Wang Huiwu, Wang Yizhi, and Cao Jinghua 曹靖华 (1897–1987), as she sought pathways to reconnect with the CCP.[90] She returned to Nanjing after a two-week stay in Beijing. Around July, Feng Xuefeng, upon learning of Ding Ling's situation, arranged her visit to Shanghai. After enduring days of anticipation, Feng Xuefeng directed Ding Ling to return to Nanjing and explore opportunities to work in Shanghai publicly.[91] It was not until September that Ding Ling's third endeavor culminated in her journey to Shaanbei.[92]

In "When I Was in Xia Village," Zhenzhen tells the narrator, "I came back here twice before. Altogether, this is my third time. I was ordered to go on this last mission. There was no choice. I was familiar with the area, the work was important, and it was impossible to find anyone else in a short time. I won't be sent back anymore. They're going to treat my disease."[93] Similar to Ding Ling, Zhenzhen had returned to the village for the third time and was preparing to travel to Yan'an. They both endured considerable mental and physical hardships. In the story, Zhenzhen battles a venereal disease, having endured excruciating pain while delivering important intelligence to the CCP. In July 1935, Ding Ling was disrupted by a two-month hospitalization due to severe typhoid fever.[94] After her recovery, she reemerged by means of her writing and subsequent publication.

Ding Ling seemingly defends her own decision to stay alive in Nanjing through Zhenzhen's words in the short story:

> People are always like that, even if they find themselves in worse situations. They brace themselves and see it through. Can you just give up and die? Later, after I made contact with our own people, I became less afraid. As I watched the Jap devils suffer defeat in battle and the guerrillas take action on all sides as a result of the tricks I was playing, I felt better by the day. I felt that even though my life was hard, I could still manage. Somehow I had to find a way to survive, and if at all possible, to live a life that was meaningful.[95]

During the Anti-Rightist Movement, Zhang Guangnian 张光年 (1913–2002), writing under his pen name Hua Fu 华夫, argued that the phrase "can you just give up and die?" (*nandao sile bucheng* 难道死了不成) served as a justification a traitor might employ.[96] Therefore, Ding Ling's defense of Zhenzhen is tantamount to a traitor's defense. The narrator in the short story, who shares both the role of a writer and that of a female CCP cadre with Ding Ling, extends sympathy to Zhenzhen and regards her as a close friend, in contrast to her relationship with comrade Agui: "After Agui left the village, I grew even closer to Zhenzhen. It seemed that neither of us could be without the other. As soon as we were apart, we thought of each other. I like people who are enthusiastic and lively, who can be really happy or sad, and at the same time are straightforward and candid. Zhenzhen was just such a person."[97]

Ding Ling expressed her love for Zhenzhen in a self-critique written during the Yan'an Rectification Movement in late 1942. In early 1939, Ding Ling underwent a two-month hospitalization for hemorrhoid surgery at the Guaimao 拐茆 Hospital, located not far from Yan'an.[98] This occurrence mirrors the narrator's experience in "When I Was in Xia Village," wherein, during her recovery, the narrator was sent to a quiet village for rehabilitation. Drawing from her hospital stay, Ding Ling wrote a short story titled "In the Hospital," which was originally published in November 1941.[99] Alongside her essay "Thoughts on March 8," "In the Hospital" faced criticism during the Yan'an Rectification Movement for exposing the dark side of the CCP-controlled liberated areas.

In her 1942 self-critique of "In the Hospital," Ding Ling confessed to a tendency to infuse her personal experiences into the development of characters in her writings.[100] She compares Zhenzhen with Lu Ping, the female protagonist in "In the Hospital," stating, "I have told many people that I prefer Zhenzhen in 'When I Was in Xia Village.' Why this favoritism toward Zhenzhen? Because I invested a greater part of my emotions in Zhenzhen, who is lonelier, prouder, and more valiant compared to Lu Ping."[101] In this self-criticism, Ding Ling acknowledges that Lu Ping fails to represent the new women in Yan'an and does not contribute positively to the revolution.[102] "When I Was in Xia Village" was not the primary focus of critique directed at Ding Ling during the Yan'an Rectification Movement. Nonetheless, it inadvertently became a point of contention during the Anti-Rightist Movement. After Mao Zedong's "Talks at the Yan'an Conference on Literature and Art" and the Rectification Movement, Ding Ling became increasingly attuned to political sensitivity. Her reportage titled "Tian Baolin," written in 1944 and endorsed by Mao Zedong, marked her transition toward writing for the masses.

As discussed earlier, Ding Ling revisited "When I Was in Xia Village" in 1950, reworking it for republication and tempering its political message. For instance, in the 1950 version, the narrator says that "a female comrade from the Propaganda Department, who was apparently on a work assignment, went with me."[103] Ding Ling here deleted the phrase "I did not ride a horse (*wo meiyou qimaqu* 我没有骑马去)" from the beginning of the sentence.[104] In Ding Ling's "Thoughts on March 8," which faced criticism during the Rectification Movement, the term "those who ride horses" (*qima de* 骑马的) symbolizes the privileged class in Yan'an.[105] The essay serves as a satirical commentary on class and gender hierarchies in Yan'an. Also published in 1942, Mo Ye's 莫耶 short story "Liping's Worries" (*Liping de fannao* 丽萍的烦恼) similarly exposed hierarchies in the Border Region, sparking controversy and criticism. In the story, the privileged revolutionaries who ride horses are referred to as having "six legs" (*liutiao tui* 六条腿).[106]

The most significant revision Ding Ling made in "When I Was a Xia Village" is that, in the original version, Zhenzhen is referred to as a hero, whereas in the 1950 version, she is simply described as a great person.[107] Zhenzhen's changing classification plays a crucial role in comprehending the perception of female revolutionary sacrifice in modern China. During the war, Zhenzhen held the status of a hero working for national salvation. However, during the Anti-Rightist Movement, Zhenzhen faced condemnation, labeled as a woman who had compromised her chastity and integrity (*shijie* 失节). This situation exemplifies Louise Edwards's concept of "crisis femininity," where women may temporarily dismiss gender norms in the pursuit of national salvation.[108] Both Zhenzhen in "When I Was in Xia Village" and Widow Chen in Lao She's *The Loyalists and Martyrs* defy the constraints of female chastity during the national crisis. However, once the crisis abated, both Zhenzhen and her creator Ding Ling faced criticism for not adhering to gender norms.

In an interview, Chen Ming recalled that "after Ding Ling published 'When I Was in Xia Village' in Yan'an, Zhou Yang wrote a letter to her expressing that he had been moved to tears by reading it."[109] However, during the Anti-Rightist Movement, Zhou Yang's perspective on the short story underwent a drastic change. He criticized Ding Ling for "glorifying Zhenzhen, a military prostitute snatched by Japanese invaders, as a goddess."[110] Hua Fu also viewed Zhenzhen as a military prostitute rather than a hero. He posited that Zhenzhen appeared to harbor disdain for her fellow villagers rather than the Japanese invaders. He calls Zhenzhen "a shameless woman who has lost her national integrity, betrayed her homeland, and abandoned her people."[111] He questioned whether Zhenzhen could be trusted to work for the CCP in intelligence collection, deeming it a grave political task unsuitable for someone who is unreliable.[112] Hua Fu argued that Ding Ling's glorification of Zhenzhen was an attempt to justify her own house arrest in Nanjing.[113]

According to Lu Yaodong, Zhenzhen had abandoned patriotism, chastity, and morality, living subserviently like a prostitute with the Japanese military.[114] He contended that Zhenzhen's loss of chastity was unforgivable, even if she worked for the CCP during the revolution.[115] Wang Liaoying 王燎熒 (1921–95) criticized both "New Faith" and "When I Was in Xia Village" for allegedly glorifying the experiences of women who were raped by the Japanese, regarding Zhenzhen as a military prostitute.[116] These accusations against Zhenzhen during the Anti-Rightist Movement were likewise directed at Ding Ling herself.

The shifting perceptions of Zhenzhen, transitioning from a revolutionary hero to a military prostitute, highlight the intricate predicament faced by female revolutionaries. In a national context, women are called upon to offer both their lives and their bodies during times of crisis. However, in "When I Was in Xia Village," Ding Ling suggests that despite Zhenzhen's profound physical and emotional dedication to the revolution, her likelihood of being embraced within the official revolutionary discourse is slim due to the loss of her chastity. Patriarchal nationalism imposed upon women an unattainable dual responsibility: to sexually sacrifice for the nation during a crisis while preserving chastity once the crisis subsided. Women could face retroactive consequences for sexual acts that had previously contributed to the nation's benefit during a crisis, even long after the events had occurred.

To some extent, engaging as a sex spy constituted a type of thankless social martyrdom, wherein the martyr would employ her body to help the cause, yet her sacrifice would inevitably lead to a loss of status and a symbolic social "death," even in the absence of physical demise. Women's individual sufferings during the national crisis often went ignored. After the national crisis, women's bodily sufferings, especially instances of sexual assault, became a reminder of unspeakable personal and national shame. The invisible power holder Mo Yu 莫俞 in "When I Was in Xia Village," whose name alludes to "no speaking" (*moyu* 莫语), mirrors the challenges that women might encounter while attempting to verbalize their sufferings.

In the context of patriarchal nationalism, women like Zhenzhen find their only option is martyrdom. In 2003, "When I Was in Xia Village" was adapted into a film titled *Zhenzhen* 贞贞 (dir. Qiao Liang 乔梁). The plot interweaves Ding Ling's short story with elements from Lao She's *The Loyalists and Martyrs*. In this cinematic rendition, Zhenzhen returns to the village after being forced by the Japanese to be a military sexual slave for years. Rejected by her fellow villagers, Zhenzhen marries Zhu Laosi 朱老四, a leader of bandits opposing the Japanese forces. After Zhu Laosi is killed by the Japanese,

Zhenzhen returns to the "comfort station" (*wei'an suo* 慰安所) where she had suffered sexual abuse, and commits suicide by detonating it.[117] The issue is not whether Zhenzhen will be remembered as a revolutionary figure, but rather the form and depth of this recognition. The 2003 cinematic adaptation of Ding Ling's short story signifies a shift in perception, a moment in history where a woman like Zhenzhen could finally receive a more sympathetic appraisal for her heroic sacrifice. Regrettably, it is through Zhenzhen's demise that such recognition is afforded, an unfortunate consequence that circumvents further discourse about her chastity.

EXHIBITION V

Liu Hulan

Contested Memories of a Girl Martyr

In his essay titled "Ding Ling's Avenging Goddess: A Criticism of 'When I Was in Xia Village,'" Hua Fu asserts that Ding Ling employed praise and elevation of her character Zhenzhen as a means to justify her own political disloyalty. He further suggests that Liu Hulan should be revered as the exemplary female revolutionary martyr and enshrined in national memory rather than the unchaste Zhenzhen.[1] Liu Hulan 刘胡兰 (1932–47) was a young female revolutionary during the Chinese Civil War between the KMT and the CCP. She was born on October 8, 1932, into a middle peasant (*zhongnong* 中农) family in Yunzhouxi village, Wenshui County, Shanxi Province.[2] In 1938, the CCP established a branch in her hometown. Due to the villagers' enthusiastic participation in the communist revolution, Yunzhouxi village became known as "Little Yan'an" (*xiao Yan'an* 小延安).[3] Growing up in this revolutionary milieu, Liu Hulan was drawn to the CCP at a young age. In 1945, she attended a communist women's cadre training session, which strengthened her revolutionary beliefs.[4] Following the training session, Liu started actively supporting the Eighth Route Army on the front lines and took leadership roles in the local women's movement and the land reform movement. On January 12, 1947, KMT troops led by Yan Xishan 阎锡山 (1883–1960) ransacked Liu Hulan's village in search of communist sympathizers.[5] Liu was arrested and beheaded at a mere fourteen years of age.

This chapter analyzes both the state-sanctioned narratives and the reinterpretations of Liu Hulan's story to explore how the process of making Liu a martyr contributed to the formation of collective memory. It examines how the notions of gender and sexuality either support or problematize the ideologies endorsed by the state, as well as how contemporary rewritings of Liu's martyrdom elaborate on the national myth, thereby posing a challenge to state ideology and nationalism. It focuses on significant artifacts and repre-

Figure 50: The entrance of the Liu Hulan Memorial Hall. Source: online Liu Hulan Memorial Hall, https://www.ijvr360.com/vr/liuhulan, accessed September 30, 2023.

sentations associated with Liu Hulan's legacy, including the state inscriptions commemorating the martyr, the hay cutter used for executing Liu Hulan, various paintings and statues, the soldiers' shoes she crafted and collected to support the Eighth Route Army, and a preserved handkerchief—all of which are relics connected to the martyr. This comprehensive approach aims to trace the evolving narratives surrounding Liu Hulan, providing insights into the shifting ideological currents in modern and contemporary China. Ultimately, this book unveils the enduring complexity in the depiction of female martyrdom, highlighting how the concept of chastity continues to pose challenges in its portrayal, even in the context of the twenty-first century.

The State Inscriptions

To commemorate Liu Hulan, the youngest female martyr of the Chinese revolution, Mao Zedong wrote the famous words "A great life, a glorious death" (*sheng de weida, si de guangrong* 生的伟大，死的光荣) in March 1947.[6] Since then, Liu Hulan has become a household name in China. Following Mao's praise for Liu, the CCP launched a series of campaigns to promote her. Numerous propaganda posters, paintings, biographies, operas, films, and picture storybooks (*lianhuan hua* 连环画) were produced to publicize Liu's

Figure 51: Inscriptions by Mao Zedong, Deng Xiaoping, and Jiang Zemin on display at the Liu Hulan Memorial Hall. Source: online Liu Hulan Memorial Hall, https://www.ijvr360.com/vr/liuhulan, accessed September 30, 2023.

heroic martyrdom. In 1956, the Liu Hulan Memorial Hall was established in her hometown.

Liu Hulan was honored by generations of Chinese leaders, as evidenced by inscriptions by Mao Zedong, Deng Xiaoping 邓小平 (1904–97), and Jiang Zemin 江泽民 (1926–2022).[7] These inscriptions, with their varying emphases, demonstrate the shifting meanings and narratives of Liu's martyrdom. Mao Zedong's inscription in 1947, which he later recapitulated in 1957, highlights Liu Hulan's honorable death.[8] At that time, China had just ended the Anti-Japanese War in 1945, and the Chinese Civil War between the CCP and the KMT had erupted in 1946. In the historical context of the initial inscription, the CCP was striving for a military victory against the KMT. Emphasizing the glorious martyrdom of Liu Hulan fostered animosity toward the KMT, who executed a young girl, and provided an emotional incentive to bolster military morale. "Seeking revenge for Liu Hulan" (*wei Liu Hulan baochou* 为刘胡兰报仇) emerged as a major slogan during the 1948 liberation of Shanxi.[9]

The promotion of Liu Hulan's sacrifice persisted in the military campaigns of the 1950s. Examining rural women's narrations of China's revolutionary past, Gail Hershatter observes that "sallying forth to do battle with the landlords in the early 1950s, women imagined themselves as successors to the revolutionary heroines who risked their lives before 1949" such as Liu Hulan.[10] Women were motivated by the revolutionary spirit of Liu Hulan and ultimately "established a women's militia regiment."[11] Liu's image played a crucial role in promoting the people's militia (*minbing* 民兵) in the late 1950s. In 1958, concerned about the growing possibility of war with the United States after the Taiwan Straits Crisis, Mao Zedong initiated the "make everyone a soldier" (*quanmin jiebing* 全民皆兵) campaign that called for civilians to undergo military training.[12] Liu was presented as a model soldier during this campaign.[13] In December 1964, the Liu Hulan Militia Squad was formed in Shanxi to honor the girl martyr, with Liu's sister appointed as its leader.[14]

In 1962, Deng Xiaoping wrote the following inscription: "With her noble character and her spirit, Liu Hulan is forever an exemplar for Chinese youth to study" (*Liu Hulan de gaogui pinzhi, ta de jingshen mianmao, yongyuan shi Zhongguo qingnian he shaonian xuexi de bangyang* 刘胡兰的高贵品质，她的精神面貌，永远是中国青年和少年学习的榜样).[15] His inscription highlights the importance of moral education for Chinese youth. It emerged during a time when the first generation of Chinese born after the establishment of the PRC were coming of age, and the newly established socialist China needed role models—ideal socialist citizens—to guide the new generation.

Jiang Zemin's inscription was written in 1994, well after the 1978 economic reforms. It encouraged citizens to "Carry on the spirit of Liu Hulan, dedicating oneself to the realization of the Four Modernizations" (*fayang Hulan jingshen, xianshen sihua daye* 发扬胡兰精神，献身四化大业),[16] shifting emphasis toward China's modernization. Unlike Mao's inscription, Deng and Jiang's writings eliminated the idea of sacrificing one's life. Both Deng and Jiang incorporated the word *jingshen* 精神 (spirit) in their inscriptions, but their explanations of the spirit of Liu Hulan remain obscure.

All these inscriptions are now exhibited in the Liu Hulan Memorial Hall in Shanxi (see fig. 51). It is worth noting that another important political leader, Lin Biao 林彪 (1907–71), who was once considered Mao Zedong's successor, also wrote an inscription for Liu, "Long live the spirit of Liu Hulan" (*Liu Hulan jingshen wansui* 刘胡兰精神万岁), honoring the sacrifice of this female martyr. However, due to his political downfall, his words were removed from the Memorial Hall.[17] As Kirk Denton points out, "State narratives and official memory are not monolithic and unchanging; indeed, they adapt continuously to changing economic and political demands."[18] The meanings and the narratives of Liu Hulan's death are constantly evolving along with changes in political power. The changes in the narratives are also reflected in the literary details of her personal story, such as representations of the hay cutter that was used to execute her. This hay cutter will thus serve as a significant exhibition piece in this book's imaginary museum commemorating this female martyr.

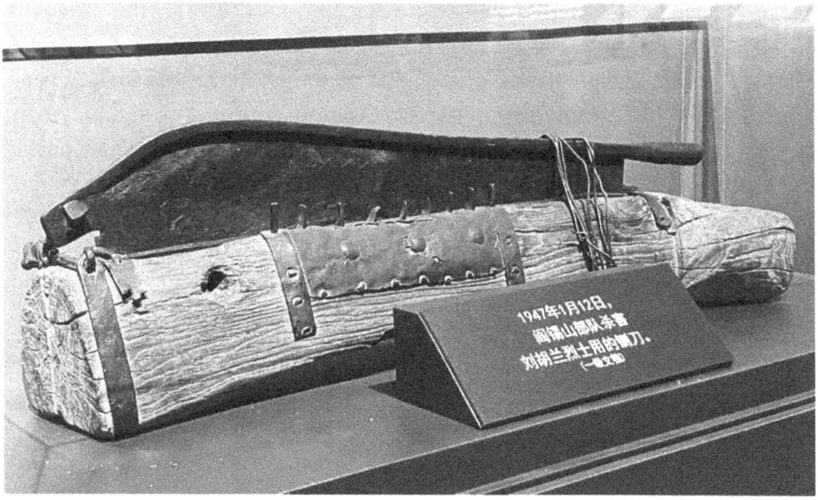

Figure 52: The hay cutter used for the execution of Liu Hulan. On display at the Museum of the Chinese Communist Party. Photo courtesy of Wu Xiyun.

The Hay Cutter

Shortly before the establishment of the PRC in 1949, the CCP initiated plans for constructing a museum aimed at preserving the cultural relics of the Chinese Communist revolution. The Museum of the Chinese Revolution was established as a commemorative site to educate visitors on the history of the communist revolution in China and to foster patriotic sentiment. In early 1949, the CCP launched nationwide campaigns to acquire revolutionary relics. Wang Yeqiu 王冶秋 (1909–87), who was in charge of collecting relics for the museum, discovered the gallows that was used to execute Li Dazhao, the pioneer of the Chinese communist revolution. The gallows was designated as "item no. 001" for display in the National Museum of China. Later that same year, Wang Yeqiu acquired the hay cutter that was used for the execution of Liu Hulan.[19]

Execution instruments used in the martyrdom of revolutionaries are a prominent feature in Chinese museums. They not only highlight the brutality of the revolution's enemies but also stand as visual representations of the heroism of the revolutionary martyrs as they confronted their imminent deaths. The display of such instruments evokes intense hatred toward the enemies, deep reverence for revolutionary martyrs, and a sense of horror. The execution of the young female martyr marks the climax of the story in literary representations of Liu Hulan. The manner in which to depict or stage the hay cutter and the execution of Liu Hulan remains a topic of constant debate.

The image of Liu Hulan as a heroic female martyr was initially established in a four-act spoken drama (*huaju* 话剧) titled *Liu Hulan*. In spring 1947, members of the Combat Dramatic Society (*Zhandou jushe* 战斗剧社), a military propaganda troupe founded by General He Long 贺龙 (1896–1969), came across the inspiring martyrdom account of Liu Hulan in *Jinsui Daily* (*Jinsui ribao* 晋绥日报). Moved by the story, Wei Feng 魏风 (1925–2010), a member of the troupe, interviewed Liu Hulan's family and local villagers in Wenshui County. Based on these interviews, the troupe collectively wrote the spoken drama within weeks. The performances of *Liu Hulan* were met with a positive reception. However, the play faced criticism for its lack of details regarding Liu's life.

Inspired by the remarkable success of the "new opera" (*xin geju* 新歌剧) *The White-Haired Girl* (*Baimao nü* 白毛女, 1945), the Combat Dramatic Society adapted the spoken drama *Liu Hulan* into a new opera in 1948. They introduced additional aspects of Liu's life into the narrative, such as her involvement in preparing food and crafting shoes for soldiers on the front lines, as well as her leadership in land reform and assistance to impoverished peasants. These additions aimed to render her final martyrdom more emotionally resonant and credible.[20]

Initially, the operatic version of Liu Hulan was primarily performed in rural China for the People's Liberation Army. Following the liberation of Beijing, the Combat Dramatic Society received an invitation from the Propaganda Department of the Central Committee of the CCP to present it for the first time in a major city in May 1949. The audiences in Beijing responded with fervor. The troupe performed for representatives attending the Chinese National Literature and Art Workers Conference (*zhonghua quanguo wenxue yishu gongzuozhe dahui* 中华全国文学艺术工作者大会) in July 1949.[21] After gathering feedback from Beijing audiences, the troupe implemented two significant modifications to the opera. First, the revised version accentuated the CCP's role as the guiding force. The other revision involved eliminating the stage direction "the blood is flying, the head falls on the ground" (*xianxue fenfei, rentou luodi* 鲜血纷飞，人头落地) from the hay cutter scene, as the performances were criticized for explicitly depicting violence and bloodshed on stage.[22]

The debate surrounding the hay cutter scene in *Liu Hulan* revolves around how the death of a communist revolutionary should be remembered after the wars. On January 21, 1950, *Guangming Daily* (*Guangming ribao* 光明日报) published Ai Wu's 艾芜 (1904–92) review of the opera *Liu Hulan*, lauding the incorporation of realistic details in the hay cutter scene presented on stage. Ai's review claims that "traditional Chinese opera resonates with the populace due to its meticulous attention to realistic details."[23] He provides an example of a lifelike hay cutter scene in a popular Chinese opera titled *The Execution of Chen Shimei* (*Zha mei an* 铡美案), which captivated audiences. Ai Wu argues that the inclusion of horrifying elements in William Shakespeare's plays, such as the wife's murder in *Othello* and the eye-gouging scene in *King Lear*, contributed to their success. He further suggests that the opera *Liu Hulan* achieves popularity for similar reasons.

Wang Zhaowen 王朝闻 (1909–2004) countered Ai Wu's praise for the execution scene in the opera *Liu Hulan* with an essay titled "A Tendency in Depicting Details in Theater" (*Xiju zhong xijie miaoxie de yizhong qingxiang* 戏剧中细节描写的一种倾向), published in *Wenyi bao*, the prominent media outlet for conveying the CCP's official views on art and literature. In his essay, Wang argues that the staging of beheading scenes was a tactic historically employed by the ruling class to instill fear among the masses in old China. He contends that art and literature in the new socialist China should focus on presenting the unyielding spirit of the heroes. According to him, the explicit depiction of Liu Hulan's beheading is unnecessary and might divert the audience's attention from the essence of the revolutionary martyr.[24] Wang Zhaowen observes that during a performance of the opera for the representatives of the Chinese National Literature and Art Workers Conference, the hay cutter scene prompted a female audience member seated beside him to scream. He points out that the realistic portrayal of beheading the martyr serves to frighten the audience rather than to praise Liu Hulan.

The debate regarding whether to depict the details of Liu Hulan's execution on stage was part of a broader discussion concerning the portrayal of socialist heroes during the 1950s. Literary and artistic representations of socialist heroes were crucial to socialist realism and play an important role in the formation of new socialist ideology and subjects. In his report on the 1949 Chinese National Literature and Art Workers Conference, Zhou Yang, the vice minister of culture and propaganda, underlined the importance of creating new socialist heroes in art and literature.[25] In accordance with the CCP's literary directives, *Wenyi bao* held several rounds of discussions on how to portray heroes in the newly established socialist China. These discussions revolved around topics such as whether to address the flaws of socialist heroes, methods to make the socialist heroes more representative (*dianxing* 典型) and exemplary for others to emulate, and approaches to depicting a socialist hero's death.

In the spring of 1950, *Wenyi bao* published a special column featuring a series of essays that commented on the debates between Ai Wu and Wang Zhaowen regarding how to stage Liu Hulan's death in the opera. Wang Zhaowen's essay titled "How to Portray the Death of a Martyr" (*Zuopin zhong ruhe chuli yingxiong jiuyi de qingjie* 作品中如何处理英雄就义的情节) in the special column expands on his previous comments in "A Tendency in Depicting Details in Theater," arguing that the death of a socialist martyr should be depicted in a sublime and optimistic manner, devoid of horrific details. He applauds the artistic representation of the heroic martyrdom of a Soviet soldier in the 1947 film *Private Aleksandr Matrosov*, in which the soldier uses his body to block machine-gun bullets. Rather than showing the soldier's bullet-riddled body, a sculpture of him appears on screen, displaying a sublime image of the martyr.[26]

The authors of the other three essays hold diverse perspectives on how to depict the execution of Liu Hulan, but all of them oppose Ai Wu's advocacy of staging the actual killing.[27] Liu Jin 刘金 and Li Guojing 李国经 argue that Liu Hulan's martyrdom reaches its pinnacle when she lies down on the hay cutter, and the story should conclude there. Zhong Dianfei 钟惦棐 (1919–87) points out that the emphasis in depicting martyrdom should be on the spirit of Liu Hulan rather than her bloody head. He Qifang 何其芳 (1912–77) contends that the hay cutter scene is necessary for demonstrating the cruelty of the war, but it could be staged in a subtle manner through the use of stage-design techniques.

By removing the stage directions that depicted "the blood is flying, the head falls on the ground," the 1952 version of the opera *Liu Hulan* achieved the aspiration to create idealized socialist heroes following the establishment of the PRC. The transformation from the 1948 version of the opera to the 1952 version reflects the CCP's shifting focus in forming collective memory. During the Chinese Civil War, the portrayal of the brutal execution of Liu Hulan on stage was effective in boosting military morale, generating public sympathy, and encouraging hatred against the CCP's rivals. As Wei Feng, the principal playwright of the production, observed, "During each performance, when the scene of Liu Hulan's heroic death took place, the entire audience cried uncontrollably. The sound of their crying drowned out the voices of the actors on stage. Some soldiers hurled stones at the actors portraying enemies on stage. Some even attempted to rush onto the stage with loaded guns to kill 'Big Beard,'"[28] the one who ordered Liu Hulan's execution.

Upon the soldiers' request, the Combat Dramatic Society later incorporated a scene into the opera that depicted the execution of "Big Beard" in revenge for Liu's death.[29] The CCP troops organized "Get Revenge for Liu Hulan Groups" (*wei Liu Hulan baochou xiaozu* 为刘胡兰报仇小组). The slogan "Seeking revenge for Liu Hulan" inspired the commandos to push forward and gain victory during the battle for the liberation of Wenshui County.[30] Preparing for the Battle of Libei (*Libei zhanyi* 荔北战役) in 1948, General Peng Dehuai 彭德怀 (1898–1974) ordered the Combat Dramatic Society to perform the opera *Liu Hulan* for the legendary 359th Brigade led by Wang Zhen 王震 (1908–93) before each battle. As Wang Zhen and his soldiers charged into the battle, they shouted, "Seeking revenge for Liu Hulan."[31] The revenge narrative in *Liu Hulan* fueled the CCP's military victories.

The theme of vengeance was prevalent in art and literature during the Yan'an era. Focusing on "class bitterness" (*jieji ku* 阶级苦) and "national grievance" (*minzu hen* 民族恨), both the Qinqiang opera *Hatred of Blood and Tears* (*Xuelei chou* 血泪仇, 1943) and the new opera *The White Haired Girl* (*Baimao nü* 白毛女, 1945) were sensations in Yan'an. The song "Hatred Is Like a Lofty Mountain, Resentment Is Like the Sea" (*hen si gaoshan chou si hai* 恨似高山仇似海) from *The White Haired Girl* became a classic. The themes of resentment and revenge persisted in the opera *Liu Hulan*. Revenge narratives proved compelling during the brutality of wartime and the land reform period, as they fueled animosity against the CCP's adversaries. Such narratives corresponded to the speaking bitterness (*suku* 诉苦) campaign launched during the land reform, encouraging peasants to openly voice their grievances, fostering hatred toward landlords responsible for their suffering. *Suku* advocated for the idea of seeking vengeance and resorting to violence when confronting opponents. It also served as a bonding mechanism for peasant communities, contributing to the formation of peasant class identity and the creation of collective memory.

In 1950, the opera *Liu Hulan* debuted in Yuncheng 运城 County, Shanxi Province, and became an instant hit. One of the executioners of Liu Hulan, Zhang Quanbao 张全宝, the aforementioned "Big Beard," had gone into hiding in Yuncheng. Fearing that he would be recognized, he attended the opera in disguise. Zhang was emotionally undone by the audience's animosity toward the performer playing Big Beard. He was captured in 1951, put on public trial, and executed.[32] In the same year, Liu Hulan's stepmother, Hu Wenxiu 胡文秀, sent her two daughters and two sons to join the army to fight in the Korean War. She made an appeal to all Chinese mothers in an open letter, urging them to send their children to the front lines. In the letter, she emphasizes the revenge narrative and calls upon mothers "to remember the blood debts owed to us by imperialists and the counterrevolutionaries. For our murdered children and to ensure that our children will no longer be harmed, please enthusiastically sign and vote on the Declaration on Defending World Peace (*Baowei shijie heping gongyue* 保卫世界和平公约), and actively participate in the Korean War."[33] Following the dissemination of the letter by the Xinhua News Agency, a nationwide movement in support of Hu Wenxiu arose. As Chang-tai Hung notes, the commemorations of revolutionary martyrs were not easily imposed through top-down decrees because "the issue of violent loss of life was also an intensely private matter among the martyrs' loved ones."[34] Through the public execution of Zhang Quanbao and the mobilization of the mother of a revolutionary martyr, the CCP successfully channeled private emotions into public memories.

The hay cutter scene in the opera *Liu Hulan* promoted hatred of the CCP's enemies at an early stage in the creation of the image of the girl martyr. Liu Hulan's extraordinary martyrdom and the extreme violence of her death were normalized, and her story served the same purpose as any other *suku* narrative: uniting the community and contributing to the formation of national memory based on the concept of vengeance.[35] In the 1950s, following the end of the Anti-Japanese War and the Chinese Civil War, the target audience of the opera *Liu Hulan* shifted from troops to new socialist citizens. During this period, the emphasis of the propaganda turned away from instilling hatred and toward establishing individuals such as Liu Hulan as heroic role models. As demonstrated in the *Wenyi bao* debate, the explicit details of a martyr's execution were deemed inappropriate for creating a sublime image of Liu Hulan in the national memory.

After engaging in the debates on how to stage the death of Liu Hulan, Wang Zhaowen, who was not only an accomplished art theorist but also a skilled sculptor, decided to apply his theories to his artistic endeavors. In 1951, he created a sculpture of Liu Hulan for the Museum of the Chinese Revolution, which became a masterpiece of socialist art and the official image of Liu. In 1954, Feng Fasi 冯法祀 (1914–2009), a renowned painter and Wang Zhaowen's colleague at the Central Academy of Fine Arts, began drafting

Figure 53: Photo of Zhu De with Konstantin Maksimov and his students in front of Feng Fasi's oil painting *The Heroic Death of Liu Hulan*. Source: Jin Shangyi and Wang Chengyi, "Huainian women de laoshi K.M. Maksimov" 怀念我们的老师K. M. 马克西莫夫 (Commemorating our teacher K.M. Maksimov), *Meishu* 7 (1994): 58.

an oil painting of Liu Hulan. It took Feng three years and numerous drafts to complete the work in 1957. During these three years, Feng attended the Soviet painter Konstantin Maksimov's class in Beijing, which introduced socialist realism into Chinese oil painting. At the class graduation exhibition, Feng Fasi's oil painting titled *The Heroic Death of Liu Hulan* (*Liu Hulan jiuyi* 刘胡兰就义) commanded center stage. General Zhu De 朱德 (1886–1976) attended the exhibition and took an iconic photo with Maksimov and his students, all of whom went on to become prominent Chinese artists, in front of Feng's painting (see fig. 53).[36] *The Heroic Death of Liu Hulan* is considered a classic socialist-realist painting.

Over the three-year span of completing the painting of Liu Hulan, Feng Fasi had drawn several sketches and colored drafts. From the initial color draft in 1954 to the final version in 1957, he made significant changes. One notable change was the representation of the hay cutter. In order to capture her heroic martyrdom in his painting, Feng Fasi traveled to Liu Hulan's hometown during the winter of 1954. He encountered a snowstorm upon his arrival. Inspired by Vasily Surikov's oil painting *The Boyarin Morozova* (1887), Feng incorporated snowy scenery into his painting to evoke a sublime atmosphere, despite the fact that the execution of Liu Hulan did not take place in snow.[37] While in Wenshui, Feng interviewed Liu Hulan's stepmother Hu Wenxiu, as well as the families of the other six martyrs who were executed alongside Liu.[38] What struck him the most were the villagers' accounts of blood flowing like a river at the execution site. "They [the villagers] believed everything appeared red because they had witnessed so much blood. When they got home, they were even afraid to lift the covers of their pots, fearing that they were filled with blood."[39] This horrifying description of the gruesome execution scene recalls the stage directions "the blood is flying, the head falls on the ground" from the original version of the opera *Liu Hulan*.

The hay cutter is depicted as a murderous machine with blood flowing all over it in Feng Fasi's 1954 color draft of *The Heroic Death of Liu Hulan* (see fig. 54). Scarlet blood spots are spread across the snow-covered ground, creating an unsettling contrast with the white snow and Liu Hulan's white blouse. However, in the final 1957 version of the painting, Liu Hulan wears a black shirt, the hay cutter remains but is without blood, and the snow is pure white and free of stains (see fig. 55). The 1957 version shifts the emphasis to the sublimity of the martyrdom, possibly influenced by the principles of socialist realism that Feng had learned in Maksimov's oil-painting class and the discussion on how to stage Li Hulan's death led by his colleague Wang Zhaowen.

The hay cutter scene was later reinterpreted in 2008 by contemporary Chinese artist Li Zhanyang 李占洋 in his scene sculpture titled *Liu Hulan* (see figs. 56 and 57). The composition of the sculpture is reminiscent of Feng Fasi's painting *The Heroic Death of Liu Hulan*.[40] However, Li Zhanyang did not follow the socialist-realist tradition, nor did he heed the directives regarding depictions of violence. He questioned the principles of socialist realism by reintroducing "the blood is flying, the head falls on the ground" to the scene in his sculpture. Unlike the socialist artists who prefer to portray heroic characters' moments before execution to avoid presenting gruesome images, Li Zhanyang reduces Liu Hulan's heroic martyrdom to a horrific murder scene.

Liu Hulan is conventionally depicted with her head held high, showcasing her fearless spirit. However, Li's sculpture portrays Liu with her head chopped off. Despite the sculpture's title being *Liu Hulan*, Li's work diminishes the importance of the heroine in this large artwork. While Liu remains

Figure 54: Feng Fasi, colored draft of *The Heroic Death of Liu Hulan*, 1954. Source: *Yi wei rensheng: Ershi shiji Zhongguo youhua mingjia Feng Fasi* 艺为人生：二十世纪中国油画名家冯法祀 (Arts for life: Twentieth-century Chinese oil painting master Feng Fasi), edited by Fan Di'an 范迪安, Hefei: Anhui meishu chubanshe, 2014, 186.

at the center of the scene, she has been reduced to meat, a mere material body on the chopping block. She is eclipsed by the multitude of people encircling her from every possible angle, scrutinizing her slaughter. In the sculpture, crowded houses dominate most of the space, creating an oppressive ambiance. The prevailing color scheme of the sculpture is gray, accentuating the somber atmosphere while drawing attention to the red hue of Liu's blood. By adopting an omniscient yet nonjudgmental viewpoint, Li Zhanyang's sculpture eliminates the sublimity of Liu Hulan's death.

In a conversation between Li Zhanyang and Dai Zhuoqun 戴卓群, Li related his artistic re-creation of Liu Hulan's martyrdom to a childhood experience of witnessing a public execution of a criminal.[41] To him, the two events are indistinguishable in terms of their shocking effects. Whether that of a revolutionary hero or a criminal, the deaths were equally bloody and terrifying. Growing up watching films and plays about Liu Hulan, Li never considered

Figure 55: Feng Fasi, part of *The Heroic Death of Liu Hulan*, 1957. Source: *Feng Fasi huaxuan* 冯法祀画选 (Selected paintings of Feng Fasi), Beijing: Renmin meishu chubanshe, 1981, 18.

the socialist depictions of Liu's martyrdom to be realistic. His artwork was inspired by this concern. He wrote a short story titled "Dead Still" (*Siji* 死寂), which detailed the execution of Liu Hulan: "The executioner gripped the hay cutter and severed Liu Hulan's head as if it were a stack of paper. The head rolled strangely on the ground, and blood spurted forth like a spring, turning the snow-covered white ground scarlet."[42]

The gruesome details in Li's fiction were later visualized in his sculpture,

Figure 56: Li Zhanyang, *Liu Hulan*, 2008. Source: "Dai Zhuoqun duihua Li Zhanyang" 戴卓群对话李占洋 (The conversation between Dai Zhuoqun and Li Zhanyang), *Dongfang yishu* 19 (2010): 56.

contradicting Wang Zhaowen's argument against providing explicit accounts of the executions of socialist martyrs. Another childhood memory that Li has mentioned in interviews and writings involves witnessing a butcher slaughter a pig. He vividly recalled details such as the pig's squeals and the blood flowing like a waterfall. This memory, according to Li, shaped his understanding of realism. He claimed that his sculptures are antimonumental, and that he aimed to shift away from socialist realism toward a more genuine form of realism.[43] Li Zhanyang incorporated his personal memories of killing and execution into his sculpture of Liu Hulan, which challenged national memory.

The literary and artistic representations of the hay cutter scene in Liu Hulan's martyrdom reflect ideological shifts in the formation of national memory. The original depiction of the brutal execution of the female martyr served the purpose of generating hatred toward the CCP's opponents and igniting military campaigns. After the end of the wars, the emphasis on commemorating the revolutionary martyr shifted to establishing heroic images in order to educate the new socialist citizens. The debates in *Wenyi bao*, Wang Zhaowen's sculpture, and Feng Fasi's painting laid the groundwork for the socialist-realist tradition of creating socialist heroes. Li Zhanyang's contemporary appropriation of the hay cutter scene resisted national memory and dismissed the monumentality of Liu Hulan's heroic death by incorporating the artist's personal memory.

Among the various artistic representations of Liu Hulan, Wang Zhaowen's sculpture stands as a significant cornerstone in shaping the monumental and sublime image of this female martyr. However, as the statues of Liu Hulan proliferated, an intriguing gender issue emerged. The following sections explore this multifaceted gender issue that surfaces in the commemoration

Figure 57: Part of the Li Zhanyang's *Liu Hulan*, 2008. Source: "Dai Zhuoqun duihua Li Zhanyang," 60.

of female revolutionary martyrdom. This examination involves an analysis of the statues, as well as a study of the literary representations of broken shoes (*poxie* 破鞋) and handkerchiefs found in the narratives of Liu Hulan.

The Statues

In 1958, the opera *Liu Hulan* was adapted into a Yu opera (*Yuju* 豫剧), with the hay cutter scene reinterpreted creatively. In the Yu opera version of *Liu Hulan*, when confronted with the hay cutter, Liu fearlessly steps on it and proceeds to sing an ode in praise of the CCP (see fig. 58).[44] While this portrayal deviates from historical accuracy, it serves to accentuate and romanticize Liu Hulan's heroic martyrdom. The act of "stepping on the hay cutter" aligns with the "two-in-one" (*liang jiehe* 两结合) principle of socialist literature, which combines revolutionary realism and revolutionary romanticism.[45] It is exemplifies the concept of *liangxiang* 亮相 (striking a pose) in Chinese opera: capturing a chosen moment in still life that best encapsulates the personality and spirit of the character in a performance.[46] In her analysis of the *liangxiang*

Figure 58: The scene of Liu Hulan stepping on the hay cutter in the Yu opera. Photo by Tian Tingxue 田庭雪. Source: Zhang Zhen 张真, "Ji Liu Hulan cai zhadao" 记刘胡兰踩铡刀 (Liu Hulan's act of stepping on the hay cutter), *Zhongguo xiju* 中国戏剧 (Chinese theater) 14 (1958): 19.

technique in Chinese revolutionary operas, Laurence Coderre observes that "at their most emblematic, revolutionary heroes are completely motionless, temporarily transposed into the realm of statuary."[47] The operatic technique of *liangxiang* enables a fleeting heroic moment to linger on stage, leaving a profound and enduring impression on the audience. It essentially transforms the character into a living statue. In the stage directions of the Yu opera, a statue of Liu Hulan stepping on the hay cutter is erected prominently in front of the village temple.[48] It was not the first time a statue of Liu Hulan had been featured on stage. In the 1955 opera version of *Liu Hulan*, her statue was placed on stage at the end of the performance (see fig. 59). In 1965, this concept was further reinforced when a statue of Liu Hulan made its appearance on stage in the new spoken drama version of *Liu Hulan* (see fig. 60).[49]

Numerous statues of Liu Hulan were constructed following her martyrdom. The most famous of these was created by Wang Zhaowen in 1951, and it became the official image of the girl martyr (see fig. 61).[50] The statues used in stage performances of Liu Hulan's story were reproductions of Wang Zhaowen's artwork. The statue displayed at the Liu Hulan Memorial Hall in Shanxi is an enlarged version of Wang's original masterpiece. Wang Zhaowen's sculpture captures the moment when Liu bravely faced her impending

Figure 59: The statue of Liu Hulan on stage in the 1955 opera. Source: Yu Cun 于村, Hai Xiao 海啸, Lu Su 卢肃, and Chen Zi 陈紫, *Liu Hulan: Er'mu jiuchang geju* 刘胡兰:二幕九场歌剧 (Liu Hulan: Two acts nine scenes opera), Beijing: Zuojia chubanshe, 1955, photo, 8.

Figure 60: On March 19, 1965, Zhou Enlai (sixth from the left in the front) watched the spoken drama *Liu Hulan* performed by Shanxi People's Drama Troupe and took a photo with the performers after the performance. The statue of Liu Hulan that appeared on stage was also included in the photo. Photo by Du Xiuxian 杜修贤. Source: "Zhou zongli deng guankan huaju Liu Hulan" 周总理等观看话剧《刘胡兰》(Premier Zhou and others watched the spoken drama *Liu Hulan*), *Renmin ribao*, March 21, 1965.

death. Inspired by a bronze *jue* (*tongjue* 铜爵), a ritual tripod vessel, he had seen at the Tsinghua University Art Museum, Wang created a bodily image in which Liu Hulan is slightly leaning forward with her feet forming a T shape, resembling the *jue*, providing full support for the weight of the body.[51] Liu's *jue*-like standing posture in the sculpture emphasizes both her firmness and fearlessness when facing death. The initial draft of Wang Zhaowen's sculpture of Liu Hulan depicted her bound before her execution, but after careful consideration, he ultimately decided not to present Liu in this restrained manner.[52] This adjustment represented a reinterpretation of the death of a socialist hero that both adhered to the principles of socialist realism and yet also corresponded to Wang's advice in *Wenyi bao*, which discouraged detailed depictions of the sufferings endured by socialist martyrs.

Wang's sculpture of Liu Hulan, characterized by its clean lines and solid structure, conveys a sublime image of the girl martyr. The artwork features Liu Hulan with her signature short hair and clenched fists, presenting her in a nearly androgynous form. She does not appear as a typical teenage girl, and her age remains ambiguous. Through analysis of the aesthetics of the sublime during the Mao era, Wang Ban notes, "What is to be sublimated can well be placed under the traditional rubric 'the feminine.' The lofty apex of sublimation, on the other hand, is commonly assumed to be the 'masculine' domain—the building of a nation, revolution, vigorous endeavors, and cultural achievements. In these grand enterprises, Chinese women are either systematically written off or viewed as subjected to masculinization."[53] Wang Zhaowen's statue, by presenting Liu Hulan in a sexless manner, serves as an embodiment of the CCP's vision for representing the bodies of female socialist heroes.

The representation of the bodies of female revolutionary heroes has constantly sparked controversies. In 1955, the Department of Sculpture at the Central Academy of Fine Arts initiated a counterformalism movement, criticizing the tendency to prioritize aesthetics over realism in sculptures. For instance, a sculpture titled *A Patriotic Overseas Chinese Woman* (*Huaqiao nü aiguo qingnian* 华侨女爱国青年) faced criticism for its exaggerated portrayal of the nude female body, particularly emphasizing the breasts.[54] The issue of how to depict the female body resurfaced in 2004 when sculptors from the Central Academy of Fine Arts conducted a field trip to Yimeng Mountain Area (*Yimeng shanqu* 沂蒙山区), the birthplace of the renowned revolutionary heroine Hongsao 红嫂, who famously fed a seriously wounded People's Liberation Army soldier with her breast milk to save his life. However, local residents vehemently opposed the idea of exposing Hongsao's breasts in her sculpture. In order to avoid controversy, the sculptors decided not to depict the iconic scene of Hongsao feeding the soldier with her breast milk. Instead, they chose to portray the moment when she unbuttons her shirt.[55]

In 2003, contemporary Chinese artist Yang Tao 杨韬 re-created Wang Zhaowen's sculpture of Liu Hulan as part of a sculpture series on revolutionary heroes, which was displayed in his "Presocialism" (*qian shehuizhuyi* 前社会主义) exhibition in Beijing in 2006.[56] In his sculpture of Liu Hulan, Yang Tao portrays the martyr's body as it was bound before her execution. This presentation evokes sadomasochistic bondage, making it drastically different from orthodox socialist representations of Liu's body. The girl martyr is overtly sexualized and objectified in Yang Tao's sculpture. Compared to the clean lines and solid structure in Wang Zhaowen's sculpture of Liu Hulan, Yang's version exaggerates her feminine features. Yang purposefully sculpts the head and body of the sculpture disproportionately, making the heroine appear ludicrous. He also deconstructs the solid structure of Wang's version, signaling that Liu is not the typical disciplined revolutionary. As Huang Xin points out, with "[her] pouting mouth, prominent cheeks, and protruding breasts,"[57] the sublime image of Liu Hulan disappears, and she is reduced to nothing more than a sexual object.

Although Liu Hulan is oversexualized in Yang's version, the overall image is disturbing rather than sexually attractive. By emphasizing the materiality of the female body, Yang Tao diminishes Liu Hulan's spirituality as a female martyr. His controversial representation of Liu Hulan is intended to disrupt the prevailing grand narrative and to unsettle the viewer. The martyr's femininity becomes a specific target in the artist's attempt to ridicule socialist narratives. In Yang Tao's portrayal, Liu Hulan is grotesquely sexualized and diminished. Her unruly breasts and cheeks, as well as her proud stance, are made contemptible by her exaggerated proportions.

Contemporary artists frequently use flesh—specifically female sexuality and materiality—to complicate and ultimately challenge official discourse. In the case of Liu Hulan, the approach to deflating female martyrdom involves exaggerating female sexuality and the material body. The female body can be symbolized and deployed as a site of national production. The bodies of revolutionary women are typically presented in a highly disciplined manner in order to embody the purity of the nation. Louise Edwards argues that in socialist China, "female chastity became a synecdoche for good governance—social stability had a sexed nature. The CCP emerges as a defender of female chastity and purity of patriotic intent."[58]

Figure 61: Wang Zhaowen, *Liu Hulan*, 1951. Source: Sun Zhenhua 孙振华, "Zhongguo dangdai juxiang diaosu gaiguan" 中国当代具象雕塑概观 (An overview of contemporary Chinese figurative sculptures), in *Qinghua meishu* 清华美术 (Tsinghua arts), vol. 15, edited by Zhang Gan 张敢, Beijing: Qinghua daxue chubanshe, 2013, 10. For a detailed process of the making of the sculpture, see Jian Ping, *Wang Zhaowen zhuan*, 102–4.

To resist the dominant ideology, postsocialist artists have chosen to present sensuous and grotesque bodies in the Bahktinian mode, in which "the artistic logic of the grotesque image ignores the closed, smooth, and impenetrable surface of the body and retains only its excrescences (sprouts, buds) and orifices, only that which leads beyond the body's limited space or into the body's depths."[59] In rejecting iconic representations of national martyrs, this boundless and transgressive grotesque body becomes a physical site of resistance to national memory. While the crucial topic of misogyny in contemporary art extends well beyond the scope of this book, it is important to note in passing that here antisocialist protest art reverts to misogynistic habits when making a mockery of a female socialist martyr. Women become the collateral damage of the counter-official-artist's ideological battle.[60]

Another contemporary Chinese artist, Yu Fan 于凡, created *Liu Hulan's Sacrifice* (*Liu Hulan de xisheng* 刘胡兰的牺牲, 2009), a statue of Liu Hulan that also addresses the gender issue in commemorating the female martyr (see fig. 62). Stone, especially marble, or bronze are the most common materials used by the state to represent martyrs. These materials imbue history and national memory with a sense of stability and gravity. Such statues symbolize both the eternal spirit of the martyr as well as of the state's enduring commemoration. In contrast, Yu Fan employs fiberglass as a medium for his artwork. In comparison to the heaviness of stone or bronze, his choice of fiberglass is distinctive as it is much lighter and has a more sensual feel. The use of fiberglass also eliminates the evocation of history and monumentality inherent in traditional materials. In Yu Fan's work, Liu Hulan has descended from her pedestal to become an ordinary and vulnerable woman. The clean, bright, flawless surface of the fiberglass stands in stark contrast to the horror of Liu Hulan's bloody death.

Sex and violence are two major themes in Yu Fan's sculpture of Liu Hulan. In this artwork, Liu Hulan is depicted lying in a pool of blood, with a shoe off to the side. Her beauty is overshadowed by the deep cut in her throat. Exposing a woman's foot carries strong sexual overtones in Chinese culture. Analyzing female images in socialist literature, Meng Yue pointed out that the state's political discourse "turned woman into an agent politicizing desire, love, and family relations by delimiting and repressing sexuality, self, and all private emotion."[61] Yu Fan, on the other hand, evokes the private emotions of Liu Hulan by portraying her as an attractive yet vulnerable woman who was the victim of a brutal murder rather than a willing martyr.

Yu Fan explained his creation of *Liu Hulan's Sacrifice* in an interview: "There have been countless sculptures of Liu Hulan made since the establishment of the PRC. Artists of the previous generation created the classical image of her clenching her fists and holding her head up high. These sculptures, in my opinion, do not reflect the reality. I was fascinated by the concept of 'reality.' Why do we want to avoid facing reality? Why can't we depict reality?"[62] Yu Fan's sculpture questions socialist realism by reintroducing violence and sexuality. The shoes in his artwork, which carry strong sexual implications, are crucial in addressing the concerns of chastity in commemorating a female martyr.

Figure 62: Yu Fan, *Liu Hulan de xisheng* 刘胡兰的牺牲 (Liu Hulan's sacrifice, 2009). Source: Yu Fan, *Zhishang: Yu Fan zuopin* 置上:于凡作品 (On high: Works of Yu Fan), Beijing: Renmin meishu chubanshe, 2013, 119.

The Broken Shoes

Making soldiers' shoes (*zuo junxie* 做军鞋) for frontline soldiers was one of the Four Mobilizations (*sida dongyuan* 四大动员) in the Northwest Shanxi Revolutionary Base Area (*Jin xibei geming genjudi* 晋西北革命根据地) during the 1940s.[63] Women in the Liberated Areas (*jiefang qu* 解放区) were often organized by the Women's Association for National Salvation (*Fujiuhui* 妇救会) to make shoes for the Eighth Route Army. This effort was also part of the Mass Production Movement (*da shengchan yundong* 大生产运动), which supported the self-reliant economy in Yan'an. In addition to providing military supplies and contributing to economic sufficiency, the act of making soldiers' shoes strengthened the emotional bond between the masses and the CCP troops. Women sewing soldiers' shoes was a recurring theme in art and literature during the Yan'an era. This includes Jiao Xinhe's 焦心河 (1917–48) famous woodblock print titled *Making Soldiers' Shoes and Sewing a Quilted*

Figure 63: Soldiers' shoes made by Liu Hulan, on display at the Liu Hulan Memorial Hall. Source: online Liu Hulan Memorial Hall, https://www.ijvr360.com/vr/liuhulan, accessed September 30, 2023.

Coat (*Zuo junxie feng mianyi* 做军鞋缝棉衣, 1940). In 1949, An Yangming 安阳明 published his woodblock print picture book *Liu Hulan* shortly after the death of Liu Hulan. The book includes a scene of Liu Hulan sewing soldiers' shoes (see fig. 64).

The first National Conference for Women Representatives (*quanguo fudai dahui* 全国妇代大会) took place in Beijing from March 24 to April 3, 1949. An accompanying exhibition was held at Zhongshan Hall during the same period. This exhibition showcased women's labor products from across the country, as well as stories of female model workers and heroines such as Liu Hulan. Large embroidered portraits of Mao Zedong and Joseph Stalin, created by sixteen women from northeast China, were prominently displayed in the center of the Hall to demonstrate women's admiration for these socialist leaders.[64] Among the most significant items in the exhibition were the soldiers' shoes made by women in the Liberated Areas.

Women skilled in needlework have long been considered virtuous in

Figure 64: "Liu Hulan making soldiers' shoes at night," illustrated by An Yangming. Source: An Yangming 安阳明, *Nü yingxiong Liu Hulan* 女英雄刘胡兰 (Liu Hulan the heroine), Shanghai: Xinhua shudian, 1949, 4.

traditional Chinese culture, a belief that has continued into socialist China. Women's needlework serves as a recurring trope in Chinese socialist propaganda, expressing affection and loyalty to the state and the CCP. As the news report for the exhibition at the first National Conference for Women Representatives states, "Through those tight and firm stitches, we can feel their deep love for the People's Liberation Army."[65] Another example is the iconic scene of the embroidering of the national flag in Luo Guangbin 罗广斌 (1924-67) and Yang Yiyan's 杨益言 (1925-2017) classic socialist novel *Red Crag* (*Hongyan* 红岩), published in 1961.

The novel *Red Crag* is based on the story of female revolutionary martyr Jiang Zhuyun 江竹筠 (1920–49), famously known as "Sister Jiang," who was executed by the KMT just before the liberation of Chongqing in late November 1949. In the novel, there is a memorable scene depicting Sister Jiang and her fellow female prisoners embroidering the national flag together upon learning the news about the establishment of the PRC.[66] The scene also appeared in opera and film versions of the story. Contrary to these depictions, historical accounts indicate that it was actually male prisoners who took on the task of embroidering the flag.[67] However, in literary depictions of the scene, women were purposely assigned traditionally gendered tasks such as doing needlework. Needlework, particularly an embroidered handkerchief given by a woman to a man, signifies romantic affection in traditional Chinese culture. Women's needlework in socialist China channeled private love into collective love, becoming a love token for the state and the CCP.

Needlework emerges as a significant motif in literary representations of Li Hulan, highlighting concerns regarding the gendered commemoration of a female martyr. The original opera *Liu Hulan* primarily focused on military mobilization and later faced criticism for lacking descriptions of Liu's heroic life. After 1949, the emphasis in literary representations of Liu Hulan shifted from her "glorious death" to her "great life."[68] Later versions of Liu Hulan's story introduced two female characters: Liu's grandmother and Second Widow (*er guafu* 二寡妇). Liu's grandmother is portrayed as a representative of the older generation who opposes the idea of women leaving their homes to join the socialist revolution. Liu Hulan fights against her grandmother, the representative of familial authority, and pledges her allegiance to the CCP.

As secretary of the Women's Association for National Salvation, Liu Hulan organizes female peasants to make soldiers' shoes and provide food for the Eighth Route Army. Despite being a socialist revolutionary, she adheres to traditional gender norms. She takes on all domestic responsibilities in the family. Chastity remains a significant concern in creating a socialist heroine. In contrast to the virtuous Liu Hulan, Second Widow is portrayed as a femme fatale who seduces a corrupt CCP cadre. A prominent plot point in literary works based on Liu Hulan's story after 1949 involves Liu's condemnation of Second Widow for making poor-quality soldiers' shoes and her public act of cutting the shoes in half. In the drum ballad version of *Liu Hulan* (1977), the scene of cutting the shoes is depicted dramatically: "The axe is flying with glittering silver lights, the sole of the shoe is split into two."[69]

The shoe cutting scene alludes to "broken shoes" (*poxie* 破鞋), a deroga-

第一場　刘胡兰剁开了地主婆二寡妇做的掺假的軍鞋。

Figure 65: "First scene: Liu Hulan chops open the counterfeit soldiers' shoes made by Second Widow." Source: Yang Wei 杨威, Guo Jian 郭健, Sun Wei 孙伟, and Fang Yan 方彦, *Liu Hulan: Bachang huaju* 刘胡兰：八场话剧 (Liu Hulan: Eight scenes spoken drama), Tianjin: Baihua wenyi chubanshe, 1965, photo, 1.

tory term for licentious women or prostitutes. In the 1956 spoken drama version of *Liu Hulan*, Second Widow is labeled "shameless broken shoes" (*buyao lian de poxie* 不要脸的破鞋).[70] In the Yan'an era, *poxie* were targets in the campaign aimed at reforming idlers (*erliuzi* 二流子), those who did not participate in collective labor. In 1939, the Yan'an-based magazine *Women in China* (*Zhongguo funü* 中国妇女) published two essays on the *poxie* issue and the women's liberation movement in the Jinxi 晋西 area. "Regarding the Issues of *Poxie*" (*Guanyu poxie wenti* 关于破鞋问题) by Liu Ying 刘英 (1905–2002) examines the social and economic causes of *poxie* in the Jinxi area. The essay advocates for educating *poxie* rather than humiliating them in order to persuade them to support national salvation and join the socialist revolution.[71] Ya Su's 亚苏 "Revisiting the Issues of *Poxie*" (*Zailun poxie wenti* 再论破鞋问题) argues that *poxie* should be viewed as normal citizens who can be mobilized in the women's liberation movement. According to the author, instead of stigmatizing *poxie* by imposing feudalistic moral standards of chastity, the women's movement should concentrate on assisting them in developing patriotic integrity.[72]

Despite efforts to destigmatize the *poxie* in Yan'an, they were still viewed as a threat to the socialist revolution. Second Widow, the widow of a landlord, who seduces and corrupts CCP cadre Shi Wuze 石五则, is portrayed as the polar opposite of the virtuous socialist heroine Li Hulan. In the literary works about Liu Hulan, Second Widow is demonized as a sexually charged creature.[73] She is vividly depicted in the drum ballad version of *Liu Hulan*, where she is referred to as an "old monster" (*lao yaoguai* 老妖怪):

> The Second Widow of a landlord has entered the courtyard, swaying her hips. Look at her; she has two taels of oil in her hair and silver earrings dangling from her ears. The makeup on her face is an inch thick, and there is a red dot between her eyebrows. She looks like a living old monster, utterly repulsive, emitting such a foul stench that no one can approach her.[74]

The demonization of Second Widow is intended to create a class enemy while highlighting Liu Hulan's virtues. In actuality, degraded women such as Second Widow were not the only women who were considered *poxie*. Women who left their households to join the revolution in the 1930s and '40s were viewed as transgressing traditional Chinese gender roles, especially in rural China. The term *poxie* was used as a derogatory term to defame female revolutionaries. The Women's Association for National Salvation was labeled as a *poxie* group (*poxie hui* 破鞋会).[75] Women who sewed shoes or provided food for the CCP troops often found their chastity being questioned.

Zhuo Shi's 灼石 short story "Blockheaded Couple" (*Erbulang fufu* 二不浪夫妇, 1941) tells a story about how a blockheaded (*erbulang*) husband in northwestern Shanxi becomes suspicious of his wife, a group leader in the Women's Association for National Salvation. He believes she is having an affair with (*gao poxie* 搞破鞋) a soldier while making shoes for the Eighth Route Army. Consumed by jealousy, the husband cuts the shoes his wife had made for the soldiers into pieces.[76] In this story, the act of cutting the shoes symbolizes the common anxiety that a woman, upon joining the revolution, might shift her loyalty to her husband to the CCP. In works about Liu Hulan, to alleviate this male fear, the socialist heroine is depicted as a virtuous girl who adheres to gender norms even after joining the revolution, as opposed to the licentious Second Widow.

During the early PRC years, the story of Liu Hulan was used to educate prostitutes, who were often humiliated as *poxie*. In 1949, The CCP launched campaigns to abolish prostitution. Prostitutes were placed in education and cultivation centers (*jiaoyang yuan* 教养院) to improve themselves through labor and undergo mind reform. Liu Hulan was an exemplary socialist woman for the prostitutes to emulate and study.[77] For the newly established PRC, prostitutes were a source of pollution and shame from the old society. In contrast, Liu Hulan, a chaste socialist heroine, represented the aspirations of the new world.

The Handkerchief

Chastity remains a constant concern in both the creation and commemoration of a female revolutionary martyr. Socialist exemplars, especially female martyrs, are often considered upholders of chastity and are thus not portrayed as having private lives. One striking feature of early socialist heroes is that they all died young. Not only do their images remain permanently youthful and robust, but they are also shielded from any potential defamatory narratives concerning romantic relationships. However, both age and romance present challenges in commemorating Liu Hulan.

Although biological age should be a historically verifiable fact, there have been constant disagreements on Liu Hulan's age.[78] Liu Hulan's girlhood at the time of her martyrdom engendered widespread sympathy for her and hatred for the KMT, the communists' adversary. In the 1950 film adaptation of Liu Hulan's story, her age was explicitly stated to be fourteen, despite the fact that she appears to be much more mature than fourteen years old.[79] However, Liu Hulan's age at her time of death became problematic in the 1990s. As Orna Naftali observes in her analysis of the rediscovery of the concept of childhood in contemporary China, in the early 1990s there was a "discernible shift in Chinese legal formulations of children and their entitlements within the family and society, together with a reconceptualization of the type of rights which children ought to possess."[80]

On September 4, 1991, China passed the Law of the PRC on Protection of Minors (*Zhonghua renmin gongheguo weichengnianren baohufa* 中华人民共和国未成年人保护法), through which the Chinese government legalized the rights of children under the age of eighteen for the first time. Articles 24 and 25 encourage writers and artists to produce works that help children grow up with a healthy mindset and prohibit organizations or individuals

Figure 66: Handkerchief used by Liu Hulan, on display at the Liu Hulan Memorial Hall. Source: online Liu Hulan Memorial Hall, https://www.ijvr360.com/vr/liuhulan, accessed September 30, 2023.

from selling, renting, or distributing works containing pornographic, violent, or horrific elements.[81] In line with this new focus on child protection, in the new 1996 version of the film *Liu Hulan*, the girl martyr appears to be a mature woman in her twenties, and her age is never mentioned.[82] After 1990, Liu Hulan was no longer specifically commemorated as a child martyr. While the two Liu Hulan films were both sanctioned by the CCP and intended to promote nationalism at different times, the discrepancies and inconstancies are evident. In recent years, the inclusion of Liu's martyrdom in textbooks has sparked controversy. Almost every child who grew up in China after 1949 learned about the story of Liu Hulan, as it appears in all major textbooks. In 2017, a parent argued that it was inappropriate to teach young children about Liu's death and to encourage them to sacrifice themselves, sparking heated debates. In response, *People's Daily* published an essay stating that it is necessary for children to have revolutionary martyrs as their role models.[83] However, the essay avoided the sensitive topic of Liu Hulan's age.

Representing the romantic relationship of a teenage girl martyr is as problematic as representing her age. According to historical records, Wang

Bengu 王本固, a company commander in the People's Liberation Army, was Liu Hulan's fiancé.[84] In 1946, Wang resided at Yunzhouxi to recover from an injury. Liu provided care for Wang, and they developed a romantic relationship. At the site of her execution, Liu Hulan handed her stepmother three items: an Essential Balm box, a silver ring, and a handkerchief.[85] The handkerchief was allegedly a token of Liu and Wang's romantic relationship. In literary renderings of the female martyr, however, the romance is either absent or inexplicit. For instance, the original opera version of Liu's story avoided any mention of romance. The army chef Lao Zhao 老赵, a fictional character, was created to replace Wang Bengu as the object of Liu's care. In different versions of the story, the symbolic meaning of the handkerchief, the love token, varies widely.

Liang Xing's 梁星 *A Brief Biography of Liu Hulan* (*Liu Hulan xiaozhuan* 刘胡兰小传, 1951) depicts the engagement of Liu Hulan and Wang Bengu. Rather than sexual attraction, their relationship is based on their mutual admiration for each another as revolutionary comrades. They believe that "if they can live together over the long term, they will be able to help each other advance."[86] The handkerchief only appears in this book as an item that Liu Hulan gives to her stepmother before her execution. The 1955 opera and 1956 spoken drama renditions of Liu Hulan's story portray a more intimate relationship between the two young revolutionaries. In the 1955 opera, Liu knits a sweater as a gift for Wang,[87] while in the 1956 spoken drama, Liu sews and patches Wang Bengu's clothing (see fig. 67).[88] Nevertheless, the handkerchief remains a cherished gift from Liu's mother, bestowed upon her before her departure to join the revolution, symbolizing the enduring love and support of her mother in both versions.[89] It becomes a symbol of parental love and support in this context. In 1964, a new opera version of *Liu Hulan* was produced to celebrate the fifteenth anniversary of the establishment of the PRC. This new version removed the romantic relationship between Liu and Wang, placing emphasis on Liu's bond with the local villagers instead.[90] In Ma Feng's *Biography of Liu Hulan* (*Liu Hulan zhuan* 刘胡兰传), Wang Gengu 王根固, a character based on Wang Bengu, gives Liu a handkerchief as a gift to thank her for taking care of him while he was recovering from an injury.[91] He claims that the handkerchief belonged to a martyred battalion commander. In this context, the handkerchief becomes a symbol of friendship between the military and civilians.

Writing about the romantic relationships of revolutionary martyrs became taboo during the Cultural Revolution. In 1968, *People's Daily* pub-

Figure 67: A still photo from the 1956 spoken drama of *Liu Hulan* depicts the heroine sewing clothes for Wang Bengu. Source: Yu Cun 于村, *Liu Hulan: Simu qichang huaju* 刘胡兰:四幕七场话剧 (Liu Hulan: Four acts seven scenes spoken drama), Beijing: Zuojia chubanshe, 1956, photo, 3.

lished an essay that fiercely criticized Zhang Geng 张庚 (1911–2003) for advocating the idea of writing about Liu Hulan's love affairs:

> We should write about Liu Hulan's sublime quality of devoting herself to the revolution wholeheartedly. . . . If we were to follow what Zhang Geng advocates, our indomitable proletarian hero would become an extremely despicable believer in the supremacy of love (*lian'ai zhishang* 恋爱至上), and the ode to the hero would become a bourgeois "love and death" tragedy.[92]

Under the guidance of aesthetic principles applied during the Cultural Revolution such as the "three prominences" (*san tuchu* 三突出), "tall, big, complete" (*gao, da, quan* 高大全), and "red, bright, shining" (*hong, guang, liang*

红光亮), socialist heroes were deified, and there was no place for individual romance. In the literary narratives, only love for Mao Zedong, the ultimate socialist hero, was permitted at the time.

In narratives of Liu Hulan during the Cultural Revolution, the handkerchief thus became a symbol of love for the socialist leader. In Li Xue'ao's 李学鳌 (1933–89) poem "Ode to Liu Hulan" (*Liu Hulan de songge* 刘胡兰的颂歌, 1973), the girl martyr is emotionally attached to the handkerchief, which she again gives to her stepmother before her execution, because she uses it to wrap Chairman Mao's works.[93] In the drum ballad *Liu Hulan*, the handkerchief is used to wrap portraits of Chairman Mao.[94] Here, Mao's works and the portraits of Mao are revered as sacred items, safeguarded by Liu Hulan's love for the socialist leader.

Romantic relationships were again permitted in representing revolutionaries in the 1990s. The 1996 film *Liu Hulan*, which aimed to celebrate the fiftieth anniversary of Liu's martyrdom, depicts a burgeoning romance between Liu Hulan and the head of Wenshui County, a CCP cadre named Gu Yongtian 顾永田. Liu is first attracted to Gu when he gives a report on the Anti-Japanese War. She is enlightened by Gu and begins to follow his lead in the revolution. After Liu Hulan takes care of the injured Gu, he gives her a handkerchief that he inherited from a martyred battalion commander.

In this film, the CCP cadre Gu Yongtian replaces the military leader Wang Bengu. Gu also serves the role of the male revolutionary who guides a female revolutionary. The handkerchief is more of an embodiment of the revolutionary spirit than a symbol of romantic love since it is a relic of a martyr. The romance is presented subtly in the film because the inclusion of romantic love creates an ambiguous space in narratives of revolution. Chastity and purity remain a central concern in the state-sanctioned narratives of female revolutionary martyrs. It is therefore only safe to have a female revolutionary fall in love with a male revolutionary, and ideally a male revolutionary who provides guidance to the female revolutionary so that their romantic relationship does not disturb the gender hierarchy.

As I have discussed in this chapter, the official narratives of Liu Hulan are constantly changing, showing that the original narratives portraying Liu Hulan as a socialist hero are fluid. The process of making Liu Hulan a revolutionary martyr reveals that national commemoration of socialist martyrs is about utilizing models and symbols to mobilize the masses and create national memory, rather than remembering individuals. However, as Kirk Denton points out, "The state is by no means the only player in the historical

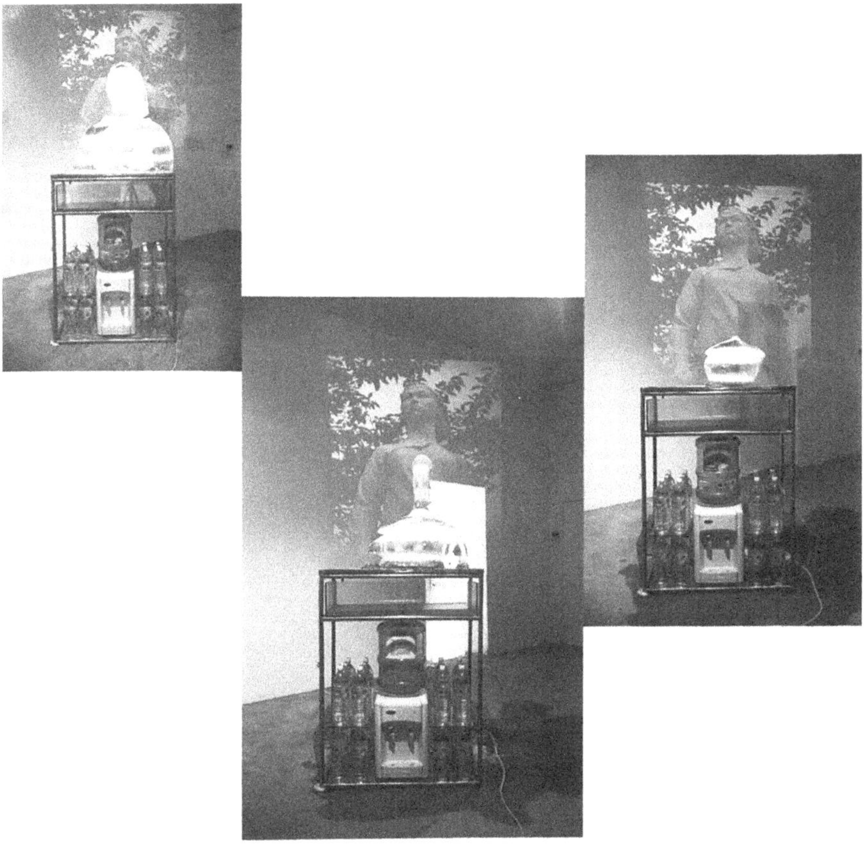

Figure 68: Zhang Xin, *Climate No. 6*, sculpture and video installation, 2000. The melting ice sculpture of Liu Hulan. Source: *Text and Subtext: An International Touring Exhibition*, edited by Binghui Huangfu, Singapore: Earl Lu Gallery, 2000, 101.

memory game in China."[95] Contemporary artistic re-representations of Liu Hulan challenge officially sanctioned martyrdom narratives, proposing alternative memories of the revolutionary past.

Chinese contemporary artist Zhang Xin 张新 completely deconstructed the official discourse of Liu Hulan in her installation artwork *Climate No. 6* (see figs. 68 and 69). Zhang Xin has been exploring the theme of climate for years in her art as a metaphor for the effects of global warming and the changing political winds. *Climate No. 6* is made up of two parts: one is a pro-

Figure 69: Zhang Xin, *Climate No. 6*, sculpture and video installation, 2000. The "Spirit" bottled water. Source: *Text and Subtext: An International Touring Exhibition*, 103.

jection of a marble statue of Liu Hulan, and the other is an identical sculpture of Liu Hulan made of ice that is melting into a water dispenser. Ironically, the original marble sculpture of Liu Hulan is absent, implying the emptiness of the official discourse. The two images of Liu Hulan in the art installation are ephemeral; the projected image is an illusion and the ice sculpture cannot last. Together they question the concept of eternity that is embedded in the statue of Liu Hulan from the Mao era. The label on the water dispenser features an introduction to Liu Hulan in both Chinese and English, an image of the marble statue of Liu Hulan, and the brand name "Spirit" (*jingshen* 精神). The "Spirit" bottled water captures the transformation of revolutionary discourse into consumer culture: revolutionary "spirit" can be commodified and consumed in contemporary China.

Although the state suggests only one way to form collective memory or intends to be the singular voice in the formation of collective memory, the memories are in fact plural. The state strictly regulates national memory and mobilizes it as needed. However, as Li Jie points out, "State surveillance can also generate important resources for unofficial, even subversive, memories in the changing media ecology of the post-Mao era."[96] Because of her high visibility in CCP propaganda, Liu Hulan is one of the most popular targets of rewritings and parodies of socialist history among netizens, intellectuals, and contemporary Chinese artists.

The fluidity of official narratives becomes evident through analyzing some of the significant objects representing the female martyr, such as the inscriptions commemorating her life and the hay cutter that ended it. The statues and the literary representations of "broken shoes" and the handkerchief illustrate that the materiality of the female body and female sexuality pose challenges in commemorating Liu Hulan in both official narratives and counternarratives. Unlike in commemorating male martyrdom, chastity proves problematic in representing female martyrdom. Liu Hulan is portrayed either as an asexualized role model or an oversexualized weapon against mainstream ideology. In contrast to Zhenzhen, who may not be included in national memory, Liu Hulan has been enshrined in history. Nonetheless, the case of commemorating Liu Hulan demonstrates that narratives of female martyrs can be both mobilized and contested.

Epilogue

The Immortal Ding Ling

A Tale of Two Female Writers: Guan Lu and Ding Ling

On September 15, 1982, Ding Ling visited her old friend Guan Lu 关露 (1907–82), a famous female writer who was a spy for the CCP during the 1930s. During this visit, Ding Ling expressed to Guan Lu, "We all barely escaped from death" (*women doushi silitaosheng ya* 我们都是死里逃生呀).[1] If Zhenzhen in "When I Was in Xia Village" serves as a fictional representation of Ding Ling, then Guan Lu embodies Ding Ling's real-life reflection. They were both female writers and members of the CCP who endured constant gossip about their personal lives and lifelong scrutiny regarding their chastity and loyalty to the party.[2] Tragically, Guan Lu committed suicide on December 5, 1982, shortly after the CCP's rehabilitation notice and Ding Ling's visit.

Guan Lu's friendship with Ding Ling began when she joined the CCP and the League of Left-wing Writers in 1932.[3] At that time, Ding Ling served as the secretary of the CCP and the Party Youth League (*dangtuan shuji* 党团书记) for the League of Left-wing Writers, and was responsible for the Creation Committee (*chuangzuo weiyuanhui* 创作委员会) of the league.[4] Guan Lu actively participated in the anti-Japanese propaganda movement led by Ding Ling and frequently attended meetings with her. After Ding Ling's abduction in 1933, Guan Lu stepped in to assume Ding Ling's role in charge of the Creation Committee and assisted Zhou Yang, who succeeded Ding Ling as the secretary of the CCP and the Party Youth League within the League of Left-wing Writers, in intelligence work.[5]

Guan Lu gained fame in the field of literature through the publication of her poem collection titled *The Song over the Pacific* (*Taipingyang shang de gesheng* 太平洋上的歌声, 1936) and the lyrics to a theme song titled "In Spring" (*Chuntian li* 春天里) for the film *Crossroads* (*Shizi jietou* 十字街头,

Figure 70: The red flag offered by people from the Great Northern Wasteland with the embroidered words "Ding Ling busi" 丁玲不死 (Ding Ling is immortal) that covered Ding Ling's body. It is on display at the National Museum of Modern Chinese Literature. Photo courtesy of Wu Xiyun.

1937). She also took on a role in Xia Yan's play, *Sai Jinhua*, performed by the 40s Drama Club in 1936.[6] In early 1939, Guan Lu wrote an essay titled "Impressions of a Female Writer—the Female Warrior Ding Ling" (*Nü zuojia yinxiangji—nü zhanshi Ding Ling* 女作家印象记—女战士丁玲) to express her admiration for Ding Ling's works and personality.[7] In late 1939, she was dispatched by the CCP to work as a spy, collaborating with Japanese and Japanese sympathizers.[8] Pan Hannian, her direct contact and leader in the CCP, instructed her that for her underground work, she could not defend herself if anyone accused her of being a traitor.[9] Guan Lu thus began to live a double life, as both a writer and a female spy, facing a lifelong struggle to prove her political purity.

In 1942, the CCP assigned Guan Lu a significant role as an editor for a magazine in Shanghai, *Women's Voice* (*Nüsheng* 女声), which had ties to the Japanese military. From then on, she faced criticism for her perceived collaboration with the Japanese. Starting that year, the Japanese Literature Patriotic Association (*Riben wenxue baoguohui* 日本文学报国会) orchestrated three Greater East Asian Writers' Conferences (*Da dongya wenxuezhe dahui* 大东亚文学者大会). These conferences were part of an ideological campaign propagating the Greater East Asia Co-Prosperity Sphere (*Da dongya gongrong quan* 大东亚共荣圈). The second of these conferences took place in Tokyo in August 1943, and *Women's Voice* sent Guan Lu as a delegate.

Though Guan Lu participated in the 1943 Tokyo Greater East Asian Writers' Conference, she grappled with being labeled a "cultural traitor" (*wenhua hanjian* 文化汉奸) by the public.[10] Instead of delivering political speeches, she spoke on cultural exchanges between Japanese and Chinese women.[11] Throughout the conference, her emotional discomfort was so profound that she experienced extreme fatigue, anxiety, and a series of other physical symptoms (a condition sometimes known as neurasthenia). After returning to China, Guan Lu wrote an essay detailing her Tokyo experience. While intended to summarize the conference, much of her essay, "Tokyo Memories: Neurotic Days" (*Dongjing yiyu: shenjing bingtai de rizi* 东京忆语：神经病态的日子), addresses her personal struggles with mental illness during the event. She also explored reflections on life and death in her essay:

> Death is a terrifying thing, but I think what is even more terrifying is to live secretly and then die secretly. When I am alive, no one feels that I am alive, and when I die, no one senses that I am dead. While I am alive, no one thinks it is beneficial, and after I die, no one thinks it is harmful. All I have are my

> tongue and nails, hair and eyes, and I will take these with me when I die, leaving nothing behind. After my death, people will immediately forget me, as if I had never been to this world, as if I had never been born. How sad that is! Thus, my vision becomes pitch black, as dark as a wasteland on a rainy night. How terrifying that is! These circumstances are much more frightening than death itself. After thinking this through, I am no longer afraid of dying; but I am still afraid. I am afraid of having lived in vain, that no one will mourn my death. Therefore, I still want to live; I want to use my remaining days to make up for those past days when my death would not cause anyone sorrow.[12]

Guan Lu's battle with neurasthenia and her contemplations on life and death reflect her internal conflict regarding her role as a spy. She chose to live and contribute to the Communist revolution, hoping that she would eventually be vindicated. Intriguingly, Ding Ling expressed comparable sentiments about life and death during her time in Nanjing, as depicted in "The Song of Death":

> I was spiritually prepared for my own death. But that didn't mean I yearned to die or welcomed death. On the contrary, I was contemplating how to elude death because I wanted to find my friends, my comrades, and my people and convey my thoughts to them. I stood by their side unwaveringly, and I would never betray them. . . . I indeed believed that death could be preferable to life, as through death, I could elucidate my convictions. My disappearance from this world would not be noticed by anyone. In that moment, society would remain oblivious to the circumstances of my demise. Yet, in the end, history would come to know that I had perished, that my life had ended in Nanjing, within the confines of KMT imprisonment. As I ruminated this way, I came to realize that, ultimately, only death could make a modest contribution to the party. I had died; I was a dead person. This encounter with death would remain etched in my memory for the entirety of my existence.[13]

Ding Ling and Guan Lu both endured lifelong struggles to defend their political integrity. Guan Lu was implicated in the Pan Hannian case and was imprisoned from 1955 to 1957.[14] In 1967, during the Cultural Revolution, she was incarcerated again and remained in prison until 1975.[15] She dedicated the rest of her life to clearing her name. On March 23, 1982, the CCP Organization Department eventually issued "The Decision regarding the Rehabilitation of Comrade Guan Lu" (*Guanyu Guan Lu tongzhi pingfan de jueding* 关于关露同志平反的决定).[16]

During Ding Ling's visit to Guan Lu in September 1982, she brought the good news Guan Lu had been waiting for: Pan Hannian, their former leader, was set to be rehabilitated. Upon hearing the news, Guan Lu was on the verge of tears. She confided in Ding Ling, "After suffering a stroke, I contemplated death several times. But every time I thought of Pan Hannian's unjust imprisonment, which has not been rectified, and the stain cast upon him that has not yet been cleansed, I realized that I must live on and wait for that day on his behalf."[17] Ding Ling mentioned to Guan Lu that she had composed an essay in memory of Pan Hannian and encouraged Guan Lu to do the same. Ding Ling was sympathetic to Guan Lu's poor living conditions and approached the China Writers Association, advocating for an improvement in Guan Lu's housing.[18] Regrettably, Guan Lu did not live long enough to enjoy better accommodations. In December 1982, before taking her own life, Guan Lu composed a brief note. It conveyed two messages: first, she wished to donate her house to the CCP Organization Department; and second, her tribute essay for Pan Hannian was complete.[19]

Upon receiving the news of the official restoration of her own reputation by the CCP in 1984, Ding Ling remarked, "Now I can die."[20] Guan Lu might have felt similar after affirming both her own and Pan Hannian's political loyalty. Believing she had no further reason to live, she committed suicide. Distraught over Guan Lu's tragic death, Ding Ling organized a symposium to commemorate her.[21] On December 18, 1982, Ding Ling spoke at the symposium. During her address, she reflected on her interactions with Guan Lu in the League of Left-wing Writers. Overwhelmed by emotion, she expressed, "Her death is like a mirror, reflecting my insignificance and selfishness. She and I were contemporaries, rolling through the waves of the same era together. I am a writer and should understand her thoughts and emotions. She was a kind person, even a bit naïve, always sacrificing herself. Her soul was wounded, alone with no family. She was very lonely. She needed love and warmth."[22] Ding Ling deeply resonated with Guan Lu's struggles, empathizing with their shared quest for vindication. Yet, in Ding Ling's case, her family and friends went the extra mile to ensure she could be appropriately commemorated.

Negotiating the Commemoration of Ding Ling

Ding Ling fell critically ill after Chinese New Year in 1986, and her allies began planning how she would be mourned upon her imminent passing.

Because of Ding Ling's complicated political reputation, her commemoration entailed negotiations between individuals and the state. On February 18, her husband, Chen Ming, visited Xi Zhongxun's 习仲勋 (1913–2002) house and documented suggestions for Ding Ling's funeral, including the widespread dissemination of a fair eulogy in accordance with "The Notification regarding the Restoration of Comrade Ding Ling's Reputation," issued by the CCP Organization Department in 1984.[23] Chen Ming was on a mission to ensure that Ding Ling would be remembered in a manner he deemed correct and appropriate. He insisted on removing Zhou Yang from the funeral planning committee, revising the memorial essay for Ding Ling to acknowledge both her contributions and sufferings during the Chinese revolution, and requested that the Chinese Communist Party flag be placed over Ding's body.

Chen Ming's request to exclude Zhou Yang from the funeral planning committee was understandable. During the Anti-Rightist Movement, Zhou Yang, who was then the vice minister of both the Central Propaganda Department and the minister of culture, accused Ding Ling of "three disloyalties" during the Nanjing, Yan'an, and PRC eras. He also criticized her for glorifying the character Zhenzhen in "When I Was in Xia Village." As the ideological spokesperson of the party, Zhou Yang's accusations against Ding Ling may be understandable given the specific political circumstances at the time. However, it remains unclear why he refused to confess to falsely accusing Ding Ling after the Cultural Revolution, despite apologizing for the majority of his other actions during the political chaos. Zhou Yang proposed the infamous idea that, while questions about Ding Ling's loyalty had been resolved, the act of having a child with the traitor Feng Da would forever be a stain on her record.[24]

After returning to Beijing from Changzhi in Shanxi, Ding Ling decided to join Chen Ming and their friend Gan Lu 甘露 (1920–87) for a visit to Zhou Yang in the hospital on May 9, 1979. This visit was Ding Ling's friendly attempt to reconnect and reconcile with Zhou, her longtime revolutionary comrade, after decades of political turmoil. The meeting, however, proved to be a disappointment to Ding Ling and failed to bridge the gap between the two literary giants. During the meeting, Zhou Yang reportedly focused only on his own hardships endured during the Cultural Revolution, without acknowledging Ding Ling's experiences.[25] The gulf between Zhou Yang and Ding Ling widened even further during the Fourth Chinese National Literature and Art Workers Conference, which took place in the fall of that year.

Ding Ling began to appeal for rehabilitation (*pingfan* 平反) upon her return to Beijing in January 1979. Her quest, however, took a long and arduous route. In May 1979, the Reexamination Office of the China Writers Association, led by Zhou Yang, issued a "Conclusion on Reexamining Ding Ling's Rightist Issue."[26] This "Conclusion" is riddled with ambiguity. While it confirms that Ding Ling is neither antiparty nor a rightist, it also upholds the findings of the 1956 investigation, stating that she made political mistakes after being arrested by the KMT in 1933. It indicates that Ding Ling's party membership would be reinstated, but provides no details regarding her branch affiliation or participation in party activities. Ding Ling was dissatisfied with the "Conclusion" and believed it should align with the 1940 investigation, which had clarified her political allegiance during her time in Nanjing.[27] Her party membership issue remained unresolved following the release of the 1979 "Conclusion." Ding Ling addressed the matter in three letters to the China Writers Association party branch but received no response.[28] She then wrote to the Central Propaganda Department, hoping to attend the Fourth Chinese National Literature and Art Workers Conference as a party member. Hu Yaobang 胡耀邦 (1915–89), the minister of the Central Propaganda Department at the time, urged that the issue be resolved.[29] Ding Ling's party membership was reinstated just in time for the conference.

The Fourth Chinese National Literature and Art Workers Conference was the first national meeting in the field of art and literature held after the Cultural Revolution, aimed at righting the past wrongs and reuniting Chinese intellectuals. Ding Ling attended the conference as a party member, while Zhou Yang delivered the keynote report. During the conference, the China Writers Association held its Third Representatives Meeting on November 8. At this meeting, Ding Ling delivered a long speech against factionalism in the fields of art and literature. She criticized Zhou Yang's assertion that there were two factions in Yan'an: the Luyi 鲁艺 (Lu Xun Academy of Art and Literature) group that he led, and the Kangda 抗大 (People's Anti-Japanese Military and Political University) group led by Ding Ling.[30]

Ding Ling's speech generated heated responses. As the host of the meeting, the poet Li Ji 李季 (1922–80) invited Zhou Yang to offer some comments.[31] Zhou Yang spoke about the persecution of intellectuals by the Gang of Four and his own suffering during the Cultural Revolution. He claimed that after a long winter of disasters, spring was finally arriving for the literary field.[32] At this, fellow author Xiao Jun exclaimed, "Zhou Yang's spring is my winter."[33] The meeting concluded on an awkward note. Two days after the meeting, He Jingzhi, who was Zhou Yang's former student and vice minister of culture at the time, persuaded Wang Zhen to invite Ding Ling and Zhou

Yang to a lunch, aiming to mend their strained relationship.[34] Zhou Yang initially agreed but changed his mind at the last moment.

After the conference, Ding Ling continued to petition the CCP Central Organization Department to uphold the 1940 verdict about her history.[35] It was not until July 14, 1984 that the CCP issued "The Notification regarding the Restoration of Comrade Ding Ling's Reputation." This officially confirmed that she had remained a loyal party member during her house arrest in Nanjing and that the conclusion of the 1940 investigation was correct. Before issuing the "Notification," the Central Organization Department sought Zhou Yang's opinion, and he was displeased. He urged He Jingzhi, who was then the vice minister of the Propaganda Department, to oppose the "Notification," asserting that the blemish on Ding Ling's record could not be erased.[36] He Jingzhi defied Zhou Yang, believing that there was no evidence to suggest that Ding Ling had betrayed the party. As a result, his relationship with his former teacher became strained over the dispute concerning Ding Ling's rehabilitation.

Ding Ling never received an apology from Zhou Yang, making Chen Ming's request to exclude him from Ding Ling's funeral planning committee understandable. Chen Ming detailed the reasoning for Zhou Yang's exclusion in a message to Wang Meng 王蒙 (1934–), the vice president of the China Writers Association, and to Deng Liqun 邓力群 (1915–2015), the secretary of the CCP Central Secretariat.[37] Deng, however, suggested retaining Zhou Yang on the list due to political considerations. On March 3, 1986, the China Writers Association released "Suggestions regarding Ding Ling's Funeral Arrangements" (*Guanyu Ding Ling houshi de anpai yijian* 关于丁玲后事的安排意见), accompanied by a list of the forty-one committee members.[38] This list includes a supplementary note explaining that, in the interest of unifying the literary community, Zhou Yang was included despite Chen Ming's reservations.[39] Ultimately, Chen Ming accepted the list, focusing instead on revising the memorial essay and requesting that the party flag be placed over Ding Ling's body.

The memorial essay for Ding Ling was drafted by Bao Chang 鲍昌 (1930–89), the secretary of the China Writers Association Secretariat. Chen Ming revised the draft with the assistance of a few of Ding Ling's friends and changed the title to "The Life of Comrade Ding Ling" (*Ding Ling tongzhi shengping* 丁玲同志生平).[40] The Central Organization Department offered further revision suggestions for "The Life of Comrade Ding Ling." Chen Ming resisted the suggested removal of two sentences, one stating that "Ding Ling was welcomed by Mao Zedong and other CCP leaders" upon her arrival in Bao'an after escaping from Nanjing, and the other asserting that "Comrade Ding Ling was a writer who had suffered for a long time under the erroneous leftist line, causing her significant trauma."[41] By refusing to remove these two sentences, Chen Ming aimed to defend Ding Ling's political loyalty and afford her posthumous justice after years of suffering during various political movements. He appealed to Xi Zhongxun and Deng Liqun, and Xi agreed to retain the sentences.[42] The official account of Ding Ling's contributions to Chinese literature and the revolution, "The Life of Comrade Ding Ling," was published in *People's Daily* on March 16, 1986.[43]

Chen Ming defended Ding Ling's political allegiance, aspiring for her to be officially acknowledged and remembered as a CCP member. The day after Ding Ling's death, Chen Ming met with the Zheng Boke 郑伯克 (1909–2008), the vice minister of the Central Organization Department, to request that Ding Ling's body be covered with the party flag. Zheng responded that Ding Ling's official rank did not qualify her for this honor.[44] On March 10, Chen Ming reiterated his plea in a meeting with Xi Zhongxun.[45] However, the Central Organization Department declined to make an exception, noting that another female CCP leader, Li Bozhao 李伯钊 (1909–85), who held a position similar to Ding Ling's, did not receive this gesture either.[46] Jiang Zulin, Ding Ling's son with Hu Yepin, stated that while regulations about draping the party flag over a deceased member were relatively flexible at the time, the rules suddenly became more restrictive just as his mother passed away.[47] Eventually, Ding Ling's body was covered by a red flag, a gift from the people of the Great Northern Wasteland, where she had lived for twelve years and which she considered her second hometown. The flag bore the embroidered words "Ding Ling busi" 丁玲不死 (Ding Ling is immortal, see fig. 70).

On March 15, 1986, the funeral ceremony for Ding Ling took place at the Babaoshan Revolutionary Cemetery Hall. Over 500 people attended, including CCP leaders such as Xi Zhongxun, Yang Shangkun 杨尚昆 (1907–98), Hu Qiaomu 胡乔木 (1912–92), Deng Liqun, Wang Zhen, and Kang Keqing.[48] The main entrance of the hall featured an elegiac couplet: "The martyr pressed forward in her later years to establish *China* magazine, the old general in the literary field endured hardships to nurture new talents."[49] Beside the entrance was a prominent photograph of Ding Ling wearing the Eighth Route Army uniform. Superimposed on the photo was her handwritten declaration: "Ding Ling forever belongs to the Chinese Communist Party. She is just an ordinary loyal soldier of the CCP"[50] (see fig. 71). Another enlarged excerpt of Ding

Figure 71: Photo of Ding Ling in Shanxi in 1937, with her handwritten message: "Ding Ling forever belongs to the Chinese Communist Party. She is just an ordinary loyal soldier of the CCP." Source: Zheng Xiaofeng 郑笑枫, *Ding Ling zai Beidahuang* 丁玲在北大荒 (Ding Ling in the Great Northern Wasteland), Beijing: Zhonggong dangshi chubanshe, 2008, 152.

Ling's handwriting in the hall declared, "Like a moth to a flame, ceaseless until its death, I will spend the rest of my life to soar on wings, continuing to pursue the truth in the fire and die for singing the praises of the flame of truth"[51] (see fig. 72). "A moth to a flame" echoes Qu Qiubai's commentary on Ding Ling, emphasizing her obsession with being a revolutionary martyr and the pursuit of truth. Although Ding Ling did not die as a martyr, the elegiac couplet, red flag, photos, and writings at her funeral collectively served to memorialize her as one in the eyes of those who loved her.

The process of negotiating the memories of Chinese female revolutionary martyrs, as explored in this book, demonstrates the challenges of including

Figure 72: Photo of Ding Ling at the Fourth Chinese National Literature and Art Workers Conference in 1979, accompanied by her handwritten message: "Like a moth to a flame, ceaseless until its death, I will spend the rest of my life to soar on wings, continuing to pursue the truth in the fire and die for singing the praises of the flame of truth." Source: Zheng Xiaofeng, *Ding Ling zai Beidahuang*, 136.

them in the national memory without constraining them to traditional gender norms. Despite the fact that the state only suggests a singular voice to form collective memory, multiple memories exist. This imaginary museum for Chinese female revolutionary martyrs shows how the state tries to control the construction and consumption of female revolutionary martyrdom and how gender dynamics affect the production of national memory. In theory, martyrs are immortalized through the sanitized and politicized narratives of their lives by the state. In contrast, this imaginary museum seeks to highlight both the personal moments of the female revolutionary martyrs before death and their circuitous paths to immortality after death. In this imaginary museum, we see the process of making Chinese female revolutionary martyrs while still celebrating them for what made them real individuals. This museum provides a space to store not only the memories of the heroic deeds of Chinese female revolutionary martyrs but also their vulnerable and intimate moments, their sufferings, joys, and tears.

NOTES

Preface

1. Mao Zedong, "Yellow Crane Tower—to the melody of *P'u Sa Man*," trans. Jerome Ch'en, in Jerome Ch'en, *Mao and the Chinese Revolution* (London: Oxford University Press, 1965), 322.

2. For discussion on the transformation of the Qingming Festival in China after 1949, see Chang-tai Hung, "The Cult of the Red Martyr: Politics of Commemoration in China," *Journal of Contemporary History* 43, no. 2 (2008): 283–84.

3. Hung, "Cult of the Red Martyr," 284.

4. James Young, *The Texture of Memory: Holocaust Memorials and Meaning* (New Haven: Yale University Press, 1994), 3.

Introduction

1. The essay was organized by Liu Chun 刘春 on July 30, 1986, based on the recordings. It was proofread and revised by Ding Ling's husband, Chen Ming 陈明. It was first published in *Hunan Literature*. See Ding Ling, "Si zhi ge" 死之歌 (The song of death), *Hunan wenxue* 湖南文学 (Hunan literature) 1 (1987): 4–9. On December 19, 1985, Ding Ling recorded her last writing, a preface to *Feng Naichao wenji* 冯乃超文集 (Collected Works of Feng Naichao), in response to a request. See Wang Zengru 王增如 and Li Xiangdong 李向东, *Ding Ling nianpu changbian* 丁玲年谱长编 (Lengthy compilation of Ding Ling's chronicle), vol. 2 (Tianjin: Tianjin renmin chubanshe, 2006), 822.

2. Ding Ling, "Si zhi ge," 4.

3. Ding Ling, "Si zhi ge," 6. Ding Ling is the pen name of Jiang Bingzhi.

4. Ding Ling, "Si zhi ge," 5.

5. The 1911 Revolution is also known as the Xinhai Revolution.

6. Ding Ling, "Si zhi ge," 6.

7. Ding Ling, "Si zhi ge," 7.

8. Wang Zengru, Li Xiangdong, *Ding Ling nianpu changbian*, vol. 1, 56.

9. Ding Ling, "Si zhi ge," 8.

10. Ding Ling, "Si zhi ge," 9.

11. Ding Ling, "Si zhi ge," 9.

12. Ding Ling, "Si zhi ge," 8.

13. For the memoir, see Ding Ling, "Wangliang shijie" 魍魉世界 (The world of demons

and monsters), in *Ding Ling quanji* 丁玲全集 (Complete works of Ding Ling), vol. 10 (Shijiazhuang: Hebei renmin chubanshe, 2001), 3–100.

14. Ding Ling, "Si zhi ge," 9.

15. Lu Weijing, *True to Her Word: The Faithful Maiden Cult in Late Imperial China* (Stanford: Stanford University Press, 2008), 41.

16. Janet Theiss, *Disgraceful Matters: The Politics of Chastity in Eighteenth-Century China* (Berkeley: University of California Press, 2004), 13.

17. Benedict Anderson, *Imagined Communities: Reflections on the Origin and Spread of Nationalism* (London: Verso, 2006), 206.

18. Louise Edwards, *Women Warriors and Wartime Spies of China* (Cambridge: Cambridge University Press, 2016), 90.

19. Anderson, *Imagined Communities*, 178.

20. Aleida Assmann, *Cultural Memory and Western Civilization: Functions, Media, Archives* (Cambridge: Cambridge University Press, 2011), 123. Maurice Halbwachs argues that "the collective memory is not the same as formal history, and 'historical memory' is a rather unfortunate expression because it connects two terms opposed in more than one aspect." See Maurice Halbwachs, *The Collective Memory*, trans. Francis J. Ditter Jr. and Vida Yazdi Ditter (New York: Harper & Row, 1980), 78.

21. Assmann, *Cultural Memory and Western Civilization*, 38.

22. Michel de Certeau, *The Practice of Everyday Life*, trans. Steven Rendall (Berkeley: University of California Press, 1984), 108.

23. See Glen Bowersock, *Martyrdom and Rome* (Cambridge: Cambridge University Press, 1995), 13–14.

24. Dou E is the heroine in Guan Hanqing's 关汉卿 (ca. 1241–1320) play *Dou E yuan* 窦娥冤 (The injustice to Dou E), who is wrongfully convicted of murder.

25. See Hua Fu 华夫, "Ding Ling de fuchou nüshen: Ping 'Wo zai Xiacun de shihou'" 丁玲的复仇女神：评"我在霞村的时候" (Ding Ling's vengeful goddess: A criticism of "When I was in Xia village"), in *Zai pipan* 再批判 (Criticism again), ed. *Wenyi bao* 文艺报 (Journal of literature and art) (Beijing: Zuojia chubanshe, 1958), 89.

Exhibition I

1. "Wenhuajie wei yingjiu Ding Pan xuanyan" 文化界为营救丁潘宣言 (Declaration from the Cultural Community for the Rescue of Ding Ling and Pan Zinian), *Wenxue zazhi* 文学杂志 (Literature magazine) 1, nos. 3 and 4 (1933): 15.

2. Ding Ling's late husband, Hu Yepin, was one of the five martyrs of the League of Left-wing Writers who were executed by the KMT in 1931. For a detailed discussion of the five martyrs, see Tsi-an Hsia, "Enigma of the Five Martyrs," in Tsi-an Hsia, *The Gate of Darkness* (Seattle: University of Washington Press, 1968), 163–233.

3. Jiu Ding 九鼎, "Wenyi jie mimi zhuidao Ding Ling suoji" 文艺界秘密追悼丁玲琐纪 (Record on the secret service for Ding Ling in the circle of art and literature), *Shanghai bao* 上海报 (Shanghai newspaper), December 25, 1933. *Sheying huabao* 摄影画报 (Photo pictorial) published an almost identical account on a secret memorial service for Ding Ling. See "Wenyijie mimi zhuidao Ding Ling" 文艺界秘密追悼丁玲 (The secret service for Ding Ling in the circle of art and literature), *Sheying huabao* 10, no. 1 (1934): 8–9.

4. The writings commemorating Ding Ling include Zhang Yinlin 张荫麟, "Dao Ding Ling" 悼丁玲 (Mourning Ding Ling), *Dagong bao* 大公报 (Dagong newspaper), September 4, 1933; Zi Jin 紫堇, "Dao Ding Ling" 悼丁玲 (Mourning Ding Ling), *Qinghua zhoukan* 清华周刊 (Tsinghua weekly) 40, nos. 3 and 4 (1933): 160; Chen Bei'ou 陈北鸥, "Dao Ding Ling" 悼丁玲 (Mourning Ding Ling), *Wenyi yuebao* 文艺月报 (Art and literature monthly) 1, no. 2 (1933): 93–94; Chen Qingzhang 陈庆璋, "Dao" 悼 (Commemoration), *Qizhong yuekan* 齐中月刊 (Central Shandong monthly) 1, nos. 5 and 6 (1933): 40–41; Xue Ye 雪野, "Jinian Ding Ling" 纪念丁玲 (Commemorating Ding Ling), *Wenxue zazhi* 文学杂志 (Literature magazine) 1, nos. 3 and 4 (1933): 132–33; Li Jinming 黎锦明, "Yi Ding Ling" 忆丁玲 (Remembering Ding Ling), *Qianqiu* 千秋 (A thousand years) 2, nos. 2 (1934): 25–26; Pengzi 蓬子, "Women de pengyou Ding Ling" 我们的朋友丁玲 (Our friend Ding Ling), in *Ding Ling xuanji* 丁玲选集 (Selected works of Ding Ling) (Shanghai: Tianma shudian, 1933), 2–42; Shen Congwen 沈从文, *Ji Ding Ling* 记丁玲 (In Memory of Ding Ling) (Shanghai: Shanghai liangyou tushu yinshu gongsi, 1934).

5. Jon Eugene von Kowallis, *The Lyrical Lu Xun: A Study of His Classical-Style Verse* (Honolulu: University of Hawai'i Press, 1996), 280. I slightly modified the translation.

6. Qu Yuan, "Li sao" 离骚 (Encountering sorrow), in *Chuci xuan* 楚辞选 (Selections from *The Lyrics of Chu*), ed. Lu Kanru 陆侃如, Gao Heng 高亨, and Huang Xiaoshu 黄孝纾 (Shanghai: Shanghai gudian wenxue chubanshe, 1956), 38. Qu Yuan was a famous poet and political martyr in early China from the state of Chu, which was also Ding Ling's birthplace. His poems pioneered the literary trope of comparing underappreciated literati with beautiful and virtuous women who were abandoned by their husbands.

7. Lu Xun's letter to Cao Juren was quoted in Ding Ling's "Lu Xun xiansheng yuwo" 鲁迅先生于我 (Mr. Lu Xun in my memory), in *Ding Ling quanji*, vol. 6, 118.

8. Ding Ling, "Lu Xun xiansheng yuwo," 118.

9. Ding Ling, "Lu Xun xiansheng yuwo," 116.

10. Ding Ling, "Lu Xun xiansheng yuwo," 110–12.

11. Ding Ling, "Lu Xun xiansheng yuwo," 114.

12. Ding Ling, "Wangliang shijie" 魍魉世界 (The world of demons and monsters), in *Ding Ling quanji*, vol. 10, 79.

13. Wang Zengru 王增如, "Mao Zedong liuci shuxie linjiang xian" 毛泽东六次书写临江仙 (Mao Zedong handwrote "The Immortals at the River: to Ding Ling" six times), *Shiji* 世纪 (Century) 4 (2018): 47.

14. Mao Zedong, "Zai Zhongguo wenyi xiehui chengli dahui shang de jianghua" 在中国文艺协会成立大会上的讲话 (Talk on the founding conference for the Chinese Literature and Art Association), *Mao Zedong wenji* 毛泽东文集 (Collected writings of Mao Zedong), vol. 1 (Beijing: Renmin chubanshe, 1993), 461–62.

15. Mao Zedong, "The Immortals at the River: To Ding Ling," in Chunhou Zhang and Edwin Vaughan, *Mao Zedong as Poet and Revolutionary Leader* (Lanham, MD: Lexington Books, 2002), 51–52.

16. Wang Zengru, "Mao Zedong liuci shuxie linjiang xian," 48–49; Wang Zengru's article has a detailed analysis of Mao Zedong's handwriting of "The Immortals at the River: To Ding Ling."

17. "1940 nian shiyue siri zhongyang zuzhibu shencha Ding Ling tongzhi beibu beijin

jingguo de jielun" 一九四零年十月四日《中央组织部审查丁玲同志被捕被禁经过的结论》(Conclusion of the review by the CCP Central Organization Department on the arrest and ban of Comrade Ding Ling on October 4, 1940), in *Ding Ling quanji*, vol. 10, 105.

18. "1940 nian shiyue siri zhongyang zuzhibu shencha Ding Ling tongzhi beibu beijin jingguo de jielun," 106. Chen Yun told Ding Ling that the last sentence of the "1940 Conclusion" was added by Mao Zedong. See Wen Liang 闻亮, "Youguan Ding Ling shengping de jige wenti—Chen Ming fangtan lu" 有关丁玲生平的几个问题—陈明访谈录 (Some issues related to Ding Ling's life—an interview with Chen Ming), *Bainian chao* 百年潮 (A hundred year tide) 1 (2001): 55.

19. Ding Ling, "Yan'an wenyi zuotanhui de qianqian houhou" 延安文艺座谈会的前前后后 (Before and after Mao Zedong's talks at the Yan'an Forum), in *Ding Ling quanji*, vol. 10, 280.

20. Ding Ling, "Mao Zhuxi gei women de yifeng xin" 毛主席给我们的一封信 (A letter Chairman Mao wrote to us), in *Ding Ling quanji*, vol. 10, 285.

21. Wang Zengru 王增如 and Li Xiangdong 李向东, *Ding Ling nianpu changbian* 丁玲年谱长编 (Lengthy compilation of Ding Ling's chronicle), vol. 1 (Tianjin: Tianjin renmin chubanshe, 2006), 178.

22. Wang Zengru and Li Xiangdong, *Ding Ling nianpu changbian*, vol. 1, 178.

23. Wang Zengru and Li Xiangdong, *Ding Ling nianpu changbian*, vol. 1, 179.

24. See Li Xiangdong 李向东, "Zui nan'ai de yinian—guanyu Ding Ling 1943 nian de jize riji" 最难挨的 — 年 — 关于丁玲1943年的几则日记 (The most difficult year—regarding some of Ding Ling's diary entries in 1943), *Xin wenxue shiliao* 新文学史料 (Historical materials on new literature) 4 (2007): 167.

25. Ding Ling, "Wangliang shijie," 39.

26. "1940 nian shiyue siri zhongyang zuzhibu shencha Ding Ling tongzhi beibu beijin jingguo de jielun," 105.

27. Ding Ling, "Huiyi Pan Hannian tongzhi" 回忆潘汉年同志 (Remembering Comrade Pan Hannian), in *Ding Ling quanji*, vol. 6, 209–10. Pan Hannian was also a cousin of Pan Zinian, who hosted Ding Ling's party admission ceremony and was arrested by the KMT along with her in 1933.

28. Ding Ling, "Huiyi Pan Hannian tongzhi," 211.

29. Wen Guang 文光, "Pan Hannian yuan'an qianqian houhou" 潘汉年冤案前前后后 (Before and after the unjust case of Pan Hannian), *Shanghai dangshi yanjiu* 上海党史研究 (Research on the history of the CCP in Shanghai) 6 (1995): 36.

30. Wen Guang, "Pan Hannian yuan'an qianqian houhou," 32–33.

31. Wen Guang, "Pan Hannian yuan'an qianqian houhou," 40.

32. Li Xiangdong, "Guanyu Ding Ling 1943 nian de jize riji," 167.

33. Wang Zengru and Li Xiangdong, *Ding Ling nianpu changbian*, vol. 1, 180.

34. Wang Zengru and Li Xiangdong, *Ding Ling nianpu changbian*, vol. 1, 190.

35. Li Xin 黎辛, "Guanyu 'Ding Ling Yuan'an jiqi lishi fansi' de bianzheng" 关于《丁玲冤案及其历史反思》的辩证 (Dialectics on "The Unjust Case of Ding Ling and Its Historical Reflection"), *Yue haifeng* 1 (2006): 63.

36. Li Xin, "Guanyu 'Ding Ling Yuan'an jiqi lishi fansi' de bianzheng," 63.

37. Ding Ling, "Yi Bishi tongzhi" 忆弼时同志 (Remembering Comrade Ren Bishi), in *Ding Ling quanji*, vol. 6, 330.

38. Chen Shuyu 陈漱渝, "Ding Ling yuan'an jiqi lishi fansi" 丁玲冤案及其历史反思 (The unjust case of Ding Ling and its historical reflection), *Yue haifeng* 4 (2005): 51.

39. Wang Zengru and Li Xiangdong, *Ding Ling nianpu changbian*, vol. 1, 337.

40. Wang Zengru 王增如 and Li Xiangdong 李向东, *Ding Ling zhuan* 丁玲传 (Biography of Ding Ling), vol. 2 (Beijing: Zhongguo da baike quanshu chubanshe, 2015), 507.

41. See Chen Shuyu, "Ding Ling yuan'an jiqi lishi fansi," 49; Li Zhilian 李之琏, "Wo canyu Ding Chen fandang xiao jituan an chuli jingguo" 我参与丁、陈"反党小集团"案处理经过 (My participation in the process of handling the Ding and Chen Anti-Party Clique case), *Yanhuang Chunqiu* 5 (1993): 13–14.

42. Wang Zengru and Li Xiangdong, *Ding Ling nianpu changbian*, vol. 1, 366.

43. Wang Zengru and Li Xiangdong, *Ding Ling nianpu changbian*, vol. 1, 383.

44. Chen Shuyu, "1957 nian pipan Ding Chen fandang jituan jishi" 1957年批判丁陈反党集团纪实 (A record of the criticism of the Ding Chen Anti-Party Group in 1957), *Xin wenxue shiliao* 4 (2014): 41.

45. Wang Zengru and Li Xiangdong, *Ding Ling nianpu changbian*, vol. 1, 395–96.

46. "Wenyi bao bianzhe anyu" 文艺报编者按语 (Editorial remarks in *Wenyi bao*), in *Zai pipan*, 2.

47. Wang Zengru and Li Xiangdong, *Ding Ling nianpu changbian*, vol. 1, 406.

48. "1979 nian wuyue sanri Zhongguo zuojia xiehui fucha bangongshi guanyu Ding Ling tongzhi youpai wenti de fucha jielun" 一九七九年五月三日中国作家协会复查办公室《关于丁玲同志右派问题的复查结论》(The review conclusion of Comrade Ding Ling's rightist issue by the China Writers Association review office on May 3, 1979), in *Ding Ling quanji*, vol. 10, 108.

49. Yi-tsi Mei Feuerwerker, *Ding Ling's Fiction* (Cambridge, MA: Harvard University Press, 1982), vii.

50. Shi Zhecun 施蛰存, "Huai Ding Ling shi sishou" 怀丁玲诗四首 (Four poems in memory of Ding Ling), *Yi tan* 4 (1981): 123–56.

51. For a detailed discussion of Zhou Yang's accusations against Ding Ling, see Chen Shuyu, "1957 nian pipan Ding Chen fandang jituan jishi," 41.

52. Chen Shuyu, "1957 nian pipan Ding Chen fandang jituan jishi," 41.

53. Ding Ling, "Wangliang shijie," 31.

54. Ding Ling, "Wangliang shijie," 30.

55. Ding Ling, "Wo suo renshi de Qu Qiubai tongzhi" 我所认识的瞿秋白同志 (Comrade Qu Qiubai as I knew him), in *Ding Ling quanji*, vol. 6, 53.

56. Ding Ling, "Wo suo renshi de Qu Qiubai tongzhi," 53.

57. Ding Ling, "Fengyu zhong yi Xiao Hong" 风雨中忆萧红 (Commemorating Xiao Hong in wind and rain), in *Ding Ling quanji*, vol. 5, 135.

58. Ding Ling, "Wo suo renshi de Qu Qiubai tongzhi," 57.

59. Li Meijie 李美皆, "Ding Ling yu Qu Qiubai" 丁玲与瞿秋白 (Ding Ling and Qu Qiubai), *Zuopin* 2 (2017): 107.

60. Wang Zengru and Li Xiangdong, *Ding Ling zhuan*, vol. 2, 723.

61. Ding Ling, "Wo suo renshi de Qu Qiubai tongzhi," 58.

62. Ding Ling, "Wo suo renshi de Qu Qiubai tongzhi," 58.

63. Zha Zhenke 查振科 and Li Xiangdong 李向东, "Chen Ming koushu: Ding Ling wan-

nian naxie shi" 陈明口述: 丁玲晚年那些事 (Chen Ming's oral account: The later life of Ding Ling), *Xin wenxue shiliao* 4 (2010): 136.

64. Li Hui 李辉, "Fengjing yi yuanqu—guanyu Xia Yan de suigan" 风景已远去—关于夏衍的随感 (The scenery has already gone—reflections on Xia Yan), *Shouhuo* 5 (1995): 101.

65. See Li Hui 李辉, "Yu Chen Ming tan Zhou Yang" 与陈明谈周扬 (Talking about Zhou Yang with Chen Ming), in Li Hui, *Yaodang de qiuqian—Shishi feifei shuo Zhou Yang* 摇荡的秋千—是是非非说周扬 (Swinging swing—discussing Zhou Yang's virtues and vices) (Shenzhen: Haitian chubanshe, 1998), 107.

66. Wang Xiaojue, *Modernity with a Cold War Face: Reimagining the Nation in Chinese Literature across the 1949 Divide* (Cambridge, MA: Harvard University Asia Center, 2013), 139.

67. Lu Xun, "My Views on Chastity," trans. Gladys Yang, in *Women in Republican China: A Sourcebook*, ed. Hua Lan and Vanessa Fong (London: Routledge, 1999), 12.

68. Ding Ling, "Wangliang shijie," 43.

69. "1940 nian shiyue siri zhongyang zuzhibu shencha Ding Ling tongzhi beibu beijin jingguo de jielun," 105.

70. Wang Zengru and Li Xiangdong, *Ding Ling nianpu changbian*, vol. 1, 102.

71. After Ding Ling's presumed martyrdom in 1933, the letters Ding Ling wrote to Feng Xuefeng were published in *Wenxue* 文学 (Literature) magazine under the title "Busuan qingshu" 不算情书 (Not love letters). See Ding Ling, "Busuan qingshu," *Wenxue* 1, no. 3 (1933): 367–70.

72. Wang Zengru and Li Xiangdong, *Ding Ling nianpu changbian*, vol. 1, 75.

73. Ding Ling, "Wangliang shijie," 5.

74. Ding Ling, "Wangliang shijie," 5.

75. Shen Congwen 沈从文, "Ji Ding Ling xuji" 记丁玲续集 (Sequel to remembering Ding Ling), in Shen Congwen, *Ji Ding Ling* 记丁玲 (Remembering Ding Ling) (Nanjing: Jingsu jiaoyu chubanshe, 2005), 199–200.

76. Wang Zengru and Li Xiangdong, *Ding Ling nianpu changbian*, vol. 1, 112.

77. Nie Gannu 聂绀弩, "Guanyu Feng Xuefeng" 关于冯雪峰 (About Feng Xuefeng), in Nie Gannu, *Ziwu yu zishu: Nie Gannu yundong dang'an huibian* 自诬与自述: 聂绀弩运动档案汇编 (Self-accusation and self-narration: Compilation of Nie Gannu's archives during the political movements) (Wuhan: Wuhan chubanshe, 2005), 222–23. In an essay she wrote in 1939, Ding Ling also mentioned that she had pleasant conversations with Nie Gannu on the train to Xi'an. See "Wo zenyang lai shaanbei de" 我怎样来陕北的 (How I arrived in Shaanbei), in *Ding Ling quanji*, vol. 5, 125–26.

In 1938, Ding Ling and Nie Gannu reunited in Xi'an. Ding invited Nie to collaborate on writing a play called *Tuji* 突击 (The sudden attack), along with Duanmu Hongliang 端木蕻良 and Xiao Hong. Nie Gannu was labeled a rightist and sent to Beidahuang in July 1958. After returning to Beijing in 1961, he remained deeply concerned about Ding Ling. During a conference in Xi'an in 1964, he even resorted to divination to inquire whether Ding Ling would return from Beidahuang. He expressed his longing for Ding Ling and Feng Xuefeng in a poem, which later served as evidence of his antirevolutionary sympathies during the Cultural Revolution. See Yuan Peili 袁培力, "Nie Gannu sanci lai Xi'an shimo" 聂绀弩三次来西安始末 (An account of Nie Gannu's three visits to Xi'an), *Gejie* 10 (2019): 73–74; Yu

Zhen 寓真, "Nie Gannu chuyu zhimi jiqi yishi" 聂绀弩出狱之谜及其轶诗 (The mystery of Nie Gannu's release from prison and his uncollected poems), *Xin wenxue shiliao* 3 (2003): 28.

78. See Ding Ling, "Wo zenyang lai Shaanbei de," in *Ding Ling quanji*, vol. 5, 125–26.

79. Ding Ling, "Wangliang shijie," 57. According to Nie Gannu's confession material, Ding Ling had a sexual relationship with someone other than Feng Da in Nanjing. He remembered Ding Ling telling him, "The KMT dispatched someone to keep an eye on her. That person initially slept outside of her room, but later moved in and had a sexual relationship with her." See Nie Gannu, "Guanyu Feng Xuefeng," 222.

In her memoir, Ding Ling mentioned that the KMT sent a couple to spy on her and Feng Da when they were on Mogan mountain. The husband had tuberculosis and thought Mogan mountain would be an ideal place for his rehabilitation. He quit his spying job shortly after realizing that the winter weather in Mogan mountain only caused worse coughs. See Ding Ling, "Wangliang shijie," 44–45.

Ding Ling wrote a few short stories during her house arrest, which were compiled and published as *Yiwai ji* 意外集 (Unexpected collection) in 1936. One of the short stories in this collection, "Chen Boxiang" 陈伯祥, was based on the story of a guard watching Ding Ling. The guards were depicted as pathetic men with no belief or purpose in their lives in both of her accounts. See Ding Ling, "Chen Boxiang" 陈伯祥, in *Yiwai ji* (Shanghai: Shanghai liangyou tushu, 1936), 89–101.

80. For Ding Ling's detailed account of her abduction in 1933, see Ding Ling, "Wangliang shijie," 6–10.

81. There are various versions of Feng Da's involvement in Ding Ling's arrest. Agnes Smedley recorded a story about Ding Ling's arrest, which was told to her by an engineer with the surname Li. Li claimed that he was apprehended by the KMT spies. At the headquarters of the KMT's secret service department, he witnessed a young man betraying his comrades and disclosing Ding Ling's address. However, the young man firmly stated that Ding Ling was not a Communist. Based on Li's descriptions, Smedley was confident that the traitor was her former secretary, Feng Da. Li was then forced to accompany the KMT spies to the address where Ding Ling and Pan Zinian were arrested. He later joined Ying Xiuren in his fight against the spies and managed to escape in the midst of the chaos caused by Ying's martyrdom. See Agnes Smedley, *Battle Hymn of China* (London: Victor Gollancz, 1944), 86–88.

On June 14, 1933, Ma Shaowu 马绍武, who was responsible for abducting Ding Ling and other communists, was assassinated by CCP secret agents. The *Shanghai Evening Post and Mercury* published details about Ding Ling's disappearance the next day, including accounts provided by Li under the pseudonym Li Chie-Chen. According to Wang Juru, Li Chie-Chen 李菊村 was the pseudonym of Xia Caixi 夏采曦 (1906–39), a graduate of Nanyang Mission College Engineering Department. He was working as a secret agent for the CCP when he was arrested by the KMT. See Wang Juru 王菊如, "Ying Xiuren shi bodou zhuilou haishi zisha zhuilou" 应修人是搏斗坠楼还是自杀坠楼 (Did Ying Xiuren fall from the building due to a struggle or as a result of suicide?), *Shiji* 4 (2019): 93–94.

The two accounts corroborated Li's role as a witness to the abduction. However, some details in the newspaper article titled "Car Number Links Sing Song Murder to Girl Kidnapping" are significantly different from what Smedley recalled from Li's accounts. For instance, the license plate number of the car associated with the abduction was 4223, rather than 1469 as recorded in Smedley's book. In the newspaper article, Li never mentioned that a traitor gave Ding Ling's address to the KMT spies, and he clearly remembered that the car started off to go to Ding Ling's place at one o'clock, not in the dark as Smedley recorded. Those details in the newspaper article align with later interviews with Ding Ling and her memoir. See Helen Snow, *Women in Modern China* (Beijing: Foreign Languages Press, 2004), 243–48; Ding Ling, "Wangliang shijie," 26–27.

Putting all of the puzzle pieces together, I believe Ding Ling and Feng Da were on the KMT spies' radar for a long time prior to their abduction. On the morning of May 14, 1933, Feng Da was followed and arrested by the KMT spies while on his way to visit two correspondents of the *Truth*. He was taken to the headquarters of the KMT's secret service department and interrogated. Not being a strong-willed revolutionary, Feng Da disclosed Ding Ling's address after 12 p.m., the time they had agreed upon to leave the house for safety concerns, thinking that no one would be present. Xia Caixi, under the pseudonym Li Chie-Chen, witnessed Feng Da's confession, the arrest of Ding Ling and Pan Zinian, and Ying Xiuren's martyrdom. Fifty years after the kidnapping, Ding Ling encountered Shen Zui 沈醉, a prominent KMT secret agent, at a study group. Shen told Ding that she was closely watched by the KMT spies and would have been arrested sooner or later even if the KMT had not obtained her address from Feng Da. See Wang Zengru 王增如, "Shen Zui xiang Ding Ling qingzui" 沈醉向丁玲请罪 (Shen Zui offers a humble apology to Ding Ling), *Lantai neiwai* 1 (2007): 58–59.

82. Ding Ling, "Wangliang shijie," 27.

83. Ding Ling, "Wangliang shijie," 56.

84. See Mei Zhi 梅志, *Hu Feng zhuan* 胡风传 (Biography of Hu Feng) (Beijing: Beijing shiyue wenyi chubanshe, 1998), 327–28.

85. Wang Zengru and Li Xiangdong, *Ding Ling nianpu changbian*, vol. 1, 110.

86. Ding Ling, "Wangliang shijie," 25–26.

87. Ping Jia 平斝, "Wei chengming yiqian de Ding Ling" 未成名以前的丁玲 (Ding Ling before her fame), *Shehui xinwen* 4, no. 13 (1933): 198.

88. Huayan Yigai 华严一丐, "Ding Ling yu Pengzi" 丁玲与蓬子 (Ding Ling and Pengzi), *Shijie chenbao*, June 26, 1932.

89. Ziye 子夜, "Ding Ling zuihou zhi airen" 丁玲最后之爱人 (Ding Ling's last lover), *Shidai ribao*, August 6, 1933.

90. See Zimo 子摩, "Ding Ling yu Pan Zinian" 丁玲与潘梓年 (Ding Ling and Pan Zinian), *Weiyan* 1, no. 3 (1933): 37–38.

91. See Lifu 戾夫, "Ding Ling zhi Shen Congwen zhi qingshu" 丁玲致沈从文之情书 (Ding Ling's love letter to Shen Congwen), *Fu'er Mosi*, August 31, 1933; Langhua 浪花, "Yao Pengzi shi Ding Ling nüshi de nanqie" 姚蓬子是丁玲女士的男妾 (Yao Pengzi is Ding Ling's male concubine), *Shanghai bao*, February 26, 1934; "Tian Han yu Ding Ling you fasheng lian'ai zhi shuo" 田汉与丁玲有发生恋爱之说 (An anecdote of a romantic relationship between Tian Han and Ding Ling), *Yule* 2, no. 28 (1936): 553; Wen Li 文丽, "Ding Ling Yang Hansheng yidu relian" 丁玲阳翰生一度热恋 (Ding Ling and Yang Hansheng were once in a romantic relationship), *Haifeng* 21 (1946): 7; Junyang 君羊, "Ding Ling zhi

tongxing lian'ai" 丁玲之同性恋爱 (Ding Ling's lesbian love affair), *Shehui ribao*, June 12, 1936.

According to Chen Bilan 陈碧兰, Ding Ling was in a lesbian relationship with Wang Jianhong, and both of them were in love with Qu Qiubai. See Chen Bilan, *Zaoqi Zhonggong yu tuopai: Wo de geming shengya huiyi* 早期中共与托派：我的革命生涯回忆 (Early Chinese Communist Party and Trotskyists: Memories of my revolutionary career) (Hong Kong: Tiandi tushu, 2010), 103.

92. "Ding Ling yi bei qiangjue" 丁玲已被枪决 (Ding Ling has been executed by firing squad), *Dagong bao* (Tianjin), June 25, 1933.

93. "Ding Ling yi bei qiangjue."

94. Quoted from Ding Ling, "Lu Xun xiansheng yuwo," 118.

95. Quoted from L. Insun, "Ding Ling zai Shaanbei" 丁玲在陕北 (Ding Ling in Shaanbei), in *Nü zhanshi Ding Ling* 女战士丁玲 (Woman warrior Ding Ling) (Shanghai: Meiri yibao she, 1938), 40.

96. Ding Ling, "Wangliang shijie," 24, 28.

Exhibition II

1. *Qiu Jin nianbiao xibian* 秋瑾年表细编 (Detailed chronological biography of Qiu Jin), ed. Wang Qubing 王去病 and Chen Dehe 陈德和 (Beijing: Huawen chubanshe, 1990), 37–38.

2. *Qiu Jin nianbiao xibian*, 72.

3. *Qiu Jin nianbiao xibian*, 74.

4. *Qiu Jin nianbiao xibian*, 79, 82.

5. See *Qiu Jin nianbiao xibian*, 75.

6. *Qiu Jin nianbiao xibian*, 94.

7. See *Qiu Jin nianbiao xibian*, 118–24.

8. Ding Ling, "Si zhi ge," 5.

9. Ding Ling, "Wo de zhongxue shenghuo de pianduan" 我的中学生活的片断 (Fragments of my middle school life), in Ding Ling, *Ding Ling zishu* 丁玲自述 (Ding Ling's self-narrative) (Zhengzhou: Daxiang chubanshe, 2006), 11–13.

10. "Lun Wan sheng dianju Guifu shi" 论皖省电据贵福事 (Regarding the news that Anhui sent a telegram declining the appointment of Guifu), *Shenbao*, April 23, 1908.

11. "Xiagu yinghun zheng shouqiu" 侠骨英魂正首邱 (The chivalrous and heroic spirit returns home), *Xinwen bao*, October 27, 1912.

12. "Xu Xilin zhulian an yuwen" 徐锡麟株连案余闻 (More news linked to Xu Xilin's case), *Shibao*, July 24, 1907.

13. "Lianhe bingqing jieshi Qiu Jin zui'an" 联合禀请揭示秋瑾罪案 (A joint plea to publicize the case of Qiu Jin), *Shibao*, July 29, 1907.

14. Wu Zhiying 吴芝瑛, "Lun Qiu Jin yu yu Huangya yu zhi bijiao" 论秋瑾狱与黄厓狱之比较 (On the comparison between the case of Qiu Jin and the case of the uprising in Huangya mountain), *Shibao*, November 22, 1907.

15. See "Qiu Jin yuansha zhi yuanyin" 秋瑾冤杀之原因 (The reason behind the wrongful execution of Qiu Jin), *Shenbao*, July 23, 1907; "Qiu Jin nüshi yuansha zhi lishi" 秋瑾女士冤杀之历史 (The history of the wrongful execution of Qiu Jin), *Shenbao*, July 28, 1907.

16. Qitian nüshi 泣天女士, "Ai Qiu Jin an" 哀秋瑾案 (Lament for Qiu Jin's case), *Shibao*, July 29, 1907.

17. Zhi Da 志达, "Qiu Jin sihou zhi yuan" 秋瑾死后之冤 (The injustice after Qiu Jin's death), *Tianyi* 15 (1908): 28.

18. "Qiu Jin nüshi aici" 秋瑾女史哀词 (Mourning for Ms. Qiu Jin), *Shenzhou ribao*, August 3, 1907.

19. Ji Sheng 旡生, "Xuanting fuhuo ji" 轩亭复活记 (Resurrection at Xuanting), *Shenzhou ribao*, from September 7 to October 5, 1907.

20. Wu Zhiying, "Ai Shanyin" 哀山阴 (Mourning Qiu Jin from Shanyin), trans. Hu Ying, in Hu Ying, *Burying Autumn: Poetry, Friendship, and Loss* (Cambridge, MA: Harvard University Asia Center, 2016), 217. Also see *Qiu Jin yanjiu ziliao* 秋瑾研究资料 (Qiu Jin research materials), ed. Guo Yanli 郭延礼 (Jinan: Shandong jiaoyu chubanshe, 1987), 566.

21. Xu Zihua 徐自华, "Jianhu nüxia Qiu Jin mubiao" 鉴湖女侠秋君墓表 (Epitaph for the female knight of Jianhu with surname Qiu), in *Qiu Jin yanjiu ziliao*, 559.

22. Qiu Yuzhang 秋誉章, "Wuti" 无题 (Untitled), in *Qiu Jin yanjiu ziliao*, 573.

23. Qiu Jin, "Zeng Jiang Lushan xiansheng yanzhi" 赠蒋鹿珊先生言志 (Expressing my aspiration in the poem addressed to Mr. Jiang Lushan), in Guo Yanli 郭延礼, *Qiu Jin wenxue lungao* 秋瑾文学论稿 (Manuscript on Qiu Jin's literary writings) (Xi'an: Shaanxi renmin chubanshe, 1987), 61.

24. Xiaoshan Xianglingzi 萧山湘灵子, "Xuanting yuan" 轩亭冤 (Tragedy at Xuanting), in *Wan Qing wenxue congchao: chuanqi zaju juan* 晚清文学丛钞:传奇杂剧卷 (Late Qing literature collection: Volume on *chuanqi* and *zaju*), ed. A Ying 阿英 (Beijing: Zhonghua shuju, 1962), 137.

25. Jingguanzi 静观子, *Liuyue shuang* 六月霜 (Frost in June) (Shanghai: Shanghai wenhua chubanshe, 1958), 7.

26. Jingguanzi, *Liuyue shuang*, 31.

27. Jingguanzi, *Liuyue shuang*, 4.

28. Jingguanzi, *Liuyue shuang*, 4.

29. Jingguanzi, *Liuyue shuang*, 69.

30. Jingguanzi, *Liuyue shuang*, 7.

31. Jingguanzi, *Liuyue shuang*, 24–25.

32. See Xiaoshan Xianglingzi, *Xuanting yuan*, 135–37. Hu Ying offered detailed analysis of Qiu Jin's crying scenes in *Xuanting yuan*. Hu Ying, "Gender and Modern Martyrology: Qiu Jin as *Lienü*, *Lieshi*, or *Nülieshi*," in *Beyond Exemplar Tales: Women's Biography in Chinese History*, ed. Joan Judge and Hu Ying (Berkeley: University of California Press, 2011), 125–26.

33. Xiaoshan Xianglingzi, *Xuanting yuan*, 136.

34. Hu Ying, "Gender and Modern Martyrology," 126.

35. Xiaoshan Xianglingzi, *Xuanting yuan*, 131.

36. Jingguanzi, *Liuyue shuang*, 63–64.

37. Jingguanzi, *Liuyue shuang*, 36.

38. Taiyan 太炎, "Ji Xu Xilin, Chen Boping, Ma Zonghan, Qiu Jin wen" 祭徐锡麟陈伯平马宗汉秋瑾文 (An essay mourning Xu Xilin, Chen Boping, Ma Zonghan, and Qiu Jin), *Minbao* 17 (1907): 117–18.

39. Taiyan 太炎, "Qiu Jin ji xu" 秋瑾集序 (Preface to a collection of Qiu Jin's works), *Minbao* 17 (1907): 118–19.

40. Hu Ying, "Gender and Modern Martyrology," 128.

41. In "Ji Qiu nüshi yishi" 纪秋女士遗事 (Anecdotal memoir of Ms. Qiu), Wu Zhiying recalls that she frequently warned Qiu Jin about her radical comments on the revolution. Qiu Jin once assured Wu that she was not a revolutionary. See Wu Zhiying, "Ji Qiu nüshi yishi," *Shibao*, July 25, 1907.

42. Wu Zhiying, "Qiu Jin yizhu xu" 秋瑾遗著序 (Preface to the posthumous works of Qiu Jin), *Minguo bao* 4 (1912): 4.

43. "Wu Zhiying fufu zhi Xu Zihua de shi'er feng xin" 吴芝瑛夫妇致徐自华的12封信 (Twelve letters from Mr. and Mrs. Wu Zhiying to Xu Zihua), compiled by Zhou Yongzhen 周永珍, in *Jindaishi ziliao* 近代史资料 (Modern history materials), no. 91 (Beijing: Zhongguo shehui kexue chubanshe, 1997), 275.

44. "Wu Zhiying fufu zhi Xu Zihua de shi'er feng xin," 277.

45. "Zhu lieshi zhuidao dahui ji" 诸烈士追悼大会纪 (Record of the memorial service for numerous martyrs), *Shenbao*, December 18, 1911. The honored revolutionary martyrs include Fu Cixiang 傅慈祥, Yang Weiyun 杨卫云, Shi Jianru 史坚如, Zheng Chenglie 郑承烈, Qin Lisan 秦力三, Cai Weizhi 蔡蔚之, Zhang Peiru 张沛如, and Qiu Jin.

46. "Zhu lieshi zhuidao dahui ji."

47. "Zai ji zhuidaohui xiangqing" 再记追悼会详情 (Additional account of the memorial service details), *Shenbao*, December 20, 1911. Huang Fu was the chief advisor for the Shanghai military government.

48. "Xu nüshi qing xiufu Qiu mu" 徐女士请修复秋墓 (Ms. Xu requests the restoration of Qiu Jin's tomb), *Shenbao*, January 12, 1912.

49. For details about the memorial service in Shaoxing, see "Cao E jiangshang zhi hanchao" 曹娥江上之寒潮 (Cold tides of the Cao E River), *Shenbao*, January 29, 1912. The Qiu Society was founded by Xu Zihua in 1908 to commemorate Qiu Jin.

50. For details about the memorial service in Hangzhou, see "Zheren zhuidao zhu xianlie" 浙人追悼诸先烈 (People in Zhejiang commemorating the martyrs), *Shenbao*, January 30, 1912.

51. "Lujun bu qing jiang qian-Qing zhaozhong ge zhuanci fenbie gaijian dahan zhonglie ci cheng" 陆军部请将前清昭忠各专祠分别改建大汉忠烈祠呈 (Ministry of the Army's request to convert all shrines dedicated to loyal soldiers from the Qing dynasty into shrines honoring the great Han loyal martyrs), *Linshi zhengfu gongbao* 临时政府公报 (Provisional Government gazette) 51 (1912): 14.

52. "Qiu xia ruci jisheng" 秋侠入祠纪盛 (Records of welcoming the spiritual tablet of the knight-errant with the surname Qiu into the ancestral hall), *Shenbao*, July 21, 1912.

53. For details about the memorial service for Qiu Jin in Changsha, see "Changsha zhuidao Qiu nüxia jisheng" 长沙追悼秋女侠纪盛 (Records of the grand memorial service for female knight-errant with the surname Qiu in Changsha), *Shenbao*, July 27, 1912.

54. Henrietta Harrison, "Martyrs and Militarism in Early Republican China," *Twentieth-Century China* 23, no. 2 (1998): 43.

55. "Qiu nüxia guigu Xihu" 秋女侠归骨西湖 (The remains of the female knight-errant with the surname Qiu return to West Lake), *Shenbao*, September 24, 1912.

56. "Qiu nüxia guigu Xihu."

57. For details about transforming and reburying Qiu Jin at West Lake, see "Yunsong nüxia lingchen xiangzhi" 运送女侠灵榇详志 (Detailed records on transforming the female knight-errant's coffin), *Shenbao*, October 27, 1912; "Qiufeng qiuyu tuo qiuhun" 秋风秋雨妥秋魂 (Autumn wind and autumn rain bring peace to the spirit of Qiu), *Shenbao*, October 29, 1912.

58. "Sun Zhongshan li hang jishi" 孙中山莅杭记事 (Accounts of Sun Yat-sen's visit in Hangzhou), *Shenbao*, December 10, 1912.

59. For his visit to Hangzhou after the death of Yuan Shikai, see "Sun Zhongshan xiansheng hang you riji" 孙中山先生杭游日记 (Diary of Mr. Sun Yat-sen's visit in Hangzhou), *Yishi bao* (Tianjin), August 26, 1916.

60. Jiang Shengmei 蒋胜眉, "Dingmu huiyilu" 丁母回忆录 (The memoir of Ding Ling's mother), in *Ding Ling quanji*, vol. 1, 343. For details about their visit to Hangzhou and the West Lake Exposition in 1929, see "Dingmu huiyilu," 340–46.

61. Other exhibition halls include Museum Hall (Bowu guan 博物馆), Art Hall (Yishu guan 艺术馆), Agriculture Hall (Nongye guan 农业馆), Education Hall (Jiaoyu guan 教育馆), Public Health Hall (Weisheng guan 卫生馆), Silk Hall (Sichou guan 丝绸馆), Industry Hall (Gongye guan 工业馆), Special Exhibition Hall (Tezhong chenliesuo 特种陈列所), and Exhibition Hall for Reference (Cankao chenliesuo 参考陈列所). See *Xihu bolanhui canguan bixie* 西湖博览会参观必携 (Essential guide for visiting the West Lake Exposition) (Shanghai: Shangwu yinshuguan, 1929), 3–6.

62. Li Chaoying 李超英, "Xuyan" 序言 (Preface), in *Xihu wenxian jicheng* 西湖文献集成 (West Lake collective archives), vol. 16, ed. Wang Guoping 王国平 (Hangzhou: Hangzhou chubanshe, 2004), 796.

63. Hu Yong 湖傭, "Danghua de Xihu bolanhui" 党化的西湖博览会 (Politicized West Lake Exposition), *Xinwen bao*, January 16, 1929.

64. Hu Yong, "Danghua de Xihu bolanhui."

65. Kirk Denton, *Exhibiting the Past: Historical Memory and the Politics of Museums in Postsocialist China* (Honolulu: University of Hawai'i Press, 2014), 51.

66. For details about the layout of the Revolutionary Memorial Hall and the visitors' guidelines, see *Xihu wenxian jicheng*, vol. 16, 804–7.

67. *Xihu wenxian jicheng*, vol. 16, 804–7.

68. For the items on display commemorating Qiu Jin in the Revolutionary Memorial Hall, see *Xihu wenxian jicheng*, vol. 16, 809; and "Xihu bolanhui canguan baogao" 西湖博览会参观报告 (West Lake Exposition visit report), *Suzhong xiaokan* 苏中校刊 (Suzhou middle school magazine) 1, no. 27/28 (1929): 30–31.

69. "Qiu Jin jiuyi guci" 秋瑾就义鼓词 (Drum lyrics version of *Qiu Jin's Martyrdom*), *Zhongyang ribao* 中央日报 (Central news daily), November 2, 1932.

70. "Qiu Jin jiuyi guci."

71. Pan Gongzhan 潘公展, "Xunling" 训令 (Command), *Shanghaishi jiaoyuju jiaoyu zhoubao* 上海市教育局教育周报 (Shanghai Educational Bureau weekly newspaper) 212 (1933): 3.

72. "Guofu mingling baoyang Qiu Jin" 国府明令褒扬秋瑾 (Nationalist government issued an order to eulogize Qiu Jin), *Zhongyang ribao*, October 15, 1935.

73. "Zhongyang dangshi shiliao chenlieguan jin xing luochengli" 中央党史史料陈列馆今行落成礼 (The opening ceremony for the Exhibition Hall for Historical Materials of the KMT was held today), *Minbao*, October 10, 1936. The Exhibition Hall for Historical Materials of the KMT is now the Second Historical Archives of China (*Zhongguo di'er lishi dang'an guan* 中国第二历史档案馆).

74. *Zhongyang dangshi shiliao chenlieguan chenlie shiliao mulu* 中央党史史料陈列馆陈列史料目录 (Catalog of historical materials on display at the Exhibition Hall for Historical Materials of the KMT), Zhongyang dangshi shiliao bianzuo weiyuanhui bianyin 中央党史史料编纂委员会编印 (Printed by the committee for editing the historical materials of the KMT), 1937, 12.

75. Xu Zihua, "Fanchuan ji" 返钏记 (A record of returning the bracelets), *Jiansu geming bowuguan yuekan* 5 (1929): 5–7. The essay first appeared in Zhang Jiya's 张寄涯 "Qiu chuan" 秋钏 (Qiu Jin's bracelets) in *Shenbao* on August 1, 1927.

76. The middle school textbooks in the Republic of China include the original classical Chinese version of the "Fanchuan ji." See *Kaiming guowen duben* 开明国文读本 (Kaiming Chinese textbook), vol. 2, ed. Wang Boxiang 王伯祥 (Shanghai: Kaiming shudian, 1932), 72–73; *Chuzhong guowen duben* 初中国文读本 (Middle school Chinese textbook), vol. 2, ed. Zhu Wenshu 朱文叔 (Shanghai: Shanghai zhonghua shuju, 1933), 16–17.

The vernacular version of "Fanchuan ji" was included in textbooks for senior elementary school students in the Republic of China. See *Fuxing Guoyu keben gaoxiao* 复兴国语课本高小 (Fuxing Chinese textbook for senior elementary school students), vol. 3, ed. Shen Baiying 沈百英, Zong Lianghuan 宗亮寰, and Ding Kouyin 丁瞉音 (Shanghai: Shangwu yinshu guan, 1935), 35–37; *Jiben jiaokeshu guoyu* 基本教科书国语 (Basic Chinese textbook), vol. 2, ed. Dai Hongheng 戴洪恒 (Shanghai: Shangwu yinshuguan, 1932), 15–17.

77. See *Jiben jiaokeshu gaoxiao guoyu jiaoxuefa* 基本教科书高小国语教学法 (Teaching methodology for *Basic Chinese Textbook*), vol. 2, ed. Dai Hongheng 戴洪恒 (Shanghai: Shangwu yinshuguan, 1932), 40.

78. Wang Canzhi, "Chengsong xianci yiwu feicui shuanglong yuzhuo yishuang chenlie gemingdang shiliao chenlieguan xu" 呈送先慈遗物翡翠双龙玉镯一双陈列革命党史料陈列馆序 (Preface for donating my late mother's emerald green jade bracelets with engraved double dragon to the Exhibition Hall for Historical Materials of the KMT), *Shanghai funü* 上海妇女 (Women in Shanghai) 1, no. 4 (1938): 14.

79. "Xinhai geming wenxianzhanlan" 辛亥革命文献展览 (Xinhai Revolution archive exhibition), *Dagong bao* (Shanghai), October 9, 1947.

80. "Weile Xinhai geming wenxian zhanlanhui Qiu Jin nügongzi Wang Canzhi gaixing" 为了辛亥革命文献展览会秋瑾女公子王灿芝改姓 (Qiu Jin's daughter Wang Canzhi changed her surname for the Xinhai Revolution Archive Exhibition), *Chengbao*, October 14, 1947.

81. For details about this exhibition, see "Qiu Jin jiuyi sishinian juxing yiji zhanlanhui" 秋瑾就义四十年举行遗迹展览会 (Relics of Qiu Jin exhibition for the fortieth anniversary of her martyrdom), *Shenbao*, April 14, 1948; and "Qiu Jin yiji zhanlan" 秋瑾遗迹展览 (Relics of Qiu Jin exhibition), *Dagong bao* (Shanghai), April 25, 1948.

82. Hu Ying, *Burying Autumn*, 143.

83. Daixi 黛茜 argues that the year 1936 should be considered as the year of Qiu Jin. See

Daixi, "Jinnian wei Qiu Jin xianlie xunguo zhi sanshinian jinian" 今年为秋瑾先烈殉国之三十年纪念 (This year marks the thirtieth anniversary of Qiu Jin's martyrdom for the nation), *Shenbao*, May 30, 1936. In "Qiu Jin nian" 秋瑾年 (The year of Qiu Jin), the author explains that in traditional Chinese culture, thirty years is considered an era (*sanshi wei yishi* 三十为一世). As a result, 1936 should be designated as the Year of Qiu Jin, and large memorial events should be held in her honor. See Wan Ye 万叶, "Qiu Jin nian," *Shibao*, June 24, 1936.

84. "Benshi funüjie kai kuoda jinianhui" 本市妇女界开扩大纪念会 (Local women's community will host an expanded commemoration meeting), *Minbao*, March 7, 1936.

85. For details about the meetings on March 8 in Nanjing and Shanghai, as well as the parade, see "Sanba funüjie jinghu liangdi juxing jinian" 三八妇女节京沪两地举行纪念 (Nanjing and Shanghai hosted commemoration meetings on March 8, International Women's Day), *Shidai ribao*, March 9, 1936; "Shoudu funüjie zuo relie qingzhu sanbajie" 首都妇女界昨热烈庆祝三八节 (Women in Nanjing celebrated March 8 yesterday), *Zhongyang ribao*, March 9, 1936; and "Shanghai juxing sanba funüjie" 上海举行三八妇女节 (Shanghai celebrates March 8, International Women's Day), *Shenghuo jiaoyu* 生活教育 (Life and education) 3, no. 3 (1936): 1.

86. Shen Zijiu 沈兹九, "Women weishenme yao jinian Qiu Jin" 我们为什么要纪念秋瑾 (Why we should commemorate Qiu Jin), *Funü shenghuo* 妇女生活 (Women's life) 3, no. 2 (1936): 6.

87. The script was initially published in *Guangming* 光明 (Light) magazine. See Xia Yan 夏衍, *Ziyou hun* 自由魂 (The spirit of freedom), *Guangming* 2, no. 1 (1936): 845–56 and vol. 2, no. 2 (1936): 941–55. It was later republished in 1937. See Xia Yan, *Ziyou hun* 自由魂 (The spirit of freedom) (Shanghai: Shanghai shenghuo shudian, 1937). The title of the play was changed to *Qiu Jin zhuan* 秋瑾传 (Biography of Qiu Jin) for the version published in 1950. See Xia Yan, *Qiu Jin zhuan* (Shanghai: Kaiming shudian, 1950).

88. In 1935, in response to the national crisis, Zhou Libo 周立波 proposed the concept of national defense literature (*guofang wenxue* 国防文学) as a means to resist the foreign invasions and combat traitors. See Libo 立波, "Guanyu guofang wenxue" 关于国防文学 (About national defense literature), *Shishi xinbao*, December 21, 1935.

In February 1936, *Shenghuo zhishi* 生活知识 (Knowledge of life) magazine dedicated a special issue to national defense theater (*guofang xiju* 国防戏剧). In this issue, Zhou Gangming 周钢鸣 emphasized the mission of national defense theater, which was to mobilize people for national salvation. He outlined two key themes for national defense dramas: anti–foreign invasion and antitraitor. See Zhou Gangming, "Minzu weiji yu guofang xiju" 民族危机与国防戏剧 (National crisis and national defense theater), *Shenghuo zhishi* 1, no. 10 (1936): 481–85.

Another article in this special issue, written by Zhang Geng 张庚, argued that the best topics for national defense theater are historical events because they can serve as allusions to contemporary events. See Zhang Geng, "Guofang xiju de ticai he ticai chuli" 国防戏剧的题材和题材处理 (The topics of national defense dramas and how to handle them), *Shenghuo zhishi* 1, no. 10 (1936): 485–87. These discussions had a significant impact on the writing of national defense dramas.

89. For details about the incident and its aftermath following the performance of *Sai Jinhua* in Nanjing, see "*Sai Jinhua* beida you zaofa" 赛金花被打又遭罚 (*Sai Jinhua* crew was beaten up and fined), *Jingang zuan*, February 28, 1937; and "Sai Jinhua shoudu chu

maobing" 赛金花首都出毛病 (Issues arising from the performance of *Sai Jinhua* in the capital), *Diansheng* 6, no. 9 (1937): 462.

90. For the reasons for changing the title of the play to *Qiu Jin*, see "Sai Jinhua, Qiu Jin" 赛金花，秋瑾, *Minbao*, January 24, 1937.

91. Xia Yan discussed the motivations behind his writing of the play in an essay commemorating Qiu Jin. See Xia Yan, "Qiu Jin buxiu" 秋瑾不朽 (Long live Qiu Jin), *Renmin ribao* 人民日报 (People's daily), December 5, 1979. Feng Keng was the only female martyr among the five martyrs of the League of Left-wing Writers.

92. Xia Yan, *Ziyou hun* 自由魂 (The spirit of freedom) (Shanghai: Shanghai shenghuo shudian, 1937), 99.

93. Xia Yan mentioned in his memoir that he was impressed and influenced by Shi Cuntong's 施存统 revolutionary essay "Feixiao" 非孝 (Against filial piety), which was published in *Zhejiang xinchao* 浙江新潮 (New waves in Zhejiang) in 1919. See Xia Yan, *Lanxun jiumeng lu* 懒寻旧梦录 (Leisurely recollecting my old dreams) (Beijing: Sanlian shudian, 2000), 29.

94. Xia Yan, *Ziyou hun*, 94.

95. Xia Yan, *Ziyou hun*, 101.

96. Xia Yan, *Ziyou hun*, 72.

97. Xia Yan, *Ziyou hun*, 82.

98. In his essay commemorating Qiu Jin, Xia Yan noted the criticism from Guo Moruo and Tian Han. See Xia Yan, "Qiu Jin buxiu."

99. Quoted from Xia Yan, "Qiu Jin buxiu." In "Nala de da'an" 娜拉的答案 (The answer to Nora), Guo Moruo eulogizes Qiu Jin's sacrifice and states that Qiu Jin's "martyrdom for the revolution was an action of seeking benevolence and receiving benevolence (*qiuren deren* 求仁得仁). Why, then, was her sacrifice considered unjust and pitiful?" See Guo Moruo 郭沫若, "Nala de da'an," *Xinhua ribao* 新华日报 (New China daily), July 19, 1942.

100. For the full text of the Publication Law, see "Chuban fa" 出版法 (Publication Law), *Guomin zhengfu gongbao* 国民政府公报 (Nationalist government gazette) 651 (1930): 3–8.

101. "Xuanchuanpin shencha biaozhun" 宣传品审查标准 (Standards for inspecting propaganda materials), *Zhongyang dangwu yuekan* 中央党务月刊 (Central Party affairs monthly), no. 45/46 (1932): 414.

102. For the full texts of the two directives, see the "Shenjing guomin duiyu youbang wudunmuyi ling" 申儆国民对于友邦务敦睦谊令 (Directive urging citizens to foster friendly relations with other nations), *Guomin zhengfu gongbao* 1764 (1935): 1; and "Weichi zhi'an jinji banfa ling" 维持治安紧急办法令 (Emergency measures for maintaining public order), *Guomin zhengfu gongbao* 1977 (1936): 1–2.

103. Xia Yan, "Gei gaibianzhe de yifeng xin" 给改编者的一封信 (A letter to the adaptors), in Wang Yan 王雁, *Qiu Jin zhuan (Jingju)* 秋瑾传 (京剧) (Biography of Qiu Jin: Peking opera adaptation) (Beijing: Beijing chubanshe, 1960), 2.

104. Xia Yan's memoir contains detailed accounts of the "strange Westerner incident" and his involvement in it. See Xia Yan, *Lanxun jiumeng lu*, 187–93. For an in-depth analysis of the Walden incident, see David Ian Chambers, "Shanghai's 'Mysterious Westerner': The Walden Affair and Soviet Military Intelligence Operations in China, 1933–1935," *Twentieth-Century China* 40, no. 2 (2015): 105–25.

105. Luo Fu 罗夫, "*Liang Hongyu* de gongyan ji qita" 《梁红玉》的公演及其他 (The pre-

miere of *Liang Hongyu* and more), *Zhongguo funü* 中国妇女 (Chinese women) 1, no. 10/11 (1940): 17.

106. Yan Yiyan studied in Japan and learned scriptwriting under Hong Shen 洪深 after returning to China in 1937. In 1938, she went to Yan'an and attended the Counter-Japanese Military and Political University. She is the screenwriter of films such as *Zhonghua nü'er* 中华女儿 (Daughters of China, 1949) and *Yiguan hairen dao* 一贯害人道 (The harmful Way of Pervading Unity, 1952), as well as the author of the spoken drama *Dongfeng shitang* 东风食堂 (Dongfeng dining hall, 1956). For a detailed introduction to Yan Yiyan, see "Yan Yiyan" 颜一烟, in *Yan'an wenyi dang'an* 延安文艺档案 (The archive of art and literature in Yan'an), vol. 3, ed. Wang Jucai 王巨才 (Xi'an: Taibai wenyi chubanshe, 2015), 891–917.

107. Yan Yiyan 颜一烟, "Yan'an shangyan de *Qiu Jin*" 延安上演的秋瑾 (*Qiu Jin* performed in Yan'an), *Zhongguo funü* 1, no. 10/11 (1940): 19.

108. Mao Zedong, "Mao Zedong zai Yan'an Zhongguo nüzi daxue kaixue dianli shang de jianghua" 毛泽东在延安中国女子大学开学典礼上的讲话 (Mao Zedong's speech at the opening ceremony of Chinese Women's University in Yan'an), *Xin zhonghua bao* 新中华报 (New China news), July 25, 1939.

109. "Wanren qingzhu zhong zhuangyan relie juxing le Zhongguo nüzi daxue kaixue dianli" 万人庆祝中庄严热烈举行了中国女子大学开学典礼 (Thousands of people celebrated as Chinese Women's University held its opening ceremony with great solemnity and enthusiasm), *Xin zhonghua bao*, July 25, 1939.

110. Wang Ming was responsible for women's affairs in Yan'an. He played a significant role in the establishment of the Chinese Women's University and *Zhongguo funü* 中国妇女 (Chinese women) magazine. Meng Qingshu 孟庆树 (1911–83), Wang Ming's wife, was also a prominent leader in the women's movement in Yan'an and served as the vice president of the Chinese Women's University.

111. Wang Ming 王明, "Wang Ming tongzhi zai Zhongguo nüzi daxue kaixue dianli dahui shang de baogao" 王明同志在中国女子大学开学典礼大会上的报告 (Comrade Wang Ming's report on the opening ceremony of Chinese Women's University), *Zhongguo funü* 1, no. 3 (1939): 4.

112. Song Qingling was married to Sun Yat-sen, He Xiangning was the widow of Liang Zhongkai 廖仲恺, Xiang Jingyu was married to Cai Hesen 蔡和森, Zhou Enlai and Deng Yingchao were considered the perfect revolutionary couple, Kang Keqing was married to Zhu De 朱德, and Cai Chang was married to Li Fuchun 李富春 and was also the sister-in-law of Xiang Jingyu.

113. For details on the New Life Movement, see Chiang Kai-shek, "Xin shenghuo yundong gangyao" 新生活运动纲要 (Essentials of the New Life Movement), *Xin shenghuo zhoukan* 新生活周刊 (New life weekly) 1, no. 4 (1934): 1–6. In it, Chiang argues that the shortcomings of communists stem from their lack of "*li, yi, lian, chi*." See "Xin shenghuo yundong gangyao," 3.

114. There were numerous reports on the virtuous wife and good mother movements in Nazi Germany and Fascist Italy in China in the 1930s. For instance: "Deguo yong jiu daode jiaoyu nüzi shicheng xianqiliangmu" 德国用旧道德教育女子使成贤妻良母 (Germany uses old virtues to educate women to become virtuous wives and good mothers), *Shengjing shibao*, July 22, 1933; Shen Yiming 沈亦鸣, "Mosuolini de furen: Yige xianqiliangmu de

dianxing" 墨索里尼的夫人：一个贤妻良母的典型 (Madame Mussolini: A representative of virtuous wife and good mother), *Shanghai zhoubao* 3, no. 20 (1934): 389–90; "Deguo xianqiliangmu yundong" 德国贤妻良母运动 (Virtuous wife and good mother movement in Germany), *Linglong* 5, no. 21 (1935): 1370–71; "Yidali peiyang xianqiliangmu de jiaoyu" 意大利培养贤妻良母的教育 (Education to cultivate virtuous wives and good mothers in Italy), *Shandong minzhong jiaoyu yuekan* 山东民众教育月刊 (Shandong citizens' education monthly) 6, no. 5 (1935): 1.

115. See Zhimin 志敏, "Xin xianqiliangmu lun" 新贤妻良母论 (On new virtuous wife and good mother), *Zhongyang ribao*, May 1, 1935; "Lusheng nüzi jiaoyu fangzhen jiang zhuyi xianqiliangmu zhi" 鲁省女子教育方针将注意贤妻良母制 (Women's education in Shandong will focus on the doctrine of virtuous wife and good mother), *Zhongyang ribao*, June 7, 1935; Zhimin 志敏 "Zailun xin xianqiliangmu" 再论新贤妻良母论 (Revisiting the new virtuous wife and good mother theory), *Zhongyang ribao*, September 4, 1935.

116. *Funü gongming* was supported by the Nationalist Party. The special issue includes essays that both promote and criticize the virtuous wife and good mother movement. However, most of them agree that women should prioritize taking care of the family. For the special issue, see *Funü gongming* 4, no. 11 (1935): 9–55.

117. Luo Qiong 罗琼, "Cong xianqiliangmu zhi xianfuliangfu: Du *Funü gongming* xianliang wenti zhuanhao yihou" 从贤妻良母至贤夫良父：读《妇女共鸣》贤良问题专号以后 (From virtuous wife and good mother to virtuous husband and good father: After reading the special issue on "the question of being virtuous" in *Funü gongming*), *Funü shenghuo* 2, no. 1 (1936): 60.

118. Shen Zijiu, "Xin qimu xuexiao" 新妻母学校 (The new wife and mother school), *Funü shenghuo* 2, no. 5 (1936): 1–2.

119. Nora is the female protagonist in Norwegian playwright Henrik Ibsen's (1828–1906) play *A Doll's House* (1879). Hu Shi 胡适 introduced Ibsen and his play *A Doll's House* to China in 1918, inspiring the women's movement in the country.

120. See "Nanjing Nala shijian de jingguo" 南京娜拉事件的经过 (The course of the Nanjing Nora Incident), *Xi zhoukan* 戏周刊 (Theater weekly) 27 (1935): 3–9.

121. Gengfu 更夫, "Sanba tan Nala" 三八谈娜拉 (Discussing Nora on March 8), *Xin shehui* 8, no. 6 (1935): 57. For the whole special issue, see *Xin shehui* 8, no. 6 (1935): 55–58.

122. Weiming 微明, "Nala de jiufen" 娜拉的纠纷 (The dispute on Nora), *Manhua shenghuo* 漫画生活 (Comic life) 7 (1935): 5.

123. "Nala zuotan" 娜拉座谈 (Nora symposium), *Funü shenghuo* 2, no. 1 (1936): 104–20.

124. Shen Zijiu, "Women weishenme yao jinian Qiu Jin," 7.

125. Lu Xun, "Nala zouhou zenyang" 娜拉走后怎样 (What happens after Nora leaves home), *Funü zazhi* 妇女杂志 (Women's magazine) 10, no. 8 (1924): 1218–22.

126. Guo Moruo, "Nala de da'an," *Xinhua ribao*, July 19, 1942.

127. "Zhonggong zhongyang fuwei guangyu muqian funü yundong de fangzhen he renwu de zhishixin" 中共中央妇委关于目前妇女运动的方针和任务的指示信 (Guidance letter from the CCP women's committee regarding the principles and tasks of the current women's movement), in *Zhongguo funü yundong lishi ziliao* (1937–1945) 中国妇女运动历史资料：1937–1945 (Historical materials on Chinese women's movements from 1937 to 1945) (Beijing: Zhongguo funü chubanshe, 1991), 144.

128. Qinqiu 琴秋, "Wei youju nüzhiyuan huyu" 为邮局女职员呼吁 (An appeal on behalf of female postal workers), *Zhongguo funü* 1, no. 8 (1940): 11–12. Women's prohibition from taking the postal office job entrance exam and their restricted access to jobs sparked heated discussions in the media in 1939. Also see "Duiyu Shanghai youju bu zhaokao nüyouwuyuan de ganxiang" 对于上海邮局不招考女邮务员的感想 (Thoughts on the Shanghai post office's exclusion of women from its recruitment exam), *Funü shenghuo* 7, no. 5 (1939): 8–9.

129. See Duanmu Luxi 端木露西, "Weilan zhong yidian andan" 蔚蓝中一点黯淡 (A touch of gray in azure), *Dagong bao*, July 6, 1940; and Deng Yingchao 邓颖超, "Guanyu 'Weilan zhong yidian andan' de pipan" 关于"蔚蓝中一点黯淡"的批判 (Regarding the criticism of "A touch of gray in azure"), *Xinhua ribao*, August 12, 1940. Duanmu Luxi was the former editor-in-chief for *Women's Weekly*, a publication that supported the "virtuous wife and good mother" campaign.

130. Bai Shuang 白霜, "Hui jiating? Dao shehui?" 回家庭?到社会? (Returning home or going out to society?), *Jiefang ribao*, March 8, 1942.

131. Zhou Enlai 周恩来, "Lun 'xianqiliangmu' yu muzhi" 论"贤妻良母"与母职 (On the "virtuous wife and good mother" and motherhood), *Jiefang ribao*, November 20, 1942.

132. Yan Yiyan, *Qiu Jin* 秋瑾, in *Yan'an wenyi dang'an*, vol. 5, 349.

133. Yan Yiyan, *Qiu Jin*, 350.

134. In an essay introducing her play, Yan Yiyan expressed her gratitude to Wang Ming and Wu Yuzhang for entrusting her with the task of writing about Qiu Jin. See Yan Yiyan, "Yan'an shangyan de *Qiu Jin*," 19.

135. Yan Yiyan, "Yi *Qiu Jin* zai Yan'an de yanchu" 忆《秋瑾》在延安的演出 (Recollections of the performance of *Qiu Jin* in Yan'an), *Xiju bao* 2 (1984): 32.

136. Mao Zedong, "Dangqian shiju de zuida weiji" 当前时局的最大危机 (The greatest crisis under current circumstances), *Zhongguo funü* 1, no. 2 (1939): 4–5.

137. For a detailed introduction to the performance of *Liang Hongyu*, see Luo Fu, "*Liang Hongyu* de gongyan ji qita," 17–18.

138. Yan Yiyan, *Qiu Jin*, 356.

139. Yan Yiyan, *Qiu Jin*, 351.

140. Yan Yiyan, *Qiu Jin*, 375.

141. Yan Yiyan, *Qiu Jin*, 380.

142. "Zhonggong zhongyang wei sanbajie gongzuo gei geji dangbu de zhishi" 中共中央为三八节工作给各级党部的指示 (The instructions issued by the Central Committee of the CCP to the party branches for celebrating International Women's Day), *Zhongguo funü* 1, no. 9 (1940): 2.

143. Xiu Yan 修岩, "Jinnian sanbajie funüjie de xin renwu" 今年三八节妇女界的新任务 (New tasks in the women's field for this year's International Women's Day), *Zhongguo funü* 1, no. 9 (1940): 5.

144. "Yan'an gejie funü sanbajie jinian dahui gao quanguo zimei shu" 延安各界妇女三八节纪念大会告全国姊妹书 (An open letter from Yan'an women's International Women's Day commemoration conference to sisters across the nation), *Zhongguo funü* 1, no. 10/11 (1940): 3.

Exhibition III

1. Edgar Snow, *Red Star over China* (New York: Grove Press, 1978), 148.

2. "Weida de sanba jieri zai Yan'an" 伟大的三八节日在延安 (The great March 8 celebration in Yan'an), *Xin zhonghua bao* 新中华报 (New China news), March 13, 1939.

3. "Wanren qingzhu zhong zhuangyan relie juxing le Zhongguo nüzi daxue kaixue dianli."

4. According to Jiang Huaxuan's 姜华宣 research, there is a lack of evidence to support that Xiang Jingyu was a member of the Central Committee or the minister for women of the CCP. See Jiang Huaxuan, "Xiang Jingyu shifou danren guo zhongyang weiyuan he funü buzhang?" 向警予是否担任过中央委员和妇女部长? (Did Xiang Jingyu ever serve as a member of the Central Committee or the minister for women?), *Dangshi ziliao* 党史资料 (Materials of the history of the CCP), vol. 3 (Shanghai: Shanghai renmin chubanshe, 1983), 112–16.

5. Andrea McElderry, "Woman Revolutionary: Xiang Jingyu," *China Quarterly* 105 (1986): 95.

6. Ding Ling, "Si zhi ge," 6–7.

7. Ding Ling, "Yige zhenshi ren de yisheng—ji Hu Yepin" 一个真实人的一生—记胡也频 (The life of a real person—remembering Hu Yepin), *Ding Ling quanji*, vol. 9, 67.

8. Ding Ling, "Xiang Jingyu lieshi liugei wo de yingxiang" 向警予烈士留给我的影响 (Martyr Xiang Jingyu's influence on me), in *Ding Ling quanji*, vol. 6, 29.

9. Ding Ling discussed her motivation to write the novel *Mother* in a letter to the editor of *Dalu xinwen* 大陆新闻 (Continental news) on June 11, 1932. See Ding Ling, "Daixu" 代序 (The substitute preface), in Ding Ling, *Muqin* 母亲 (Mother) (Beijing: Renmin wenxue chubanshe, 1980), 1–3.

10. For details on Ding Ling's process of writing the novel, see Wang Zhousheng 王周生, *Ding Ling nianpu* 丁玲年谱 (The chronicle of Ding Ling) (Shanghai: Shanghai shehui kexueyuan chubanshe, 1997), 42–44.

11. Zhao Jiabi 赵家璧, "Chongjian Ding Ling hua dangnian: *Muqin* chuban de qianqian houhou" 重见丁玲话当年:《母亲》出版的前前后后 (Talking about the past upon meeting with Ding Ling again: Before and after the publication of *Mother*), in Zhao Jiabi, *Bianji yijiu* 编辑忆旧 (An editor's remembrance of the past) (Beijing: Sanlian shudian, 2008), 50–51.

12. Qiu Jin, "Jingwei shi" 精卫石 (The stones of Jingwei), in *Qiu Jin ji* 秋瑾集 (Collection of Qiu Jin's works) (Shanghai: Zhonghua shuju, 1965), 121–64.

13. Dai Xugong 戴绪恭 and Cai Bo 蔡博, "Xiang Jingyu shengping dashi nianbiao" 向警予生平大事年表 (Chronicle of events in Xiang Jingyu's life), in *Xiang Jingyu wenji* 向警予文集 (Collected writings of Xiang Jingyu), ed. Dai Xugong and Yao Weidou 姚维斗 (Beijing: Renmin chubanshe, 2011), 316–17.

14. Ding Ling's mother changed her name from Yu Manzhen to Jiang Shengmei after the death of her husband. See Wang Zengru and Li Xiangdong, *Ding Ling nianpu changbian*, vol. 1, 3.

15. "Xiang Jingyu shengping dashi nianbiao," 316.

16. "Qi zimei shici" 七姊妹誓词 (Oath of the seven sisters), in *Xiang Jingyu wenji* (2011), 1.

17. Ding Ling, "Xiang Jingyu lieshi liugei wo de yingxiang," 26.

18. Jiang Shengmei, "Dingmu huiyilu," 273. To avoid censorship, Jiang Shengmei used a friend with the surname Bai 白 to represent Xiang Jingyu in her memoir.

19. Ding Ling, *Muqin*, 89.

20. Ding Ling, *Muqin*, 94–95.

21. "Xiang Jingyu shengping dashi nianbiao," 317.

22. "Xiang Jingyu shengping dashi nianbiao," 317.

23. "Xiang Jingyu shengping dashi nianbiao," 318.

24. Xiang Jingyu, "Xupu xianli nüxiao xiaoge" 溆浦县立女校校歌 (The song for Xupu Girls' School), in *Xiang Jingyu wenji* (2011), 313.

25. Xiang Jingyu, "Qing chuling gequ song nüzi jiuxue wen" 请出令各区送女子就学文 (The request to order each district to send girls to school), in *Xiang Jingyu wenji* (2011), 289–90.

26. Dai Xugong 戴绪恭, *Xiang Jingyu zhuan* 向警予传 (Biography of Xiang Jingyu) (Beijing: Renmin chubanshe, 1985), 26.

27. For details about Xiang Jingyu's contributions to Xupu Girls' School, see Dai Xugong, *Xiang Jingyu zhuan*, 18–28.

28. Christina Kelley Gilmartin, *Engendering the Chinese Revolution: Radical Women, Communist Politics, and Mass Movements in the 1920s* (Berkeley: University of California Press, 1995), 76.

29. Xu Fangping 徐方平, *Cai Hesen pingzhuan* 蔡和森评传 (Critical biography of Cai Hesen) (Beijing: Zhongguo shehui kexue chubanshe, 2013), 51.

30. "Xiang Jingyu shengping dashi nianbiao," 319.

31. Ding Ling, "Wo muqin de shengping" 我母亲的生平 (My mother's life), *Ding Ling quanji*, vol. 6, 67–69; and "Xiang Jingyu shengping dashi nianbiao," 319.

32. Dai Xugong, *Xiang Jingyu zhuan*, 33–34.

33. "Xiang Jingyu shengping dashi nianbiao," 320.

34. Some of the essays published in Changsha *Dagong bao* on Zhao Wuzhen's suicide include Mao Zedong 毛泽东, "Duiyu Zhao nüshi zisha de piping" 对于赵女士自杀的批评 (Critique of Miss Zhao's suicide), November 16, 1919; Jiangong 兼公, "Wo duiyu Zhao nüshi zisha de zagan" 我对于赵女士自杀的杂感 (My miscellaneous thoughts on Miss Zhao's suicide), November 17, 1919; Dun 盾, "Wo ye shuoshuo Zhao nüshi zisha shijian" 我也说说赵女士自杀事件 (My thoughts on Miss Zhao's suicide), November 18, 1919; Rulin 汝霖, "Wo duiyu Zhao nüshi zisha an de zhuzhang" 我对于赵女士自杀案的主张 (My views on the case of Miss Zhao's suicide), November 19, 1919; Mao Zedong, "Shehui wan'e yu Zhao nüshi" 社会万恶与赵女士 (The evils of society and Miss Zhao), November 21, 1919; Maijun 迈君, "Wo duiyu Zhao nüshi zisha de ganxiang" 我对于赵女士自杀的感想 (My reflections on Miss Zhao's suicide), November 21, 1919; Pingzi 平子, "Wo bu zancheng fumu zhuhun" 我不赞成父母主婚 (I disapprove of parental arranged marriages), November 22, 1919; Yuying 毓莹, "Yige wenti" 一个问题 (One problem), November 22, 1919; Mao Zedong, "Dapo meiren zhidu" 打破媒人制度 (Breaking the matchmaking system), November 27, 1919.

35. Mao Zedong, "Shehui wan'e yu Zhao nüshi."

36. Dai Xugong, *Xiang Jingyu zhuan*, 41–42.

37. Dai Xugong, *Xiang Jingyu zhuan*, 41–42.

38. For the life of Li Chao, see Hu Shi 胡适, "Li Chao zhuan" 李超传 (The biography of Li Chao), *Xinchao* 新潮 (New wave) 2, no. 2 (1919): 266–75.

39. Hu Shi, "Li Chao zhuan," 274–75.

40. Yanren 衍仁, "Kelian de Zhongguo funü" 可怜的中国妇女 (Pitiful Chinese women), *Dagong bao*, November 30, 1919.

41. "Li Chao nüshi zhi zangli" 李超女士之葬礼 (The funeral of lady Li Chao), *Minguo ribao* 民国日报 (Republican daily), January 4, 1920.

42. "Li Chao nüshi zhuidaohui jishi" 李超女士追悼会纪事 (Records of the memorial service for lady Li Chao), *Minguo ribao*, December 4, 1919.

43. "Li Chao nüshi zhuidaohui jishi."

44. "Xiang Jingyu shengping dashi nianbiao," 321.

45. Dai Xugong, *Xiang Jingyu zhuan*, 48–50.

46. Xiang Jingyu, "Nüzi jiefang yu gaizao de shangque" 女子解放与改造的商榷 (Discussions on women's liberation and transformation), in *Xiang Jingyu wenji* (2011), 17. It was first published in *Shaonian Zhongguo* 少年中国 (Young China) 2, no. 2 (1920): 29–37.

47. Xiang Jingyu, "Nüzi jiefang yu gaizao de shangque," 11–15.

48. Xiang Jingyu, "Nüzi jiefang yu gaizao de shangque," 12.

49. Xiang Jingyu, "Nüzi jiefang yu gaizao de shangque," 15–21.

50. Dai Xugong, *Xiang Jingyu zhuan*, 51.

51. Helen Snow, *Women in Modern China*, 275.

52. "Xinmin xuehui huiwu baogao (diyi hao)" 新民学会会务报告第一号 (Report of the affairs of the New Citizen Study Society, no. 1), in *Xinmin xuehui ziliao* 新民学会资料 (Materials of the New Citizen Study Society) (Beijing: Renmin chubanshe, 1980), 2.

53. "Xinmin xuehui huiwu baogao (diyi hao)," 3.

54. "Xinmin xuehui huiwu baogao (di'er hao)" 新民学会会务报告第二号 (Report of the affairs of the New Citizen Study Society, no. 2), in *Xinmin xuehui ziliao*, 20.

55. Xiang Jingyu, "Gei diedie mama" 给爹爹妈妈 (To my parents), December 29, 1920, in *Xiang Jingyu wenji* (2011), 304. Jiu'er 九儿 refers to Xiang Jingyu, who is the ninth child in the family.

56. Xiang Jingyu, "Gei diedie mama," 304.

57. Cai Hesen, "Cai Linbin gei Mao Zedong" 蔡林彬给毛泽东 (Letter from Cai Linbin to Mao Zedong, dated May 28, 1920), *Xinmin xuehui ziliao*, 127. Cai Linbin was a name Cai Hesen used. The brochure mentioned in the letter refers to the poem collection *Looking Upward Together*.

58. Xiang Jingyu, "Xiang Jingyu gei Tao Yi, Ren Peidao" 向警予给陶毅任培道 (Letter from Xiang Jingyu to Tao Yi and Ren Peidao, dated June 7, 1920), in *Xinmin xuehui ziliao*, 85–87.

59. Xiao Zizhang, "Xiao Zizhang gei Mao Zedong, Peng Huang" 萧子暲给毛泽东彭璜 (Letter from Xiao Zizhang to Mao Zedong and Peng Huang, dated June 22, 1920), in *Xinmin xuehui ziliao*, 93.

60. Mao Zedong, "Mao Zedong gei Luo Xuezan" 毛泽东给罗学瓒 (Letter from Mao Zedong to Luo Xuezan, dated November 26, 1920), in *Xinmin xuehui ziliao*, 121.

61. For a detailed account of the meeting in Montargis, see Yu Siao, *Mao Tse-Tung and I Were Beggars* (Syracuse, NY: Syracuse University Press, 1959), 183–87. Siao Yu 萧瑜 is another name of Xiao Zisheng.

62. "Xiang Jingyu shengping dashi nianbiao," 322.

63. Following the Montargis meeting, Cai Hesen wrote two extensive letters to Mao Zedong, emphasizing the importance of establishing the CCP and urging him to take action. For their correspondence, see Cai Hesen, "Cai Linbin gei Mao Zedong" 蔡林彬给毛泽东 (Letter from Cai Linbin to Mao Zedong, dated August 13, 1920), in *Xinmin xuehui ziliao*, 130; Cai Hesen, "Cai Linbin gei Mao Zedong" 蔡林彬给毛泽东 (Letter from Cai Linbin to Mao Zedong, dated September 16, 1920), in *Xinmin xuehui ziliao*, 153–62; Mao Zedong, "Mao Zedong gei Cai Hesen" 毛泽东给蔡和森 (Letter from Mao Zedong to Cai Hesen, dated January 21, 1921), in *Xinmin xuehui ziliao*, 163.

On July 23, 1921, the CCP was founded in Shanghai. Almost simultaneously, the World Work-study Society (*gongxue shijie she* 工学世界社), with the assistance of Cai Hesen and Xiang Jingyu, shifted its focus to socialism. The society convened its second conference in Montargis to deliberate on its action principles and attempted to rename itself as the Chinese Communist Party. See "Xiang Jingyu shengping dashi nianbiao," 325.

64. Luo Xuezan, "Luo Xuezan gei Mao Zedong" 罗学瓒给毛泽东 (Letter from Luo Xuezan to Mao Zedong, dated July 14, 1920), in *Xinmin xuehui ziliao*, 118.

65. "Xinmin xuehui huiwu baogao (di'er hao)," 29.

66. Kang Youwei 康有为, *Datong shu* 大同书 (The book of great unity) (Shenyang: Liaoning renmin chubanshe, 1994), 193–98.

67. Cai Yuanpei 蔡元培, "Xinnian meng" 新年梦 (New Year's dream), in *Cai Yuanpei quanji* 蔡元培全集 (The complete works of Cai Yuanpei), vol. 1 (Beijing: Zhonghua shuju, 1984), 241.

68. Hanyi 汉一, "Huijia lun" 毁家论 (On destroying families), *Tianyi bao* 4 (1907): 43. Hanyi is likely Liu Shipei's 刘师培 pen name.

69. Zhen 真, "Sangang geming" 三纲革命 (Revolution in the three bonds), *Xin shiji* 11 (1907): 1. Zhen is Li Shizeng's pen name.

70. Some of the essays and corresponding letters in the debate published in *Juewu* include Zhemin 哲民, "Feichu hunyin zhidu di taolun" 废除婚姻制度底讨论 (Discussion on abolishing the marriage system), *Juewu*, May 8, 1920; Lizi 力子, "Feichu hunzhi wenti di taolun" 废除婚制问题底讨论 (Discussion on the issues with abolishing the marriage system), *Juewu*, May 20, 1920; Cuntong 存统, "Bianlun de taidu he feichu hunzhi" 辩论的态度和废除婚制 (Attitude in debate and the abolishment of the marriage system), *Juewu*, May 21, 1920; Ke Qingshi 柯庆施, "Feichu hunzhi wenti de taolun" 废除婚制问题的讨论 (Discussion on abolishing the marriage system), *Juewu*, May 23, 1920. Fei Zhemin, Shao Lizi, and Shi Cuntong wrote under their pen names of Zhemin, Lizi, and Cuntong.

71. "Zhou Enlai, Zhou Enlai lüri riji" 周恩来旅日日记 (Zhou Enlai's travel diary in Japan), February 9, 1918, in *Zhou Enlai zaoqi wenji* 周恩来早期文集 (Early writings of Zhou Enlai), vol. 1, ed. Liu Yan 刘焱 (Tianjin: Nankai University Press, 1993), 279–80.

72. "Zhou Enlai lüri riji," February 9, 1918, 279.

73. "Zhou Enlai lüri riji," February 15, 1918, 282.

74. Deng Yingchao, "Cong Xihuating haitanghua yiqi" 从西花厅海棠花忆起 (Recalling the Chinese crabapple from the Western Flower Hall), *Renmin ribao*, March 5, 1997.

75. Deng Yingchao, "Cong Xihuating haitanghua yiqi."

76. Xiang Jingyu, "Gei Peng Huang Mao Zedong" 给彭璜毛泽东 (Letter to Peng Huang

and Mao Zedong, dated June 2, 1920), in *Xiang Jingyu wenji* (2011), 23.

77. Mao Zedong, "Mao Zedong gei Xiao Xudong Cai Linbin bing zaifa zhu huiyou" 毛泽东给萧旭东蔡林彬并在法诸会友 (Letter from Mao Zedong to Xiao Xudong, Cai Linbin, and our members in France), in *Xinmin xuehui ziliao*, 148. Xiao Xudong is the original name of Xiao Zisheng.

78. "Xiang Jingyu shengping dashi nianbiao," 323.

79. "Xiang Jingyu shengping dashi nianbiao," 324.

80. "Xiang Jingyu shengping dashi nianbiao," 324.

81. "Liufa nüsheng dui haiwai daxue zhi yaoqiu" 留法女生对海外大学之要求 (Requests of female students studying in France to the overseas Chinese university), in *Xiang Jingyu wenji* (2011), 31. The overseas Chinese university refers to the Lyon Sino-French University.

82. Enlai 恩来, "Lü'ou tongxin: Li'ang zhongfa daxue zhi tonggao" 旅欧通信: 里昂中法大学之通告 (Correspondence from Europe: Lyon Sino-French University's announcement), *Yishi bao* (Tianjin), December 29, 1921. Zhou Enlai wrote the correspondence from Europe series for *Yishi bao* under the pen name Enlai.

83. "Xiang Jingyu shengping dashi nianbiao," 326.

84. "Xiang Jingyu shengping dashi nianbiao," 326.

85. "Xiang Jingyu shengping dashi nianbiao," 326.

86. "Xiang Jingyu shengping dashi nianbiao," 327.

87. Li Yongchun 李永春, *Cai Hesen nianpu* 蔡和森年谱 (Chronicle of Cai Hesen) (Xiangtan: Xiangtan daxue chubanshe, 2008), 108.

88. Li Yongchun, *Cai Hesen nianpu*, 112.

89. According to Dai Xugong and Yao Weidou's research, "Zhenyu" is the pen name used by Xiang Jingyu for her publications in *Xiangdao*. Fumiko Niki argues that the essays published in *Xiangdao* under the pen name "Zhenyu" were written by Xiang Jingyu, Cai Hesen, or both. Ke Qin 柯秦 and Gu Ci 谷茨 raise questions about whether Xiang Jingyu authored all the essays in *Xiangdao* under the pen name "Zhenyu."

For detailed discussions on the pen name "Zhenyu," see Dai Xugong and Yao Weidou, "Zhenyu wei Xiang Jingyu biming kao" 振宇为向警予笔名考 (Evidential research on whether "Zhenyu" is Xiang Jingyu's pen name), in *Xiang Jingyu: Zhuanji, jinian yu huiyi, lunshu, ziliao* 向警予:传记,纪念与回忆,论述,资料 (Xiang Jingyu: Biography, commemoration and recollection, discussion, and material), ed. Liu Maoshu 刘茂舒 (Wuhan: Wuhan chubanshe, 1995), 250–55; Fumiko Niki, "Zhenyu shi Xiang Jingyu de biming ma" 振宇是向警予的笔名吗? (Is "Zhenyu" Xiang Jingyu's pen name?), trans. Wang Zhixin 王智新, in *Xiang Jingyu: Zhuanji, jinian yu huiyi, lunshu, ziliao*, 256–69; Ke Qin, Gu Ci, "Biming, niandai ji qita" 笔名、年代及其他 (Pen name, periods, and others), in *Xiang Jingyu: Zhuanji, jinian yu huiyi, lunshu, ziliao*, 270–73.

According to Yang Zilie's 杨子烈 recollection, Xiang Jingyu frequently wrote short essays for *Xiangdao*. See Yang Zilie, *Zhang Guotao furen huiyilu* 张国焘夫人回忆录 (The memoir of Zhang Guotao's wife) (Hong Kong: Zilian chubanshe, 1970), 131. The most recent collected writings of Xiang Jingyu include all the essays published in *Xiangdao* under the pen name "Zhenyu." See *Xiang Jingyu wenji*, 2011.

90. Dai Xugong, *Xiang Jingyu zhuan*, 85–86.

91. Dai Xugong, *Xiang Jingyu zhuan*, 86.

92. Dai Xugong, *Xiang Jingyu zhuan*, 86. For Ding Ling's participation in supporting women workers during the strikes, see Helen Snow, *Women in Modern China*, 229.

93. Wang Zengru and Li Xiangdong, *Ding Ling nianpu changbian*, vol. 1, 18.

94. Ding Ling, "Xiang Jingyu lieshi liugei wo de yingxiang," 28.

95. Wang Yizhi, "Jinian Xiangjingyu tongzhi" 纪念向警予同志 (Commemorating Comrade Xiang Jingyu), in *Lieshi Xiang Jingyu* 烈士向警予 (Martyr Xiang Jingyu), ed. Zhongguo funü zazhishe 中国妇女杂志社 (Chinese women magazine) (Beijing: Zhongguo funü zazhi chubanshe, 1958), 7.

96. Wang Yizhi, "Jinian Xiangjingyu tongzhi," 8–9.

97. Helen Snow, *Women in Modern China*, 229.

98. This experience also prepared Ding Ling to promote revolutionary literature among workers in the 1930s after she joined the League of Left-wing Writers. She changed into a cloth *qipao* and flat shoes so she could blend in with the workers. However, she admitted that it was difficult for intellectuals to integrate with the workers because their walking styles differed, even though they dressed similarly. The workers knew each other, but the intellectuals were strangers to them. Ding Ling attempted to connect with the workers by visiting their homes and participating in their literature groups. See Ding Ling, "Guanyu zuolian de pianduan huiyi" 关于左联的片断回忆 (Fragmentary memories of the League of Left-wing Writers), in *Ding Ling quanji*, vol. 10, 243.

99. Dai Xugong, *Xiang Jingyu zhuan*, 86.

100. "Funü yundong jueyi'an" 妇女运动决议案 (Resolution about the women's movement), *Zhongguo Gongchandang di'erci zhi diliuci quanguo daibiao dahui wenjian huibian* 中国共产党第二次至第六次全国代表大会文件汇编 (Compiled materials of the Second to the Sixth National Congress of the CCP), ed. Zhongyang dang'an guan 中央档案馆 (The Central Archive) (Beijing: Renmin chubanshe, 1981), 66. Also see "Zhongguo Gongchandang di sanci quanguo daibiao dahui 'Guanyu funü yundong de jueyi'an'" 中国共产党第三次全国代表大会《关于妇女运动的决议案》(Resolution about the women's movement passed by the Third National Congress of the CCP), in *Xiang Jingyu wenji* 向警予文集 (Collected writings of Xiang Jingyu) (Changsha: Hunan renmin chubanshe, 1980), 216-17.

101. Xiang Jingyu, "Zhongguo zuijin funü yundong" 中国最近妇女运动 (Recent women's movements in China), in *Xiang Jingyu wenji* (2011), 92.

102. Xiang Jingyu, "Zhongguo zuijin funü yundong," 98.

103. Xiang Jingyu, "Zhongguo zuijin funü yundong," 96.

104. Xiang Jingyu, "Zhongguo zuijin funü yundong," 100.

105. "Xiang Jingyu shengping dashi nianbiao," 328.

106. Sima Qian, "Xiangyu benji" 项羽本纪 (Annals of Xiang Yu), in *Shiji* 史记 (The records of a grand historian), vol. 1, annotated by Han Zhaoqi 韩兆琦 (Beijing: Zhonghua shuju, 2010), 680. For detailed accounts of the Three Household Mansion, see Luo Zhanglong 罗章龙, *Chunyuan zaiji* 椿园载记 (Memories from the Chun garden) (Beijing: Sanlian shudian, 1984), 287–90.

107. "Xiang Jingyu shengping dashi nianbiao," 330.

108. Xiang Jingyu's essays on reforming women's education and supporting female students' movements, published in *Funü zhoubao*, include "Cong pingmin jiaoyu zhong huafen nüzi pingmin jiaoyu de wojian" 从平民教育中划分女子平民教育的我见 (My view

on separating mass education for women from mass education), January 30, 1924; "Zhili Di'er Nüshi xuechao zai nüzi jiaoyu gexin yundong shang de jiazhi" 直隶第二女师学潮在女子教育革新运动上的价值 (The value of students' movement at Zhili No. 2 Women's Normal School in women's education reform movement), April 9, 1924; "Duiyu genben gaige Beijing nüzi shifan daxue de yijian bing zhi Beijing nüzi shifan daxue quanti tongxue" 对于根本改革北京女子师范大学的意见并质北京女子师范大学全体同学 (My suggestions on the fundamental reform of Beijing Women's Normal University and questions to all the students at Beijing Women's Normal University), February 9, 1925; "Ping E nüshi xuechao bing gao huaibao gaige nüzi jiaoyu sixiang de zimei" 评鄂女师学潮并告怀抱改革女子教育思想的姊妹 (Comments on the students' movement at Hubei Women's Normal School and an appeal to the sisters who have ideas to reform women's education), April 19, 1925.

Additionally, Xiang Jingyu published an essay on reforming women's education in *Funü zazhi* titled "Zhongdeng yishang nüxuesheng de dushu wenti" 中等以上女学生的读书问题 (The problems of education for female students in middle schools and above), *Funü zazhi* 10, no. 3 (1924): 448–53. She published all of these essays in *Funü zhoubao* and *Funü zazhi* under the pen name Jingyu 警予.

109. Jingyu, "Zhili Di'er Nüshi xuechao zai nüzi jiaoyu gexin yundong shang de jiazhi," *Funü zhoubao*, April 9, 1924.

110. Jingyu, "Zhili Di'er Nüshi xuechao zai nüzi jiaoyu gexin yundong shang de jiazhi."

111. Sun Yat-sen, "Sun Zhongshan duiyu shiju zhi xuanyan" 孙中山对于时局之宣言 (Sun Yat-sen's manifesto on the current situation), *Shenbao*, November 18, 1924.

112. "Xiang Jingyu shengping dashi nianbiao," 331.

113. Article 13 of the Regulations on People's Representatives Meeting states that only men above twenty-five years old in the Republic of China can elect and be elected as representatives. See "Guomin daibiao huiyi tiaoli" 国民代表会议条例 (Regulations on People's Representatives Meeting), *Guowen zhoubao* 国闻周报 (National news weekly) 2, no. 16 (1925): 42.

114. Jingyu, "Zai Shanghai nüjie guomin huiyi cuchenghui de chengli dahui shang de jianghua" 在上海女界国民会议促成会的成立大会上的讲话 (The speech at the inaugural meeting of the Shanghai Women's Association for Facilitating the People's Assembly), *Funü zhoubao*, December 7, 1924.

115. Jingyu, "Guomin huiyi yu funü" 国民会议与妇女 (Women and the People's Assembly), *Funü zhoubao*, December 14, 1924.

116. These essays, published in *Funü zhoubao*, include "Guomin huiyi yu funü" 国民会议与妇女 (Women and the People's Assembly), December 14, 1924; "Hanjia zhong nüxuesheng ying nuli de yijian dashi" 寒假中女学生应努力的一件大事 (An important thing female students should do during the winter break), December 27, 1924; "Nüjie guomin huiyi cuchenghui zai Zhongguo funü yundong zhong de diwei" 女界国民会议促成会在中国妇女运动中的地位 (The status of the Women's Association for Facilitating the People's Assembly in Chinese women's movements), January 11, 1925; "Ying lizheng funü tuanti canjia guomin huiyi" 应力争妇女团体参加国民会议 (We should strive for women's groups to participate in the People's Assembly), April 13, 1925; "Shibai geiyu women de jiaoxun" 失败给予我们的教训 (The lessons we learned from our failure), April 26, 1925.

She also published another essay on the issue in *Juewu* titled "Funü yundong yu guomin yundong" 妇女运动与国民运动 (Women's movements and citizens' movements) on December 30, 1924.

117. For Xiang Jingyu's speech at the meeting, see Jingyu, "Nü guomin dahui de sanda yiyi" 女国民大会的三大意义 (Three significances of the female citizens' meeting), *Funü zhoubao*, March 29, 1925.

118. Jingyu, "Jiu guniang fanle hezui?" 九姑娘犯了何罪? (What crime did the Ninth Girl commit?), *Funü zhoubao*, September 26, 1923. The Ninth Girl refers to Wang Xichun, who organized strikes in Shanghai silk factories and also worked as a secretary at the Three Household Mansion. See Luo Zhanglong, *Chunyuan zaiji*, 288.

119. Xiang Jingyu's writings in *Funü zhoubao* supporting women workers in Shanghai silk factories include "Gao sichang laoku nütongbao" 告丝厂劳苦女同胞 (Appeal to the our toiling female workers in the silk factories), September 26, 1923; "Yige jinji de tiyi" 一个紧急的提议 (An urgent proposal), September 26, 1923; "Shanghai funü tuanti jiang lianhe yuanzhu sichang nügong" 上海妇女团体将联合援助丝厂女工 (Women's organizations in Shanghai will unite to help women workers in silk factories), November 14, 1923; "Sichang nügong tuanjie qilai" 丝厂女工团结起来 (Please unite, women silk workers), November 21, 1923.

120. Jingyu, "Zhongguo zhishi funü de sanpai" 中国知识妇女的三派 (The three groups of Chinese female intellectuals), *Funü zhoubao*, November 28, 1923.

121. "Xiang Jingyu shengping dashi nianbiao," 329.

122. Dai Xugong, *Xiang Jingyu zhuan*, 93–94.

123. Dai Xugong, *Xiang Jingyu zhuan*, 94–95.

124. "Duiyu funü yundong zhi yijue'an" 对于妇女运动之议决案 (Resolution about the women's movement), in *Zhongguo Gongchandang di'erci zhi diliuci quanguo daibiao dahui wenjian huibian*, 119.

125. Dai Xugong, *Xiang Jingyu zhuan*, 111.

126. Zhong Fuguang 钟复光, "Funü yundong de jiechu lingxiu" 妇女运动的杰出领袖 (The outstanding leader of women's movements), in *Xiang Jingyu: Zhuanji, jinian yu huiyi, lunshu, ziliao*, 121.

127. Dai Xugong, *Xiang Jingyu zhuan*, 110.

128. Jingyu, "Shanghai nüquan yundonghui jinhou ying zhuyi de sanjianshi" 上海女权运动会今后应注意的三件事 (Three things the Shanghai Feminist Movement Association should pay attention to in the future), *Funü zhoubao*, November 8, 1923.

129. Jingyu, "Zai Zhongguo funü xiehui chenglihui shang de yanshuo" 在中国妇女协会成立会上的演说 (The speech at the inaugural meeting of the Chinese Women's Association), *Funü zhoubao*, May 10, 1925.

130. "Xiang Jingyu shengping dashi nianbiao," 334.

131. Zhong Fuguang, "Funü yundong de jiechu lingxiu," 123.

132. "Duiyu minzu geming yundong zhi yijue'an" 对于民族运动之议决案 (Resolution on national revolutionary movements), *Zhongguo Gongchandang di'erci zhi diliuci quanguo daibiao dahui wenjian huibian*, 86–95.

133. Peng Shuzhi 彭述之, *Peng Shuzhi huiyilu* 彭述之回忆录 (The memoir of Peng Shuzhi), vol. 2 (Hong Kong: Tiandi tushu, 2016), 14.

134. Ren Wuxiong 任武雄, "Xiang Jingyu," in *Xiang Jingyu: Zhuanji, jinian yu huiyi, lunshu, ziliao*, 14.

135. Zhang Guotao 张国焘, *Wo de huiyi* 我的回忆 (My memories), vol. 2 (Beijing: Dongfang chubanshe, 1980), 26.

136. Zhang Guotao, *Wo de huiyi*, 26.

137. For the CCP's meeting records during the May Thirtieth Movement, see "Zhonggong Shanghai diwei guanyu kangyi riren qiangsha Xiaoshadu gongren taolun bing yijue fanri shiwei yundong gexiang shishi banfa deng wenti de huiyi lu" 中共上海地委关于抗议日人枪杀小沙渡工人讨论并议决反日示威运动各项实施办法等问题的会议录 (The meeting records of the CCP Shanghai branch's discussions on protesting the shooting death of the worker at Xiaoshadu by the Japanese and making decisions on how to implement the anti-Japanese protests), *Wusa yundong* 五卅运动, (The May Thirtieth Movement), vol. 1, ed. Shanghaishi dang'anguan 上海市档案馆 (Shanghai Archives) (Shanghai: Shanghai renmin chubanshe, 1991), 12–21.

138. Li Yongchun, *Cai Hesen nianpu*, 200.

139. The two official announcements are "Zhonggong zhongyang guanyu yuanzhu Shanghai rishang neiwai mianshachang bagong gongren de tonggao" 中共中央关于援助上海日商内外棉纱厂罢工工人的通告 (The Central Committee of the CCP's announcement regarding assistance to the strikers of the Shanghai Naga Wata Kaisha Cotton Mill); and "Zhonggong zhongyang guanyu fadong fandui riben diguozhuyi yundong de tonggao" 中共中央关于发动反对日本帝国主义运动的通告 (The Central Committee of the CCP's announcement regarding the initiation of the anti-Japanese imperialism movement), in *Wusa yundong*, vol. 1, 22–24.

140. Dai Xugong, *Xiang Jingyu zhuan*, 113.

141. "Zhonggong zhongyang wei fankang diguo zhuyi yeman canbao de datusha gao quanguo minzhong shu" 中共中央为反抗帝国主义野蛮残暴的大屠杀告全国民众书 (The Central Committee of the CCP's letter to the nation protesting the brutal massacre by imperialism), in *Wusa yundong*, vol. 1, 25–29.

142. Ren Wuxiong, "Xiang Jingyu," in *Xiang Jingyu: Zhuanji, jinian yu huiyi, lunshu, ziliao*, 15.

143. The flyers include "Shanghai nüjie guomin huiyi cuchenghui wei riren cansha tongbao xuanyan" 上海女界国民会议促成会为日人惨杀同胞宣言 (The declaration from Shanghai Women's Association for Facilitating the People's Assembly in response to the killing of Chinese citizens by the Japanese) and "Shanghai shi Zhongguoren de Shanghai" 上海是中国人的上海 (Shanghai is Chinese people's Shanghai), in *Xiang Jingyu wenji*, 2011, 244–48.

144. Dai Xugong, *Xiang Jingyu zhuan*, 114.

145. Li Yongchun, *Cai Hesen nianpu*, 206.

146. Li Yongchun, *Cai Hesen nianpu*, 209.

147. Helen Snow, *Women in Modern China*, 235–36.

148. *Zhongguo Gongchandang de qishinian* 中国共产党的七十年 (Seventy years of the Chinese Communist Party), ed. Hu Sheng 胡绳 (Beijing: Zhonggong dangshi chubanshe, 2005), 43.

149. Dai Jitao 戴季陶, *Guomin geming yu Zhongguo Guomindang* 国民革命与中国国民党 (The national revolution and the KMT), printed by Dai Jitao's office, 1925.

150. See Qu Qiubai, "Zhongguo guomin geming yu Dai Jitao zhuyi" 中国国民革命与戴

季陶主义 (Chinese national revolution and Dai Jitaoism), in *Zhonggong zhongyang wenjian xuanji* 中共中央文件选集 (Selected documents of the Central Committee of the CCP), vol. 1, ed. Zhongyang dang'an guan 中央档案馆 (National Archives Administration of China) (Beijing: Zhonggong zhongyang dangxiao chubanshe, 1991), 651–65; and Chen Duxiu, "Gei Dai Jitao de yifeng xin" 给戴季陶的一封信 (A letter to Dai Jitao), in *Zhonggong zhongyang wenjian xuanji*, vol. 1, 666–76. The two writings were originally published in *Fan Dai Jitao de guomin gemingguan* 反戴季陶的国民革命观 (Countering Dai Jitao's views on the national revolution) (Shanghai: Xiangdao congshu, 1925).

151. For discussions on the different opinions of Central Committee members regarding how to lead the CCP after the May Thirtieth Movement, see Zhang Guotao, *Wo de huiyi*, vol. 2, 13–14.

152. Li Yongchun, *Cai Hesen nianpu*, 206.

153. Peng Shuzhi, *Peng Shuzhi huiyilu*, vol. 1, 182.

154. Peng Shuzhi, *Peng Shuzhi huiyilu*, vol. 1, 208.

155. Peng Shuzhi, *Peng Shuzhi huiyilu*, vol. 1, 256.

156. Peng Shuzhi, *Peng Shuzhi huiyilu*, vol. 1, 351.

157. Wang Zengru and Li Xiangdong, *Ding Ling nianpu changbian*, vol. 1, 25.

158. Peng Shuzhi, *Peng Shuzhi huiyilu*, vol. 1, 373. According to Peng Shuzhi, Qu Yunbai and Ding Ling were in a romantic relationship.

159. Peng Shuzhi, *Peng Shuzhi huiyilu*, vol. 1, 460.

160. Peng Shuzhi, *Peng Shuzhi huiyilu*, vol. 2, 19.

161. Zheng Chaolin, "Lian'ai yu geming" 恋爱与革命 (Love and revolution), in Zheng Chaolin, *Shishi yu huiyi: Zheng Chaolin wannian wenxuan* 史事与回忆：郑超麟晚年文选 (History and memory: Selected writings from Zheng Chaolin's late years), vol. 1 (Hong Kong: Tiandi tushu, 1998), 287.

162. For Zheng Chaolin's account of the dinner party and Xiang and Peng's affair, see Zheng Chaolin, "Lian'ai yu geming," 287–88.

163. For detailed accounts of the meeting, see Zhang Guotao, *Wo de huiyi*, vol. 2, 92–93; Peng Shuzhi, *Peng Shuzhi huiyilu*, vol. 2, 48–49. Zheng Chaolin's version of the meeting differs from that of Zhang Guotao and Peng Shuzhi. According to Zheng Chaolin, he and representatives of the Communist Youth League and the CCP Shanghai branch all attended the meeting. At the end of the meeting, Cai Hesen stood up abruptly and claimed that Xiang and Peng were in love. Everyone was shocked and remained silent for a while. Chen Duxiu finally broke the silence by asking Xiang Jingyu to choose between Cai and Peng. Xiang Jingyu did not say a word but instead cried. The Central Committee then decided to send both Xiang and Cai to Moscow. After the meeting, Xiang Jingyu scolded Cai for raising the issue during the meeting because Cai knew that the Central Committee would side with him. See Zheng Chaolin, "Lian'ai yu geming," 288–89. In Zheng Chaolin's account, Xiang Jingyu was passive during the meeting, and the party made the decision for her to be separated from Peng Shuzhi.

164. Zhang Guotao, *Wo de huiyi*, vol. 2, 95.

165. Zhang Guotao, *Wo de huiyi*, vol. 2, 95–96.

166. Zhang Guotao, *Wo de huiyi*, vol. 2, 96–97.

167. Zhang Guotao, *Wo de huiyi*, vol. 2, 97. Zhang Guotao believed that Peng Shuzhi

spread the rumor. However, Peng denied it in his memoir. See Peng Shuzhi, *Peng Shuzhi huiyilu*, vol. 2, 47.

168. Qu Qiubai, *Zhongguo geming zhong zhi zhenglun wenti* 中国革命中之争论问题 (Controversial issues in the Chinese revolution) (Nagoya: Caihua shulin, 1976), 176. The book has been reprinted according to the 1928 version. The original version was published in 1927.

169. Zhang Guotao, *Wo de huiyi*, vol. 2, 266.

170. Zhang Guotao, *Wo de huiyi*, vol. 2, 339–40.

171. Zheng Chaolin, "Lian'ai yu geming," 289.

172. Andrea McElderry, "Woman Revolutionary: Xiang Jingyu," 118.

173. Zhang Guotao, *Wo de huiyi*, vol. 2, 94, 100.

174. Yang Zilie, *Zhang Guotao furen huiyilu*, 131.

175. Wang Yizhi, "Jinian Xiangjingyu tongzhi," 8.

176. Zheng Chaolin, "Lian'ai yu geming," 287.

177. Jingyu, "Funü weishenme hao zhuangshi" 妇女为什么好装饰 (Why women like adornments), *Funü zhoubao*, October 24, 1922.

178. Chen Xiuliang 陈修良, "Xiang Jingyu lieshi zai Wuhan" 向警予烈士在武汉 (The martyr Xiang Jingyu in Wuhan), in *Xiang Jingyu: Zhuanji, jinian yu huiyi, lunshu, ziliao*, 143.

179. Zheng Chaolin, "Lian'ai yu geming," 287.

180. Cai Hesen, "Xiang Jingyu tongzhi zhuan" 向警予同志传 (Biography of Comrade Xiang Jingyu), in *Xiang Jingyu: Zhuanji, jinian yu huiyi, lunshu, ziliao*, 3.

181. Cai Hesen, "Xiang Jingyu tongzhi zhuan," 3; and Dai Xugong, *Xiang Jingyu zhuan*, 11–12. Shuai Mengqi 帅孟奇 also mentioned that Xiang Jingyu's classmates in middle school called her Saint Xiang (*Xiang shengren* 向圣人). See Gu Ci 谷茨, "Shuai dajie tan Xiang Jingyu tongzhi" 帅大姐谈向警予同志 (Sister Shuai talks about Comrade Xiang Jingyu), in *Xiang Jingyu: Zhuanji, jinian yu huiyi, lunshu, ziliao*, 34.

182. *Xiang Jingyu wenji*, 2011, 278.

183. *Xiang Jingyu wenji*, 2011, 280.

184. Zheng Chaolin, "Lian'ai yu geming," 287.

185. Peng Shuzhi, *Peng Shuzhi huiyilu*, vol. 2, 50.

186. Zhang Guotao, *Wo de huiyi*, vol. 2, 93.

187. Cai Hesen, "Xiang Jingyu tongzhi zhuan," 3; Dai Xugong, *Xiang Jingyu zhuan*, 7.

188. Chen Huanqiao 陈桓乔, "Wo he Xiang Jingyu dajie xiangchu de rizi" 我和向警予大姐相处的日子 (My days spent living and working with Sister Xiang Jingyu), in *Xiang Jingyu: Zhuanji, jinian yu huiyi, lunshu, ziliao*, 176.

189. Yang Zilie, *Zhang Guotao furen huiyilu*, 138.

190. Cai Hesen, "Xiang Jingyu tongzhi zhuan," 3.

191. Helen Snow, *Women in Modern China*, 275.

192. Peng Shuzhi, *Peng Shuzhi huiyilu*, vol. 2, 47.

193. Cai Hesen, "Xiang Jingyu tongzhi zhuan," 3; Yang Zilie, *Zhang Guotao furen huiyilu*, 131.

194. Helen Snow, *Women in Modern China*, 275.

195. Helen Snow, *Women in Modern China*, 275.

196. Zhang Guotao, *Wo de huiyi*, vol. 2, 93.

197. Zhang Guotao, *Wo de huiyi*, vol. 2, 93.

198. Zhang Guotao, *Wo de huiyi*, vol. 2, 94.

199. Yang Zilie, *Zhang Guotao furen huiyilu*, 146; Li Yongchun, *Cai Hesen nianpu*, 209.

200. Yang Zilie, *Zhang Guotao furen huiyilu*, 146–47. Yang Zilie did not leave Vladivostok with Xiang Jingyu and Cai Hesen because she was about to give birth.

201. Li Yongchun, *Cai Hesen nianpu*, 231. According to Zheng Chaolin, Cai Hesen's affair with Li Yichun caused pain for Li Lisan and intensified the conflict between the two men at the Sixth Congress of the CCP. See Zheng Chaolin, "Lian'ai yu geming," 290.

202. Xiang Jingyu admitted to Yang Zilie that she had fallen in love with other comrades after returning to Shanghai from France. She claimed that she was uncertain about her relationship with the Mongolian student but loved both Cai Hesen and Peng Shuzhi. Yang Zilie believed that Xiang Jingyu was influenced by the "glass of water" theory (*beishui zhuyi* 杯水主义), which views the need for love and sex as just as natural as drinking a glass of water. See Yang Zilie, *Zhang Guotao furen huiyilu*, 161–62. Peng Shuzhi stated in his memoir that Xiang Jingyu had told him about her romantic relationships with Mao Zedong and Zhang Guotao. See Peng Shuzhi, *Peng Shuzhi huiyilu*, vol. 2, 50.

203. Yang Zilie, *Zhang Guotao furen huiyilu*, 127.

204. Yang Zilie, *Zhang Guotao furen huiyilu*, 127. Wang Yizhi was Shi Cuntong's wife; Kong Xianzhi (original name Kong Dezhi 孔德沚) married Mao Dun; Yang Zhihua was Qu Qiubai's wife; Zhang Qinqiu and Shen Zemin were a couple; and He Baozhen married Liu Shaoqi.

205. Peng Shuzhi, *Peng Shuzhi huiyilu*, vol. 1, 459.

206. Cai Hesen, "Xiang Jingyu tongzhi zhuan," 4.

207. Cai Hesen, "Xiang Jingyu tongzhi zhuan," 4.

208. Cai Hesen, "Xiang Jingyu tongzhi zhuan," 4.

209. Lee Haiyan, *Revolution of the Heart: A Genealogy of Love in China* (Stanford: Stanford University Press, 2010), 91.

210. Dai Xugong, *Xiang Jingyu zhuan*, 36.

211. "Shijie tuchen lu" 史屆兔尘录 (Records of anecdotes in history), *Xinmin congbao* 7 (1902): 89.

212. Xuanyuan Zhengyi 轩辕正裔, "Guafen canhuo yuyan ji" 瓜分惨祸预言记 (Prophecy about the tragic fate of the dissection of China), reprinted in *Zhongguo jindai xiaoshuo daxi* 中国近代小说大系 (Modern Chinese fiction series) (Nanchang: Baihuazhou wenyi chubanshe, 1991), 387.

213. Yi Shengli 伊胜利 and Chen Shuzhi 陈书智, "Zhongguo gongchandang diyi wei nü dangyuan: Miu Boying zhuanlüe" 中国共产党第一位女党员:缪伯英传略 (The first female Chinese Communist Party member: A brief biography of Miao Boying), in *Zhonggong dangshi ziliao* 中共党史资料 (The CCP history materials), vol. 56 (Beijing: Zhonggong dangshi chubanshe, 1996), 166.

214. For information on Xiang Jingyu's activities after returning from Moscow, see "Xiang Jingyu shengping dashi nianbiao," 336–40.

215. Cai Hesen, "Xiang Jingyu tongzhi zhuan," 4.

216. Cai Hesen, "Xiang Jingyu tongzhi zhuan," 6.

217. The early CCP leaders' writings about Xiang Jingyu's love affairs were published by either Hong Kong or foreign presses. Zheng Chaolin and Zhang Guotao's memoirs were published as "internal materials" (*neibu ziliao* 内部资料) by Dongfang Press, a subsidiary of Renmin Press. The chapter detailing Xiang Jingyu's love affairs in Zheng Chaolin's memoir was deleted from the version published by Dongfang Press.

Exhibition IV

1. Ding Ling, "Wo zai Xiacun de shihou" 我在霞村的時候 (When I was in Xia village), *Zhongguo wenhua* 中国文化 (Chinese culture) 3, no. 1 (June 20, 1941): 24–31.

2. For the 1944 version, see Ding Ling, "Wo zai Xiacun de shihou," in Ding Ling, *Wo zai Xiacun de shihou* (Guilin: Yuanfang shudian, 1944), 97–128; for the 1946 version, see Ding Ling, "Wo zai Xiacun de shihou," in *Jiefangqu duanpian chuangzuo xuan*, ed. Zhou Yang (Shenyang: Dongbei shudian, 1946), 1–18.

3. Ding Ling, "Wo zai Xiacun de shihou," in Ding Ling, *Wo zai Xiacun de shihou* (Beijing: Sanlian shudian, 1950), 13–41.

4. Earl Leaf, "Ting Ling, Herald of a New China," *T'ien Hsia Monthly* 5, no. 3 (1937): 234–35.

5. Ding Ling, "Yike wei chutang de qiangdan" 一颗未出膛的枪弹 (An unfired bullet), in *Ding Ling quanji*, vol. 4, 122–32.

6. Ding Ling, "Dongcun shijian" 东村事件 (Affair in East Village), in *Ding Ling quanji*, vol. 4, 133–54.

7. For a detailed account of the group's initiation, see Ding Ling, *Yinian* 一年 (One year) (Chongqing: Shenghuo shudian, 1939), 2–5.

8. Wang Zengru and Li Xiangdong, *Ding Ling nianpu changbian*, vol. 1, 128.

9. Ding Ling, *Yinian*, 15. Other talks include "Zhanshi zhengzhi gongzuo" 战时政治工作 (Political work during the wartime) by Mo Zhihua 莫之骅; "Xingjun xuzhi" 行军须知 (Rules for marching) by He Changgong 何长工; "Zhanshi de difang qunzhong gongzuo" 战时的地方群众工作 (Local mass work during wartime) by Li Fuchun 李富春; "Tongyi zhanxian" 统一战线 (The united front) by Kai Feng 凯丰; "Tongpai lilun" 托派理论 (Theories of Trotskyism) by Wu Liangping 吴亮平; and "Zhongri wenti" 中日问题 (Issues between China and Japan) by Li Fanfu 李凡夫. See Ding Ling, *Yinian*, 14–15.

10. In the first published version of the play, the female and male protagonists are named Li Baizhi 李白芝 and Zhang Daming 张达明. See Ding Ling, "Chongfeng" 重逢 (Reunion), *Qiyue*, no. 5, December 16, 1937: 137–42.

11. Ding Ling, "Chongfeng" 重逢 (Reunion), in *Ding Ling quanji*, vol. 4, 357.

12. Ding Ling, "Chongfeng," in *Ding Ling quanji*, vol. 4, 357.

13. Ding Ling, "Chongfeng," in *Ding Ling quanji*, vol. 4, 359.

14. Ding Ling, "*Henei Yilang* houji" 《河内一郎》后记 (The afterword of *Kawachi Ichiro*), in *Ding Ling quanji*, vol. 9, 30.

15. Quoted from Wang Zengru and Li Xiangdong, *Ding Ling nianpu changbian*, vol. 1, 128.

16. Wang Zengru and Li Xiangdong, *Ding Ling nianpu changbian*, vol. 1, 131.

17. Ting Ling, "An Unexpected Reunion," trans. Lu Yung, *Far Eastern Mirror*, August 10, 1938: 60–70. For a detailed account of the performance of the English version of Ding

Ling's play in India, see Ba Zhou 巴宙, "Guanyu Ding Ling de 'buqi'eryu'—Zai Yindu guoji daxue paiyan jingguo" 关于丁玲的"不期而遇"—在印度国际大学的排演经过 (The process of performing Ding Ling's "An Unexpected Reunion" at Visva-Bharati University in India), *Yuzhou feng* 宇宙风 (The wind of the universe) 100 (1940): 142–44. The play was also performed in Batavia in 1946. See "Ding Ling mingju Chongfeng liangge jingcai jingtou" 丁玲名剧"重逢"两个精彩镜头 (Two remarkable scenes from Ding Ling renowned play *Reunion*), *Nanyang Post* 5 (1946): 21.

18. Ding Ling, "Cong Linfen jidao Wuhan" 从临汾寄到武汉 (A letter from Linfen to Wuhan), *Qiyue*, no. 8, February 1, 1938, 227.

19. Ding Ling, "Cong Linfen jidao Wuhan."

20. "Guomindang zhongyang xuanchuanbu guanyu jinyan Ding Ling bianzhou zhi 'Chongfeng' juben shi zhi junweihui zhengzhibu gonghan" 国民党中央宣传部关于禁演丁玲编著之《重逢》剧本事致军委会政治部公函 (The KMT Propaganda Department's official letter addressed to the Political Department of the Military Committee regarding the prohibition of the performance of Ding Ling's *Reunion*), dated November 7, 1939, in *Zhonghua minguoshi dang'an ziliao huibian* 中华民国史档案资料汇编 (Compilation of archival materials of the Republic of China), vol. 5, no. 2, culture (2), ed. Second Historical Archives of China (Nanjing: Jiangsu guji chubanshe, 1998), 22–23.

21. Quoted from Ding Ling, "Yan'an wenyi zuotanhui de qianqian houhou," vol. 10, 264.

22. Jiang Heng 江横, "Ding Ling fangwen ji" 丁玲访问记 (The interview with Ding Ling), *Xinhua ribao*, April 27, 1938.

23. The concept of "new wine in old bottles" generated heated discussions in the late 1930s and early '40s. With the intent of disseminating anti-Japanese invasion messages through popular culture, the historian Gu Jiegang 顾颉刚 established *Tongsu duwu biankan she* 通俗读物编刊社 (Popular Reading Press) in 1932 and *Minzhong zhoubao* 民众周报 (The people's weekly) in 1936. He advocated for the idea of "new wine in old bottles" and wrote several essays on the topic. See Gu Jiegang, "Weishenme yaoba xinjiu zhuangzai jiuping li" 为什么要把新酒装在旧瓶里 (Why new wine should be put in old bottles), *Minzhong zhoubao* 1, no. 5 (1936): 8–10; "Zailun Weishenme yaoba xinjiu zhuangzai jiuping li" 再论为什么要把新酒装在旧瓶里 (Another discussion on why new wine should be put in old bottles), *Minzhong zhoubao* 1, no. 6 (1936): 9–11; "Jiuping zhuang xinjiu de chuangzuo fangfa lun" 旧瓶装新酒的创作方法论 (The methodology of writing "new wine in old bottles" literature), *Minzhong zhoubao* 2, no. 2 (1937): 7–9.

In April 1938, the literary journal *Qiyue*, edited by Hu Feng, organized a panel discussion on "new wine in old bottles" literature and its limitations. See "Xuanchuan, wenxue, jiu xingshi de liyong: Zuotanhui jilu" 宣传•文学•旧形式的利用：座谈会纪录 (Propaganda, literature, and the use of traditional forms: The records of a panel discussion), *Qiyue* 3, no. 1 (1938): 2–8. In response to the panel discussion organized by the journal *Qiyue*, the Popular Reading Press organized its own panel discussion on "new wine in old bottles" in May. See "Guanyu 'jiuping zhuang xinjiu' de chuangzuo fangfa zuotanhui jilu" 关于"旧瓶装新酒"的创作方法座谈会纪录 (The records of a panel discussion on the methodology of writing "new wine in old bottles" literature), in *Tongsu duwu lunwen ji* 通俗读物论文集 (Collected essays on popular readings) (Chongqing: Shenghuo shudian, 1938), 87–111. The discussion on "new wine in old bottles" also sparked discussions on national forms in literature (*wenxue de minzu xingshi* 文学的民族形式).

24. Lao She, "Zhonglie tu" 忠烈图 (The loyalists and martyrs), *Wenyi zhendi* 文艺阵地 (Literary battlefield), April 16, 1938: 9–12; "Liefu xunguo" 烈妇殉国 (A chaste woman martyred for the nation), *Kangzhan xiju* 抗战戏剧 (War of Resistance drama) 2, no. 1 (May 25, 1938): 23–27.

Lao She shifted his focus to the "new wine in old bottles" literary style at the beginning of the War of Resistance against Japan. He wrote three big drum songs, four Peking operas, and one traditional novel, all of which were included in the book titled *San si yi* 三四一 (Three, four, one). In the book, "Liefu xunguo" was published under the title "Xue Erniang" 薛二娘 (Second lady Xue). See Lao She, *San si yi* (Chongqing: Duli chubanshe, August 1938).

25. Ding Ling, "Xiezai disan ci gongyan qianmian" 写在第三次公演前面 (Written before the third public performance), in *Ding Ling quanji*, vol. 5, 106–7.

26. Ding Ling, "Chongfeng" 重逢 (Reunion), *Qiyue*, no. 5, December 16, 1937: 138.

27. Liu Long-hsin, "Popular Readings and Wartime Historical Writings in Modern China," in *The Challenge of Linear Time: Nationhood and the Politics of History in East Asia*, ed. Viren Murthy and Axel Schneider (Leiden: Brill, 2014), 191.

28. Lao She, "Nü'er jing" 女儿经 (Classic for girls), in *Lao She quyi wenxuan* 老舍曲艺文选 (Selected works of Lao She's folk literature) (Beijing: Zhongguo quyi chubanshe, 1982), 275.

29. Lao She, "Zhonglie tu," 11.

30. Lao She, "Zhonglie tu," 9.

31. Wang Zengru and Li Xiangdong, *Ding Ling nianpu changbian*, vol. 1, 141.

32. Wang Zengru and Li Xiangdong, *Ding Ling nianpu changbian*, vol. 1, 142.

33. Chen Xuezhao 陈学昭, *Yan'an fangwen ji* 延安访问记 (A visit to Yan'an) (Hong Kong: Beiji shudian, 1940), 80.

34. Ding Ling, "Lüetan gailiang pingju" 略谈改良平剧 (A brief discussion on reforming Peking opera), in *Ding Ling quanji*, vol. 7, 30–36.

35. Wang Zengru and Li Xiangdong, *Ding Ling nianpu changbian*, vol. 1, 146.

36. Chen Ming 陈明, *Wo yu Ding Ling wushi nian* 我与丁玲五十年 (My fifty years with Ding Ling), ed. Zha Zhenke 查振科 and Li Xiangdong 李向东 (Beijing: Zhongguo dabaike quanshu chubanshe, 2015), 65.

37. Ding Ling, "Yi Bishi tongzhi," 329.

38. For the original version of the story, see Ding Ling, "Leiyan mohu zhong zhi xinnian" 泪眼模糊中之信念 (Faith in the eyes dimmed by tears), *Wenyi zhanxian* 文艺战线 (Literary front) 1, no. 4 (September 1939): 1–9.

39. Ding Ling, "New Faith," in *I Myself Am a Woman: Selected Writings of Ding Ling*, ed. Tani Barlow and Gary J. Bjorge, trans. Jean James and Tani Barlow (Boston: Beacon Press, 1989), 287–88.

40. Yan Haiping, *Chinese Women Writers and the Feminist Imagination, 1905–1948* (London: Routledge, 2006), 215.

41. Ding Ling, "New Faith," 289–90.

42. Ding Ling, "New Faith," 290.

43. Tani Barlow and Gary J. Bjorge, eds., *I Myself Am a Woman: Selected Writings of Ding Ling* (Boston: Beacon Press, 1989), 281.

44. Ding Ling, "New Faith," 297.

45. Ding Ling, "New Faith," 297.

46. For the original version of the story, see Ma Feng 马烽, "Jinbao niang" 金宝娘 (Jinbao's mother), *Jinsui ribao* 晋绥日报 (Jinsui daily), from February 28 to March 3, 1949. It was republished in *Xinhua zhoubao* 新华周报 (Xinhua weekly). See Ma Feng, "Jinbao niang," *Xinhua zhoubao* 1, no. 12 (1949): 11–15. The title was later changed to "Yige xiajian nüren" 一个下贱女人 (A despicable woman) in Ma Feng's short story collection. See "Yige xiajian nüren," in Ma Feng, *Yige xiajian nüren* (Beijing: Tianxia tushu gongsi, November 1949), 1–23.

47. Ma Feng, "Jinbao niang," *Xinhua zhoubao*, 11.

48. Ma Feng, "Jinbao niang," *Xinhua zhoubao*, 15.

49. Cao Ming, "Shouru zhe" 受辱者 (The humiliated), in *Cao Ming wenji* 草明文集 (Collected works of Cao Ming), vol. 2 (Beijing: Guangming ribao chubanshe, 1992), 289–301; Liu Qing, "Bei wuru le de nüren" 被污辱了的女人 (A woman who has been humiliated), *Jiefang ribao*, September 2, 1941 and September 3, 1941.

50. Cao Ming, "Shouru zhe," 291.

51. Cao Ming, "Shouru zhe," 301.

52. Liu Qing, "Bei wuru le de nüren," *Jiefang ribao*, September 3, 1941.

53. See Lu Xun, "The New Year's Sacrifice," in *Selected Stories of Lu Hsun*, trans. Yang Hsien-yi and Gladys Yang (Beijing: Foreign Languages Press, 1960), 125–43.

54. Ding Ling and Xiao Jun were close friends in their early days in Yan'an. In late March 1938, Ding Ling went back to Yan'an to report on the activities of the Northwest Front Service Corps. During her two-week stay in Yan'an, she persuaded Xiao Jun to join the Corps for propagandist works in Xi'an.

Ding Ling and Xiao Jun arrived in Xi'an in April and reunited with Xiao Hong, Xiao Jun's former lover. Duanmu Hongliang, who later married Xiao Hong, was also there. According to Duanmu, in Xi'an, Xiao Jun once claimed that he would marry Ding Ling in front of Duanmu and Xiao Hong. Xiao Jun's words could have been intended to irritate the two at the time. He did, however, admit in his diary (dated September 2, 1940) that he loved Ding Ling.

According to Xiao Jun's diary (dated September 2, 1940), he and Ding Ling discussed their future and agreed that they could not be together because they both prioritized individual freedom. Their close relationship caused quarrels between Xiao Jun and his wife Wang Defen 王德芬 (see Xiao Jun's diary entry dated September 10, 1940).

Ding Ling and Xiao Jun parted ways in Yan'an over disputes regarding Wang Shiwei's issues during the Rectification Movement in 1942. Xiao Jun argued that Wang still believed in revolution, and the CCP's attitude in criticizing Wang was inappropriate (see his diary entry dated May 25, 1942), while Ding Ling sided with the CCP to criticize Wang for opposing the party. See Wang Zengru and Li Xiangdong, *Ding Ling nianpu changbian*, vol. 1, 139; Kong Haili 孔海立, *Duanmu Hongliang zhuan* 端木蕻良传 (Biography of Duanmu Hongliang) (Shanghai: Fudan daxue chubanshe, 2011), 80; Xiao Jun, *Yan'an riji* 延安日记 1940–1945 (Yan'an diary, 1940–1945), vol. 1 (Oxford: Oxford University Press, 2013), 22, 23, 31, 476; and Ding Ling, "Wenyijie dui Wang Shiwei yingyou de taidu ji fanxing" 文艺界对王实味应有的态度及反省 (The attitude and introspection that the literary and art fields should have toward Wang Shiwei), *Jiefang ribao*, June 16, 1942.

55. Xiao Jun, *Yan'an riji*, vol. 1, 6 and 8–9. The letter "T" in Xiao Jun's diary refers to Ding Ling.

56. Wang Zengru and Li Xiangdong, *Ding Ling zhuan*, vol. 1, 245; Dong Xiao 冬晓, "Zoufang Ding Ling" 走访丁玲 (Interview with Ding Ling), in *Ding Ling yanjiu ziliao* 丁玲研究资料 (Research materials on Ding Ling), ed. Yuan Liangjun 袁良骏 (Tianjin: Tianjin renmin chubanshe, 1982), 195–96; Ding Ling, "Tan ziji de chuangzuo" 谈自己的创作 (A discussion on my creative writing), *Ding Ling quanji*, vol. 8, 87–88; Ding Ling, "He Beijing yuyan xueyuan liuxuesheng de yici tanhua" 和北京语言学院留学生的一次谈话 (A conversation with study abroad students at Beijing Language and Culture University), *Ding Ling quanji*, vol. 8, 290–91.

57. Xiao Jun, *Yan'an riji*, vol. 1, 51–52.

58. Xiao Jun, *Yan'an riji*, vol. 1, 54.

59. Xiao Jun, *Yan'an riji*, vol. 1, 53, 68.

60. Ding Ling, "Wo zai Xiacun de shihou," 1941: 24.

61. Ding Ling, "When I Was in Xia Village," in *I Myself Am a Woman*, trans. Gary J. Bjorge (1989), 302.

62. Ding Ling, "Wo zai Xiacun de shihou," 1941: 25.

63. Lu Yaodong 陆耀东, "Ping 'Wo zai Xiacun de shihou'" 评"我在霞村的时候" (A critique of "When I was in Xia Village"), in *Zai pipan*, 98–99.

64. Ding Ling, "Wo zai Xiacun de shihou," 1941, 24.

65. Ding Ling, "When I Was in Xia Village," trans. Gary J. Bjorge (1989), 299.

66. Ding Ling, "When I Was in Xia Village," 299.

67. Ding Ling, "When I Was in Xia Village," 303.

68. Ding Ling, "When I Was in Xia Village," 303.

69. Ding Ling, "When I Was in Xia Village," 303.

70. Ding Ling, "When I Was in Xia Village," 299.

71. Chen Ming, "Xibei zhandi fuwutuan diyinian jishi" 西北战地服务团第一年纪实 (Records of the first year of the Northwest Front Service Corps), *Xin wenxue shiliao* 2 (1982): 69.

72. Chen Ming, "Xibei zhandi fuwutuan diyinian jishi," 69.

73. Ding Ling, "Yan'an wenyi zuotanhui de qianqian houhou," 267.

74. *Yan'an wenyi dang'an*, vol. 4, 149–50.

75. He Huoren 何火任, "He Jingzhi nianbiao" 贺敬之年表 (Chronicle of He Jingzhi), in *He Jingzhi shixuan* 贺敬之诗选 (Selected poems of He Jingzhi) (Beijing: Renmin wenxue chubanshe, 2004), 503–5.

76. He Jingzhi, "Buyao zhujiao: xiangei Luyi" 不要注脚:献给鲁艺 (No explanation: Dedicated to Lu Xun Academy of Art and Literature), in *He Jingzhi shixuan*, 42–43.

77. Wei Mingxing 危明星, "Jieji yu xingbie huayu gaixie xia de jiaotang kongjian—1940 nian qianhou Yan'an wenxue zhong de jiaotang shuxie" 阶级与性别话语改写下的教堂空间—1940年前后延安文学中的教堂书写 (Rewriting church space under the class and gender discourse—the representation of churches in Yan'an literature around 1940), *Wenyi lilun yu piping* 文艺理论与批评 (Literary theory and criticism) 6 (2019): 50.

78. He Jingzhi, "Zai jiaotang li" 在教堂里 (In the church), in *He Jingzhi shixuan*, 111; He Jingzhi, *Shengdan jie* 圣诞节 (Christmas), in *He Jingzhi shixuan*, 112–13.

79. Chen Huangmei 陈荒煤, "Zai jiaotang gechang de ren" 在教堂歌唱的人 (The person who sings at the church), *Jiefang ribao*, from May 26 to May 28, 1941.

80. For a detailed discussion of the church image in Chen Huangmei's short story, "Zai jiaotang gechang de ren," see Wei Mingxing, "Jieji yu xingbie huayu gaixie xia de jiaotang kongjian," 47-48.

81. Gu Yuan 古元, "Wo zai Yan'an chuangzuo de liangfu muke" 我在延安创作的两幅木刻 (Two woodblock prints I made in Yan'an), in *Yan'an yishu jia* 延安艺术家 (Artists in Yan'an), ed. Ai Ke'en 艾克恩 (Xi'an: Shaanxi renmin jiaoyu chubanshe, 1992), 484.

Another woodblock print by Gu Yuan, "Taowang dizhu you guilai" 逃亡地主又归来 (The runaway landlord returns, 1941), also explores issues related to religious belief and ideological change in Yan'an. To find more information about this woodblock print and the discussion related to it, see Gu Yuan, "Wo zai Yan'an chuangzuo de liangfu muke," 485–86.

82. Gu Yuan, "Wo zai Yan'an chuangzuo de liangfu muke," 484.

83. Gu Yuan, "Wo zai Yan'an chuangzuo de liangfu muke," 484.

84. Mao Dun, "Kaihuang" 开荒 (Cultivate the wasteland), *Bitan* 笔谈 (Brush talks) 6 (1941): 1.

85. Mao Dun, "Ji Lu Xun yishu wenxueyuan" 记鲁迅艺术文学院 (An account of Lu Xun Academy of Art and Literature), *Xuexi* 学习 (Studies) 5, no. 2 (1941): 66–67.

86. Li Qun 力群, "Yan'an Luyi xiaojing" 延安鲁艺校景 (The landscape of Lu Xun Academy of Art and Literature), see https://auction.artron.net/paimai-art5149490716, accessed August 15, 2023.

87. Ding Ling, "Tian Baolin" 田保霖, in *Ding Ling quanji*, vol. 5, 156.

88. Ding Ling, "When I Was in Xia Village," trans. Gary J. Bjorge (1989), 315. I highlighted the word "seemed."

89. David Der-Wei Wang, *The Monster That Is History: History, Violence, and Fictional Writing in Twentieth-Century China* (Berkeley: University of California Press, 2004), 68.

90. Wang Zengru and Li Xiangdong, *Ding Ling nianpu changbian*, vol. 1, 107–8.

91. Wang Zengru and Li Xiangdong, *Ding Ling nianpu changbian*, vol. 1, 108–9.

92. Wang Zengru and Li Xiangdong, *Ding Ling nianpu changbian*, vol. 1, 112.

93. Ding Ling, "When I Was in Xia Village," trans. Gary J. Bjorge (1989), 307. The original version of the story did not explain why Zhenzhen was sent back to the Japanese army. Ding Ling added the sentence "I was familiar with the area, the work was important, and it was impossible to find anyone else in a short time" in a later revision. In the original version, Ding Ling wrote, "[I] have heard that they are going to cure my disease" instead of "they're going to treat my disease." In the 1950 revision, Ding Ling justified sending Zhenzhen back for intelligence work and expressed more optimism about Zhenzhen's upcoming journey to Yan'an. For the original version, see Ding Ling, "Wo zai Xiacun de shihou," 1941, 28.

94. Wang Zengru and Li Xiangdong, *Ding Ling nianpu changbian*, vol. 1, 104.

95. Ding Ling, "When I Was in Xia Village," trans. Gary J. Bjorge (1989), 308. The sentences "later, after I made contact with our own people, I became less afraid. As I watched the Jap devils suffer defeat in battle and the guerrillas take action on all sides as a result of the tricks I was playing, I felt better by the day" were not in the original version.

96. Hua Fu, "Ding Ling de fuchou nüshen: Ping 'Wo zai Xiacun de shihou,'" 88.

97. Ding Ling, "When I Was in Xia Village," trans. Gary J. Bjorge (1989), 309.

98. Wang Zengru and Li Xiangdong, *Ding Ling nianpu changbian*, vol. 1, 146.

99. The original version of this short story was published under the title "Zai yiyuan zhong shi" 在医院中时 (When in the hospital). See Ding Ling, "Zai yiyuan zhong shi," *Guyu* 谷雨 (Grain rain), inaugural issue, November 15, 1941: 1–7. It was later republished in *Wenyi zhendi* 文艺阵地 (Literary battlefield) under the title "Zai yiyuan zhong" 在医院中 (In the hospital). See Ding Ling, "Zai yiyuan zhong," *Wenyi zhendi* 7, no. 1 (1942): 3–10.

100. Ding Ling, "Guanyu 'Zai yiyuan zhong' (caogao)" 关于《在医院中》(草稿) (On 'In the hospital': Draft), *Zhongguo xiandai wenxue yanjiu congkan* 中国现代文学研究丛刊 (Journal of modern Chinese literature studies) 6 (2007):105.

101. Ding Ling, "Guanyu 'Zai yiyuan zhong' (caogao)," 105.

102. Ding Ling, "Guanyu 'Zai yiyuan zhong' (caogao)," 111.

103. Ding Ling, "When I Was in Xia Village," trans. Gary J. Bjorge (1989), 299; and Ding Ling, "Wo zai Xiacun de shihou," 1950, 13.

104. Ding Ling, "Wo zai Xiacun de shihou," 1941, 24.

105. Ding Ling, "Sanba jie yougan" 三八节有感 (Thoughts on March 8), in *Ding Ling quanji*, vol. 7, 60–63.

106. Mo Ye 莫耶, "Liping de fannao" 丽萍的烦恼 (Liping's worries), in *Yan'an wenyi dang'an*, vol. 35, 344.

107. In the original version, Comrade Ma says that "Liu Dama's daughter, Zhenzhen, came back. I never thought she could be such a hero." See Ding Ling, "Wo zai Xiacun de shihou," 1941, 25. In the 1950 version, Comrade Ma says, "I never thought she could be so great." See Ding Ling, "When I Was in Xia Village," trans. Gary J. Bjorge (1989), 302. For the Chinese text, see Ding Ling, "Wo zai Xiacun de shihou," 1950, 19.

108. For the concept of "crisis femininity," see Edwards, *Women Warriors and Wartime Spies of China*, 90.

109. Xing Xiaoqun 邢小群, "Chen Ming fangtan" 陈明访谈 (Interview with Chen Ming), in Xing Xiaoqun, *Ding Ling yu wenxue yanjiusuo de xingshuai* 丁玲与文学研究所的兴衰 (Ding Ling and rise and fall of the Literature Study Institute) (Zhengzhou: Henan wenyi chubanshe, 2013), 264.

110. Zhou Yang 周扬, "Wenyi zhanxian shang de yichang da bianlun" 文艺战线上的一场大辩论 (A major debate on the frontline of art and literature), *Renmin ribao*, February 28, 1958.

111. Hua Fu, "Ding Ling de fuchou nüshen: Ping 'Wo zai Xiacun de shihou,'" 86.

112. Hua Fu, "Ding Ling de fuchou nüshen: Ping 'Wo zai Xiacun de shihou,'" 87.

113. Hua Fu, "Ding Ling de fuchou nüshen: Ping 'Wo zai Xiacun de shihou,'" 92.

114. Lu Yaodong, "Ping 'Wo zai Xiacun de shihou,'" 95.

115. Lu Yaodong, "Ping 'Wo zai Xiacun de shihou,'" 97.

116. Wang Liaoying 王燎荧, "Kangzhan shiqi Ding Ling xiaoshuo de sixiang qingxiang" 抗战时期丁玲小说的思想倾向 (The ideological tendencies in Ding Ling's wartime stories), *Wenxue yanjiu* 文学研究 (Literary studies) 4 (1957): 98–101.

117. *Zhenzhen* 贞贞, directed by Qiao Liang 乔梁, DVD (Beijing: Beijing jiuzhou tongying shuzi dianying yuanxian youxian gongsi, 2003).

Exhibition V

1. Hua Fu, "Ding Ling de fuchou nüshen: Ping 'Wo zai Xiacun de shihou,'" 89.

2. For a detailed account of Liu Hulan's life, see "Liu Hulan lieshi de shengping" 刘胡兰烈士的生平 (Biography of the martyr Liu Hulan), *Renmin ribao*, January 12, 1957.

3. "Liu Hulan lieshi de shengping."

4. "Liu Hulan lieshi de shengping."

5. "Liu Hulan lieshi de shengping."

6. Lei Yunfeng 雷云峰, "Mao zhuxi wei Liu Hulan lieshi tici jingguo" 毛主席为刘胡兰烈士题词经过 (The process of Chairman Mao's inscription for Liu Hulan), *Renwen zazhi* 人文杂志 (Humanity magazine) 6 (1983): 100.

7. Wang Xueli 王学礼, "Deng Xiaoping wei Liu Hulan tici shimo" 邓小平为刘胡兰题词始末 (The full story of Deng Xiaoping's inscription for Liu Hulan), *Dangshi wenhui* 党史文汇 (Collective essays on the history of the party) 9 (2013): 35–36.

8. Mao Zedong wrote the memorial words in 1947 after hearing the story of Liu Hulan. However, the original inscription was lost during the war. In 1957, on the tenth anniversary of Liu Hulan's death, Mao rewrote the same words. Mao's two-time inscription emphasizes the significance of promoting Liu Hulan in the early years of the PRC. See Lei Yunfeng, "Mao zhuxi wei Liu Hulan lieshi tici jingguo," 100.

9. Wei Feng 魏风, "*Liu Hulan* juben xiezuo qianhou"《刘胡兰》剧本写作前后 (Before and after the scriptwriting of *Liu Hulan*), *Dangshi tiandi* 党史天地 (The world of party history) 1 (1997): 32.

10. Gail Hershatter, *The Gender of Memory: Rural Women and China's Collective Past* (Berkeley: University of California Press, 2011), 104.

11. Hershatter, *Gender of Memory*, 104.

12. For the "make everyone a soldier" campaign, see "Zhonggong zhongyang guanyu minbing wenti de jueding" 中共中央关于民兵问题的决定 (The Central Committee of the CCP's decision on the People's Militia issue, August 1958), in *Jianguo yilai zhongyao wenxian xuanbian* 建国以来重要文献选编 (Selected important documents since the founding of the PRC), vol. 11, ed. Central Committee of the CCP's Document Research Office (Beijing: Zhongyang wenxian chubanshe, 2011), 406–8.

13. For details about Liu Hulan's role in the campaign, see Edwards, *Women Warriors and Wartime Spies of China*, 175–78.

14. Li Guixiang 李桂香, "Chuancheng Liu Hulan jingshen de minbing ban" 传承刘胡兰精神的民兵班 (The militia squad that inherited the spirit of Liu Hulan), *Dangshi wenhui* 1 (2019): 42–45.

15. Wang Xueli, "Deng Xiaoping wei Liu Hulan tici shimo," 35.

16. Wang Xueli, "Deng Xiaoping wei Liu Hulan tici shimo," 35.

17. Wang Xueli, "Deng Xiaoping wei Liu Hulan tici shimo," 36.

18. Denton, *Exhibiting the Past*, 3.

19. For detailed accounts of the collection of relics for the Museum of the Chinese Revolution, see Chang-tai Hung, *Mao's New World*, 115–16; and Xie Bingzhi 谢炳志, "Zhongguo geming bowuguan de choujian yu Wang Yeqiu" 中国革命博物馆的筹建与王冶秋 (Wang Yeqiu and the preparation for the establishment of the Museum of the Chinese Revolution), *Xin wenhua shiliao* 2 (1996): 57. The Museum of the Chinese Revolution and

the Chinese History Museum were merged into the National Museum of China in 2003, making it the largest museum in China.

20. For the writing process of the *huaju* and opera versions of *Liu Hulan*, see Liu Lianchi 刘莲池, "Xiezai *Liu Hulan* qianmian" 写在"刘胡兰"前面 (Writing in front of *Liu Hulan*), in Xibei zhandou jushe 西北战斗剧社 (Northwest Combat Dramatic Society), *Liu Hulan* 刘胡兰 (Beijing: Renmin wenxue chubanshe, 1952), 1–2.

21. Chen Bo 陈播, "Zhandou jushe zai jiefang zhanzheng shiqi jishi" 战斗剧社在解放战争时期纪事(下) (Records of the Combat Dramatic Society in the Liberation War, part 2), *Xin wenhua shiliao* 3 (1998): 54–55.

22. Liu Lianchi, "Guanyu xiudingben de shuoming" 关于修订本的说明 (Explanations for the revised version), in Xibei zhandou jushe, *Liu Hulan*, 1952, 8–9. Founded by General He Long, the Combat Propaganda Troupe (*zhandou xuanchuan dui* 战斗宣传队), the predecessor of the Combat Dramatic Society, regularly performed *Liu shi dou tou* 刘氏兜头 (Mrs. Liu held the head), a traditional Chinese opera based on the story of He Long's great-grandparents.

He Long's great-grandfather was sentenced to be beheaded by the Qing government for leading a peasants' revolt in 1854. Mrs. Liu, He Long's great-grandmother, used her apron to hold her husband's bloody head to avoid having it touch the ground after the execution. The explicit scene of violence and blood in the opera generated sympathy toward peasants and hatred toward the ruling class in He Long's troops. It also offered an example of writing about the execution of Liu Hulan in its original version. For the performance of *Liu shi dou tou*, see Yan Jizhou 严寄洲, "He Long yu Zhandou jushe" 贺龙与战斗剧社 (He Long and the Combat Dramatic Society), *Zhonggong dangshi ziliao* 1 (2008): 31.

23. Ai Wu 艾芜, "*Liu Hulan* geju guanhou de ganxiang" 刘胡兰歌剧观后的感想 (Thoughts after watching the opera *Liu Hulan*), *Guangming ribao*, January 21, 1950.

24. Wang Zhaowen 王朝闻, "Xiju zhong xijie miaoxie de yizhong qingxiang" 戏剧中细节描写的一种倾向 (A tendency in depicting details in theater), *Wenyi bao* 10 (1949): 16–17.

25. Zhou Yang 周扬, "Xin de renmin de wenyi" 新的人民的文艺 (The new people's art and literature), in *Zhou Yang Wenji* 周扬文集 (Collected works of Zhou Yang), vol. 1 (Beijing: Renmin wenxue chubanshe, 1984), 517.

26. Wang Zhaowen, "Zuopin zhong ruhe chuli yingxiong jiuyi de qingjie" 作品中如何处理英雄就义的情节 (How to portray the death of a martyr), *Wenyi bao* 2, no. 3 (1950): 23–24.

27. Liu Jin 刘金, Li Guojing 李国经, "Du 'Xiju zhong xijie miaoxie de yizhong qingxiang' hou" 读《戏剧中细节描写的一种倾向》后 (Reflections on "A tendency in depicting details in theater"), *Wenyi bao* 2, no. 3 (1950): 28; Zhong Dianfei 钟惦棐, "Guanyu wenyi shang de xijie miaoxie wenti" 关于文艺上的细节描写问题 (Regarding the issue of writing about details in art and literature), *Wenyi bao* 2, no. 3 (1950): 21–22; He Qifang 何其芳, "Shilun xiju shang de Liu Hulan de zhatou" 试论戏剧上的刘胡兰的铡头 (On beheading Liu Hulan in theater), *Wenyi bao* 2, no. 3 (1950): 25–27.

28. Wei Feng, "*Liu Hulan* juben xiezuo qianhou," 32.

29. Liu Lianchi, "Xiezai *Liu Hulan* qianmian," 5.

30. Wei Feng, "*Liu Hulan* juben xiezuo qianhou," 32.

31. Chen Bo, "Zhandou jushe zai jiefang zhanzheng shiqi jishi," 52.

32. Cheng Shigang 程世刚, "Shahai Liu Hulan xiongshou de xiachang" 杀害刘胡兰凶手的下场 (The fate of Liu Hulan's killer), *Dangshi bocai* 6 (2007): 36.

33. Quoted from Ma Ming 马明, "Wei minzu jiefang benbo, wei guojia duli juanqu" 为民族解放奔波，为国家独立捐躯 (Rushing for the liberation of the nation, sacrificing for the independence of the country), *Dangshi wenhui* 1 (2007): 10. Also see Edwards, *Women Warriors and Wartime Spies of China*, 194.

34. Chang-tai Hung, "The Cult of the Red Martyr: Politics of Commemoration in China," 281.

35. Guo Wu convincingly argues that bitterness (*ku* 苦) and hatred (*chou* 仇) are two central themes in the CCP's narratives for reshaping collective memories. See Guo Wu, "Recalling Bitterness: Historiography, Memory, and Myth in Maoist China," *Twentieth-Century China* 39, no. 3 (2014): 259. The article has detailed discussions on how "class bitterness" (*jieji ku* 阶级苦) and "national grievance" (*minzu hen* 民族恨) were integrated into collective memory construction during the Mao era.

36. Jin Shangyi 靳尚谊 and Wang Chengyi 汪诚一, "Huainian women de laoshi K.M. Maksimov" 怀念我们的老师 K. M. 马克西莫夫 (Commemorating our teacher K. M. Maksimov), *Meishu* 7 (1994): 57.

37. Zhu Liang 朱亮, "Feng Fasi yu *Liu Hulan jiuyi*" 冯法祀与《刘胡兰就义》(Feng Fasi and *The Heroic Death of Liu Hulan*), *Zhongguo meishuguan* 7 (2007): 75.

38. Zhu Liang, "Feng Fasi yu *Liu Hulan jiuyi*," 70–71.

39. Zhu Liang, "Feng Fasi yu *Liu Hulan jiuyi*," 71.

40. One of the themes in Li Zhanyang's sculptures is the appropriation of artwork in socialist China. Another of his scene sculptures, *Zu—shouzu yuan* "租"—收租院 (*"Rent"—Rent Collection Yard*, 2007), parodically appropriates the famous *Shouzu yuan* 收租院 (*Rent Collection Yard*, 1965) group of sculptures.

41. "Dai Zhuoqun duihua Li Zhanyang" 戴卓群对话李占洋 (The conversation between Dai Zhuoqun and Li Zhanyang), *Dongfang yishu* 19 (2010): 59.

42. Quoted from Lu Mingjun 鲁明军, "Shijue, wenben yu geren xushi—Li Zhanyang de yishu shijian" 视觉、文本与个人叙事—李占洋的艺术实践 (Visual, text and individual narrative—Li Zhanyang's artistic practices), *Zhongguo yishu shikong* 2 (2013): 31.

43. Li Zhanyang 李占洋, "Shazhu shi de houjiao—wo de xianshi zhuyi" 杀猪时的吼叫—我的现实主义 (Pig's roar when it was being slaughtered—my realism), *Diaosu* 2 (2017): 39–40.

44. Yu Cun 于村, Hai Xiao 海啸, Lu Su 卢肃, and Chen Zi 陈紫, *Yuju Liu Hulan: Juben yu qupu* 豫剧《刘胡兰》:剧本与曲谱 (Yu opera *Liu Hulan*, script and score) (Zhengzhou: Henan renmin chubanshe, 1959), 159.

45. "Liang jiehe," a socialist writing principle advocated by Mao Zedong and Zhou Yang in the 1950s, was a reinforced version of socialist realism. This principle guided artists and writers to create idealized socialist heroes.

46. Zhang Zhen 张真, "Ji Liu Hulan cai zhadao" 记刘胡兰踩铡刀 (Liu Hulan's act of stepping on the hay cutter), *Zhongguo xiju* 中国戏剧 (Chinese theater) 14 (1958): 19.

47. Laurence Coderre, *Newborn Socialist Things: Materiality in Maoist China* (Durham, NC: Duke University Press, 2021), 147.

48. Yu Cun, Hai et al., *Yuju Liu Hulan*, 162.

49. Yang Wei 杨威, Guo Jian 郭健, Sun Wei 孙伟, and Fang Yan 方彦, *Liu Hulan: Bachang huaju* 刘胡兰：八场话剧 (Liu Hulan: Eight scenes spoken drama) (Tianjin: Baihua wenyi chubanshe, 1965), 99.

50. Wang Zhaowen is renowned for creating official images for the CCP. He crafted the relief sculptures of Lu Xun in 1941 and Mao Zedong in 1950. The latter sculpture became the cover image of *Mao Zedong xuanji* 毛泽东选集 (The selected works of Mao Zedong, 1951). Additionally, Wang's relief sculptures of Vladimir Lenin and Joseph Stalin were used as cover images of *Lie Ning xuanji* 列宁选集 (The selected works of Lenin, 1960) and *Si Dalin quanji* 斯大林全集 (The complete collection of Stalin, 1953), respectively. See Jian Ping 简平, *Wang Zhaowen zhuan* 王朝闻传 (Biography of Wang Zhaowen) (Yinchuan: Ningxia renmin chubanshe, 2009, 56), 100–101.

51. For the inspiration from a bronze *jue*, see Jian Ping, *Wang Zhaowen zhuan*, 102–3.

52. Jian Ping, *Wang Zhaowen zhuan*, 103.

53. Wang Ban, *The Sublime Figure of History: Aesthetics and Politics in Twentieth-Century China* (Stanford: Stanford University Press, 1997), 114.

54. Pan Shaotang 潘绍棠, "Zhongyang meishu xueyuan diaosuxi dui xingshi zhuyi qingxiang de douzheng" 中央美术学院雕塑系对形式主义倾向的斗争 (Fighting against formalism in the sculpture department at the Central Academy of Fine Arts), *Meishu* 3 (1955): 17.

55. Sun Zhenhua 孙振华, "Mao Zedong shidai diaosu zhong de shenti zhengzhi" 毛泽东时代雕塑中的身体政治 (Body politics in sculpture during the Maoist era), *Yishu tansuo* 19, no. 2 (2005): 15.

56. For Yang Tao's hero series, which includes the sculpture of Liu Hulan, see Yang Tao 杨韬, "Jingshen wanju" 精神玩具 (Spiritual toys), *Yishu jie* 艺术界 (Art field) 4 (2006): 102–3; and https://baike.baidu.com/pic/%E6%9D%A8%E9%9F%AC/12061968/1199799645/f31fbe096b63f6249fc95d2e8544ebf81a4ca303?fr=newalbum#aid=1199799645&pic=9358d109b3de9c8285f29da26e81800a19d84303, accessed October 17, 2023.

57. Huang Xin, "From 'Hyper-Feminine' to Androgyny: Changing Notions of Femininity in Contemporary China," in *Asian Popular Culture in Transition*, ed. Lorna Fitzsimmons and John Lent (London: Routledge, 2013), 137.

58. Edwards, *Women Warriors and Wartime Spies of China*, 165.

59. Mikhail Bakhtin, *Rabelais and His World*, trans. Helene Iswolsky (Bloomington: Indiana University Press, 1984), 317–18.

60. I am grateful for this comment from Louise Edwards.

61. Meng Yue, "Female Images and National Myth," in *Gender Politics in Modern China*, ed. Tani Barlow (Durham, NC: Duke University Press, 1993), 118.

62. "Yu Fan & Zhu Qi fangtan: Fofa yide, mojing nanru" 于凡&朱其访谈: 佛法易得，魔境难入 (Zhu Qi's interview with Yu Fan: The dharma is easy to get, but the magic world is hard to get into), http://www.cafa.com.cn/cn/figures/article/details/8320554, accessed May 22, 2022.

63. In response to economic and military difficulties, the Northwest Shanxi Revolutionary Base Area government launched the Four Mobilizations in 1940, which included expanding military forces, making soldiers' shoes, and donating money and food (*kuobing,*

zuo junxie, xianjin, xianliang 扩兵、做军鞋、献金、献粮). See *Jinsui geming genjudi dashi ji* 晋绥革命根据地大事记 (Significant events of the Jinsui Revolutionary Base Area), ed. CCP Shanxi Provincial Party History Research Office (Taiyuan: Shanxi renmin chubanshe, 1989), 123.

64. For a detailed account of the exhibition, see Bai Sheng 柏生, "Ji quanguo fudai dahui zhanlanhui"记全国妇代大会展览会 (Records of the exhibition at the first National Conference for Women Representatives), *Renmin ribao*, March 30, 1949.

65. Bai Sheng, "Ji quanguo fudai dahui zhanlanhui."

66. Luo Guangbin 罗广斌 and Yang Yiyan 杨益言, *Hongyan* 红岩 (Red crag) (Beijing: Zhongguo qingnian chubanshe, 1961), 518–20. "Embroidering the national flag," as canonized in *Hongyan*, is still a common practice in contemporary China demonstrating patriotism. *Xiu hongqi* 绣红旗 (embroidering the red flag) or *lianye xiu hongqi* 连夜绣红旗 (embroidering the red flag overnight) is a popular phrase among Chinese netizens that refers to people who change their political views overnight to show loyalty to the CCP and avoid potential criticism for not being sufficiently patriotic.

67. He Jianming 何建明, "Zuihou de douzheng—Hongyan geming lieshi xisheng xianchang shilu" 最后的斗争—红岩革命烈士牺牲现场实录 (The last battle—records of the sacrifices of the red crag revolutionary martyrs), *Zhongguo zuojia* 16 (2011): 24.

68. The literary works on Liu Hulan after 1949 include Liang Xing 梁星, *Liu Hulan xiaozhuan* 刘胡兰小传 (A brief biography of Liu Hulan) (Beijing: Qingnian chubanshe, 1951); Yu Cun 于村, Hai Xiao 海啸, Lu Su 卢肃, and Chen Zi 陈紫, *Liu Hulan: Er'mu jiuchang geju* 刘胡兰：二幕九场歌剧 (Liu Hulan: Two acts nine scenes opera) (Beijing: Zuojia chubanshe, 1955); Yu Cun 于村, *Liu Hulan: Simu qichang huaju* 刘胡兰：四幕七场话剧 (Liu Hulan: four acts seven scenes spoken drama), Beijing: Zuojia chubanshe, 1956; Chen Lingxi 陈灵犀, *Liu Hulan: Pingtan* 刘胡兰：评弹 (Liu Hulan: pingtan), Shanghai: Shanghai wenhua chubanshe, 1957; Yu Cun 于村, Hai Xiao 海啸, Lu Su 卢肃, Chen Zi 陈紫, *Yuju Liu Hulan: juben yu qupu* 豫剧《刘胡兰》：剧本与曲谱 (Yu opera *Liu Hulan*, script and score), Zhengzhou: Henan renmin chubanshe, 1959; Yang Wei 杨威, Guo Jian 郭健, Sun Wei 孙伟, and Fang Yan 方彦, *Liu Hulan: Bachang huaju* 刘胡兰：八场话剧 (Liu Hulan: Eight scenes spoken drama) (Tianjin: Baihua wenyi chubanshe, 1965); Peng Huagao 彭化高 and Zhang Youluo 张友洛, *Liu Hulan: Guci* 刘胡兰：鼓词 (Liu Hulan: Drum lyrics) (Taiyuan: Shanxi renmin chubanshe, 1977); Ma Feng 马烽, *Liu Hulan zhuan* 刘胡兰传 (Biography of Li Hulan) (Beijing: Zhongguo qingnian chubanshe, 1978).

69. Peng Huagao 彭化高 and Zhang Youluo 张友洛, *Liu Hulan: Guci*, 55.

70. Yu Cun, *Liu Hulan: Simu qichang huaju*, 5.

71. Liu Ying 刘英, "Guanyu poxie wenti" 关于破鞋问题 (Regarding the issues of *poxie*), *Zhongguo funü* 1, no. 2 (1939): 6–7.

72. Ya Su 亚苏, "Zailun poxie wenti" 再论破鞋问题 (Revisit the issues of *poxie*), *Zhongguo funü* 1, nos. 5 and 6 (1939): 15–18.

73. The term used to describe her is "bewitching" (*yaoliyaoqi* 妖里妖气). See Chen Lingxi, *Liu Hulan: Pingtan*, 18; also see Ma Feng, *Liu Hulan zhuan* (Beijing: Zhongguo qingnian chubanshe, 1978), 254.

74. Peng Huagao and Zhang Youluo, *Liu Hulan: Guci*, 51.

75. Sun Pujin 孙普金, "Beiping xijiao di funü" 北平西郊底妇女 (Women in the Xijiao area of Beiping), *Zhongguo funü* 2, no. 4 (1940): 23.

76. Zhuo Shi 灼石, "Erbulang fufu" 二不浪夫妇 (Blockheaded couple), *Jiefang ribao*, August 1, 1941.

77. For information on the reform of prostitutes during the early years of the PRC, see "Qianyu jinü kaishi xin shenghuo" 千余妓女开始新生活 (Thousands of prostitutes began their new lives), *Renmin ribao*, November 23, 1949; Pei Lan 培蓝, "Tiaochu huokeng de jiemeimen" 跳出火坑的姐妹们 (The sisters who jumped out of the fire pit), *Renmin ribao*, December 26, 1949. Louise Edwards also discussed how Liu Hulan was used to educate sex workers in the early PRC. See Edwards, *Women Warriors and Wartime Spies*, 192.

78. Louise Edwards provides a detailed discussion of contradictory records of Liu Hulan's age in official narratives.

See Edwards, *Women Warriors and Wartime Spies of China*, 178.

79. *Liu Hulan* 刘胡兰, directed by Feng Bailu 冯白鲁, DVD (Shenyang: Bandao yinxiang chubanshe, (1950) 2005.

80. Orna Naftali, *Children, Rights and Modernity in China: Raising Self-Governing Citizens* (London: Palgrave Macmillan, 2014), 38.

81. "Zhonghua renmin gongheguo weichengnianren baohufa" 中华人民共和国未成年人保护法 (Law of the PRC on Protection of Minors), *Zhonghua renmin gongheguo guowuyuan gongbao* 中华人民共和国国务院公报 (Gazette of the State Council of the PRC) 32 (1991): 1116.

82. *Liu Hulan* 刘胡兰, directed by Shen Yaoting 沈耀庭, DVD (Guangzhou: Guangdong Haiyan dianzi yinxiang chubanshe, (1996) 1998.

83. Zhou Renjie 周人杰, "Rang yingxiong zhiguang zhaoliang haizimen de xingkong" 让英雄之光照亮孩子们的星空 (Let the light of heroes illuminate the children's starry sky). *Renmin ribao*, June 1, 2017.

84. Liang Hongyi 梁红一, "Liu Hulan de shi" 刘胡兰的事 (Facts about Liu Hulan), *Shanxi dang'an* 山西档案 (Archives of Shanxi) 1 (2007): 48–49.

85. Liang Hongyi, "Liu Hulan de shi," 48–49.

86. Liang Xing, *Liu Hulan xiaozhuan*, 51.

87. Yu Cun et al., *Liu Hulan: Er'mu jiuchang geju*, 8.

88. Yu Cun, *Liu Hulan: Simu qichang huaju*, 51.

89. Yu Cun et al., *Liu Hulan: Er'mu jiuchang geju*, 63; and Yu Cun, *Liu Hulan: Simu qichang huaju*, 67.

90. For a detailed discussion on the 1964 opera version of *Liu Hulan*, see Wan Weizhou 万苇周, "Ping geju *Liu Hulan* xinmao ji qita" 评歌剧刘胡兰新貌及其它 (Comments on the new opera version of *Liu Hulan* and others), *Renmin yinyue* 人民音乐 (People's music), no. 10/11 (1964): 20–21.

91. Ma Feng 马烽, "Liu Hulan zhuan," *Huohua* 火花 (Spark), 1 (1964): 60. Ma Feng's *Liu Hulan zhuan* was first published in *Huohua* magazine in a series from 1962 to 1964. Due to its prohibition by the Gang of Four, the book was not released until 1978.

92. Jiang Zhanbing 江战兵, "Zhang Geng shi geming xiandaixi de sidi" 张庚是革命现代戏的死敌 (Zhang Geng is the ultimate enemy of the revolutionary opera), *Renmin ribao*, August 29, 1968.

93. Li Xue'ao 李学鳌, "Liu Hulan de songge" 刘胡兰的颂歌 (Ode to Liu Hulan), in *Li Xue'ao Changshi Xuan* 李学鳌长诗选 (Selected long poems by Li Xue'ao) (Shijiazhuang: Huashan wenyi chubanshe, 1985), 98.

94. Peng Huagao and Zhang Youluo, *Liu Hulan: Guci*, 107.

95. Denton, *Exhibiting the Past*, 267.

96. Li Jie, *Utopian Ruins: A Memorial Museum of the Mao Era* (Durham, NC: Duke University Press, 2020), 8.

Epilogue

1. Wang Zengru, "Ding Ling daiwo kanwang Guan Lu" 丁玲带我看望关露 (Ding Ling took me to visit Guan Lu), in Wang Zengru, *Wunai de niepan: Ding Ling zuihou de rizi* 无奈的涅槃：丁玲最后的日子 (Helpless nirvana: The last days of Ding Ling) (Shanghai: Shanghai shudian chubanshe, 2003), 155.

2. For detailed discussion of Guan Lu's private life and the gossip surrounding her, see Louise Edwards, "Commemorating China's Wartime Spies: Red Agents Guan Lu and Jiang Zhuyun, and the Problem of Female Fidelity," in *Women Warriors and National Heroes: Global Histories*, ed. Boyd Cothran, Joan Judge, and Adrian Shubert (London: Bloomsbury Academic, 2020), 220–22.

3. Ding Yanzhao 丁言昭, "Guan Lu shengping nianbiao" 关露生平年表 (Chronological biography of Guan Lu), in *Guan Lu a Guan Lu* 关露啊关露 (Guan Lu, oh Guan Lu), ed. Ding Yanzhao (Beijing: Renmin wenxue chubanshe, 2001), 261.

4. Guan Lu, "Wo xiangqi le Zuolian" 我想起了左联 (I remembered the League of Left-wing Writers), in *Guan Lu a Guan Lu*, 256; and Ding Yanzhao, "Guan Lu shengping nianbiao," 261.

5. Ding Yanzhao, "Guan Lu shengping nianbiao," 261.

6. Ding Yanzhao, "Guan Lu shengping nianbiao," 262.

7. See Guan Lu, "Nü zuojia yinxiangji—nü zhanshi Ding Ling" 女作家印象记—女战士丁玲 (Impressions of a female writer—the female warrior Ding Ling), *Shanghai funü* 上海妇女 (Women in Shanghai) 2, no. 8 (1939): 27–28.

8. Ding Yanzhao, "Guan Lu shengping nianbiao," 263.

9. See Wang Zengru, "Ding Ling daiwo kanwang Guan Lu," 217.

10. As Louise Edwards noted, "Once she [Guan Lu] joined the Japanese-sponsored magazine, she was branded a 'cultural traitor' (*wenhua hanjian*)." Louise Edwards, "Commemorating China's Wartime Spies: Red Agents Guan Lu and Jiang Zhuyun, and the Problem of Female Fidelity," 218.

11. Ding Yanzhao, "Guan Lu shengping nianbiao," 263.

12. Guan Lu, "Dongjing yiyu: Shenjing bingtai de rizi" 东京忆语：神经病态的日子 (Tokyo memories: Neurotic days), *Nüsheng* 女声 (Women's voice) 2, no. 6 (1943): 15.

13. Ding Ling, "Si zhi ge," 9.

14. Ding Yanzhao, "Guan Lu shengping nianbiao," 264–65.

15. Ding Yanzhao, "Guan Lu shengping nianbiao," 265.

16. Ding Yanzhao, "Guan Lu shengping nianbiao," 266.

17. Wang Zengru, "Ding Ling daiwo kanwang Guan Lu," 156.

18. Wang Zengru, "Ding Ling daiwo kanwang Guan Lu," 157.

19. Wang Zengru, "Ding Ling daiwo kanwang Guan Lu," 158.

20. Wang Zengru, Li Xiangdong, *Ding Ling zhuan*, vol. 2, 723.

21. Wang Zengru, "Ding Ling daiwo kanwang Guan Lu," 158.

22. Xiao Yang 萧阳, "Daonian Guan Lu zuotanhui jishi" 悼念关露座谈会纪实 (Record of the memorial symposium for Guan Lu), in *Guan Lu a Guan Lu*, 186.

23. Wang Zengru and Li Xiangdong, *Ding Ling nianpu changbian*, vol. 2, 830. Xi Zhongxun was then a member of the Politburo of the CCP Central Committee and the secretary of the CCP Central Secretariat. He praised Ding Ling's advocacy for freedom of artistic creation in 1985, and he supported *Zhongguo* 中国 (China) magazine, which was founded by Ding Ling. He visited her in the hospital in February 1986 and helped acquire medical equipment for her treatment. See Tu Shaojun, *Tuben Ding Ling zhuan*, 302; Ding Ling, "Zhi Xi Zhongxun" 致习仲勋 (Letter to Xi Zhongxun), in *Ding Ling quanji*, vol. 12, 298; and Jiang Zulin, *Ding Ling zhuan*, 551–52.

24. Zha Zhenke and Li Xiangdong, "Chen Ming koushu: Ding Ling wannian naxie shi," 136.

25. For a detailed account of this meeting, see Gan Lu, "Yici nanwang de tanshi—yi Ding Ling tanwang Zhou Yang" 一次难忘的探视—忆丁玲探望周扬 (An unforgettable visit: A recollection of Ding Ling's visit to Zhou Yang), *Xin wenxue shiliao* 3 (1991): 86–87.

26. For the full text of "Guanyu Ding Ling tongzhi youpai wenti de fucha jielun" 关于丁玲同志右派问题的复查结论 (Conclusion on reexamining Ding Ling's Rightist issue), see Yang Guixin 杨桂欣, *Ding Ling yu Zhou Yang de enyuan* 丁玲与周扬的恩怨 (The gratitude and grudge between Ding Ling and Zhou Yang) (Wuhan: Hubei renmin chubanshe, 2006), 200–202.

27. Chen Ming, *Wo yu Ding Ling wushi nian*, 266.

28. Chen Ming, *Wo yu Ding Ling wushi nian*, 266.

29. Chen Ming, *Wo yu Ding Ling wushi nian*, 266.

30. For Ding Ling's speech, see Ding Ling, "Jiang yidian xinli hua" 讲一点心里话 (Some words from my heart), in *Ding Ling quanji*, vol. 8, 64–79. In an interview with Zhao Haosheng 赵浩生 in 1978, Zhou Yang discussed the two factions in Yan'an. For the interview, see Zhao Haosheng, "Zhou Yang xiaotan lishi gongguo" 周扬笑谈历史功过 (Zhou Yang talks about historical achievements and mistakes), *Xin wenxue shiliao* 2 (1979): 228–42.

31. Zhou Liangpei 周良沛, *Ding Ling zhuan* 丁玲传 (Biography of Ding Ling) (Beijing: Beijing shiyue wenyi chubanshe, 1993), 753.

32. Zhou Liangpei, *Ding Ling zhuan*, 753.

33. Quoted from Zhou Liangpei, *Ding Ling zhuan*, 753.

34. Wang Zengru and Li Xiangdong, *Ding Ling nianpu changbian*, vol. 2, 550.

35. Wang Zengru and Li Xiangdong, *Ding Ling nianpu changbian*, vol. 2, 552.

36. Yang Guixin, *Ding Ling yu Zhou Yang de enyuan*, 212–13.

37. Wang Zengru and Li Xiangdong, *Ding Ling nianpu changbian*, vol. 2, 831.

38. Wang Zengru and Li Xiangdong, *Ding Ling nianpu changbian*, vol. 2, 832.

39. Wang Zengru and Li Xiangdong, *Ding Ling nianpu changbian*, vol. 2, 832.

40. Wang Zengru and Li Xiangdong, *Ding Ling nianpu changbian*, vol. 2, 835.

41. Wang Zengru and Li Xiangdong, *Ding Ling nianpu changbian*, vol. 2, 835.

42. Wang Zengru and Li Xiangdong, *Ding Ling nianpu changbian*, vol. 2, 837; Zhou Liangpei, *Ding Ling zhuan*, 829.

43. "Ding Ling tongzhi shengping" 丁玲同志生平 (The life of Comrade Ding Ling), *Renmin ribao*, March 16, 1986.

44. Wang Zengru and Li Xiangdong, *Ding Ling nianpu changbian*, vol. 2, 833–34.

45. Wang Zengru and Li Xiangdong, *Ding Ling nianpu changbian*, vol. 2, 835.

46. Wang Zengru and Li Xiangdong, *Ding Ling nianpu changbian*, vol. 2, 835. For details on Chen Ming's appeal to cover Ding Ling's body with the party flag, also see Chen Ming, *Wo yu Ding Ling wushi nian*, 287.

47. Jiang Zulin, *Ding Ling zhuan*, 552.

48. "Ding Ling tongzhi yiti gaobie yishi zai jing juxing" 丁玲同志遗体告别仪式在京举行 (The funeral ceremony for Comrade Ding Ling was held in Beijing), *Renmin ribao*, March 16, 1986.

49. Wang Zengru and Li Xiangdong, *Ding Ling nianpu changbian*, vol. 2, 837.

50. Wang Zengru and Li Xiangdong, *Ding Ling nianpu changbian*, vol. 2, 837–38.

51. Zhou Liangpei, *Ding Ling zhuan*, 833. Ding Ling's writing is from her essay, "Wo suo renshi de Qu Qiubai tongzhi," 58.

BIBLIOGRAPHY

Ai Wu 艾芜. "*Liu Hulan* geju guanhou de ganxiang" 刘胡兰歌剧观后的感想 [Thoughts after watching the opera *Liu Hulan*]. *Guangming ribao*, January 21, 1950.

An Yangming 安阳明. *Nü yingxiong Liu Hulan* 女英雄刘胡兰 [Liu Hulan the heroine]. Shanghai: Xinhua shudian, 1949.

Anderson, Benedict. *Imagined Communities: Reflections on the Origin and Spread of Nationalism*. London: Verso, 2006.

Assmann, Aleida. *Cultural Memory and Western Civilization: Functions, Media, Archives*. Cambridge: Cambridge University Press, 2011.

Bai Sheng 柏生. "Ji quanguo fudai dahui zhanlanhui" 记全国妇代大会展览会 [Records of the exhibition at the first National Conference for Women Representatives]. *Renmin ribao*, March 30, 1949.

Bai Shuang 白霜. "Hui jiating? Dao shehui?" 回家庭?到社会? [Returning home or going out to society?]. *Jiefang ribao*, March 8, 1942.

Bakhtin, Mikhail. *Rabelais and His World*. Translated by Helene Iswolsky. Bloomington: Indiana University Press, 1984.

Baoji 宝记. "Shanghai zhi nü guomin dahui" 上海之女国民大会 [Shanghai Women Citizens' Meeting]. *Tuhua shibao* 图画时报 [Pictorial times] 243 (1925): 7.

Barlow, Tani, and Gary J. Bjorge, eds. *I Myself Am a Woman: Selected Writings of Ding Ling*. Boston: Beacon Press, 1989.

"Benshi funüjie kai kuoda jinianhui" 本市妇女界开扩大纪念会 [Local women's community will host an expanded commemoration meeting]. *Minbao*, March 7, 1936.

Bowersock, Glen. *Martyrdom and Rome*. Cambridge: Cambridge University Press, 1995.

Cai Yuanpei quanji 蔡元培全集 [The complete works of Cai Yuanpei], vol. 1. Beijing: Zhonghua shuju, 1984.

"Cao E jiangshang zhi hanchao" 曹娥江上之寒潮 [Cold tides of the Cao E River]. *Shenbao*, January 29, 1912.

Cao Ming 草明. "Shouru zhe" 受辱者 [The humiliated]. In *Cao Ming wenji* 草明文集 [Collected works of Cao Ming], vol. 2, 289–301. Beijing: Guangming ribao chubanshe, 1992.

CCP Shanxi Provincial Party History Research Office, ed. *Jinsui geming genjudi dashi ji* 晋绥革命根据地大事记 [Significant events of the Jinsui Revolutionary Base Area]. Taiyuan: Shanxi renmin chubanshe, 1989.

Central Committee of the CCP's Document Research Office, ed. *Jianguo yilai zhongyao wenxian xuanbian* 建国以来重要文献选编 [Selected important documents since the founding of the PRC]. Beijing: Zhongyang wenxian chubanshe, 2011.

Certeau, Michel de. *The Practice of Everyday Life*. Translated by Steven Rendall. Berkeley: University of California Press, 1984.

Chambers, David Ian. "Shanghai's 'Mysterious Westerner': The Walden Affair and Soviet Military Intelligence Operations in China, 1933–1935." *Twentieth-Century China* 40, no. 2 (2015): 105–25.

"Changsha zhuidao Qiu nüxia jisheng" 长沙追悼秋女侠纪盛 [Records of the grand memorial service for female knight-errant with the surname Qiu in Changsha]. *Shenbao*, July 27, 1912.

Chen Bilan 陈碧兰. *Zaoqi Zhonggong yu tuopai: Wo de geming shengya huiyi* 早期中共与托派：我的革命生涯回忆 [Early Chinese Communist Party and Trotskyists: Memories of my revolutionary career]. Hong Kong: Tiandi tushu, 2010.

Chen Bo 陈播. "Zhandou jushe zai jiefang zhanzheng shiqi jishi" 战斗剧社在解放战争时期纪事(下) [Records of the Combat Dramatic Society in the Liberation War, part 2]. *Xin wenhua shiliao* 3 (1998): 52–55.

Chen Huangmei 陈荒煤. "Zai jiaotang gechang de ren" 在教堂歌唱的人 [The person who sings at the church]. *Jiefang ribao*, from May 26 to May 28, 1941.

Chen Lingxi 陈灵犀. *Liu Hulan: Pingtan* 刘胡兰：评弹 [Liu Hulan: Pingtan]. Shanghai: Shanghai wenhua chubanshe, 1957.

Chen Ming 陈明. *Wo yu Ding Ling wushi nian* 我与丁玲五十年 [My fifty years with Ding Ling], edited by Zha Zhenke 查振科 and Li Xiangdong 李向东. Beijing: Zhongguo dabaike quanshu chubanshe, 2015.

Chen Ming. "Xibei zhandi fuwutuan diyinian jishi" 西北战地服务团第一年纪实 [Records of the first year of the Northwest Front Service Corps]. *Xin wenxue shiliao* 2 (1982): 65–72.

Chen Shuyu 陈漱渝. "1957 nian pipan Ding Chen fandang jituan jishi" 1957年批判丁陈反党集团纪实 [A record of the criticism of the Ding Chen Anti-Party Group in 1957]. *Xin wenxue shiliao* 4 (2014): 39–65.

Chen Shuyu. "Ding Ling yuan'an jiqi lishi fansi" 丁玲冤案及其历史反思 [The unjust case of Ding Ling and its historical reflection]. *Yue haifeng* 4 (2005): 45–52.

Chen Xuezhao 陈学昭. *Yan'an fangwen ji* 延安访问记 [A visit to Yan'an]. Hong Kong: Beiji shudian, 1940.

Cheng Shigang 程世刚. "Shahai Liu Hulan xiongshou de xiachang" 杀害刘胡兰凶手的下场 [The fate of Liu Hulan's killer]. *Dangshi bocai* 6 (2007): 34–37.

Chiang Kai-shek. "Xin shenghuo yundong gangyao" 新生活运动纲要 [Essentials of the New Life Movement]. *Xin shenghuo zhoukan* 新生活周刊 [New life weekly] 1, no. 4, 1934: 1–6.

"Chuban fa" 出版法 [Publication Law]. *Guomin zhengfu gongbao* 国民政府公报 [Nationalist government gazette] 651 (1930): 3–8.

Coderre, Laurence. *Newborn Socialist Things: Materiality in Maoist China*. Durham, NC: Duke University Press, 2021.

Dai Hongheng 戴洪恒, ed. *Jiben jiaokeshu gaoxiao guoyu jiaoxuefa* 基本教科书高小国语

教学法 [Teaching methodology for *Basic Chinese Textbook*], vol. 2. Shanghai: Shangwu yinshuguan, 1932.

Dai Jitao 戴季陶. *Guomin geming yu Zhongguo Guomindang* 国民革命与中国国民党 [The national revolution and the KMT]. Printed by Dai Jitao's office, 1925.

Daixi 黛茜. "Jinnian wei Qiu Jin xianlie xunguo zhi sanshinian jinian" 今年为秋瑾先烈殉国之三十年纪念 [This year marks the thirtieth anniversary of Qiu Jin's martyrdom for the nation]. *Shenbao*, May 30, 1936.

Dai Xugong 戴绪恭. *Xiang Jingyu zhuan* 向警予传 [Biography of Xiang Jingyu]. Beijing: Renmin chubanshe, 1985.

Dai Xugong and Yao Weidou 姚维斗, eds. *Xiang Jingyu wenji* 向警予文集 [Collected writings of Xiang Jingyu]. Beijing: Renmin chubanshe, 2011.

"Dai Zhuoqun duihua Li Zhanyang" 戴卓群对话李占洋 [The conversation between Dai Zhuoqun and Li Zhanyang]. *Dongfang yishu* 19 (2010): 56–61.

Deng Yingchao. "Cong Xihuating haitanghua yiqi" 从西花厅海棠花忆起 [Recalling the Chinese crabapple from the Western Flower Hall]. *Renmin ribao*, March 5, 1997.

Deng Yingchao 邓颖超. "Guanyu 'Weilan zhong yidian andan' de pipan" 关于"蔚蓝中一点黯淡"的批判 [Regarding the criticism of "A touch of gray in azure"]. *Xinhua ribao*, August 12, 1940.

Denton, Kirk. *Exhibiting the Past: Historical Memory and the Politics of Museums in Postsocialist China*. Honolulu: University of Hawai'i Press, 2014.

Ding Ling 丁玲. "Busuan qingshu" 不算情书 [Not love letters]. *Wenxue* 1, no. 3 (1933): 367–70.

Ding Ling. "Chongfeng" 重逢 [Reunion]. *Qiyue*, no. 5, December 16, 1937: 137–42.

Ding Ling. "Cong Linfen jidao Wuhan" 从临汾寄到武汉 [A letter from Linfen to Wuhan]. *Qiyue*, no. 8, February 1, 1938: 227.

Ding Ling. *Ding Ling zishu* 丁玲自述 [Ding Ling's self-narrative]. Zhengzhou: Daxiang chubanshe, 2006.

Ding Ling. "Guanyu 'Zai yiyuan zhong' (caogao)" 关于《在医院中》(草稿) [On 'In the hospital': Draft]. *Zhongguo xiandai wenxue yanjiu congkan* 中国现代文学研究丛刊 [Journal of modern Chinese literature studies] 6 (2007): 97–114.

Ding Ling. "Leiyan mohu zhong zhi xinnian" 泪眼模糊中之信念 [Faith in the eyes dimmed by tears]. *Wenyi zhanxian* 文艺战线 [Literary front] 1, no. 4 (September 1939): 1–9.

Ding Ling. *Muqin* 母亲 [Mother]. Beijing: Renmin wenxue chubanshe, 1980.

Ding Ling. *Ding Ling quanji* 丁玲全集 [Complete works of Ding Ling]. Shijiazhuang: Hebei renmin chubanshe, 2001.

Ding Ling. "Si zhi ge" 死之歌 [The song of death]. *Hunan wenxue* 湖南文学 [Hunan literature] 1 (1987): 4–9.

"Ding Ling tongzhi shengping" 丁玲同志生平 [The life of Comrade Ding Ling]. *Renmin ribao*, March 16, 1986.

"Ding Ling tongzhi yiti gaobie yishi zai jing juxing" 丁玲同志遗体告别仪式在京举行 [The funeral ceremony for Comrade Ding Ling was held in Beijing]. *Renmin ribao*, March 16, 1986.

Ding Ling. "Wenyijie dui Wang Shiwei yingyou de taidu ji fanxing" 文艺界对王实味应有的态度及反省 [The attitude and introspection that the literary and art fields should have toward Wang Shiwei]. *Jiefang ribao*, June 16, 1942.

Ding Ling. "Wo zai Xiacun de shihou" 我在霞村的時候 [When I was in Xia village]. *Zhongguo wenhua* 中国文化 [Chinese culture] 3, no. 1 (June 20, 1941): 24–31.

Ding Ling. *Wo zai Xiacun de shihou*. Guilin: Yuanfang shudian, 1944.

Ding Ling. "Wo zai Xiacun de shihou." In *Jiefangqu duanpian chuangzuo xuan* 解放区短篇创作选 [Collection of short stories in the liberated areas], edited by Zhou Yang 周扬, 1–18. Shenyang: Dongbei shudian, 1946.

Ding Ling. *Wo zai Xiacun de shihou*. Beijing: Sanlian shudian, 1950.

"Ding Ling yi bei qiangjue" 丁玲已被枪决 [Ding Ling has been executed by firing squad]. *Dagong bao* (Tianjin), June 25, 1933.

Ding Ling. *Yinian* 一年 [One year]. Chongqing: Shenghuo shudian, 1939.

Ding Ling. *Yiwai ji* 意外集 [Unexpected collection]. Shanghai: Shanghai liangyou tushu, 1936.

Ding Yanzhao 丁言昭, ed. *Guan Lu a Guan Lu* 关露啊关露 [Guan Lu, oh Guan Lu]. Beijing: Renmin wenxue chubanshe, 2001.

Duanmu Luxi 端木露西. "Weilan zhong yidian andan" 蔚蓝中一点黯淡 [A touch of gray in azure]. *Dagong bao*, July 6, 1940.

Edwards, Louise. "Commemorating China's Wartime Spies: Red Agents Guan Lu and Jiang Zhuyun, and the Problem of Female Fidelity." In *Women Warriors and National Heroes: Global Histories*, edited by Boyd Cothran, Joan Judge, and Adrian Shubert, 217–32. London: Bloomsbury Academic, 2020.

Edwards, Louise. *Women Warriors and Wartime Spies of China*. Cambridge: Cambridge University Press, 2016.

Fan Di'an 范迪安, ed. *Yi wei rensheng: Ershi shiji Zhongguo youhua mingjia Feng Fasi* 艺为人生：二十世纪中国油画名家冯法祀 [Arts for life: Twentieth century Chinese oil painting master Feng Fasi]. Hefei: Anhui meishu chubanshe, 2014.

Feng Bailu 冯白鲁, dir. *Liu Hulan* 刘胡兰. DVD. Shenyang: Bandao yinxiang chubanshe, (1950) 2005.

Feng Fasi huaxuan 冯法祀画选 [Selected paintings of Feng Fasi]. Beijing: Renmin meishu chubanshe, 1981.

Feuerwerker, Yi-tsi Mei. *Ding Ling's Fiction*. Cambridge, MA: Harvard University Press, 1982.

Gan Lu 甘露. "Yici nanwang de tanshi—yi Ding Ling tanwang Zhou Yang" 一次难忘的探视—忆丁玲探望周扬 [An unforgettable visit—A recollection of Ding Ling's visit to Zhou Yang]. *Xin wenxue shiliao* 3 (1991): 86–87.

Gengfu 更夫. "Sanba tan Nala" 三八谈娜拉 [Discussing Nora on March 8]. *Xin shehui* 8, no. 6 (1935): 56–57.

Gilmartin, Christina Kelley. *Engendering the Chinese Revolution: Radical Women, Communist Politics, and Mass Movements in the 1920s*. Berkeley: University of California Press, 1995.

Gu Menghe 顾梦鹤. "Sishi niandai jushe gongyan 'Qiu Jin' yu Nanjing 四十年代剧社公演《秋瑾》于南京" [Public performance of Qiu Jin by the 40s Drama Club at Nanjing]. *Xinhua huabao* 新华画报 [New China pictorial] 4 (1937): 15.

Gu Yuan 古元. "Wo zai Yan'an chuangzuo de liangfu muke" 我在延安创作的两幅木刻 [Two woodblock prints I made in Yan'an]. In *Yan'an yishu jia* 延安艺术家 [Artists in

Yan'an], edited by Ai Ke'en 艾克恩, 483–86. Xi'an: Shaanxi renmin jiaoyu chubanshe, 1992.

Guan Lu 关露. "Dongjing yiyu: Shenjing bingtai de rizi" 东京忆语：神经病态的日子 [Tokyo memories: Neurotic days]. *Nüsheng* 女声 [Women's voice] 2, no. 6 (1943): 14–15.

Guan Lu. "Nü zuojia yinxiangji—nü zhanshi Ding Ling" 女作家印象记—女战士丁玲 [Impressions of a female writer—the female warrior Ding Ling]. *Shanghai funü* 上海妇女 [Women in Shanghai] 2, no. 8 (1939): 27–28.

"Guofu mingling baoyang Qiu Jin" 国府明令褒扬秋瑾 [Nationalist government issued an order to eulogize Qiu Jin]. *Zhongyang ribao*, October 15, 1935.

"Guomin daibiao huiyi tiaoli" 国民代表会议条例 [Regulations on People's Representatives Meeting]. *Guowen zhoubao* 国闻周报 [National news weekly] 2, no. 16 (1925): 41–43.

"Guomindang zhongyang xuanchuanbu guanyu jinyan Ding Ling bianzhou zhi 'Chongfeng' juben shi zhi junweihui zhengzhibu gonghan" 国民党中央宣传部关于禁演丁玲编著之《重逢》剧本事致军委会政治部公函 [The KMT Propaganda Department's official letter addressed to the Political Department of the Military Committee regarding the prohibition of the performance of Ding Ling's *Reunion*], dated November 7, 1939. In *Zhonghua minguoshi dang'an ziliao huibian* 中华民国史档案资料汇编 [Compilation of archival materials of the Republic of China], vol. 5, no. 2, culture (2), edited by the Second Historical Archives of China, 22–23. Nanjing: Jiangsu guji chubanshe, 1998.

Guo Moruo 郭沫若. "Nala de da'an" 娜拉的答案 [The answer to Nora]. *Xinhua ribao* 新华日报 [New China daily], July 19, 1942.

Guo Yanli 郭延礼. *Qiu Jin wenxue lungao* 秋瑾文学论稿 [Manuscript on Qiu Jin's literary writings]. Xi'an: Shaanxi renmin chubanshe, 1987.

Guo Yanli, ed. *Qiu Jin yanjiu ziliao* 秋瑾研究资料 [Qiu Jin research materials]. Jinan: Shandong jiaoyu chubanshe, 1987.

Halbwachs, Maurice. *The Collective Memory*. Translated by Francis J. Ditter Jr. and Vida Yazdi Ditter. New York: Harper & Row, 1980.

Hanyi 汉一. "Huijia lun" 毁家论 [On destroying families]. *Tianyi bao* 4 (1907): 43–46.

Harrison, Henrietta. "Martyrs and Militarism in Early Republican China." *Twentieth-Century China* 23, no. 2 (1998): 41–70.

He Jianming 何建明. "Zuihou de douzheng—Hongyan geming lieshi xisheng xianchang shilu" 最后的斗争—红岩革命烈士牺牲现场实录 [The last battle—records of the sacrifices of the red crag revolutionary martyrs]. *Zhongguo zuojia* 16 (2011): 19–83.

He Jingzhi 贺敬之. *He Jingzhi shixuan* 贺敬之诗选 [Selected poems of He Jingzhi]. Beijing: Renmin wenxue chubanshe, 2004.

He Qifang 何其芳. "Shilun xiju shang de Liu Hulan de zhatou" 试论戏剧上的刘胡兰的铡头 [On beheading Liu Hulan in theater]. *Wenyi bao* 2, no. 3 (1950): 25–27.

Hershatter, Gail. *The Gender of Memory: Rural Women and China's Collective Past*. Berkeley: University of California Press, 2011.

Hsia, Tsi-an. *The Gate of Darkness*. Seattle: University of Washington Press, 1968.

Hu Sheng 胡绳. *Zhongguo Gongchandang de qishinian* 中国共产党的七十年 [Seventy years of the Chinese Communist Party]. Beijing: Zhonggong dangshi chubanshe, 2005.

Hu Shi 胡适. "Li Chao zhuan" 李超传 [The biography of Li Chao]. *Xinchao* 新潮 [New wave] 2, no. 2 (1919): 266–75.

Hu, Ying. *Burying Autumn: Poetry, Friendship, and Loss*. Cambridge, MA: Harvard University Asia Center, 2016.

Hu, Ying. "Gender and Modern Martyrology: Qiu Jin as *Lienü, Lieshi,* or *Nülieshi*." In *Beyond Exemplar Tales: Women's Biography in Chinese History*, edited by Joan Judge and Hu Ying, 121–36. Berkeley: University of California Press, 2011.

Hu Yong 湖傭. "Danghua de Xihu bolanhui" 党化的西湖博览会 [Politicized West Lake Exposition]. *Xinwen bao*, January 16, 1929.

Huang, Xin. "From 'Hyper-feminine' to Androgyny: Changing Notions of Femininity in Contemporary China." In *Asian Popular Culture in Transition*, edited by Lorna Fitzsimmons and John Lent, 133–55. London: Routledge, 2013.

Huayan Yigai 华严一丐. "Ding Ling yu Pengzi" 丁玲与蓬子 [Ding Ling and Pengzi]. *Shijie chenbao*, June 26, 1932.

Hung, Chang-tai. "The Cult of the Red Martyr: Politics of Commemoration in China." *Journal of Contemporary History* 43, no. 2 (2008): 279–304.

Hung, Chang-tai. *Mao's New World: Political Culture in the Early People's Republic*. Ithaca: Cornell University Press, 2011.

Jiang Heng 江横. "Ding Ling fangwen ji" 丁玲访问记 [The interview with Ding Ling]. *Xinhua ribao*, April 27, 1938.

Jiang Huaxuan 姜华宣. "Xiang Jingyu shifou danren guo zhongyang weiyuan he funü buzhang?" 向警予是否担任过中央委员和妇女部长？ [Did Xiang Jingyu ever serve as a member of the Central Committee or the minister for women?]. *Dangshi ziliao* 党史资料 [Materials of the history of the CCP] vol. 3, 112–16. Shanghai: Shanghai renmin chubanshe, 1983.

Jiang Zhanbing 江战兵. "Zhang Geng shi geming xiandaixi de sidi" 张庚是革命现代戏的死敌 [Zhang Geng is the ultimate enemy of the revolutionary opera]. *Renmin ribao*, August 29, 1968.

Jiang Zulin 蒋祖林. *Ding Ling zhuan* 丁玲传 [Biography of Ding Ling]. Beijing: Renmin wenxue chubanshe, 2015.

Jian Ping 简平. *Wang Zhaowen zhuan* 王朝闻传 [Biography of Wang Zhaowen]. Yinchuan: Ningxia renmin chubanshe, 2009.

Jingguanzi 静观子. *Liuyue shuang* 六月霜 [Frost in June]. Shanghai: Shanghai wenhua chubanshe, 1958.

Jin Shangyi 靳尚谊 and Wang Chengyi 汪诚一. "Huainian women de laoshi K .M. Maksimov" 怀念我们的老师K. M. 马克西莫夫 [Commemorating our teacher K. M. Maksimov]. *Meishu* 7 (1994): 57–60.

Ji Sheng 无生. "Xuanting fuhuo ji" 轩亭复活记 [Resurrection at Xuanting]. *Shenzhou ribao*, from September 7 to October 5, 1907.

Jiu Ding 九鼎. "Wenyi jie mimi zhuidao Ding Ling suoji" 文艺界秘密追悼丁玲琐纪 [Record on the secret service for Ding Ling in the circle of art and literature]. *Shanghai bao* 上海报 [Shanghai newspaper], December 25, 1933.

Kang Youwei 康有为. *Datong shu* 大同书 [The book of great unity]. Shenyang: Liaoning renmin chubanshe, 1994.

Kong Haili 孔海立. *Duanmu Hongliang zhuan* 端木蕻良传 [Biography of Duanmu Hongliang]. Shanghai: Fudan daxue chubanshe, 2011.

Kowallis, Jon Eugene von. *The Lyrical Lu Xun: A Study of His Classical-Style Verse*. Honolulu: University of Hawai'i Press, 1996.

Lao She 老舍. "Liefu xunguo" 烈妇殉国 [A chaste woman martyred for the nation]. *Kangzhan xiju* 抗战戏剧 [War of Resistance drama] 2, no. 1 (May 25, 1938): 23–27.

Lao She quyi wenxuan 老舍曲艺文选 [Selected works of Lao She's folk literature]. Beijing: Zhongguo quyi chubanshe, 1982.

Lao She. *San si yi* 三四一 [Three, four, one]. Chongqing: Duli chubanshe, August 1938.

Lao She. "Zhonglie tu" 忠烈图 [The loyalists and martyrs]. *Wenyi zhendi* 文艺阵地 [Literary battlefield], April 16, 1938: 9–12.

Leaf, Earl. "Ting Ling, Herald of a New China." *T'ien Hsia Monthly* 5, no. 3 (1937): 225–36.

Lee, Haiyan. *Revolution of the Heart: A Genealogy of Love in China*. Stanford: Stanford University Press, 2010.

Lei Yunfeng 雷云峰. "Mao zhuxi wei Liu Hulan lieshi tici jingguo" 毛主席为刘胡兰烈士题词经过 [The process of Chairman Mao's inscription for Liu Hulan]. *Renwen zazhi* 人文杂志 [Humanity magazine] 6 (1983): 100.

Liang Hongyi 梁红一. "Liu Hulan de shi" 刘胡兰的事 [Facts about Liu Hulan]. *Shanxi dang'an* 山西档案 [Archives of Shanxi] 1 (2007): 47–52.

Liang Xing 梁星. *Liu Hulan xiaozhuan* 刘胡兰小传 [A brief biography of Liu Hulan]. Beijing: Qingnian chubanshe, 1951.

"Lianhe bingqing jieshi Qiu Jin zui'an" 联合禀请揭示秋瑾罪案 [A joint plea to publicize the case of Qiu Jin]. *Shibao*, July 29, 1907.

"Li Chao nüshi zhi zangli" 李超女士之葬礼 [The funeral of lady Li Chao]. *Minguo ribao* 民国日报 [Republican daily], January 4, 1920.

"Li Chao nüshi zhuidaohui jishi" 李超女士追悼会纪事 [Records of the memorial service for lady Li Chao]. *Minguo ribao*, December 4, 1919.

Li Guixiang 李桂香. "Chuancheng Liu Hulan jingshen de minbing ban" 传承刘胡兰精神的民兵班 [The militia squad that inherited the spirit of Liu Hulan]. *Dangshi wenhui* 1 (2019): 42–45.

Li Hui 李辉. "Fengjing yi yuanqu—guanyu Xia Yan de suigan" 风景已远去—关于夏衍的随感 [The scenery has already gone—reflections on Xia Yan]. *Shouhuo* 5 (1995): 98–108.

Li Hui. *Yaodang de qiuqian—Shishi feifei shuo Zhou Yang* 摇荡的秋千—是是非非说周扬 [Swinging swing—discussing Zhou Yang's virtues and vices]. Shenzhen: Haitian chubanshe, 1998.

Li, Jie. *Utopian Ruins: A Memorial Museum of the Mao Era*. Durham, NC: Duke University Press, 2020.

Li Meijie 李美皆. "Ding Ling yu Qu Qiubai" 丁玲与瞿秋白 [Ding Ling and Qu Qiubai]. *Zuopin* 2 (2017): 94–110.

L. Insun. "Ding Ling zai Shaanbei" 丁玲在陕北 [Ding Ling in Shaanbei]. In *Nü zhanshi Ding Ling* 女战士丁玲 [Woman warrior Ding Ling]. Shanghai: Meiri yibao she, 1938.

Li Qun 力群. "Yan'an Luyi xiaojing" 延安鲁艺校景 [The landscape of Lu Xun Academy of Art and Literature]. https://auction.artron.net/paimai-art5149490716, accessed August 15, 2023.

Li Xiangdong 李向东. "Zui nan'ai de yinian—guanyu Ding Ling 1943 nian de jize riji" 最难

挨的一年—关于丁玲1943年的几则日记 [The most difficult year—regarding some of Ding Ling's diary entries in 1943]. *Xin wenxue shiliao* 4 (2007): 164–68.

Li Xin 黎辛. "Guanyu 'Ding Ling Yuan'an jiqi lishi fansi' de bianzheng" 关于《丁玲冤案及其历史反思》的辩证 [Dialectics on "The Unjust Case of Ding Ling and its Historical Reflection"]. *Yue haifeng* 1 (2006): 62–65.

Li Xue'ao 李学鳌. "Liu Hulan de songge" 刘胡兰的颂歌 [Ode to Liu Hulan]. In *Li Xue'ao Changshi Xuan* 李学鳌长诗选 [Selected long poems by Li Xue'ao], 53–109. Shijiazhuang: Huashan wenyi chubanshe, 1985.

Li Yongchun 李永春. *Cai Hesen nianpu* 蔡和森年谱 [Chronicle of Cai Hesen]. Xiangtan: Xiangtan daxue chubanshe, 2008.

Li Zhanyang 李占洋. "Shazhu shi de houjiao—wo de xianshi zhuyi" 杀猪时的吼叫—我的现实主义 [Pig's roar when it was being slaughtered—my realism]. *Diaosu* 2 (2017): 39–41.

Li Zhilian 李之琏. "Wo canyu Ding Chen fandang xiao jituan an chuli jingguo" 我参与丁、陈"反党小集团"案处理经过 [My participation in the process of handling the Ding and Chen Anti-Party Clique case]. *Yanhuang Chunqiu* 5 (1993): 10–17.

"Liu Hulan lieshi de shengping" 刘胡兰烈士的生平 [Biography of the martyr Liu Hulan]. *Renmin ribao*, January 12, 1957.

Liu Jin 刘金 and Li Guojing 李国经. "Du 'Xiju zhong xijie miaoxie de yizhong qingxiang' hou" 读《戏剧中细节描写的一种倾向》后 [Reflections on "A tendency in depicting details in theater"]. *Wenyi bao* 2, no. 3 (1950): 28.

Liu, Long-hsin. "Popular Readings and Wartime Historical Writings in Modern China." In *The Challenge of Linear Time: Nationhood and the Politics of History in East Asia*, edited by Viren Murthy and Axel Schneider, 181–214. Leiden: Brill, 2014.

Liu Maoshu 刘茂舒, ed. *Xiang Jingyu: Zhuanji, jinian yu huiyi, lunshu, ziliao* 向警予:传记,纪念与回忆,论述,资料 [Xiang Jingyu: Biography, commemoration and recollection, discussion, and material]. Wuhan: Wuhan chubanshe, 1995.

Liu Qing 柳青. "Bei wuru le de nüren" 被污辱了的女人 [A woman who has been humiliated]. *Jiefang ribao*, September 2, 1941 and September 3, 1941.

Liu Shuiqing 刘水清. "Lingyuan li de yipian ye" 陵园里的一片叶 [A leaf in the cemetery]. *Changjiang ribao* 长江日报 [Yangtze River daily], March 21, 2021.

Liu Yan 刘焱, ed. *Zhou Enlai zaoqi wenji* 周恩来早期文集 [Early writings of Zhou Enlai], vol. 1. Tianjin: Nankai University Press, 1993.

Liu Ying 刘英. "Guanyu poxie wenti" 关于破鞋问题 [Regarding the issues of *poxie*]. *Zhongguo funü* 1, no. 2 (1939): 6–7.

"Lujun bu qing jiang qian-Qing zhaozhong ge zhuanci fenbie gaijian dahan zhonglie ci cheng" 陆军部请将前清昭忠各专祠分别改建大汉忠烈祠呈 [Ministry of the Army's request to convert all shrines dedicated to loyal soldiers from the Qing dynasty into shrines honoring the great Han loyal martyrs]. *Linshi zhengfu gongbao* 临时政府公报 [Provisional Government gazette] 51 (1912): 14–15.

Lu Mingjun 鲁明军. "Shijue, wenben yu geren xushi—Li Zhanyang de yishu shijian" 视觉、文本与个人叙事—李占洋的艺术实践 [Visual, text and individual narrative—Li Zhanyang's artistic practices]. *Zhongguo yishu shikong* 2 (2013): 30–35.

Lu, Weijing. *True to Her Word: The Faithful Maiden Cult in Late Imperial China*. Stanford: Stanford University Press, 2008.

Lu Xun. "My Views on Chastity." Translated by Gladys Yang. In *Women in Republican China: A Sourcebook*, edited by Hua Lan and Vanessa Fong, 8–18. London: Routledge, 1999.

Lu Xun 鲁迅. "Nala zouhou zenyang" 娜拉走后怎样 [What happens after Nora leaves home], *Funü zazhi* 妇女杂志 [Women's magazine] 10, no. 8 (1924): 1218–22.

Lu Xun. "The New Year's Sacrifice." In *Selected Stories of Lu Hsun*, translated by Yang Hsien-yi and Gladys Yang, 125–43. Beijing: Foreign Languages Press, 1960.

"Lun Wan sheng dianju Guifu shi" 论皖省电据贵福事 [Regarding the news that Anhui sent a telegram declining the appointment of Guifu]. *Shenbao*, April 23, 1908.

Luo Fu 罗夫. "*Liang Hongyu* de gongyan ji qita" 《梁红玉》的公演及其他 [The premiere of *Liang Hongyu* and more]. *Zhongguo funü* 中国妇女 [Chinese women] 1, no. 10/11 (1940): 17–18.

Luo Guangbin 罗广斌 and Yang Yiyan 杨益言. *Hongyan* 红岩 [Red crag]. Beijing: Zhongguo qingnian chubanshe, 1961.

Luo Guangda 罗光达 and Jiang Zulin, eds. *Ding Ling* 丁玲. Shenyang: Liaoning meishu chubanshe, 1993.

Luo Qiong 罗琼. "Cong xianqiliangmu zhi xianfuliangfu: du *Funü gongming* xianliang wenti zhuanhao yihou" 从贤妻良母至贤夫良父:读《妇女共鸣》贤良问题专号以后 [From virtuous wife and good mother to virtuous husband and good father: After reading the special issue on "the question of being virtuous" in *Funü gongming*]. *Funü shenghuo* 2, no. 1 (1936): 59–67.

Luo Zhanglong 罗章龙. *Chunyuan zaiji* 椿园载记 [Memories from the Chun garden]. Beijing: Sanlian shudian, 1984.

Ma Feng 马烽. "Jinbao niang" 金宝娘 [Jinbao's mother]. *Xinhua zhoubao* 新华周报 [Xinhua weekly] 1, no. 12 (1949): 11–15.

Ma Feng. *Liu Hulan zhuan* 刘胡兰传 [Biography of Li Hulan]. Beijing: Zhongguo qingnian chubanshe, 1978.

Ma Feng. "Liu Hulan zhuan." *Huohua* 火花 [Spark] 1 (1964): 57–63.

Ma Ming 马明. "Wei minzu jiefang benbo, wei guojia duli juanqu" 为民族解放奔波,为国家独立捐躯 [Rushing for the liberation of the nation, sacrificing for the independence of the country]. *Dangshi wenhui* 1 (2007): 9–11.

Mao Dun 茅盾. "Ji Lu Xun yishu wenxueyuan" 记鲁迅艺术文学院 [An account of Lu Xun Academy of Art and Literature]. *Xuexi* 学习 [Studies] 5, no. 2 (1941): 66–68.

Mao Dun. "Kaihuang" 开荒 [Cultivate the wasteland]. *Bitan* 笔谈 [Brush talks] 6 (1941): 1.

Mao Zedong 毛泽东. "Dangqian shiju de zuida weiji" 当前时局的最大危机 [The greatest crisis under current circumstances]. *Zhongguo funü* 1, no. 2 (1939): 4–5.

Mao Zedong. "The Immortals at the River: To Ding Ling." In Chunhou Zhang and Edwin Vaughan, *Mao Zedong as Poet and Revolutionary Leader*, 51–52. Lanham, MD: Lexington Books, 2002.

Mao Zedong. "Mao Zedong zai Yan'an Zhongguo nüzi daxue kaixue dianli shang de jianghua" 毛泽东在延安中国女子大学开学典礼上的讲话 [Mao Zedong's speech at the opening ceremony of Chinese Women's University in Yan'an]. *Xin zhonghua bao* 新中华报 [New China news], July 25, 1939.

Mao Zedong. "Shehui wan'e yu Zhao nüshi" 社会万恶与赵女士 [The evils of society and Miss Zhao]. *Dagong bao* (Changsha), November 21, 1919.

Mao Zedong wenji 毛泽东文集 [Collected writings of Mao Zedong]. Beijing: Renmin chubanshe, 1993.

Mao Zedong. "Yellow Crane Tower—to the melody of *P'u Sa Man*." Translated by Jerome Ch'en. In Jerome Ch'en, *Mao and the Chinese Revolution*, 322. London: Oxford University Press, 1965.

McElderry, Andrea. "Woman Revolutionary: Xiang Jingyu." *China Quarterly* 105 (1986): 95–122.

Mei Zhi 梅志. *Hu Feng zhuan* 胡风传 [Biography of Hu Feng]. Beijing: Beijing shiyue wenyi chubanshe, 1998.

Meng, Yue. "Female Images and National Myth." In *Gender Politics in Modern China*, edited by Tani Barlow, 118–36. Durham, NC: Duke University Press, 1993.

Naftali, Orna. *Children, Rights and Modernity in China: Raising Self-Governing Citizens*. London: Palgrave Macmillan, 2014.

"Nala zuotan" 娜拉座谈 [Nora symposium]. *Funü shenghuo* 2, no. 1 (1936): 104–20.

"Nanjing Nala shijian de jingguo" 南京娜拉事件的经过 [The course of the Nanjing Nora Incident]. *Xi zhoukan* 戏周刊 [Theater weekly] 27 (1935): 3–9.

Nie Gannu 聂绀弩. *Ziwu yu zishu: Nie Gannu yundong dang'an huibian* 自诬与自述: 聂绀弩运动档案汇编 [Self-accusation and self-narration: Compilation of Nie Gannu's archives during the political movements]. Wuhan: Wuhan chubanshe, 2005.

Online Liu Hulan Memorial Hall. https://www.ijvr360.com/vr/liuhulan, accessed September 30, 2023.

Pan Gongzhan 潘公展. "Xunling" 训令 [Command]. *Shanghaishi jiaoyuju jiaoyu zhoubao* 上海市教育局教育周报 [Shanghai Educational Bureau weekly newspaper] 212 (1933): 3.

Pan Shaotang 潘绍棠. "Zhongyang meishu xueyuan diaosuxi dui xingshi zhuyi qingxiang de douzheng" 中央美术学院雕塑系对形式主义倾向的斗争 [Fighting against formalism in the sculpture department at the Central Academy of Fine Arts]. *Meishu* 3 (1955): 16–18.

Pei Lan 培蓝. "Tiaochu huokeng de jiemeimen" 跳出火坑的姐妹们 [The sisters who jumped out of the fire pit]. *Renmin ribao*, December 26, 1949.

Peng Huagao 彭化高 and Zhang Youluo 张友洛. *Liu Hulan: Guci* 刘胡兰:鼓词 [Liu Hulan: Drum lyrics]. Taiyuan: Shanxi renmin chubanshe, 1977.

Peng Shuzhi 彭述之. *Peng Shuzhi huiyilu* 彭述之回忆录 [The memoir of Peng Shuzhi]. Hong Kong: Tiandi tushu, 2016.

Ping Jia 平斝. "Wei chengming yiqian de Ding Ling" 未成名以前的丁玲 [Ding Ling before her fame]. *Shehui xinwen* 4, no. 13 (1933): 196–98.

"Qianyu jinü kaishi xin shenghuo" 千余妓女开始新生活 [Thousands of prostitutes began their new lives]. *Renmin ribao*, November 23, 1949.

Qiao Liang 乔梁, dir. *Zhenzhen* 贞贞. DVD. Beijing: Beijing jiuzhou tongying shuzi dianying yuanxian youxian gongsi, 2003.

Qitian nüshi 泣天女士. "Ai Qiu Jin an" 哀秋瑾案 [Lament for Qiu Jin's case]. *Shibao*, July 29, 1907.

"Qiufeng qiuyu tuo qiuhun" 秋风秋雨妥秋魂 [Autumn wind and autumn rain bring peace to the spirit of Qiu]. *Shenbao*, October 29, 1912.

Qiu Jin 秋瑾. "Jingwei shi" 精卫石 [The stones of Jingwei]. In *Qiu Jin ji* 秋瑾集 [Collection of Qiu Jin's works], 121–64. Shanghai: Zhonghua shuju, 1965.

"Qiu Jin jiuyi guci" 秋瑾就义鼓词 [Drum lyrics version of *Qiu Jin's Martyrdom*]. *Zhongyang ribao* 中央日报 [Central news daily], November 2, 1932.

"Qiu Jin jiuyi sishinian juxing yiji zhanlanhui" 秋瑾就义四十年举行遗迹展览会 [Relics of Qiu Jin exhibition for the fortieth anniversary of her martyrdom]. *Shenbao*, April 14, 1948.

"Qiu Jin nüshi aici" 秋瑾女史哀词 [Mourning for Ms. Qiu Jin]. *Shenzhou ribao*, August 3, 1907.

"Qiu Jin nüshi yuansha zhi lishi" 秋瑾女士冤杀之历史 [The history of the wrongful execution of Qiu Jin]. *Shenbao*, July 28, 1907.

Qiu Jin shiji 秋瑾史迹 [Historical materials on Qiu Jin]. Shanghai: Zhonghua shuju, 1958.

Qiu Jin shiji 秋瑾史迹 [Historical materials on Qiu Jin]. Shanghai: Shanghai guji chubanshe, 1991.

"Qiu Jin yiji zhanlan" 秋瑾遗迹展览 [Relics of Qiu Jin exhibition]. *Dagong bao* (Shanghai), April 25, 1948.

"Qiu Jin yuansha zhi yuanyin" 秋瑾冤杀之原因 [The reason behind the wrongful execution of Qiu Jin]. *Shenbao*, July 23, 1907.

"Qiu nüxia guigu Xihu" 秋女侠归骨西湖 [The remains of the female knight-errant with the surname Qiu return to West Lake]. *Shenbao*, September 24, 1912.

"Qiu xia ruci jisheng" 秋侠入祠纪盛 [Records of welcoming the spiritual tablet of the knight-errant with the surname Qiu into the ancestral hall]. *Shenbao*, July 21, 1912.

Qu Qiubai 瞿秋白. *Zhongguo geming zhong zhi zhenglun wenti* 中国革命中之争论问题 [Controversial issues in the Chinese revolution]. Nagoya: Caihua shulin, 1976.

Qu Yuan 屈原. "Li sao" 离骚 [Encountering sorrow]. In *Chuci xuan* 楚辞选 [Selections from *The Lyrics of Chu*], edited by Lu Kanru 陆侃如, Gao Heng 高亨, and Huang Xiaoshu 黄孝纾, 23–46. Shanghai: Shanghai gudian wenxue chubanshe, 1956.

"*Sai Jinhua* beida you zaofa" 赛金花被打又遭罚 [*Sai Jinhua* crew was beaten up and fined]. *Jingang zuan*, February 28, 1937.

"Sai Jinhua, Qiu Jin" 赛金花，秋瑾. *Minbao*, January 24, 1937.

"Sai Jinhua shoudu chu maobing" 赛金花首都出毛病 [Issues arising from the performance of *Sai Jinhua* in the capital]. *Diansheng* 6, no. 9 (1937): 462.

Shanghaishi dang'anguan 上海市档案馆 [Shanghai Archives], ed. *Wusa yundong* 五卅运动 [The May Thirtieth Movement], vol. 1. Shanghai: Shanghai renmin chubanshe, 1991.

Shen Congwen 沈从文. *Ji Ding Ling* 记丁玲 [Remembering Ding Ling]. Nanjing: Jingsu jiaoyu chubanshe, 2005.

Shen Yaoting 沈耀庭, dir. *Liu Hulan* 刘胡兰. DVD. Guangzhou: Guangdong Haiyan dianzi yinxiang chubanshe, (1996) 1998.

Shen Zijiu 沈兹九. "Women weishenme yao jinian Qiu Jin" 我们为什么要纪念秋瑾 [Why we should commemorate Qiu Jin]. *Funü shenghuo* 妇女生活 [Women's life] 3, no. 2 (1936): 6–7.

Shen Zijiu. "Xin qimu xuexiao" 新妻母学校 [The new wife and mother school]. *Funü shenghuo* 2, no. 5 (1936): 1–2.

"Shenjing guomin duiyu youbang wudunmuyi ling" 申儆国民对于友邦务敦睦谊令 [Directive urging citizens to foster friendly relations with other nations]. *Guomin zhengfu gongbao*, 1764 (1935): 1–2.

"Shijie tuchen lu" 史屆兔尘录 [Records of anecdotes in history]. *Xinmin congbao* 7 (1902): 89–90.

Shi Zhecun 施蛰存. "Huai Ding Ling shi sishou" 怀丁玲诗四首 [Four poems in memory of Ding Ling]. *Yi tan* 4 (1981): 123–56.

Siao, Yu. *Mao Tse-Tung and I Were Beggars*. Syracuse, NY: Syracuse University Press, 1959.

Smedley, Agnes. *Battle Hymn of China*. London: Victor Gollancz, 1944.

Snow, Edgar. *Red Star over China*. New York: Grove Press, 1978.

Snow, Helen. *Women in Modern China*. Beijing: Foreign Languages Press, 2004.

Sun Pujin 孙普金. "Beiping xijiao di funü" 北平西郊底妇女 [Women in the Xijiao area of Beiping]. *Zhongguo funü* 2, no. 4 (1940): 22–24.

Sun Yat-sen. "Sun Zhongshan duiyu shiju zhi xuanyan" 孙中山对于时局之宣言 [Sun Yat-sen's manifesto on the current situation]. *Shenbao*, November 18, 1924.

Sun Zhenhua 孙振华. "Mao Zedong shidai diaosu zhong de shenti zhengzhi" 毛泽东时代雕塑中的身体政治 [Body politics in sculpture during the Maoist era]. *Yishu tansuo* 19, no. 2 (2005): 15–22.

Sun Zhenhua. "Zhongguo dangdai juxiang diaosu gaiguan" 中国当代具象雕塑概观 [An overview of contemporary Chinese figurative sculptures]. In *Qinghua meishu* 清华美术 [Tsinghua arts], vol. 15, ed. Zhang Gan 张敢, 9–21. Beijing: Qinghua daxue chubanshe, 2013.

"Sun Zhongshan li hang jishi" 孙中山莅杭记事 [Accounts of Sun Yat-sen's visit in Hangzhou]. *Shenbao*, December 10, 1912.

"Sun Zhongshan xiansheng hang you riji" 孙中山先生杭游日记 [Diary of Mr. Sun Yat-sen's visit in Hangzhou]. *Yishi bao* (Tianjin), August 26, 1916.

Theiss, Janet. *Disgraceful Matters: The Politics of Chastity in Eighteenth-Century China*. Berkeley: University of California Press, 2004.

Ting, Ling. "An Unexpected Reunion." Translated by Lu Yung. *Far Eastern Mirror*, August 10, 1938, 60–70.

Tu Shaojun 涂绍钧. *Tuben Ding Ling zhuan* 图本丁玲传 [Illustrated biography of Ding Ling]. Changchun: Changchun chubanshe, 2015.

"Wanren qingzhu zhong zhuangyan relie juxing le Zhongguo nüzi daxue kaixue dianli" 万人庆祝中庄严热烈举行了中国女子大学开学典礼 [Thousands of people celebrated as Chinese Women's University held its opening ceremony with great solemnity and enthusiasm]. *Xin zhonghua bao*, July 25, 1939.

Wan Weizhou 万苇周. "Ping geju *Liu Hulan* xinmao ji qita" 评歌剧刘胡兰新貌及其它 [Comments on the new opera version of *Liu Hulan* and others]. *Renmin yinyue* 人民音乐 [People's music], no. 10/11 (1964): 20–21.

Wan Ye 万叶. "Qiu Jin nian" 秋瑾年 [The year of Qiu Jin]. *Shibao*, June 24, 1936.

Wang, Ban. *The Sublime Figure of History: Aesthetics and Politics in Twentieth-Century China*. Stanford: Stanford University Press, 1997.

Wang Canzhi 王灿芝. "Chengsong xianci yiwu feicui shuanglong yuzhuo yishuang chenlie gemingdang shiliao chenlieguan xu" 呈送先慈遗物翡翠双龙玉镯一双陈列革命党史料陈列馆序 [Preface for donating my late mother's emerald green jade bracelets with engraved double dragon to the Exhibition Hall for Historical Materials of the KMT]. *Shanghai funü* 上海妇女 [Women in Shanghai] 1, no. 4 (1938): 13–14.

Wang Canzhi, ed. *Qiu Jin nüxia yiji* 秋瑾女侠遗集 [Remaining works of the woman warrior Qiu Jin]. Beijing: Zhaohua chubanshe, 2018.

Wang, David Der-Wei. *The Monster That Is History: History, Violence, and Fictional Writing in Twentieth-Century China*. Berkeley: University of California Press, 2004.

Wang Guoping 王国平, ed. *Xihu wenxian jicheng* 西湖文献集成 [West Lake collective archives], vol. 16. Hangzhou: Hangzhou chubanshe, 2004.

Wang Jucai 王巨才, ed. *Yan'an wenyi dang'an* 延安文艺档案 [The archive of art and literature in Yan'an]. Xi'an: Taibai wenyi chubanshe, 2015.

Wang Juru 王菊如. "Ying Xiuren shi bodou zhuilou haishi zisha zhuilou" 应修人是搏斗坠楼还是自杀坠楼 [Did Ying Xiuren fall from the building due to a struggle or as a result of suicide?]. *Shiji* 4 (2019): 92–95.

Wang Li 王莉 and Yu Changfei 于长飞. *Shaanbei jindai jianzhu yanjiu* 陕北近代建筑研究 [Research on modern architecture in Northern Shaanxi]. Xi'an: Xibei gongye daxue chubanshe, 2015.

Wang Liaoying 王燎荧. "Kangzhan shiqi Ding Ling xiaoshuo de sixiang qingxiang" 抗战时期丁玲小说的思想倾向 [The ideological tendencies in Ding Ling's wartime stories]. *Wenxue yanjiu* 文学研究 [Literary studies] 4 (1957): 98–101.

Wang Ming 王明. "Wang Ming tongzhi zai Zhongguo nüzi daxue kaixue dianli dahui shang de baogao" 王明同志在中国女子大学开学典礼大会上的报告 [Comrade Wang Ming's report on the opening ceremony of the Chinese Women's University]. *Zhongguo funü* 1, no. 3 (1939): 2–6.

Wang Qubing 王去病 and Chen Dehe 陈德和, eds. *Qiu Jin nianbiao xibian* 秋瑾年表细编 [Detailed chronological biography of Qiu Jin]. Beijing: Huawen chubanshe, 1990.

Wang, Xiaojue. *Modernity with a Cold War Face: Reimagining the Nation in Chinese Literature across the 1949 Divide*. Cambridge, MA: Harvard University Asia Center, 2013.

Wang Xueli 王学礼. "Deng Xiaoping wei Liu Hulan tici shimo" 邓小平为刘胡兰题词始末 [The full story of Deng Xiaoping's inscription for Liu Hulan]. *Dangshi wenhui* 9 (2013): 35–36.

Wang Yan 王雁. *Qiu Jin zhuan (Jingju)* 秋瑾传 (京剧) [Biography of Qiu Jin: Peking opera adaptation]. Beijing: Beijing chubanshe, 1960.

Wang Zengru 王增如. "Jiaru meiyou nachang bangjia—Ding Ling yu Feng Da zai Bansong yuan de yizhang heying" 假如没有那场绑架—丁玲与冯达在半淞园的一张合影 [If there hadn't been that kidnapping—a photo of Ding Ling and Feng Da at Bansong garden]. *Shiji* 2 (2016): 41–46.

Wang Zengru. "Mao Zedong liuci shuxie linjiang xian" 毛泽东六次书写临江仙 [Mao Zedong handwrote "The Immortals at the River: To Ding Ling" six times]. *Shiji* 世纪 [Century] 4 (2018): 46–51.

Wang Zengru. "Shen Zui xiang Ding Ling qingzui" 沈醉向丁玲请罪 [Shen Zui offers a humble apology to Ding Ling]. *Lantai neiwai* 1 (2007): 58–59.

Wang Zengru. *Wunai de niepan: Ding Ling zuihou de rizi* 无奈的涅槃：丁玲最后的日子 [Helpless nirvana: the last days of Ding Ling]. Shanghai: Shanghai shudian chubanshe, 2003.

Wang Zengru and Li Xiangdong 李向东. *Ding Ling nianpu changbian* 丁玲年谱长编 [Lengthy compilation of Ding Ling's chronicle]. Tianjin: Tianjin renmin chubanshe, 2006.

Wang Zengru and Li Xiangdong. *Ding Ling zhuan* 丁玲传 [Biography of Ding Ling]. Beijing: Zhongguo da baike quanshu chubanshe, 2015.

Wang Zhaowen 王朝闻. "Xiju zhong xijie miaoxie de yizhong qingxiang" 戏剧中细节描写的一种倾向 [A tendency in depicting details in theater]. *Wenyi bao* 10 (1949): 16–17.

Wang Zhaowen. "Zuopin zhong ruhe chuli yingxiong jiuyi de qingjie" 作品中如何处理英雄就义的情节 [How to portray the death of a martyr]. *Wenyi bao* 2, no. 3 (1950): 23–24.

Wang Zhousheng 王周生. *Ding Ling nianpu* 丁玲年谱 [The chronicle of Ding Ling]. Shanghai: Shanghai shehui kexueyuan chubanshe, 1997.

"Weichi zhi'an jinji banfa ling" 维持治安紧急办法令 [Emergency measures for maintaining public order]. *Guomin zhengfu gongbao* 1977 (1936): 1–2.

"Weida de sanba jieri zai Yan'an" 伟大的三八节日在延安 [The great March 8 celebration in Yan'an]. *Xin zhonghua bao* 新中华报 [New China news], March 13, 1939.

Wei Feng 魏风. "*Liu Hulan* juben xiezuo qianhou"《刘胡兰》剧本写作前后 [Before and after the scriptwriting of *Liu Hulan*]. *Dangshi tiandi* 党史天地 [The world of party history] 1 (1997): 30–32.

"Weile Xinhai geming wenxian zhanlanhui Qiu Jin nügongzi Wang Canzhi gaixing" 为了辛亥革命文献展览会秋瑾女公子王灿芝改姓 [Qiu Jin's daughter Wang Canzhi changed her surname for the Xinhai Revolution Archive Exhibition]. *Chengbao*, October 14, 1947.

Weiming 微明. "Nala de jiufen" 娜拉的纠纷 [The dispute on Nora]. *Manhua shenghuo* 漫画生活 [Comic life] 7 (1935): 5.

Wei Mingxing 危明星. "Jieji yu xingbie huayu gaixie xia de jiaotang kongjian—1940 nian qianhou Yan'an wenxue zhong de jiaotang shuxie" 阶级与性别话语改写下的教堂空间—1940年前后延安文学中的教堂书写 [Rewriting church space under the class and gender discourse—the representation of churches in Yan'an literature around 1940]. *Wenyi lilun yu piping* 文艺理论与批评 [Literary theory and criticism] 6 (2019): 43-57.

Wen Guang 文光. "Pan Hannian yuan'an qianqian houhou" 潘汉年冤案前前后后 [Before and after the unjust case of Pan Hannian]. *Shanghai dangshi yanjiu* 上海党史研究 [Research on the history of the CCP in Shanghai] 6 (1995): 32–41.

Wen Liang 闻亮. "Youguan Ding Ling shengping de jige wenti—Chen Ming fangtan lu" 有关丁玲生平的几个问题—陈明访谈录 [Some issues related to Ding Ling's life—an interview with Chen Ming]. *Bainian chao* 百年潮 [A hundred year tide] 1 (2001): 54–57.

"Wenhuajie wei yingjiu Ding Pan xuanyan" 文化界为营救丁潘宣言 [Declaration from the Cultural Community for the Rescue of Ding Ling and Pan Zinian]. *Wenxue zazhi* 文学杂志 [Literature magazine] 1, nos. 3 and 4 (1933): 15.

"Wenyijie mimi zhuidao Ding Ling" 文艺界秘密追悼丁玲 [The secret service for Ding Ling in the circle of art and literature]. *Sheying huabao* 10, no. 1 (1934): 8–9.

Wu, Guo. "Recalling Bitterness: Historiography, Memory, and Myth in Maoist China." *Twentieth-Century China* 39, no. 3 (2014): 245–68.

Wu Zhiying 吴芝瑛. "Ji Qiu nüshi yishi" 纪秋女士遗事 [Anecdotal memoir of Ms. Qiu]. *Shibao*, July 25, 1907.

Wu Zhiying. "Lun Qiu Jin yu yu Huangya yu zhi bijiao" 论秋瑾狱与黄厓狱之比较 [On the comparison between the case of Qiu Jin and the case of the uprising in the Huangya mountain]. *Shibao*, November 22, 1907.

Wu Zhiying. "Qiu Jin yizhu xu" 秋瑾遗著序 [Preface to the posthumous works of Qiu Jin]. *Minguo bao* 4 (1912): 4–5.

"Wu Zhiying fufu zhi Xu Zihua de shi'er feng xin" 吴芝瑛夫妇致徐自华的12封信 [Twelve letters from Mr. and Mrs. Wu Zhiying to Xu Zihua]. Compiled by Zhou Yongzhen 周永珍. In *Jindaishi ziliao* 近代史资料 [Modern history materials], no. 91, 265–78. Beijing: Zhongguo shehui kexue chubanshe, 1997.

"Xiagu yinghun zheng shouqiu" 侠骨英魂正首邱 [The chivalrous and heroic spirit returns home]. *Xinwen bao*, October 27, 1912.

Xia Yan 夏衍. *Lanxun jiumeng lu* 懒寻旧梦录 [Leisurely recollecting my old dreams]. Beijing: Sanlian shudian, 2000.

Xia Yan. "Qiu Jin buxiu" 秋瑾不朽 [Long live Qiu Jin]. *Renmin ribao* 人民日报 [People's daily], December 5, 1979.

Xia Yan. *Qiu Jin zhuan* 秋瑾传 [Biography of Qiu Jin]. Shanghai: Kaiming shudian, 1950.

Xia Yan. *Ziyou hun* 自由魂 [The spirit of freedom]. Shanghai: Shanghai shenghuo shudian, 1937.

"Xihu bolanhui canguan baogao" 西湖博览会参观报告 [West Lake Exposition visit report]. *Suzhong xiaokan* 苏中校刊 [Suzhou middle school magazine] 1, no. 27/28 (1929): 30–31.

Xihu bolanhui canguan bixie 西湖博览会参观必携 [Essential guide for visiting the West Lake Exposition]. Shanghai: Shangwu yinshuguan, 1929.

(Xiang) Jingyu 警予. "Funü weishenme hao zhuangshi" 妇女为什么好装饰 [Why women like adornments]. *Funü zhoubao*, October 24, 1922.

(Xiang) Jingyu. "Guomin huiyi yu funü" 国民会议与妇女 [Women and the People's Assembly]. *Funü zhoubao*, December 14, 1924.

(Xiang) Jingyu. "Jiu guniang fanle hezui?" 九姑娘犯了何罪? [What crime did the Ninth Girl commit?]. *Funü zhoubao*, September 26, 1923.

(Xiang) Jingyu. "Shanghai nüquan yundonghui jinhou ying zhuyi de sanjianshi" 上海女权运动会今后应注意的三件事 [Three things the Shanghai Feminist Movement Association should pay attention to in the future]. *Funü zhoubao*, November 8, 1923.

(Xiang) Jingyu. "Zai Shanghai nüjie guomin huiyi cuchenghui de chengli dahui shang de jianghua" 在上海女界国民会议促成会的成立大会上的讲话 [The speech at the inaugural meeting of the Shanghai Women's Association for Facilitating the People's Assembly]. *Funü zhoubao*, December 7, 1924.

(Xiang) Jingyu. "Zai Zhongguo funü xiehui chenglihui shang de yanshuo" 在中国妇女协会成立会上的演说 [The speech at the inaugural meeting of the Chinese Women's Association]. *Funü zhoubao*, May 10, 1925.

(Xiang) Jingyu, "Zhili Di'er Nüshi xuechao zai nüzi jiaoyu gexin yundong shang de jiazhi" 直隶第二女师学潮在女子教育革新运动上的价值 [The value of the students' movement at Zhili No. 2 Women's Normal School in women's education reform movement]. *Funü zhoubao*, April 9, 1924.

(Xiang) Jingyu. "Zhongguo zhishi funü de sanpai" 中国知识妇女的三派 [The three groups of Chinese female intellectuals]. *Funü zhoubao*, November 28, 1923.

Xiang Jingyu jinian wenji 向警予纪念文集 [Collected works in memory of Xiang Jingyu]. Changsha: Hunan renmin chubanshe, 2005.

Xiang Jingyu wenji 向警予文集 [Collected writings of Xiang Jingyu]. Changsha: Hunan renmin chubanshe, 1980.

Xiao Jun 萧军. *Yan'an riji* 延安日记 1940–1945 [Yan'an diary, 1940–1945]. Oxford: Oxford University Press, 2013.

Xiaoshan Xianglingzi 萧山湘灵子. "Xuanting yuan" 轩亭冤 [Tragedy at Xuanting]. In *Wan Qing wenxue congchao chuanqi zaju juan* 晚清文学丛钞:传奇杂剧卷 [Late Qing literature collection: Volume on *chuanqi* and *zaju*], edited by A Ying 阿英, 108–47. Beijing: Zhonghua shuju, 1962.

Xibei zhandou jushe 西北战斗剧社 [Northwest Combat Dramatic Society]. *Liu Hulan* 刘胡兰. Beijing: Renmin wenxue chubanshe, 1952.

Xie Bingzhi 谢炳志. "Zhongguo geming bowuguan de choujian yu Wang Yeqiu" 中国革命博物馆的筹建与王冶秋 [Wang Yeqiu and the preparation for the establishment of the Museum of Chinese Revolution]. *Xin wenhua shiliao* 2 (1996): 56–59.

Xing Xiaoqun 邢小群. *Ding Ling yu wenxue yanjiusuo de xingshuai* 丁玲与文学研究所的兴衰 [Ding Ling and rise and fall of the Literature Study Institute]. Zhengzhou: Henan wenyi chubanshe, 2013.

"Xinhai geming wenxianzhanlan" 辛亥革命文献展览 [Xinhai Revolution archive exhibition]. *Dagong bao* (Shanghai), October 9, 1947.

Xinhai geming wenxian zhanlanhui jiniance 辛亥革命文献展览会纪念册 [Memorial brochure for the Xinhai Revolution Archive Exhibition]. Xinhai geming tongzhihui 辛亥革命同志会 [Alliance of the Comrades of the Xinhai Revolution], 1947.

Xinmin xuehui ziliao 新民学会资料 [Materials of the New Citizen Study Society]. Beijing: Renmin chubanshe, 1980.

Xiong Guanqin 熊广琴. "Qiu Jin maigu, Xiling chuanqi—du Wu Zhiying zhi Xu Zihua xinzha" 秋瑾埋骨,西泠传奇—读吴芝瑛致徐自华信札 [Qiu Jin's resting place, a legendary tale in Xiling—reading Wu Zhiying's letters to Xu Zihua]. *Rongbaozhai* 6 (2017): 246–55.

Xiu Yan 修岩. "Jinnian sanbajie funüjie de xin renwu" 今年三八节妇女界的新任务 [New tasks in the women's field for this year's International Women's Day]. *Zhongguo funü* 1, no. 9 (1940): 5–6.

Xu Fangping 徐方平. *Cai Hesen pingzhuan* 蔡和森评传 [Critical biography of Cai Hesen]. Beijing: Zhongguo shehui kexue chubanshe, 2013.

"Xu nüshi qing xiufu Qiu mu" 徐女士请修复秋墓 [Ms. Xu requests the restoration of Qiu Jin's tomb]. *Shenbao*, January 12, 1912.

"Xu Xilin zhulian an yuwen" 徐锡麟株连案余闻 [More news linked to Xu Xilin's case]. *Shibao*, July 24, 1907.

Xu Zihua 徐自华. "Fanchuan ji" 返钏记 [A record of returning the bracelets]. *Jiansu geming bowuguan yuekan* 5 (1929): 5–7.

"Xuanchuanpin shencha biaozhun" 宣传品审查标准 [Standards for inspecting propaganda materials]. *Zhongyang dangwu yuekan* 中央党务月刊 [Central party affairs monthly], no. 45/46 (1932): 414–15.

Xuanyuan Zhengyi 轩辕正裔. "Guafen canhuo yuyan ji" 瓜分惨祸预言记 [Prophecy about the tragic fate of the dissection of China]. Reprinted in *Zhongguo jindai xiaoshuo daxi* 中国近代小说大系 [Modern Chinese fiction series], 287–388. Nanchang: Baihuazhou wenyi chubanshe, 1991.

Ya Su 亚苏. "Zailun poxie wenti" 再论破鞋问题 [Revisiting the issues of *poxie*]. *Zhongguo funü* 1, nos. 5 and 6 (1939): 15–18.

Yan, Haiping. *Chinese Women Writers and the Feminist Imagination, 1905–1948*. London: Routledge, 2006.

Yan Jizhou 严寄洲. "He Long yu Zhandou jushe" 贺龙与战斗剧社 [He Long and the Combat Dramatic Society]. *Zhonggong dangshi ziliao* 1 (2008): 29–46.

Yanren 衍仁. "Kelian de Zhongguo funü" 可怜的中国妇女 [Pitiful Chinese women]. *Dagong bao*, November 30, 1919.

Yan Yiyan 颜一烟. *Qiu Jin* 秋瑾. In *Yan'an wenyi dang'an*, vol. 5, 342–96.

Yan Yiyan. "Yan'an shangyan de *Qiu Jin*" 延安上演的秋瑾 [*Qiu Jin* performed in Yan'an]. *Zhongguo funü* 1, no. 10/11 (1940): 18–19.

Yan Yiyan. "Yi *Qiu Jin* zai Yan'an de yanchu" 忆《秋瑾》在延安的演出 [Recollections of the performance of *Qiu Jin* in Yan'an]. *Xiju bao* 2 (1984): 32.

"Yan'an gejie funü sanbajie jinian dahui gao quanguo zimei shu" 延安各界妇女三八节纪念大会告全国姊妹书 [An open letter from Yan'an women's International Women's Day commemoration conference to sisters across the nation]. *Zhongguo funü* 1, nos. 10 and 11 (1940): 2–3.

Yang Guixin 杨桂欣. *Ding Ling yu Zhou Yang de enyuan* 丁玲与周扬的恩怨 [The gratitude and grudge between Ding Ling and Zhou Yang]. Wuhan: Hubei renmin chubanshe, 2006.

Yang Tao 杨韬. "Jingshen wanju" 精神玩具 [Spiritual toys]. *Yishu jie* 艺术界 [Art field] 4 (2006): 102–7.

Yang Wei 杨威, Guo Jian 郭健, Sun Wei 孙伟 and Fang Yan 方彦. *Liu Hulan: Bachang huaju* 刘胡兰：八场话剧 [Liu Hulan: Eight scenes spoken drama]. Tianjin: Baihua wenyi chubanshe, 1965.

Yang Zilie 杨子烈. *Zhang Guotao furen huiyilu* 张国焘夫人回忆录 [The memoir of Zhang Guotao's wife]. Hong Kong: Zilian chubanshe, 1970.

Yi Shengli 伊胜利 and Chen Shuzhi 陈书智. "Zhongguo gongchandang diyi wei nü dangyuan: Miu Boying zhuanlüe" 中国共产党第一位女党员：缪伯英传略 [The first female Chinese Communist Party member: A brief biography of Miu Boying]. In *Zhonggong dangshi ziliao* 中共党史资料 [The CCP history materials], vol. 56, 162–66. Beijing: Zhonggong dangshi chubanshe, 1996.

Young, James. *The Texture of Memory: Holocaust Memorials and Meaning*. New Haven: Yale University Press, 1994.

Yu Cun 于村. *Liu Hulan: Simu qichang huaju* 刘胡兰：四幕七场话剧 [Liu Hulan: Four acts seven scenes spoken drama]. Beijing: Zuojia chubanshe, 1956.

Yu Cun 于村, Hai Xiao 海啸, Lu Su 卢肃, and Chen Zi 陈紫. *Liu Hulan: Er'mu jiuchang geju* 刘胡兰：二幕九场歌剧 [Liu Hulan: Two acts nine scenes opera]. Beijing: Zuojia chubanshe, 1955.

Yu Cun 于村, Hai Xiao 海啸, Lu Su 卢肃, and Chen Zi 陈紫. *Yuju Liu Hulan: Juben yu qupu* 豫剧《刘胡兰》：剧本与曲谱 [Yu opera *Liu Hulan*: Script and score]. Zhengzhou: Henan renmin chubanshe, 1959.

Yu Fan 于凡. *Zhishang: Yu Fan zuopin* 置上:于凡作品 [On high: Works of Yu Fan]. Beijing: Renmin meishu chubanshe, 2013.

"Yu Fan and Zhu Qi fangtan: Fofa yide, mojing nanru" 于凡&朱其访谈: 佛法易得，魔境难入 [Zhu Qi's interview with Yu Fan: The dharma is easy to get, but the magic world is hard to get into]. http://www.cafa.com.cn/cn/figures/article/details/8320554, accessed May 22, 2022.

Yu Zhen 寓真. "Nie Gannu chuyu zhimi jiqi yishi" 聂绀弩出狱之谜及其轶诗 [The mystery of Nie Gannu's release from prison and his uncollected poems]. *Xin wenxue shiliao* 3 (2003): 25–30.

Yuan Liangjun 袁良骏, ed. *Ding Ling yanjiu ziliao* 丁玲研究资料 [Research materials on Ding Ling]. Tianjin: Tianjin renmin chubanshe, 1982.

Yuan Peili 袁培力. "Kangzhan chuqi Xizhantuan zai Xi'an de sanci gongyan" 抗战初期西战团在西安的三次公演 [Three public performances of the Northwest Front Service Corps in Xi'an during the early stage of the Anti-Japanese War]. *Gejie* 9 (2019): 72–75.

Yuan Peili. "Nie Gannu sanci lai Xi'an shimo" 聂绀弩三次来西安始末 [An account of Nie Gannu's three visits to Xi'an]. *Gejie* (10) 2019: 72–74.

"Yunsong nüxia lingchen xiangzhi" 运送女侠灵榇详志 [Detailed records on transforming the female knight-errant's coffin]. *Shenbao*, October 27, 1912.

"Zai ji zhuidaohui xiangqing" 再记追悼会详情 [Additional account of the memorial service details]. *Shenbao*, December 20, 1911.

Zai pipan 再批判 [Criticism again], edited by *Wenyi bao* 文艺报 [Journal of literature and art]. Beijing: Zuojia chubanshe, 1958.

"Zai qianxian de nüzi" 在前线的女子 [Girls at the front]. *Dongfang huakan* 东方画刊 [The eastern pictorial] 1, no. 2 (1938): 8.

Zha Zhenke 查振科 and Li Xiangdong 李向东. "Chen Ming koushu: Ding Ling wannian naxie shi" 陈明口述: 丁玲晚年那些事 [Chen Ming's oral account: The later life of Ding Ling]. *Xin wenxue shiliao* 4 (2010): 128–42.

Zhang Geng 张庚. "Guofang xiju de ticai he ticai chuli" 国防戏剧的题材和题材处理 [The topics of national defense dramas and how to handle them]. *Shenghuo zhishi* 1, no. 10 (1936): 485–87.

Zhang Guotao 张国焘. *Wo de huiyi* 我的回忆 [My memories]. Beijing: Dongfang chubanshe, 1980.

(Zhang) Qinqiu 琴秋. "Wei youju nüzhiyuan huyu" 为邮局女职员呼吁 [An appeal on behalf of female postal workers]. *Zhongguo funü* 1, no. 8 (1940): 11–12.

(Zhang) Taiyan 太炎. "Ji Xu Xilin, Chen Boping, Ma Zonghan, Qiu Jin wen" 祭徐锡麟陈伯平马宗汉秋瑾文 [An essay mourning Xu Xilin, Chen Boping, Ma Zonghan, and Qiu Jin]. *Minbao* 17 (1907): 117–18.

(Zhang) Taiyan. "Qiu Jin ji xu" 秋瑾集序 [Preface to a collection of Qiu Jin's works]. *Minbao* 17 (1907): 118–19.

Zhang, Xin. "Climate No. 6." *Text and Subtext: An International Touring Exhibition*, edited by Binghui Huangfu, 100–103. Singapore: Earl Lu Gallery, 2000.

Zhang Zhen 张真. "Ji Liu Hulan cai zhadao" 记刘胡兰踩铡刀 [Liu Hulan's act of stepping on the hay cutter]. *Zhongguo xiju* 中国戏剧 [Chinese theater] 14 (1958): 19.

Zhao Dingming 赵定明. "Xibei zhandi fuwutuan" 西北战地服务团 [The Northwest Front Service Corps]. *Zhonghua* 中华 [The China pictorial] 68 (1938): 22–23.

Zhao Haosheng 赵浩生. "Zhou Yang xiaotan lishi gongguo" 周扬笑谈历史功过 [Zhou Yang talks about historical achievements and mistakes]. *Xin wenxue shiliao* 2 (1979): 228–42.

Zhao Jiabi 赵家璧. *Bianji yijiu* 编辑忆旧 [An editor's remembrance of the past]. Beijing: Sanlian shudian, 2008.

Zhen 真. "Sangang geming" 三纲革命 [Revolution in the three bonds]. *Xin shiji* 11 (1907): 1–2.

Zheng Chaolin 郑超麟. *Shishi yu huiyi: Zheng Chaolin wannian wenxuan* 史事与回忆：郑超麟晚年文选 [History and memory: Selected writings from Zheng Chaolin's late years]. Hong Kong: Tiandi tushu, 1998.

Zheng Xiaofeng 郑笑枫. *Ding Ling zai Beidahuang* 丁玲在北大荒 [Ding Ling in the Great Northern Wasteland]. Beijing: Zhonggong dangshi chubanshe, 2008.

"Zheren zhuidao zhu xianlie" 浙人追悼诸先烈 [People in Zhejiang commemorating the martyrs]. *Shenbao*, January 30, 1912.

Zhi Da 志达. "Qiu Jin sihou zhi yuan" 秋瑾死后之冤 [The injustice after Qiu Jin's death]. *Tianyi* 15 (1908): 28.

Zhong Dianfei 钟惦棐. "Guanyu wenyi shang de xijie miaoxie wenti" 关于文艺上的细节描写问题 [Regarding the issue of writing about details in art and literature]. *Wenyi bao* 2, no. 3 (1950): 21–22.

"Zhonggong zhongyang wei sanbajie gongzuo gei geji dangbu de zhishi" 中共中央为三八节工作给各级党部的指示 [The instructions issued by the Central Committee of the CCP to the party branches for celebrating International Women's Day]. *Zhongguo funü* 1, no. 9 (1940): 2.

Zhongguo funü yundong lishi ziliao (1937–1945) 中国妇女运动历史资料: 1937–1945 [Historical materials on Chinese women's movements from 1937 to 1945]. Beijing: Zhongguo funü chubanshe, 1991.

Zhongguo funü zazhishe 中国妇女杂志社 [Chinese women's magazine], ed. *Lieshi Xiang Jingyu* 烈士向警予 [Martyr Xiang Jingyu]. Beijing: Zhongguo funü zazhi chubanshe, 1958.

"Zhonghua renmin gongheguo weichengnianren baohufa" 中华人民共和国未成年人保护法 [Law of the PRC on Protection of Minors]. *Zhonghua renmin gongheguo guowuyuan gongbao* 中华人民共和国国务院公报 [Gazette of the State Council of the PRC] 32 (1991): 1113–20.

Zhongyang dang'an guan 中央档案馆 [The Central Archive], ed. *Zhongguo Gongchandang di'erci zhi diliuci quanguo daibiao dahui wenjian huibian* 中国共产党第二次至第六次全国代表大会文件汇编 [Compiled materials of the Second to the Sixth National Congress of the CCP]. Beijing: Renmin chubanshe, 1981.

Zhongyang dang'an guan 中央档案馆 [National Archives Administration of China], ed. *Zhonggong zhongyang wenjian xuanji* 中共中央文件选集 [Selected documents of the

Central Committee of the CCP], vol. 1. Beijing: Zhonggong zhongyang dangxiao chubanshe, 1991.

Zhongyang dangshi shiliao chenlieguan chenlie shiliao mulu 中央党史史料陈列馆陈列史料目录 [Catalog of historical materials on display at the Exhibition Hall for Historical Materials of the KMT]. Zhongyang dangshi shiliao bianzuo weiyuanhui bianyin 中央党史史料编纂委员会编印 [Printed by the committee for editing the historical materials of the KMT], 1937.

"Zhongyang dangshi shiliao chenlieguan jin xing luochengli" 中央党史史料陈列馆今行落成礼 [The opening ceremony for the Exhibition Hall for Historical Materials of the KMT was held today]. *Minbao*, October 10, 1936.

Zhou Enlai 周恩来. "Lun 'xianqiliangmu' yu muzhi" 论"贤妻良母"与母职 [On "virtuous wife and good mother" and motherhood]. *Jiefang ribao*, November 20, 1942.

(Zhou) Enlai 恩来. "Lü'ou tongxin: Li'ang zhongfa daxue zhi tonggao" 旅欧通信: 里昂中法大学之通告 [Correspondence from Europe: Lyon Sino-French University's announcement]. *Yishi bao* (Tianjin), December 29, 1921.

Zhou Gangming 周钢鸣. "Minzu weiji yu guofang xiju" 民族危机与国防戏剧 [National crisis and national defense theater]. *Shenghuo zhishi* 1, no. 10 (1936): 481–85.

Zhou Liangpei 周良沛. *Ding Ling zhuan* 丁玲传 [Biography of Ding Ling]. Beijing: Beijing shiyue wenyi chubanshe, 1993.

(Zhou) Libo 立波. "Guanyu guofang wenxue" 关于国防文学 [About the national defense literature]. *Shishi xinbao*, December 21, 1935.

Zhou Renjie 周人杰. "Rang yingxiong zhiguang zhaoliang haizimen de xingkong" 让英雄之光照亮孩子们的星空 [Let the light of heroes illuminate the children's starry sky]. *Renmin ribao*, June 1, 2017.

Zhou Yang 周扬. "Wenyi zhanxian shang de yichang da bianlun" 文艺战线上的一场大辩论 [A major debate on the frontline of art and literature]. *Renmin ribao*, February 28, 1958.

Zhou Yang. *Zhou Yang Wenji* 周扬文集 [Collected works of Zhou Yang], vol. 1. Beijing: Renmin wenxue chubanshe, 1984.

"Zhou zongli deng guankan huaju Liu Hulan" 周总理等观看话剧《刘胡兰》[Premier Zhou and others watched the spoken drama Liu Hulan]. *Renmin ribao*, March 21, 1965.

Zhu Liang 朱亮. "Feng Fasi yu *Liu Hulan jiuyi*" 冯法祀与《刘胡兰就义》[Feng Fasi and *The Heroic Death of Liu Hulan*]. *Zhongguo meishuguan* 7 (2007): 69–75.

"Zhu lieshi zhuidao dahui ji" 诸烈士追悼大会纪 [Record of the memorial service for numerous martyrs]. *Shenbao*, December 18, 1911.

Zhuo Shi 灼石. "Erbulang fufu" 二不浪夫妇 [Blockheaded couple]. *Jiefang ribao*, August 1, 1941.

Zimo 子摩. "Ding Ling yu Pan Zinian" 丁玲与潘梓年 [Ding Ling and Pan Zinian]. *Weiyan* 1, no. 3 (1933): 37–38.

Ziye 子夜. "Ding Ling zuihou zhi airen" 丁玲最后之爱人 [Ding Ling's last lover]. *Shidai ribao*, August 6, 1933.

"Zuijin luocheng zhi dangshi shiliao chenlieguan" 最近落成之党史史料陈列馆 [The recently completed Exhibition Hall for Historical Materials of the KMT]. *Zhongyang dangwu yuekan* 中央党务月刊 [Central party affairs monthly] 100 (1936): 9.

INDEX